NEW OFFICES

NEW OFFICES

Edited by Cristina Montes

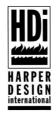

HDi

HARPER
DESIGN
international

An Imprint of HarperCollins*Publishers*

Editor: Cristina Montes

Editorial coordination: Haike Falkenberg

Art director: Mireia Casanovas Soley

Layout: Emma Termes Parera

Copy-editing: Karen Capria and Gyda Arber

Translation: Michael Brunelle and Beatriz Cortabarria

2003 © Loft Publications S.L. and Harper Design International, an
imprint of HarperCollins Publishers

First published in 2003 by LOFT and Harper Design International,
an imprint of HarperCollins Publishers
10 East 53rd St.,
New York, NY 10022-5299

Distributed throughout the world by:
HarperCollins International
10 East 53rd Street
New York, NY 10022
Fax: (212) 207-7654

HarperCollins books may be purchased for educational, business, or sales promotional use.
For information, please write:
Special Markets Department
HarperCollins Publishers Inc.
10 East 53rd Street
New York, NY 10022

Editorial project:

2003 © **LOFT** Publications
Via Laietana 32, 4º Of. 92. 08003 Barcelona. Spain
Tel.: +34 932 688 088
Fax: +34 932 687 073
loft@loftpublications.com
www.loftpublications.com

Library of Congress Control Number: 2003103504

ISBN: 0-06-054470-8

D.L.: B-07.878-03

Printed by: Anman Gràfiques del Vallès. Spain
First Printing, 2003

Contents

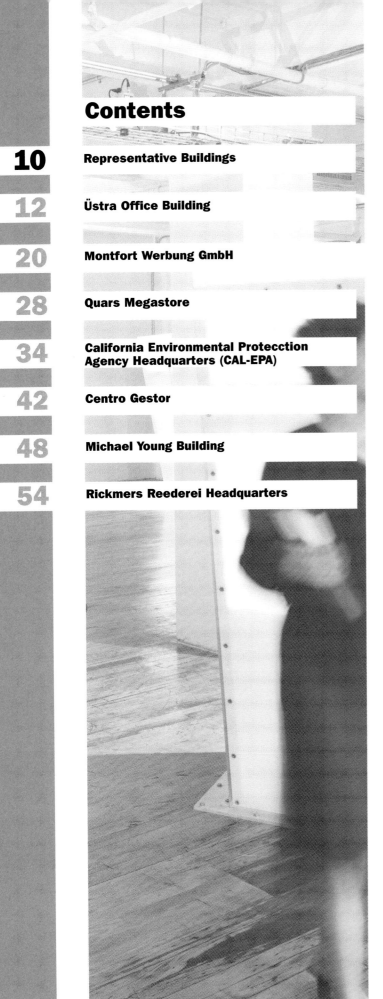
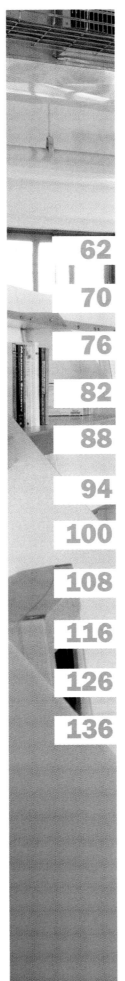
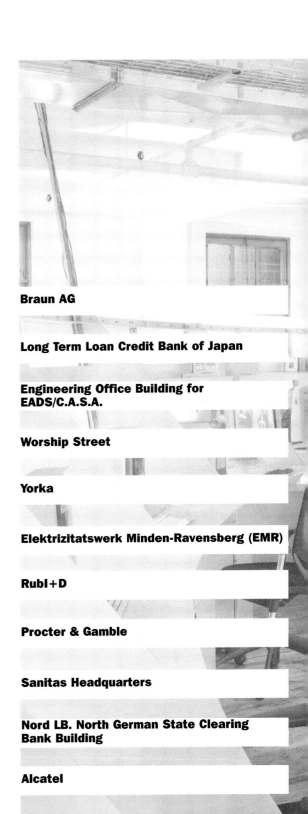

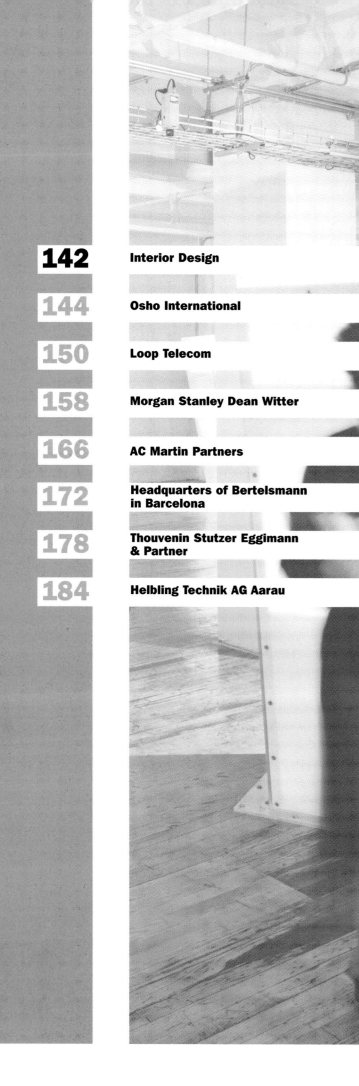
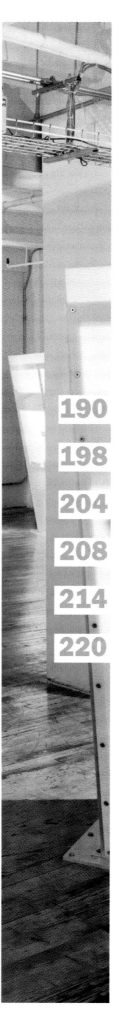

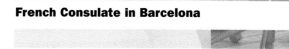

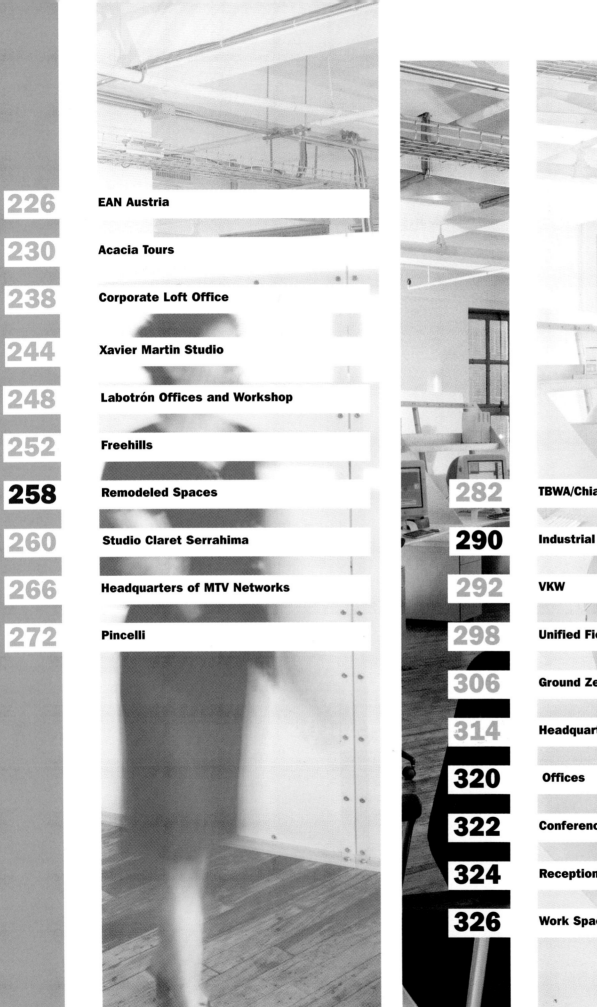
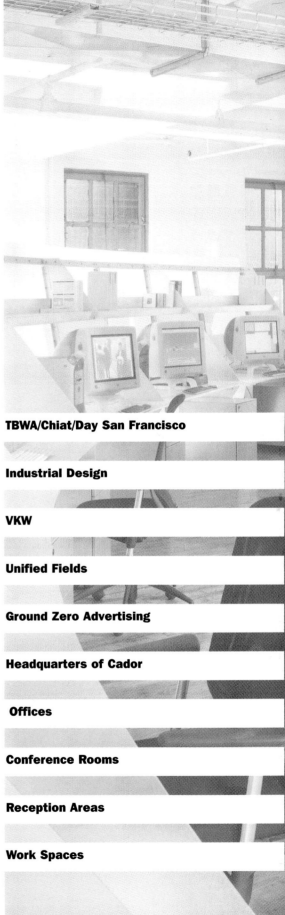

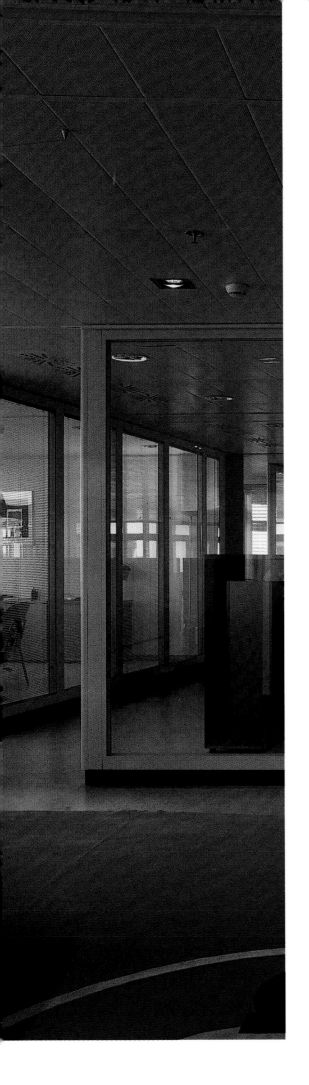

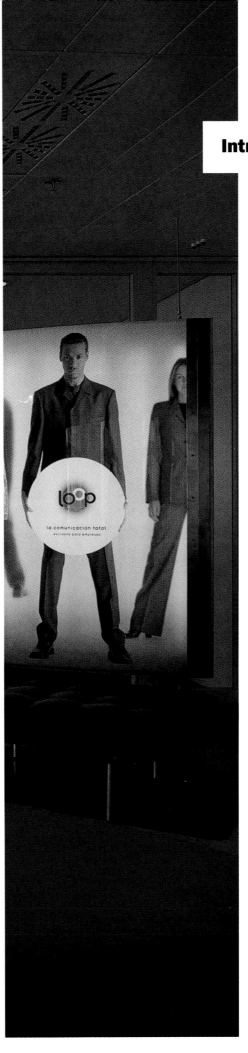

Introduction

New Offices presents carefully selected buildings that incorporate the most current ideas in workspaces. The innovative spaces displayed here are characterized by flexible and dynamic floor plans that can be adapted to multiple purposes and functions, where workers can carry out their duties in comfort and with efficiency. The innovative places examined in the following pages exhibit the latest trends in office design. The resulting collection is a tour of some of the most interesting office designs of the most prestigious contemporary architects. Frank O. Gehry, Fletcher + Priest Architects, Marmol & Radziner Associates, Shubin + Donaldson Architects, and Hemmi Fayet are some of the great names of modern architecture that are presented in these pages. These professionals have devoted their talent and imagination to the service of these new spaces.

The selected projects are a faithful reflection of the evolution and revolution of workspace. In these designs one can see the most avant-garde and daring ideas, as well as highly functional and effective solutions to common problems. Many different ways of planning spaces are presented, including offices where the areas are kept open and flowing, the boundaries blurred and the work areas shared. Other design concepts are introduced, including interiors where color floods every corner—something unheard of for offices until relatively recently—and environments treated more like domestic spaces than a workplace, with combinations of styles previously considered impossible.

This book shows that the image of the traditional office, gray and boring, has become a thing of the past. Current needs call for a renewal of these spaces and new requirements have caused offices to greatly evolve in recent years. Advances in technology and security have influenced the planning, distribution, and especially the interior design of modern workspaces. Even though the particular activity of each company dictates its needs, now that almost everything can be saved in a CD-ROM, the idea of reserving large spaces for information storage has fallen out of use. The bulky, heavy shelves and storage furniture of the past are giving way to stylized auxiliary elements. Dull colors are being abandoned in favor of bright and pleasing chromatic schemes. Materials, textures, and finishes like glass, aluminum, plastic, and Plexiglas are now more frequently used.

Office buildings have experienced such a vast transformation that there are no fixed rules any more. The new designs are surprising and innovative: Ingenuity, mixture of styles, disparity of architectural solutions, new uses of resources, and an eclectic spirit are all at the service of functionality. One of the basic requirements that each space must fulfill is to guarantee the comfort of the people that work there. Changes in aesthetics, in construction and architectural methods, and, of course, in technical advances have played a major role in the transformation of offices. All of these factors have favorably influenced the transformation that these pages reflect. The result is a book displaying ingenuity, mastery, and solutions that, by showing us what offices are like today, puts us within reach of what offices will be like in the future.

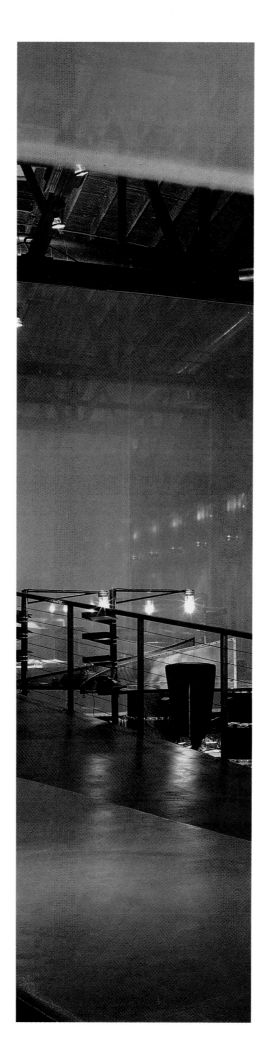

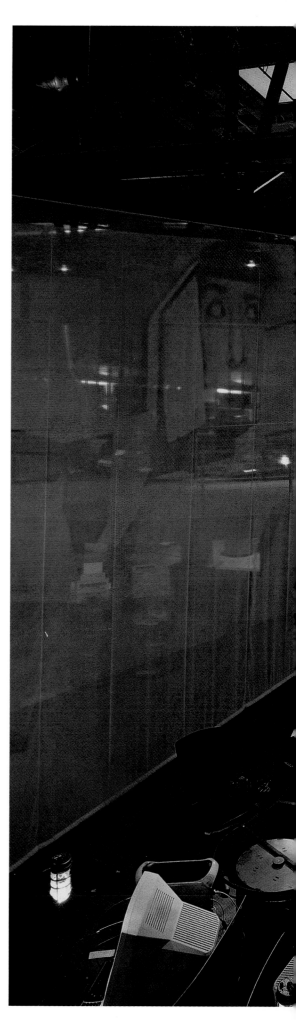

Representative Buildings

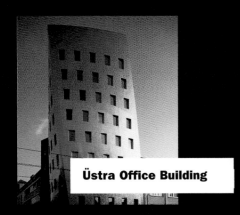

Üstra Office Building

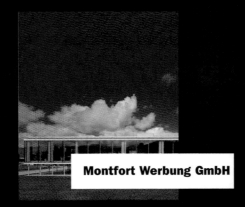

Montfort Werbung GmbH

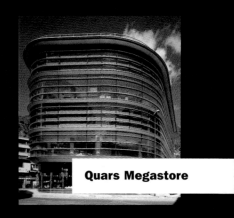

Quars Megastore

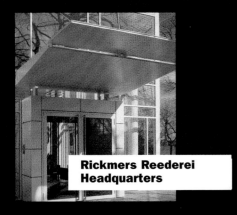

Rickmers Reederei Headquarters

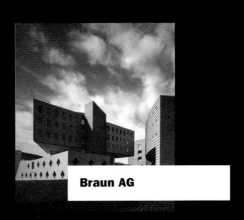

Braun AG

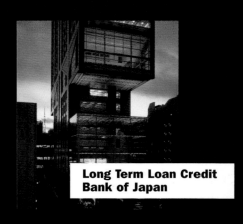

Long Term Loan Credit Bank of Japan

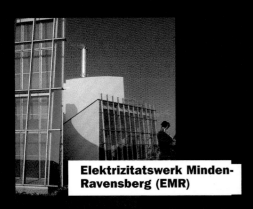

Elektrizitatswerk Minden-Ravensberg (EMR)

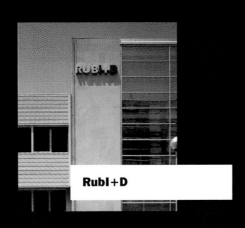

Rubl+D

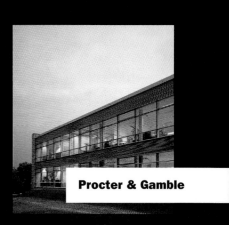

Procter & Gamble

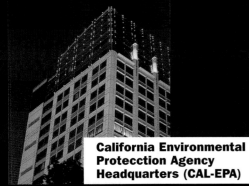

California Environmental Protecction Agency Headquarters (CAL-EPA)

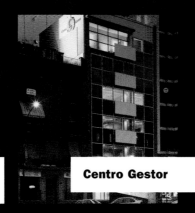

Centro Gestor

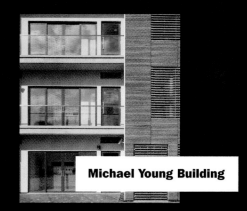

Michael Young Building

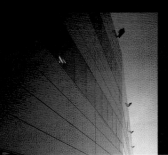

Engineering Office Building for EADS/C.A.S.A.

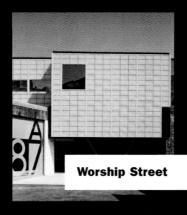

Worship Street

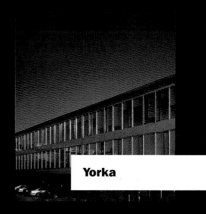

Yorka

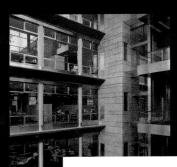

Sanitas Headquarters

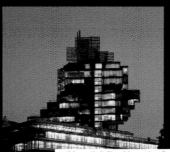

Nord LB. North German State Clearing Bank Building

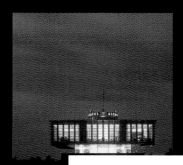

Alcatel

Üstra Office Building

Üstra Transportation headquarters are located at the corner of one of the main streets in downtown Hanover in a unique nine-story building. The construction is yet another example of the creative talent of architect Frank O. Gehry, and its striking and attractive lines are another expression of the typically impossible shapes that characterize the architecture of this professional.

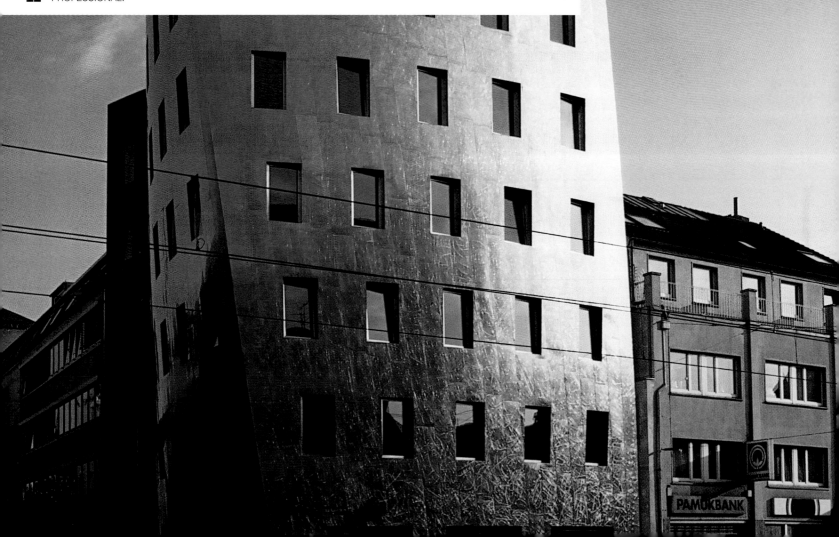

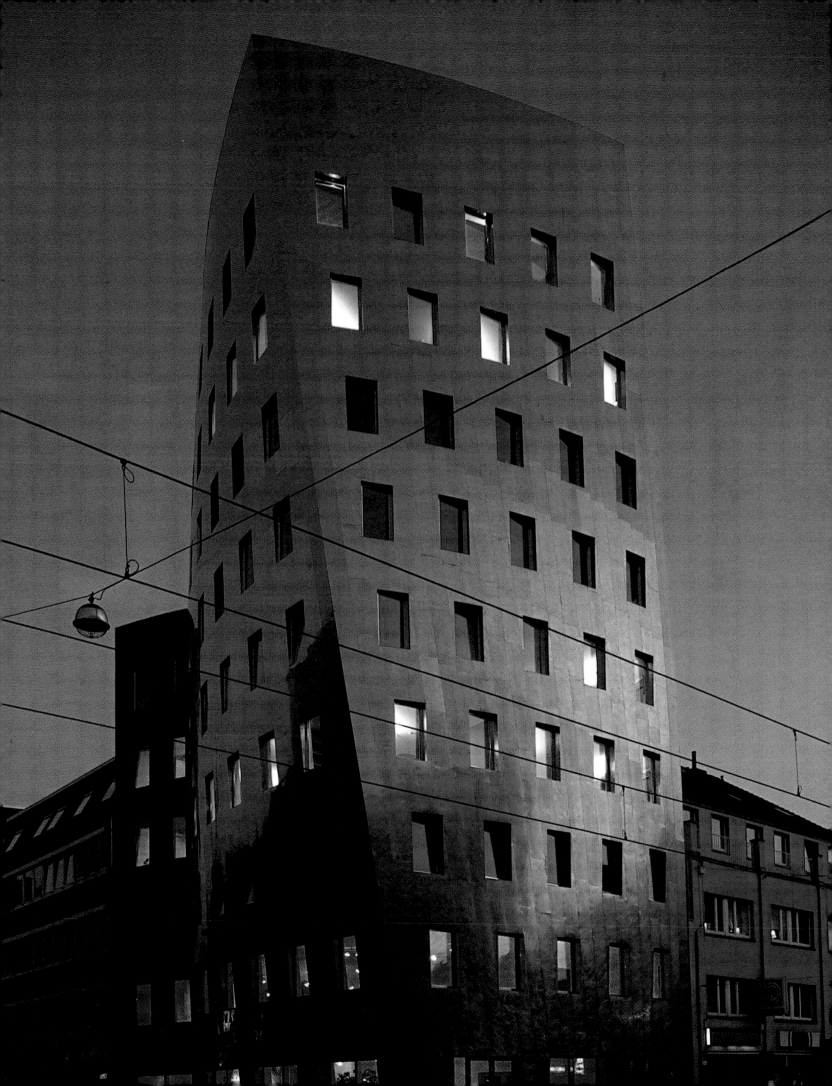

Üstra Office Building

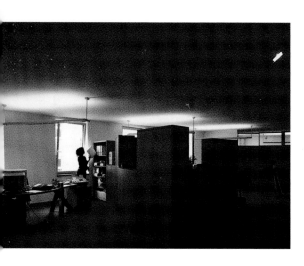

Architect: **Frank O. Gehry**
Client: **Üstra Hanover Public Transportation**
Location: **Hanover, Germany**
Construction Date: **2001**
Photography: **Thomas Mayer**

The office building contains approximately 22,604 square feet, and its particular location had an influence on its lines. The building was designed as a tower that stretches vertically; its attractive and spectacular outlines extend beyond the buildings that surround it.

Formally, the construction contains multipurpose and multifunctional space capable of accommodating different groups of employees according to their activities. The spatial distribution and the way the interiors were designed had to respond to the demands of the different activities carried out within a single space. The results of all these requirements translated into an avant-garde and functional building that is far from the typical forms that define the most traditional offices, and very much in line with the curves that identify Gehry's work.

Seen from the outside, the tower is highly evocative and full of power. It is a smooth and regular structure replete with window-shaped openings on all four sides. This obsessive repetition becomes an architectural solution that, besides being an important compositional element, provides natural ventilation to the interiors while connecting them with the outdoors.

The interior spaces are light, bright, perfectly organized, and functional, adapting to the forms dictated by the volumes of the exterior. Contemporary and functional furniture is arranged in a space where light, natural or artificial, plays an important role.

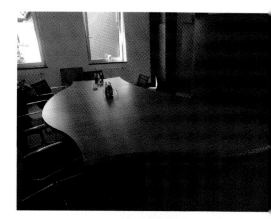

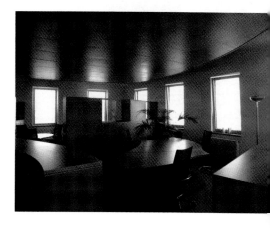

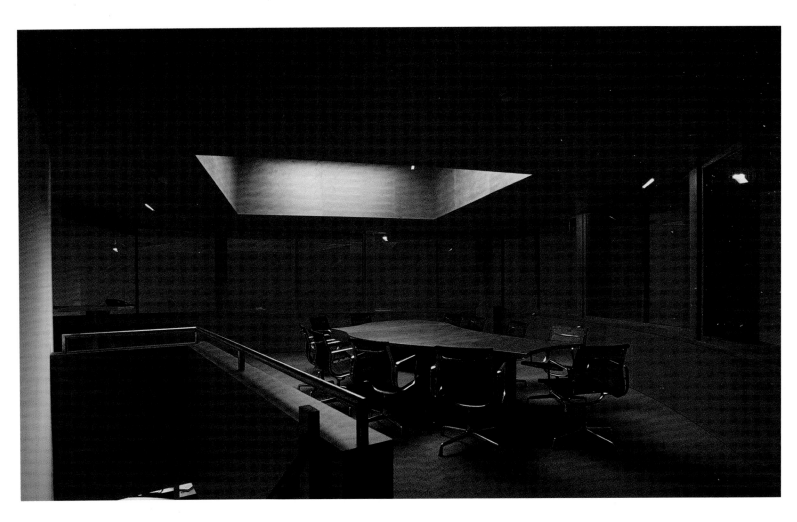

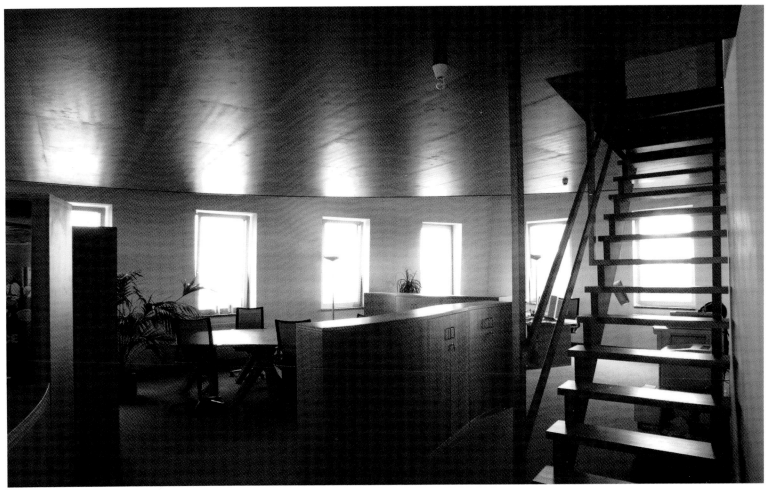

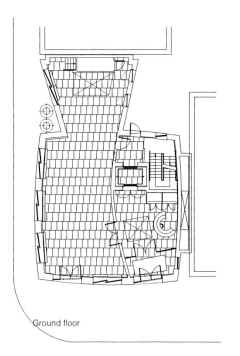

Ground floor

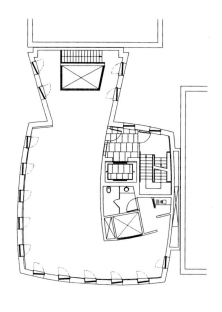

First floor

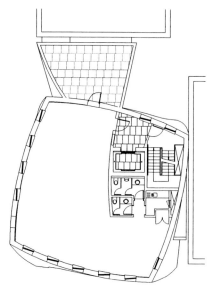

Sixth floor

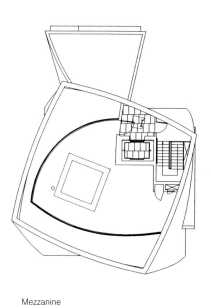

Mezzanine

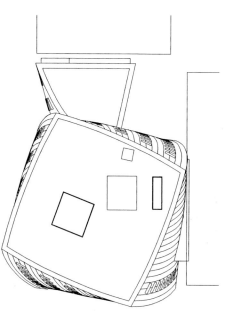

Roof floor

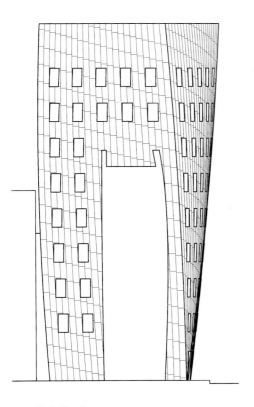

North Elevation

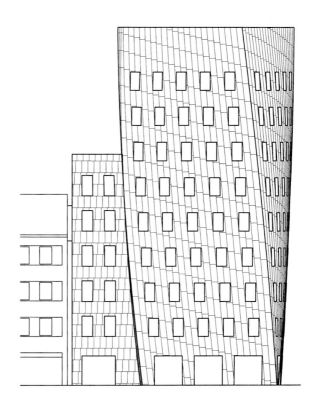

East Elevation

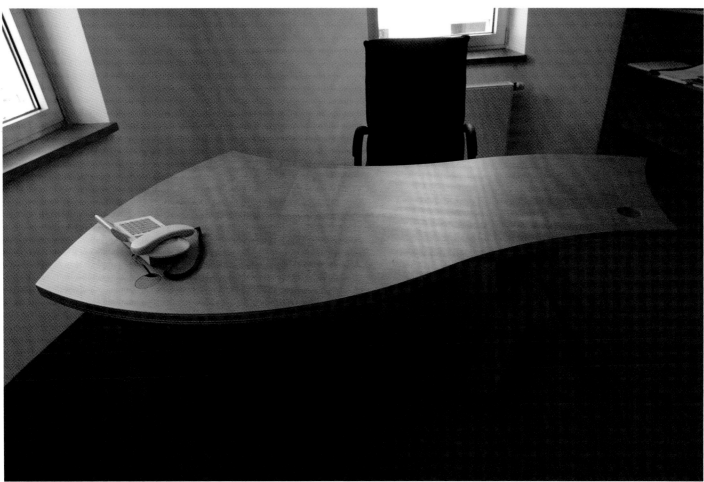

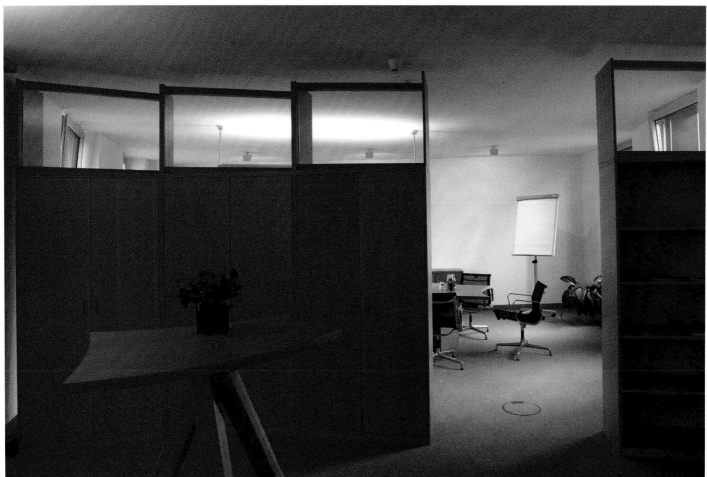

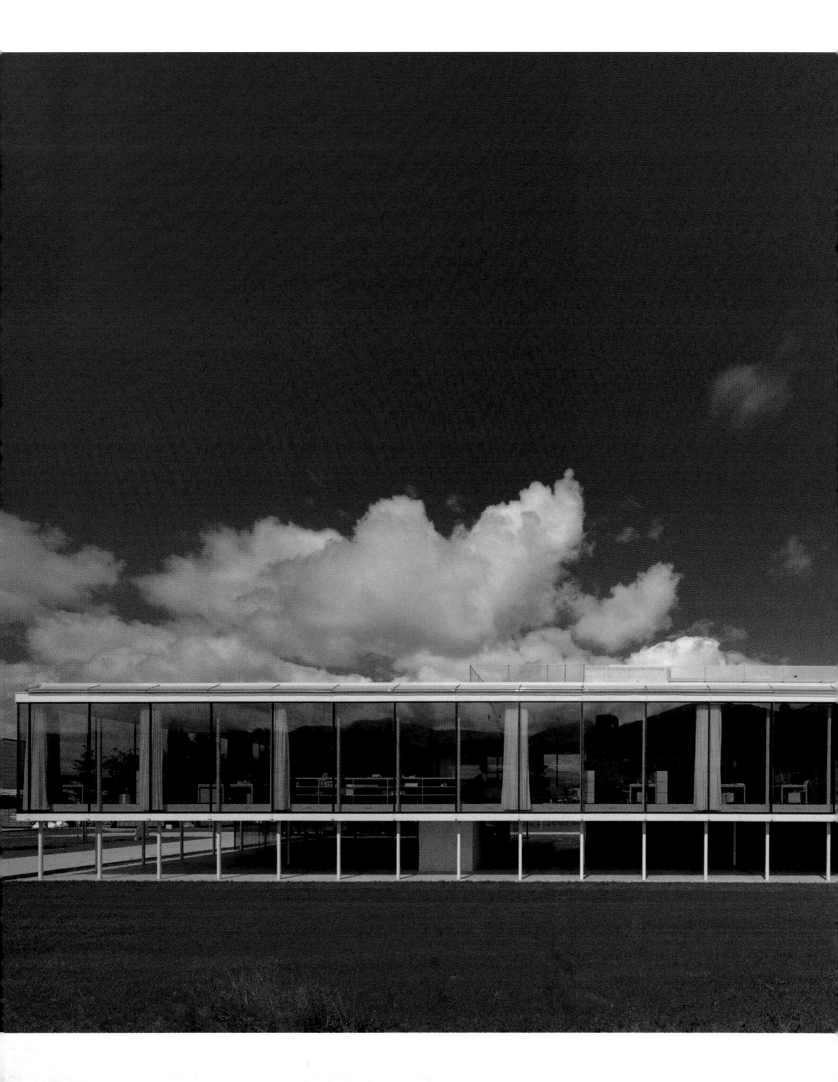

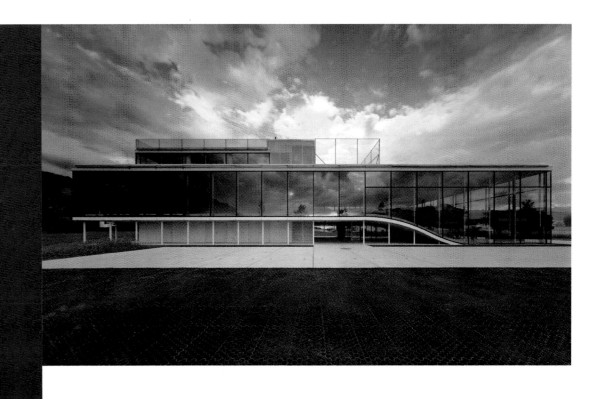

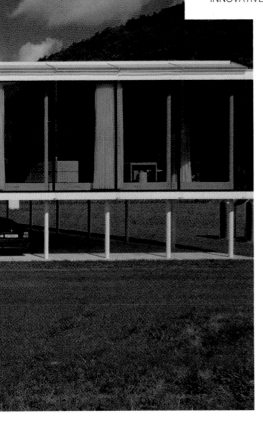

Montfort Werbung GmbH

DESIGNED FOR A PUBLICITY AGENCY BY THE ARCHITECTURE STUDIO OF OSKAR LEO KAUFMANN, THIS BUILDING IS INEVITABLY SHAPED BY ITS FUNCTIONAL REQUIREMENTS AND THE TERRAIN WHERE IT IS LOCATED, BUT IT IS DEFINED BY ITS SUBDUED LINES AND PURITY OF EXPRESSION. THE RATIONALITY AND SIMPLICITY OF ITS ARCHITECTURE SERVE AS A BACKDROP TO THE INTERIORS, WHICH ARE AS ATTRACTIVE AND EFFICIENT AS THEY ARE INNOVATIVE. IT IS AN EXERCISE OF ARCHITECTURAL MASTERY.

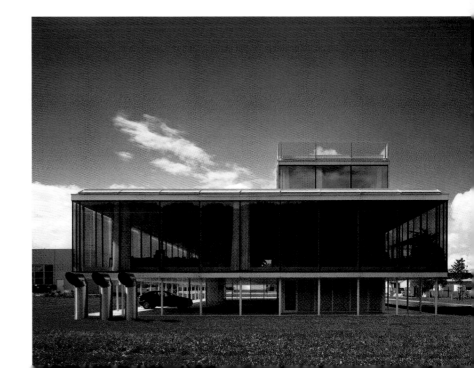

Montfort Werbung GmbH

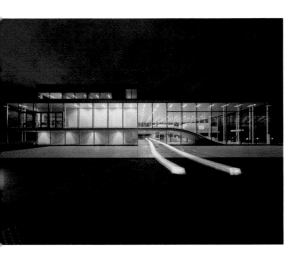

Architect: **Oskar Leo Kaufmann Architects**
Client: **Montfort Werbung GmbH**
Location: **Klaus, Austria**
Construction Date: **2001**
Photography: **Adolf Bereuter**

The construction, conceived as a large transparent rectangle, is an ingenious and rational design. The light, the glass, the polished surfaces, the fluidity, and the spatial continuity are the protagonists. The only element that breaks up the straightness of the lines is the evocative entrance, symbolically designed in the shape of a gentle wave penetrating the interior of the building.

The structure, which consists of different levels, was built of steel and glass. Replacing solid walls with transparent ones allows a clear view of the various areas and establishes an interesting dialog between the interior and exterior while letting in plenty of natural light. The metaphorical wave that becomes the entrance is made of concrete with an insulated covering. Inside, the arrangement of the spaces is defined through the use of the different materials that cover the floors.

The work areas have been placed on the upper floors and are connected to the lobby and reception through evocative carpeted stairs, a material that is also used on the floor in the workspaces. The use of materials, textures, and colors, such as steel, glass, chrome, and the whites, greens, or grays, contribute to an overall feeling of industrial starkness, luxury, and serenity.

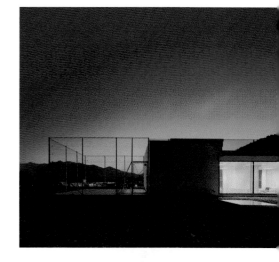

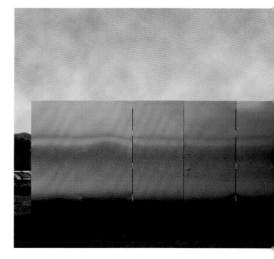

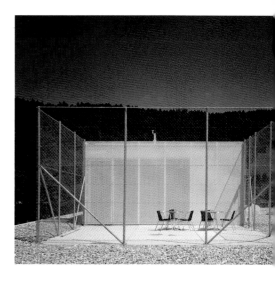

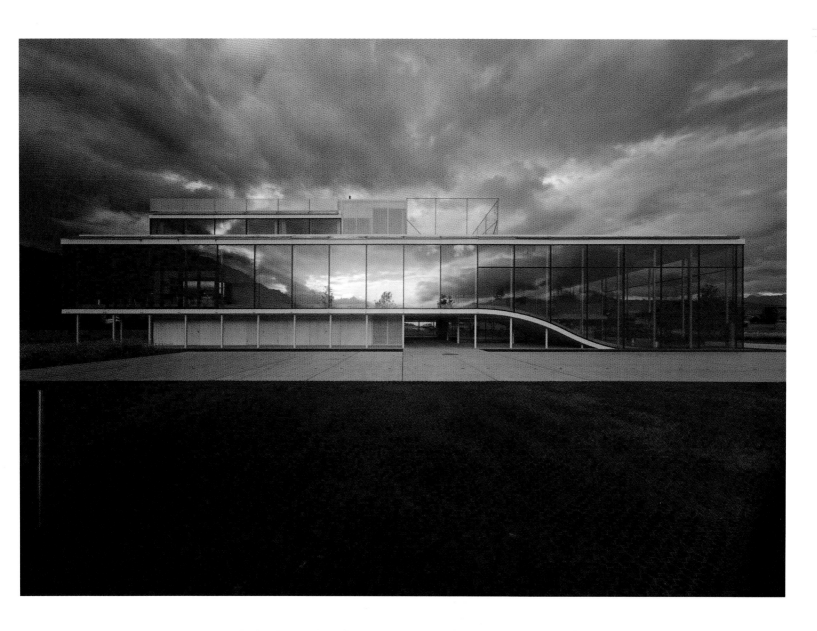

At the top level, the building is crowned with a terrace for the enjoyment of the outdoors. A simple, transparent geometric structure surrounds the finished open space. Delicate, subtle, and practically imperceptible lines have been used to be consistent with the overall design.

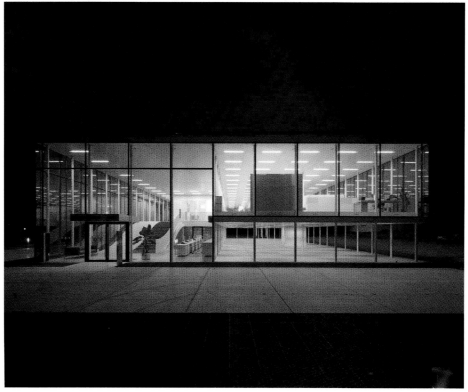

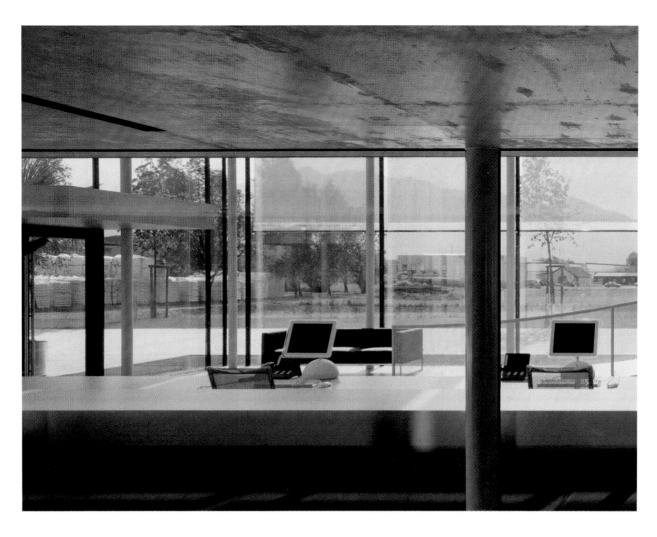

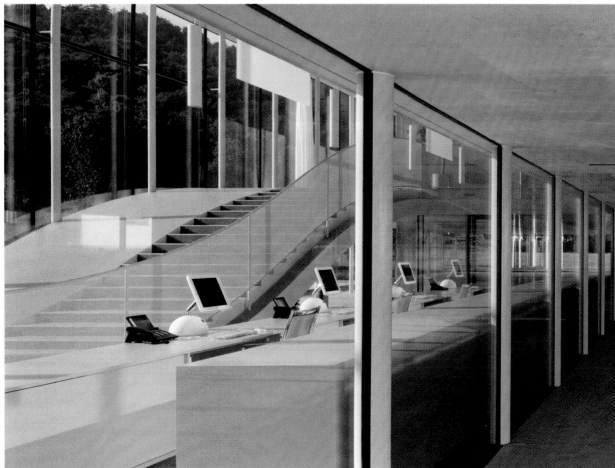

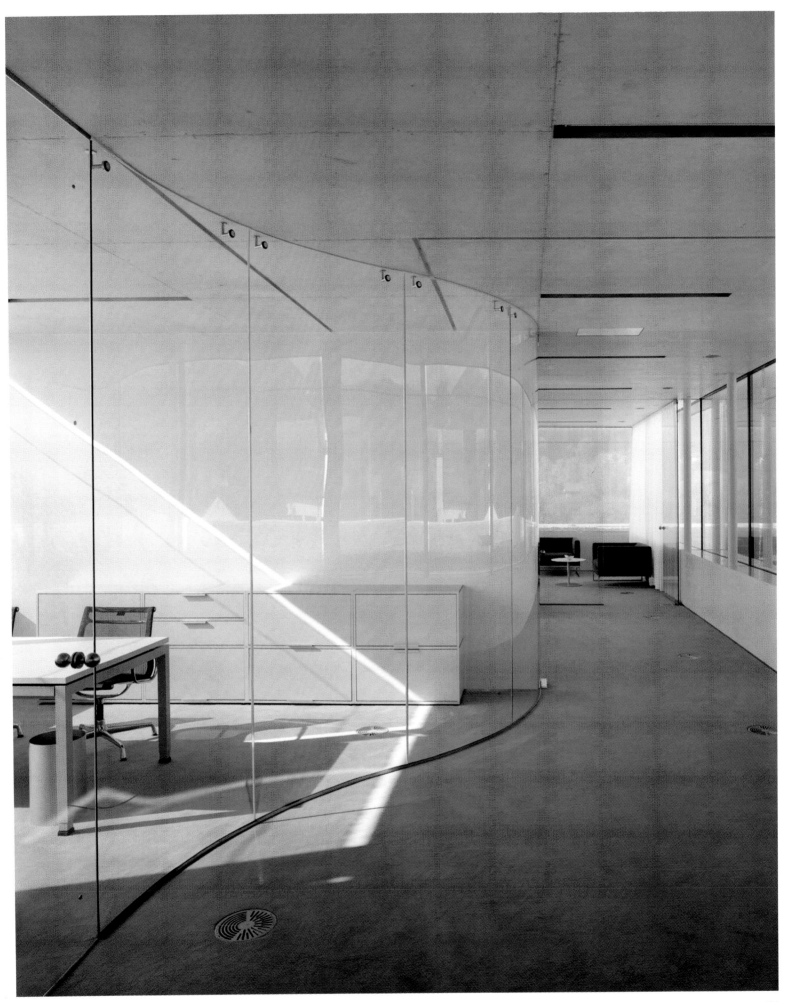

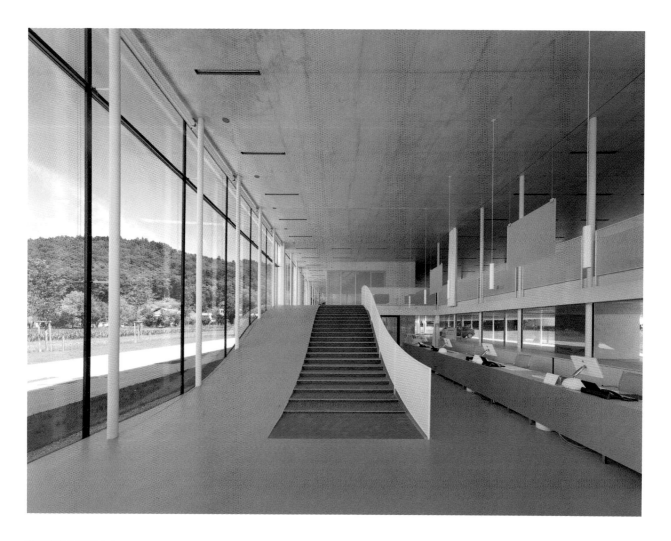

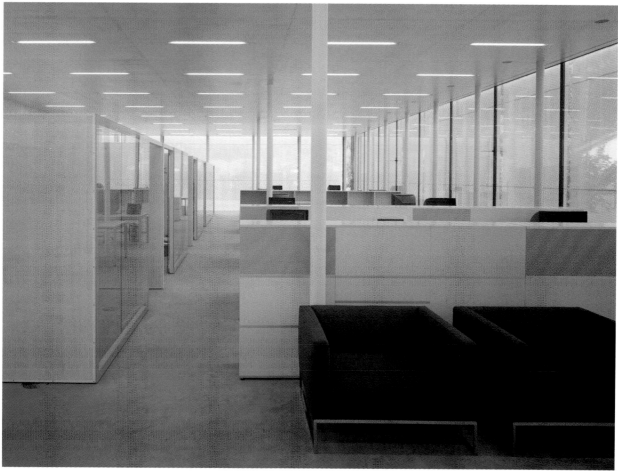

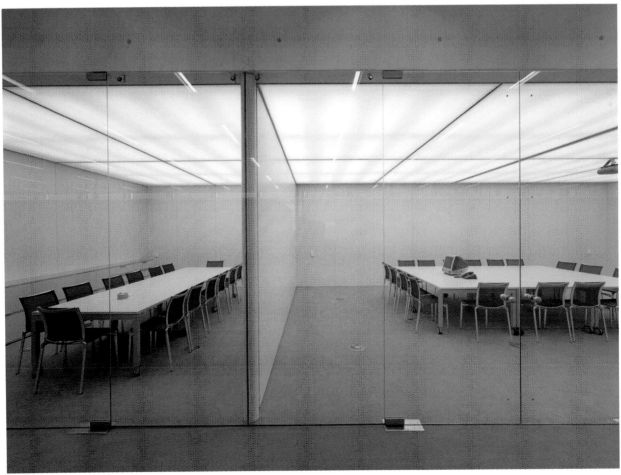

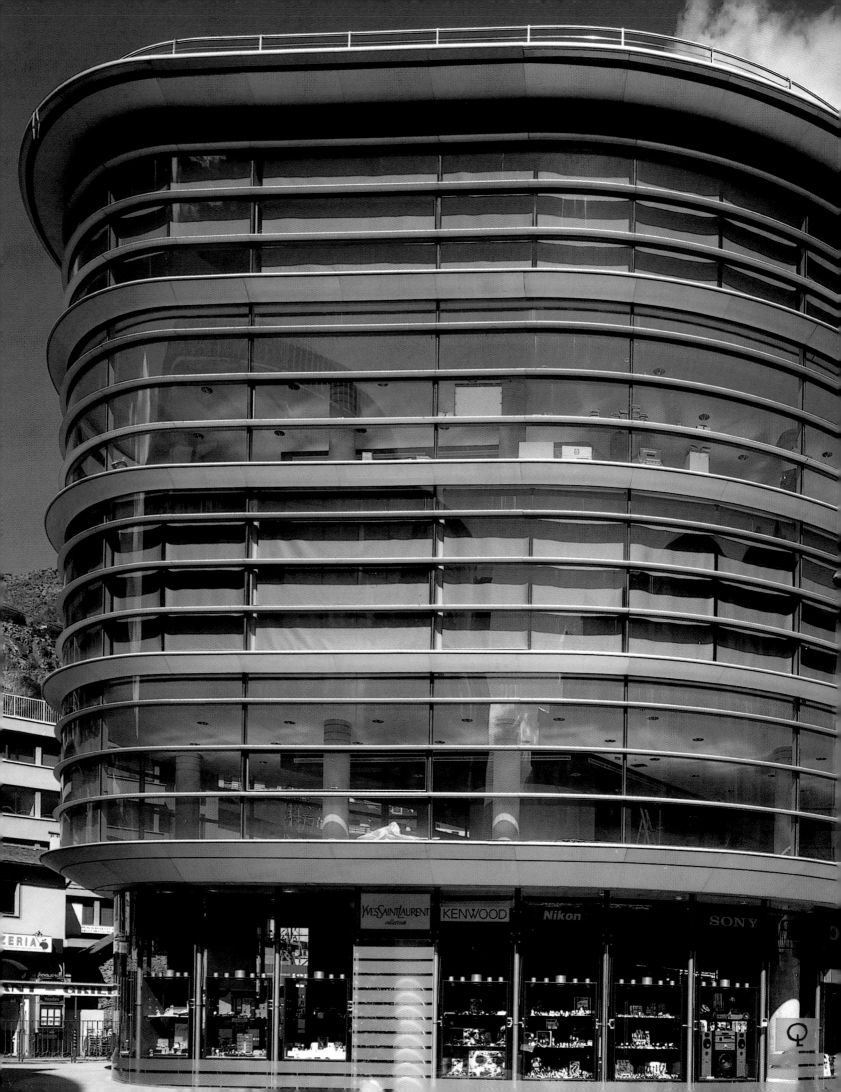

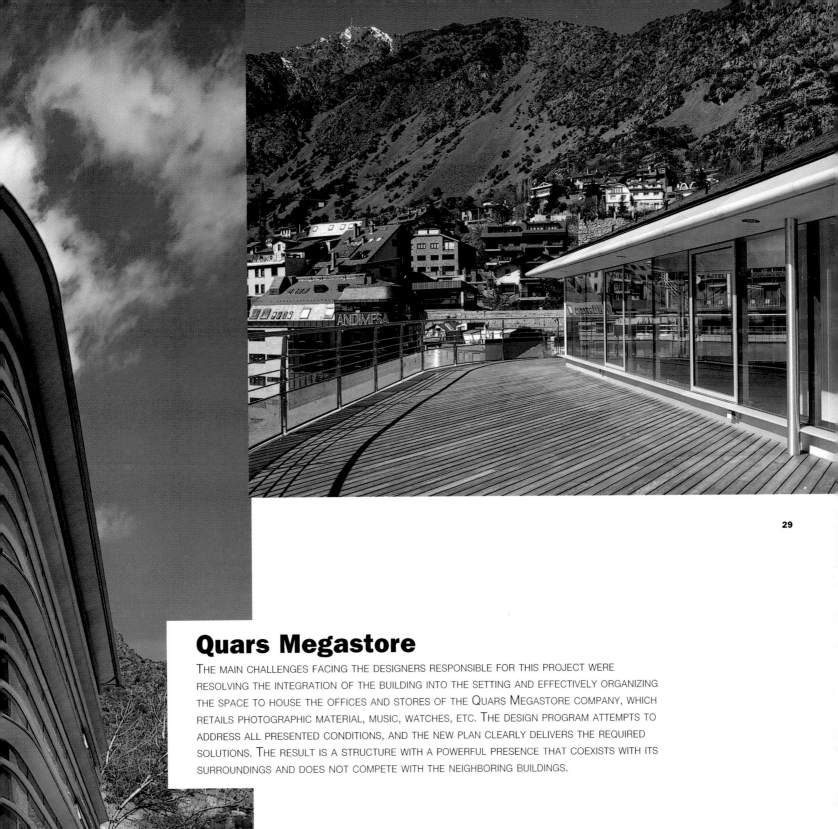

Quars Megastore

THE MAIN CHALLENGES FACING THE DESIGNERS RESPONSIBLE FOR THIS PROJECT WERE RESOLVING THE INTEGRATION OF THE BUILDING INTO THE SETTING AND EFFECTIVELY ORGANIZING THE SPACE TO HOUSE THE OFFICES AND STORES OF THE QUARS MEGASTORE COMPANY, WHICH RETAILS PHOTOGRAPHIC MATERIAL, MUSIC, WATCHES, ETC. THE DESIGN PROGRAM ATTEMPTS TO ADDRESS ALL PRESENTED CONDITIONS, AND THE NEW PLAN CLEARLY DELIVERS THE REQUIRED SOLUTIONS. THE RESULT IS A STRUCTURE WITH A POWERFUL PRESENCE THAT COEXISTS WITH ITS SURROUNDINGS AND DOES NOT COMPETE WITH THE NEIGHBORING BUILDINGS.

Quars Megastore

Architect: **Patrick Genard Associates**
Client: **Quars Megastore**
Location: **Andorra la Vella, Andorra**
Construction Date: **1999**
Photography: **Eugeni Pons**

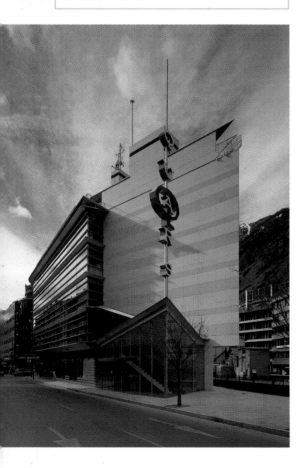

The plan specifies three different levels: The street level and the second floor have been reserved for retail stores, while the remaining levels house the administrative and management offices of the company.

Visually, the most outstanding feature is the curved form, which takes advantage of the point where two streets merge. The wave shape begins to lose its strength and gradually becomes straighter and more geometric as the volume of the building develops. The glass walls, the true skin of the body at the main facade that lets in the light that bathes the interior, extends along the structure and, together with other materials, becomes a main feature. The concept of designing the architecture of the facades differently helps strengthen the sense of contrast.

The transparency, dynamics, and coolness of the glass and steel facade contrast with the warmth of the interiors, which were redefined and organized to make them highly functional. This did not prevent the architects from creating a multifunctional, practical, attractive, and serene atmosphere.

The attractive exterior structure is representative of what lies in the interior. There, everything is clearly calculated to achieve the desired effect, where the architectural solutions and the decorative features flow throughout the building.

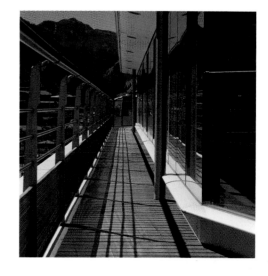

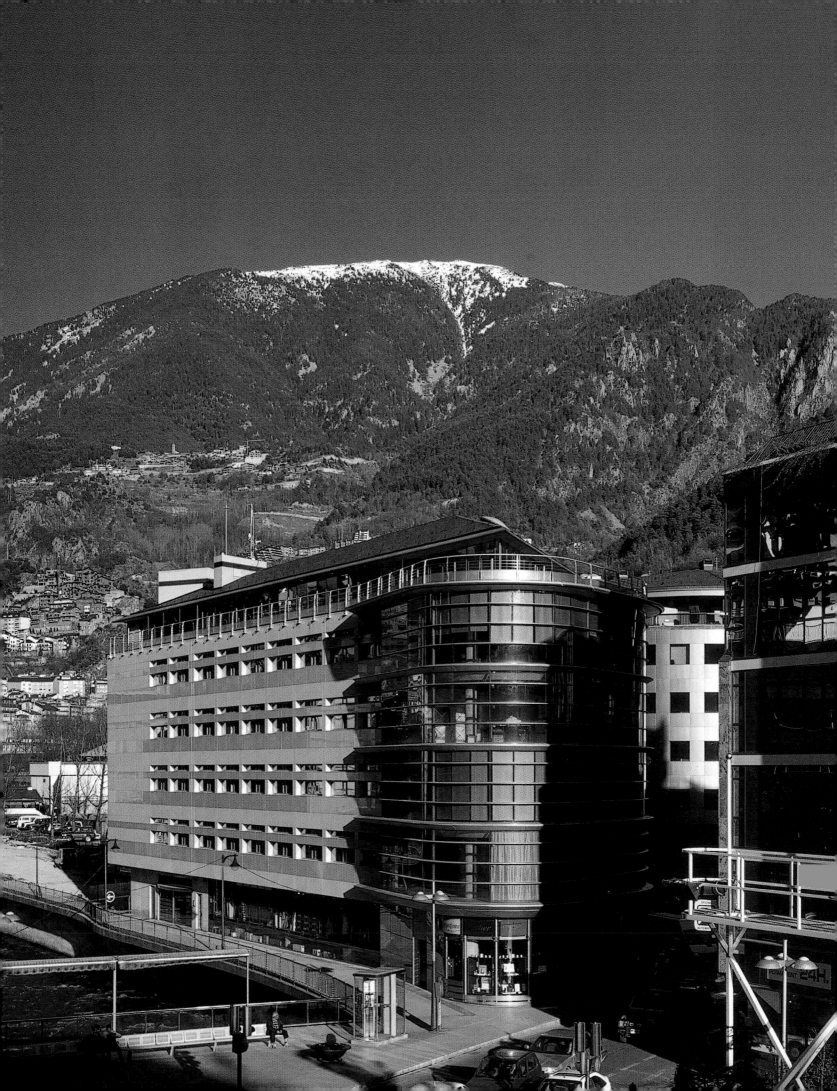

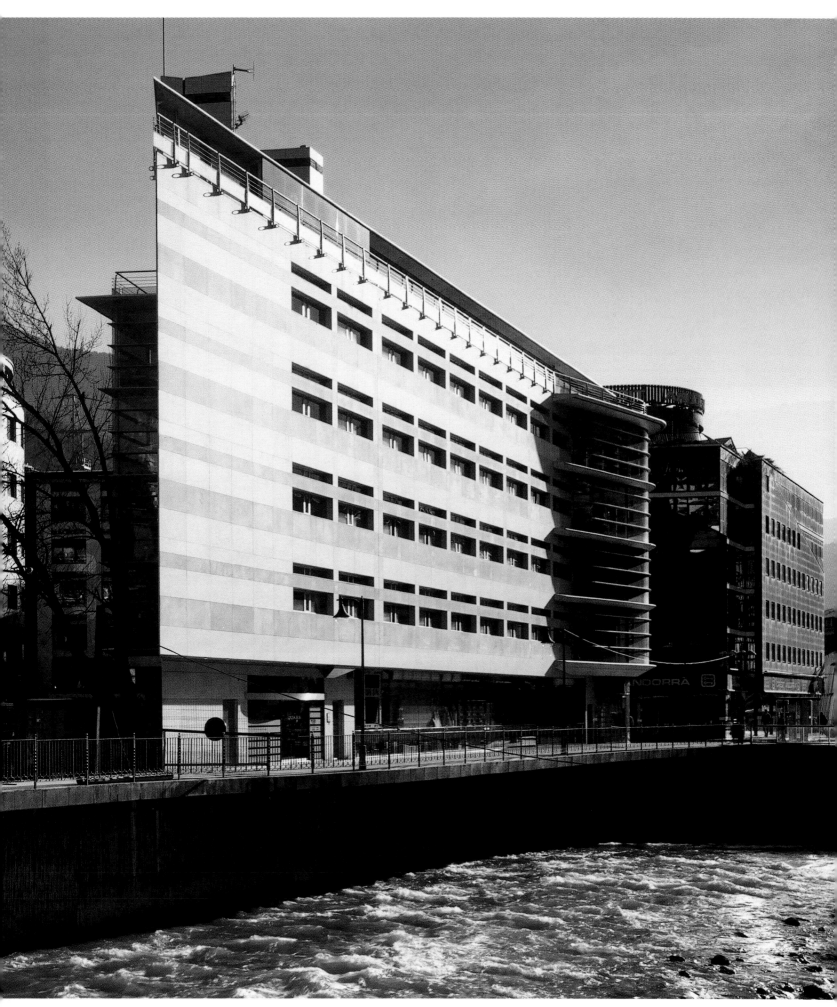

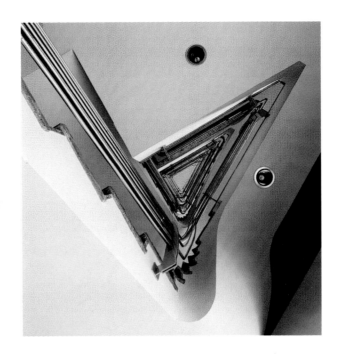

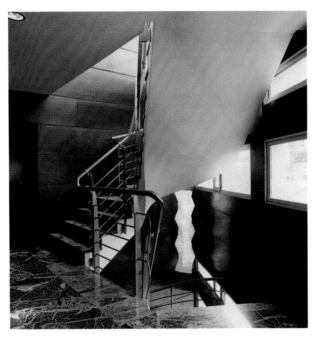

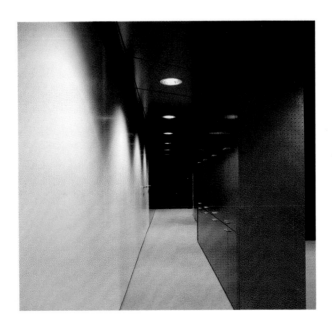

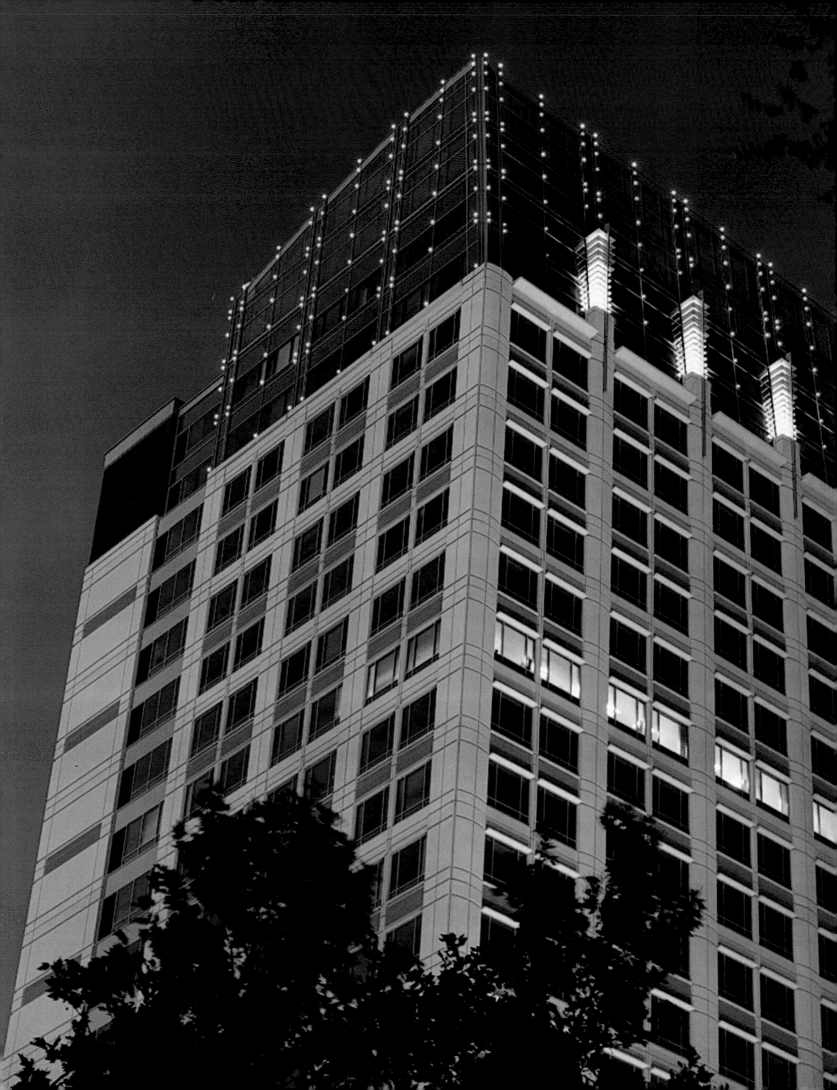

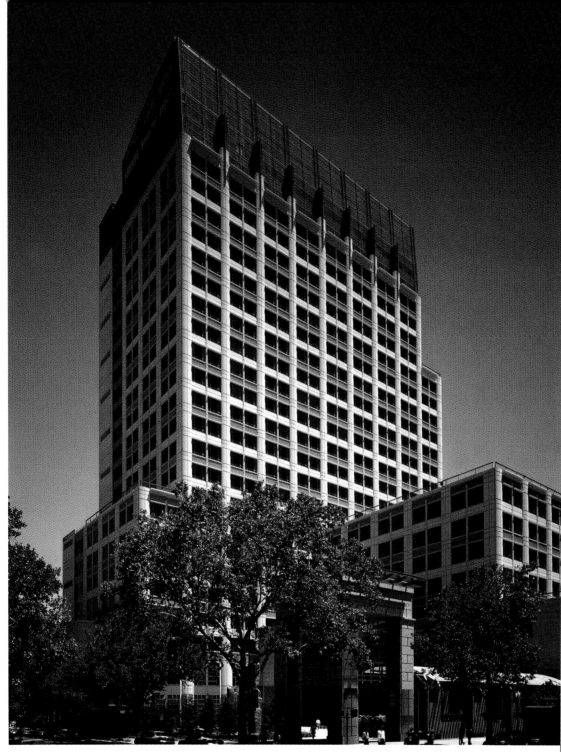

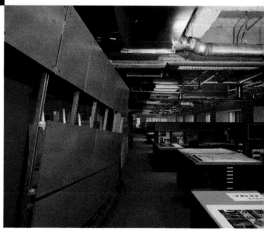

California Environmental Protecction Agency Headquarters (CAL-EPA)

THE STATE OF CALIFORNIA NEEDED A BUILDING FOR THEIR SACRAMENTO OFFICES. THE GOAL WAS TO CREATE A CONTEMPORARY BUILDING WHERE MORE THAN 3,000 EMPLOYEES COULD GO ABOUT THEIR JOBS. THE ARCHITECTURE STUDIO OF AC MARTIN PARTNERS (ACMP), A COMPANY SPECIALIZING IN CIVIL ARCHITECTURE, WAS ENTRUSTED WITH THE PROJECT, AND THEY WERE CHARGED WITH INCORPORATING THE NEEDS AND WISHES OF THE CLIENT INTO A MODERN AND FUNCTIONAL 25-STORY-HIGH BUILDING.

California Environmental Protecction Agency Headquarters (CAL-EPA)

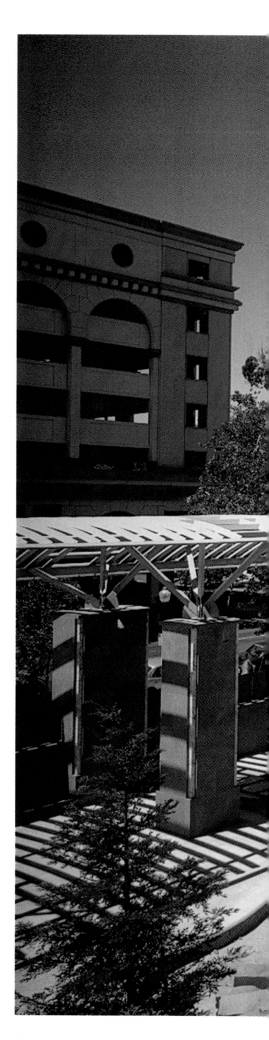

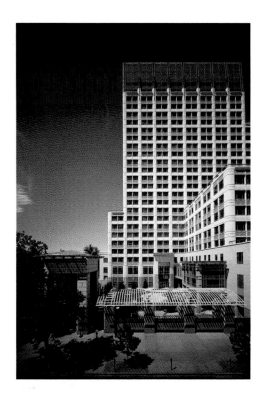

Architect: **AC Martin Partners, Inc.**
Client: **The City of Sacramento**
Location: **Sacramento, California, United States**
Construction Date: **2000**
Photography: **David Wakely**

ACMP conceived an elegant building of vertical design with offices, an auditorium, conference rooms, a day-care center, entertainment areas, a bar, sports facilities, and other services. The project, which easily fits into the surrounding metropolitan environment, was planned as an urban forum that would promote social interaction and cultural exchange. The striking and attractive exterior structure was built of stone, metal, and glass. The first thing a visitor encounters upon entering the building is a spectacular lobby with high ceilings, where marble, wood, and light become the focal points. The functional diversity and spatial dynamics involved in all the activities contrast the simplicity and elegance of the forms.

The development of a complex with these characteristics required the creation of a functional and flexible plan that would simplify the distribution of the various areas according to the activities that would take place in them. Without a doubt, all this required the application of a careful and specific design, whether in the most private areas, the common spaces, or those spaces set aside for public use. The end result is a sober and contained building where functionality and use have dictated its interior distribution.

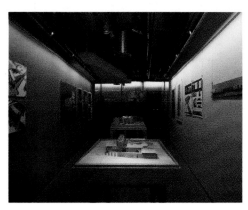

The project required careful landscape planning, and the extreme verticality of the architecture is in harmony with the green spaces around it and fits perfectly with the surroundings.

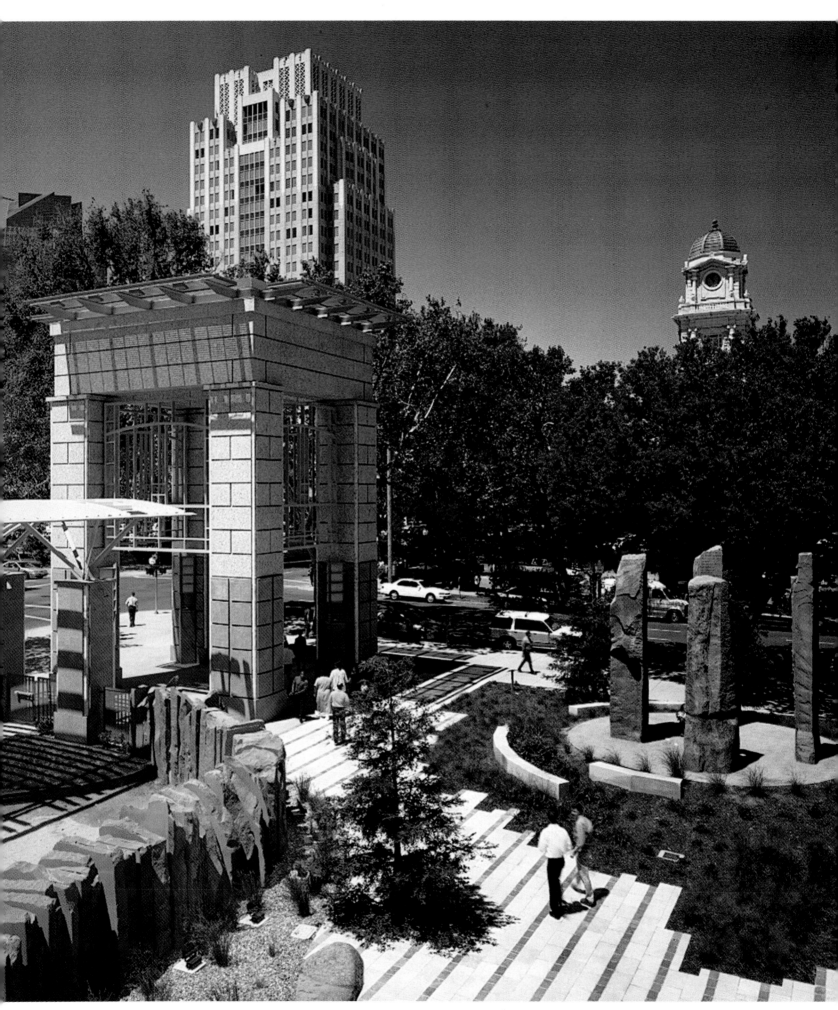

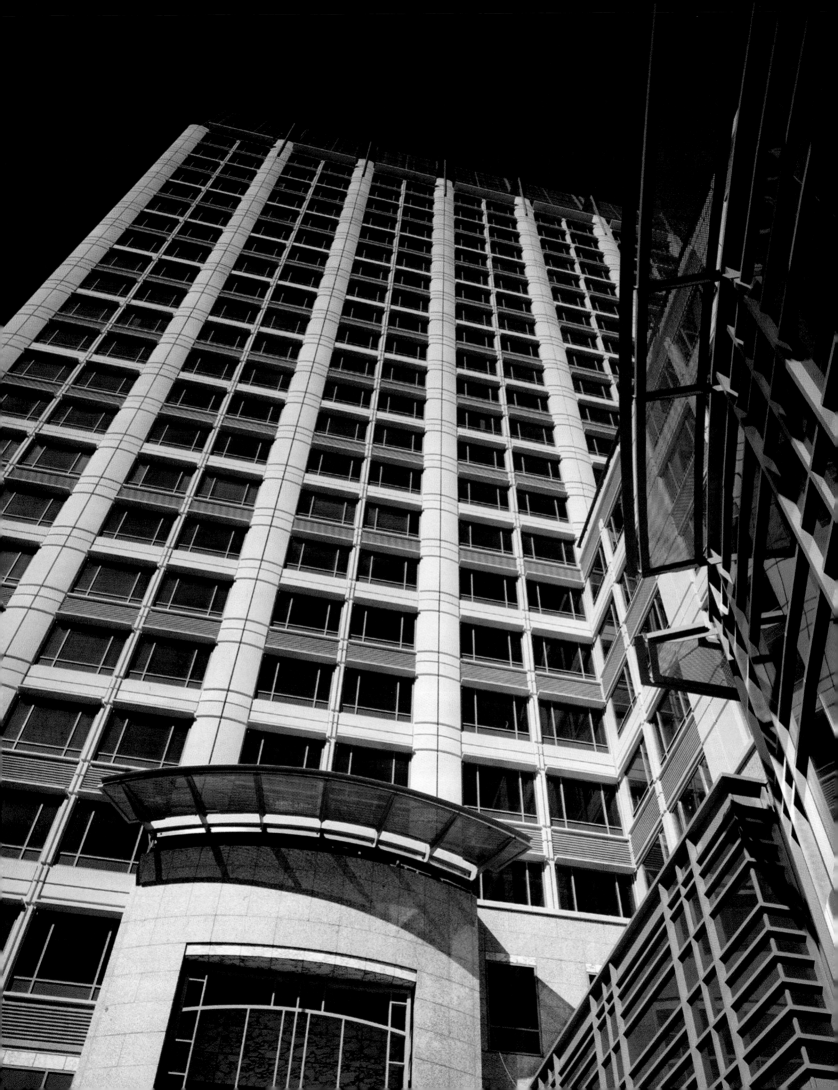

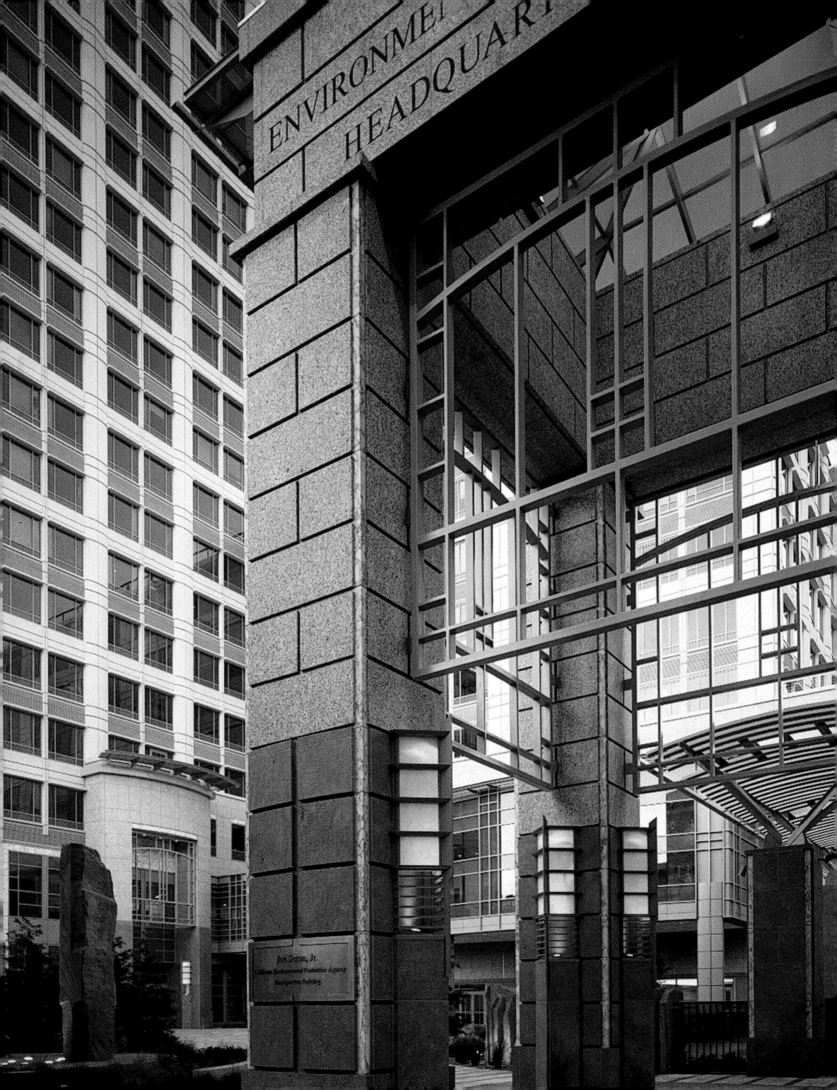

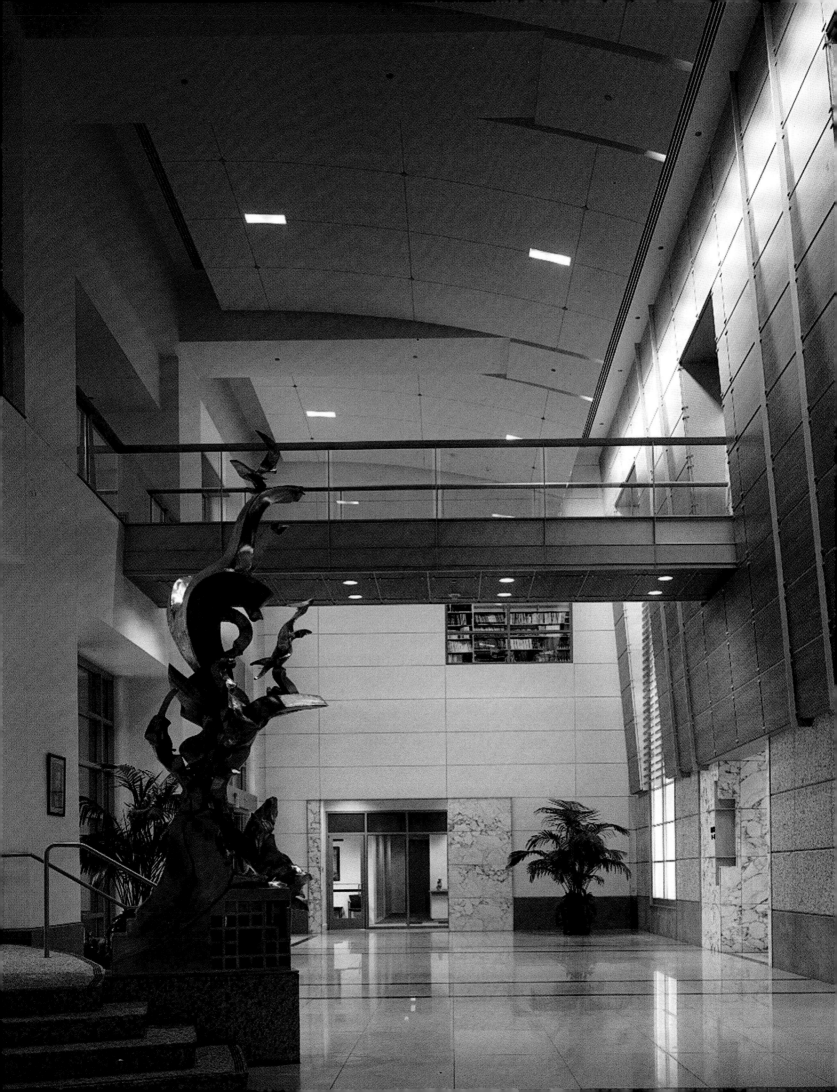

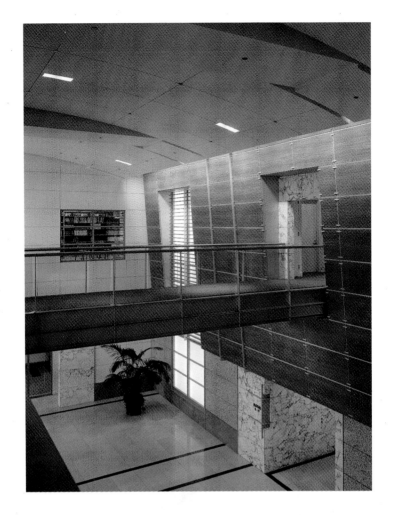

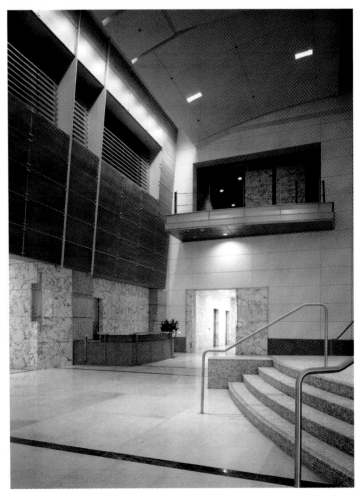

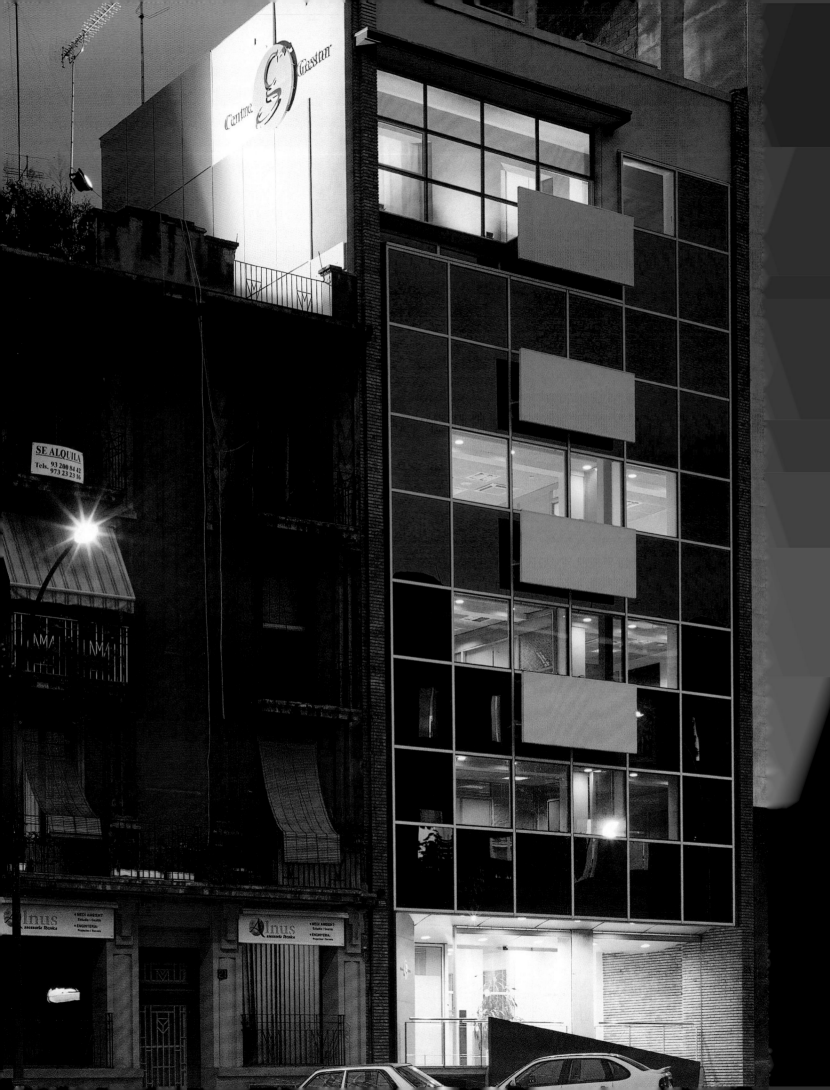

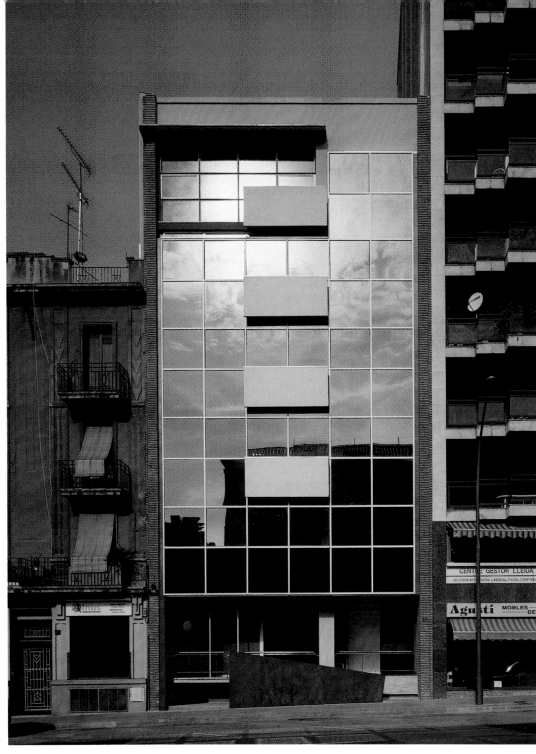

Centro Gestor

The remodeling and expansion of this already existing building—previously the headquarters of an electric company—afforded the planning of the new offices for this firm that provides labor, financial, fiscal, legal, and management services. The goal was to design a plan capable of incorporating the needs of the new company to include all the services in one building and to update the installations.

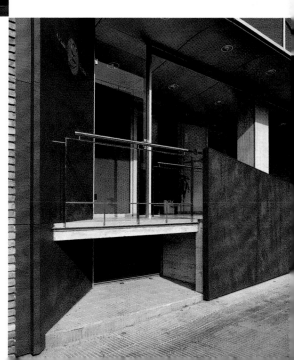

Centro Gestor

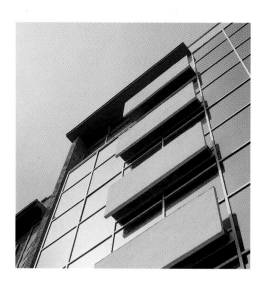

Architect: **Salvador Giné**
Client: **Centro Gestor de Lleida, S.A.**
Location: **Lleida, Spain**
Construction Date: **1999**
Photography: **Jordi Miralles**

The new building consists of seven floors, including the basement and the mezzanine. The remodeling has made it possible to increase the depth of the building (in the original structure, depth decreased progressively with height) in the basement, first and second floors, and mezzanine within the permitted limits. It was a matter of devising an architectural solution that allowed the coexistence of the old building and the new construction. A natural architectural dialogue was needed; it could not be forced. To that end, the space was made visually larger and, at the same time, the interior of the building was emptied out by creating an opening through the center of the first and second floors and the mezzanine in order to install a large skylight. This solution allowed, on the one hand, visual communication between levels to be maintained and, on the other, to articulate the areas and the traffic around them.

The treatment of the facade was also important. It was planned with the curtain-wall technique, but certain decorative and architectural elements were preserved. The result showed a new facade that neither closes nor hides anything but that defines and highlights the existing volumes.

The final project consists of a building full of personality, where preserving certain original elements and applying new, imaginative, and successful architectural solutions create a coherent and attractive balance capable of accommodating the functional needs of the resident.

The large space in the center, where the reception area is located, is created by perforating the first and second floors and the mezzanine. Visually, this space, connected with various areas of the building, is perfectly illuminated with the natural light that enters through the skylight and that floods every corner.

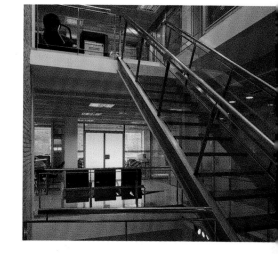

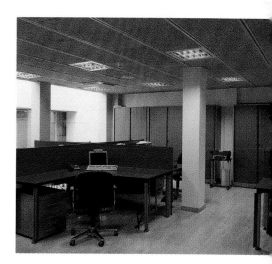

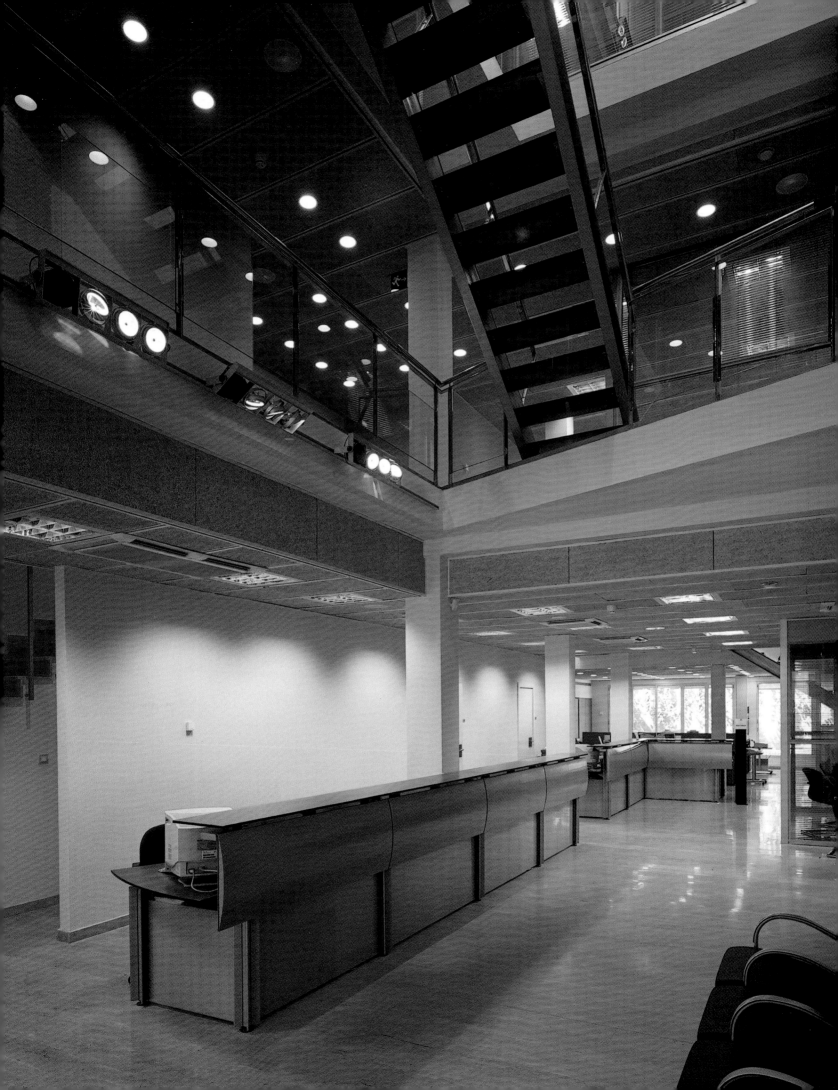

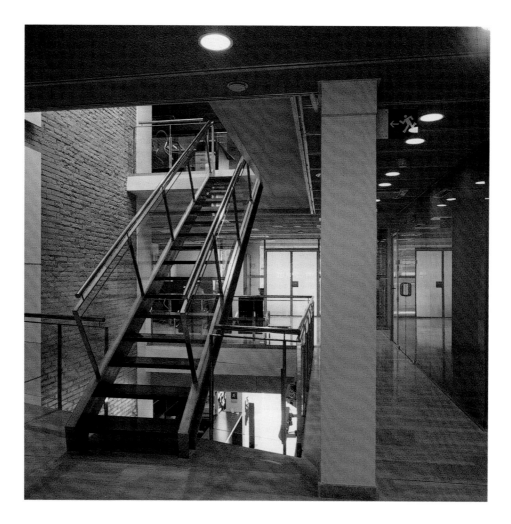

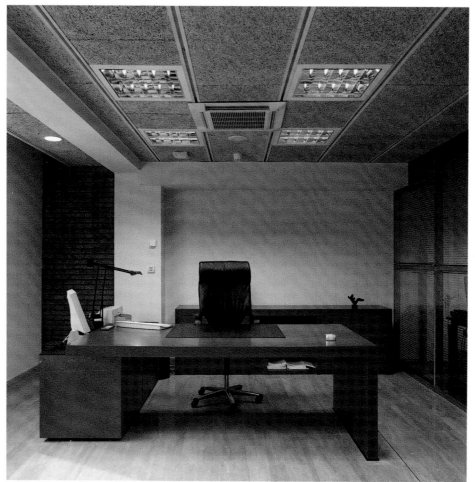

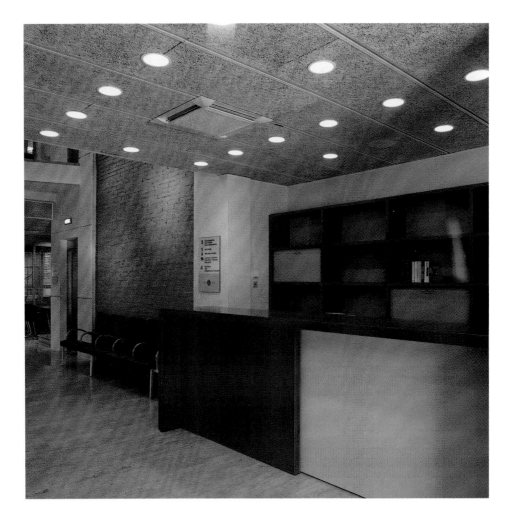

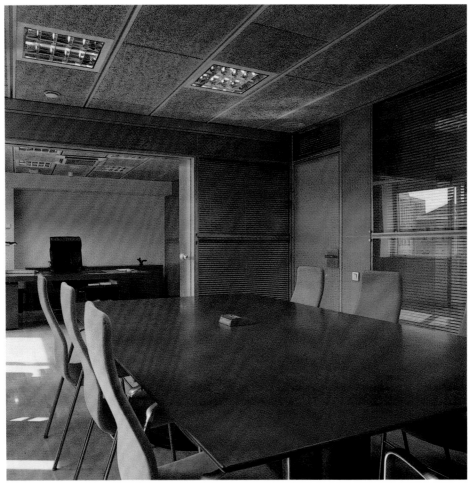

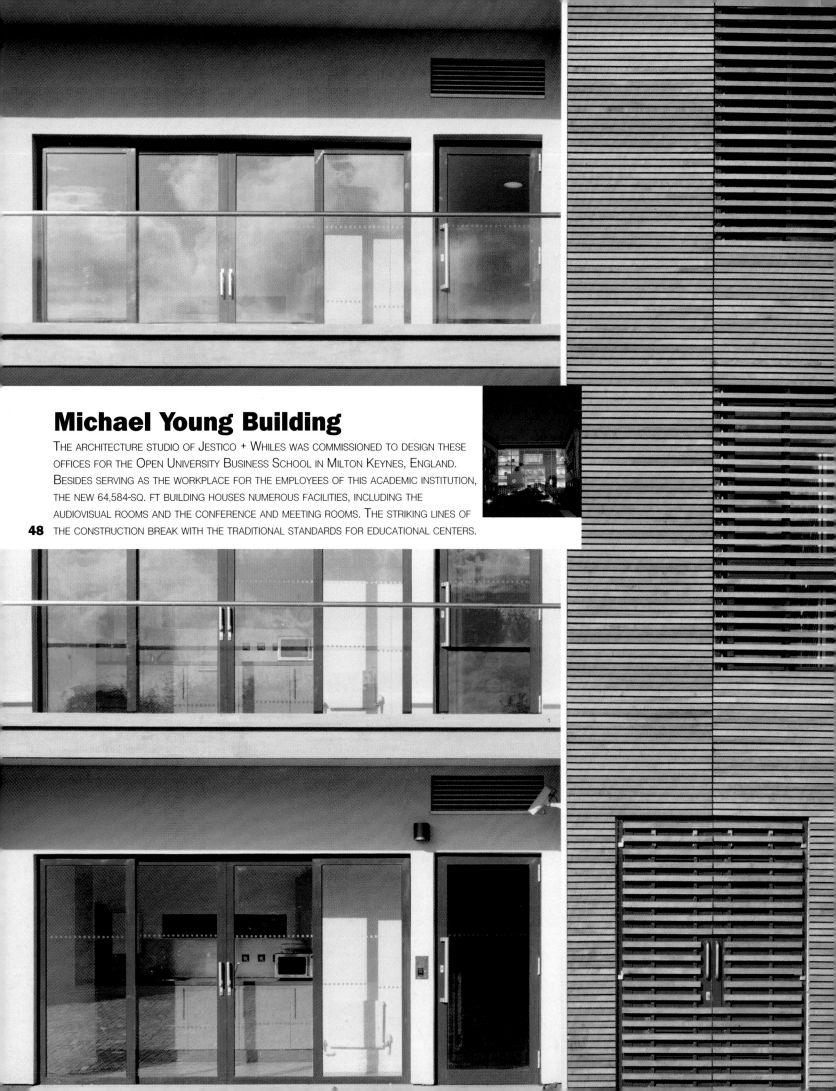

Michael Young Building

THE ARCHITECTURE STUDIO OF JESTICO + WHILES WAS COMMISSIONED TO DESIGN THESE OFFICES FOR THE OPEN UNIVERSITY BUSINESS SCHOOL IN MILTON KEYNES, ENGLAND. BESIDES SERVING AS THE WORKPLACE FOR THE EMPLOYEES OF THIS ACADEMIC INSTITUTION, THE NEW 64,584-SQ. FT BUILDING HOUSES NUMEROUS FACILITIES, INCLUDING THE AUDIOVISUAL ROOMS AND THE CONFERENCE AND MEETING ROOMS. THE STRIKING LINES OF THE CONSTRUCTION BREAK WITH THE TRADITIONAL STANDARDS FOR EDUCATIONAL CENTERS.

48

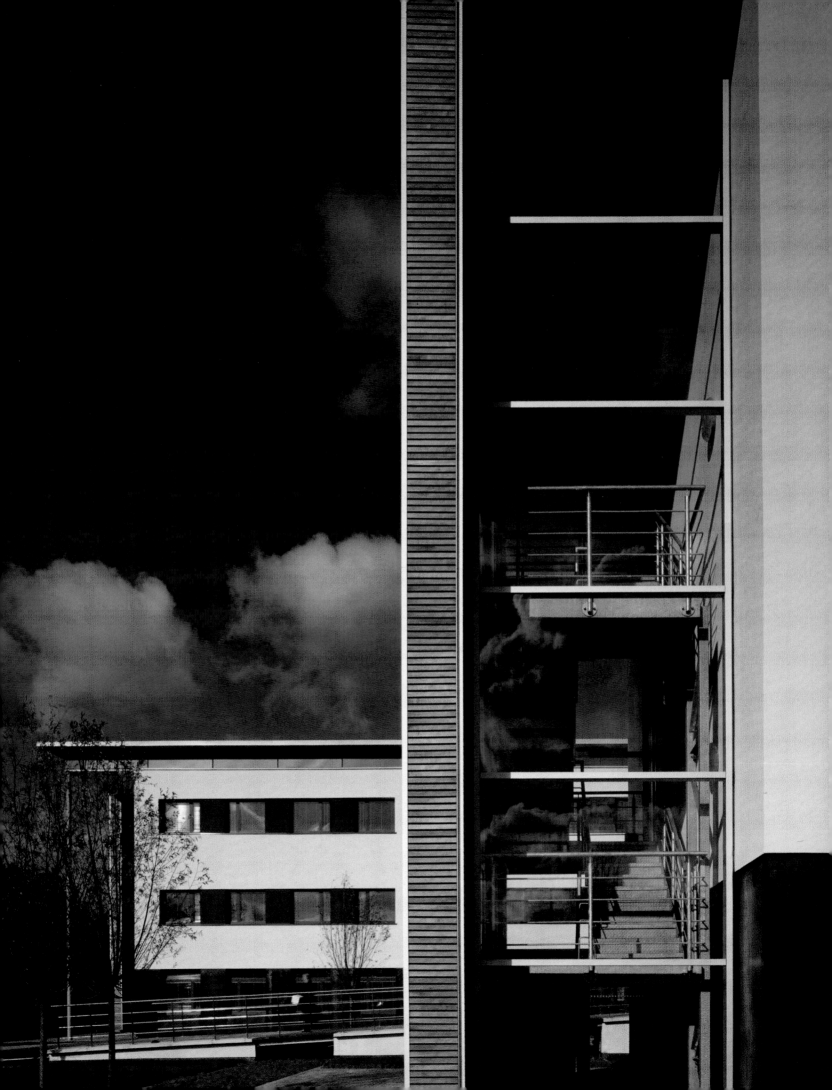

Michael Young Building

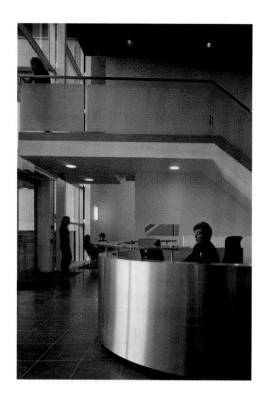

Architect: Jestico + Whiles
Client: **Open University Business School**
Location: **Milton Keynes, United Kingdom**
Construction Date: **2001**
Photography: **Peter Cook / VIEW**

Designed on three levels, the building has a peculiar configuration. A central block where the general services are located becomes the area with the most pedastrian traffic. The rooms that surround the perimeter of this body house the copying and printing facilities and the cafeteria. This central body becomes the heart and the hub of the building, from which the rest of the volumes extend. This arrangement creates a complex that is extraordinarily organized, where order and balance rule.

The work areas were deliberately conceived as open, clean, bright spaces free of columns, so they can be adapted to many spatial configurations. The areas are flexible and multifunctional, naturally ventilated, and perfectly illuminated. The present concern of architects in designing buildings that are energy efficient is reflected here through the use of passive energy and new technologies that are applied to building materials. The result is a spectacular work of structural expressiveness that demonstrates the mastery of Jestico + Whiles in creating pure structures stripped of anything unnecessary, in the handling of materials and details, as well as in the way that light is molded to become another architectural element.

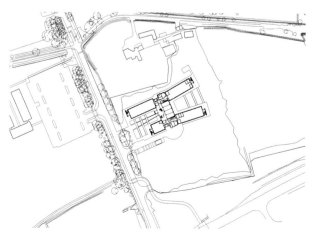

Site plan

The selection of materials for either the exterior or the interior was based on the pursuit of clarity and transparency. This is why glass and polished surfaces that reflect light and color abound. Aluminum, concrete, and steel are the structural elements that make up the restrained palette of materials, colors, and textures that dominate the project.

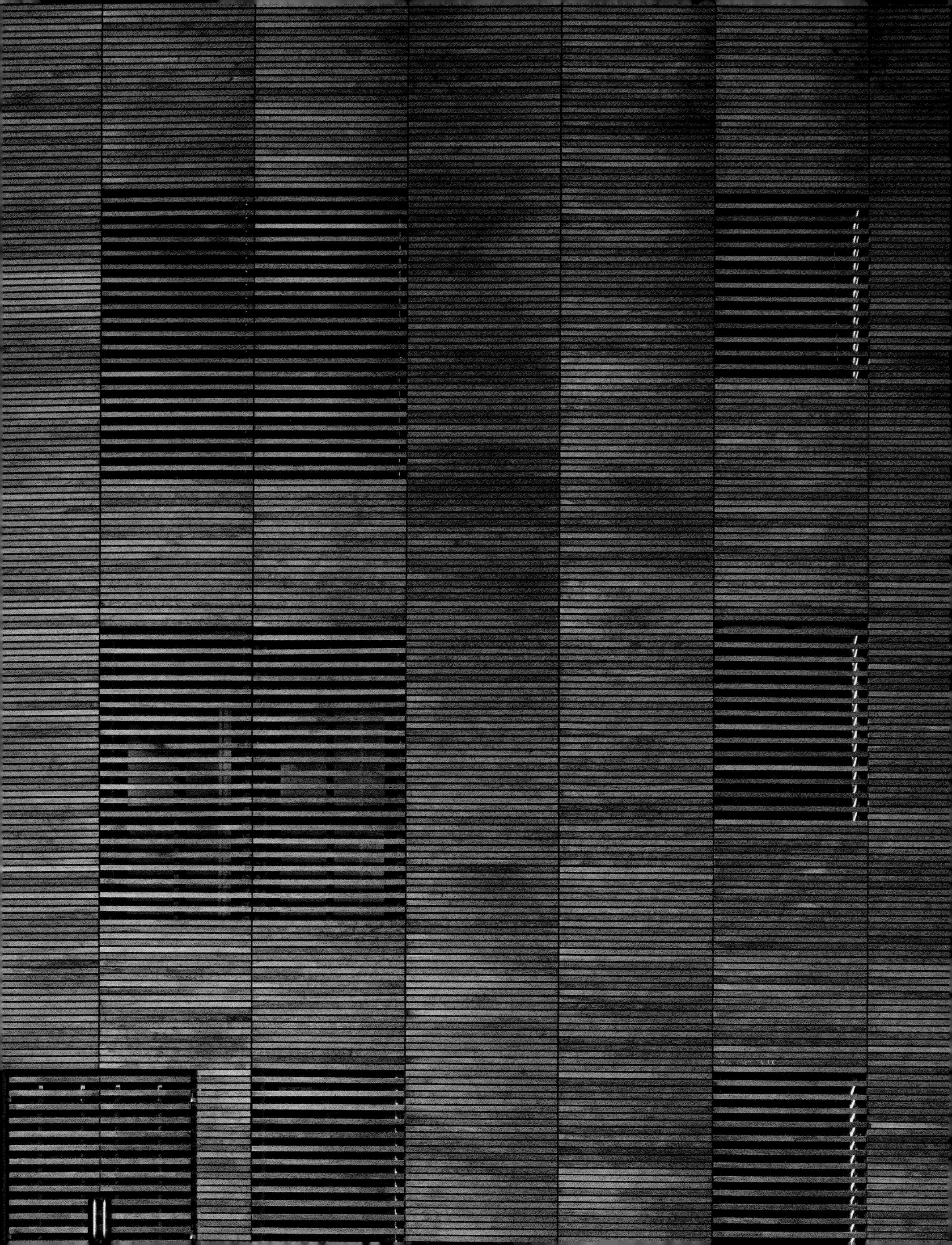

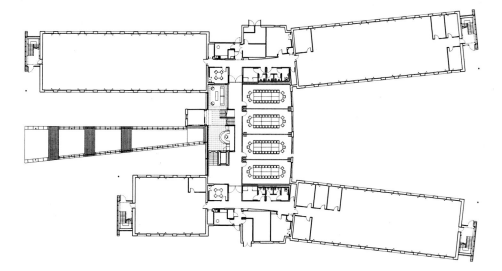

Ground floor

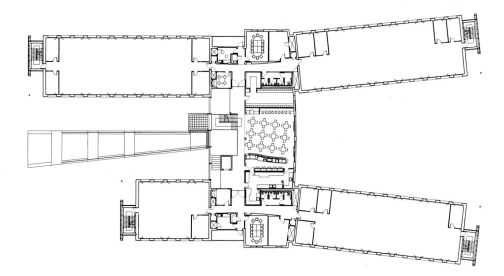

First floor

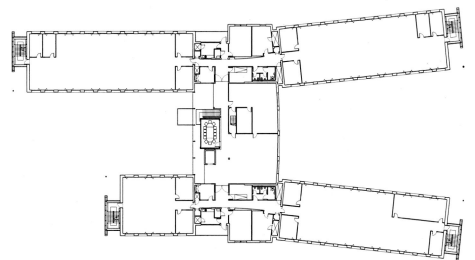

Second floor

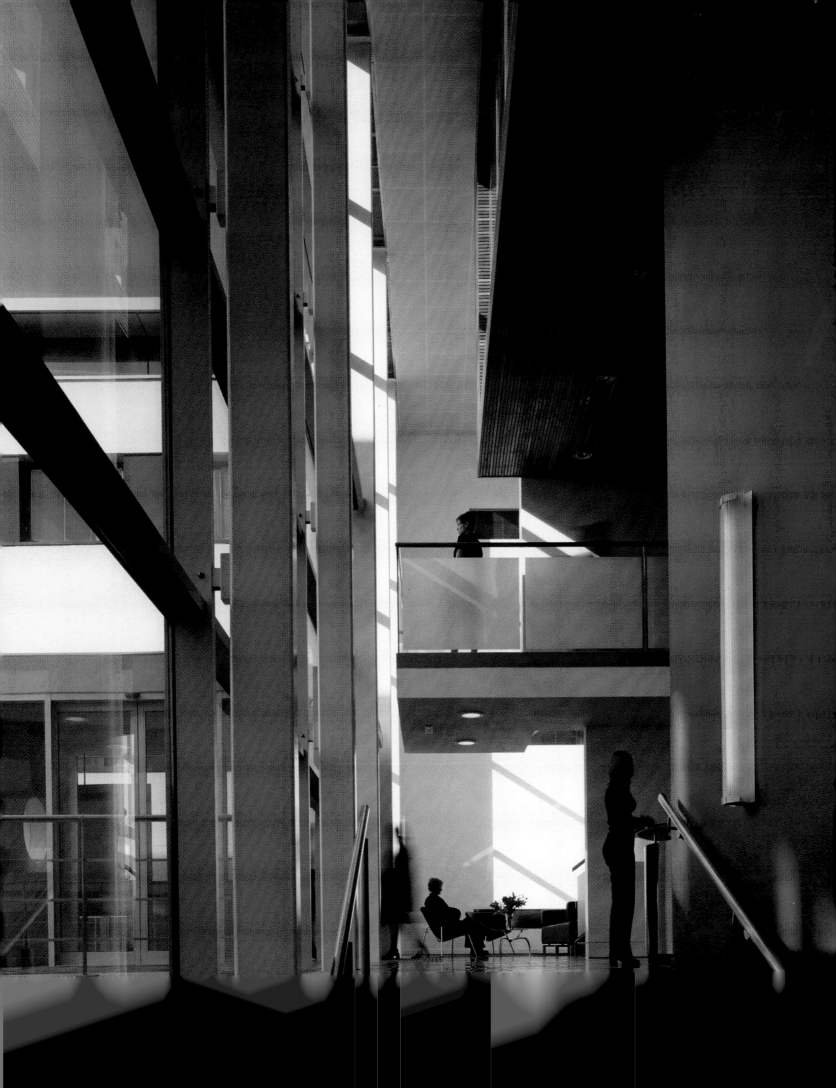

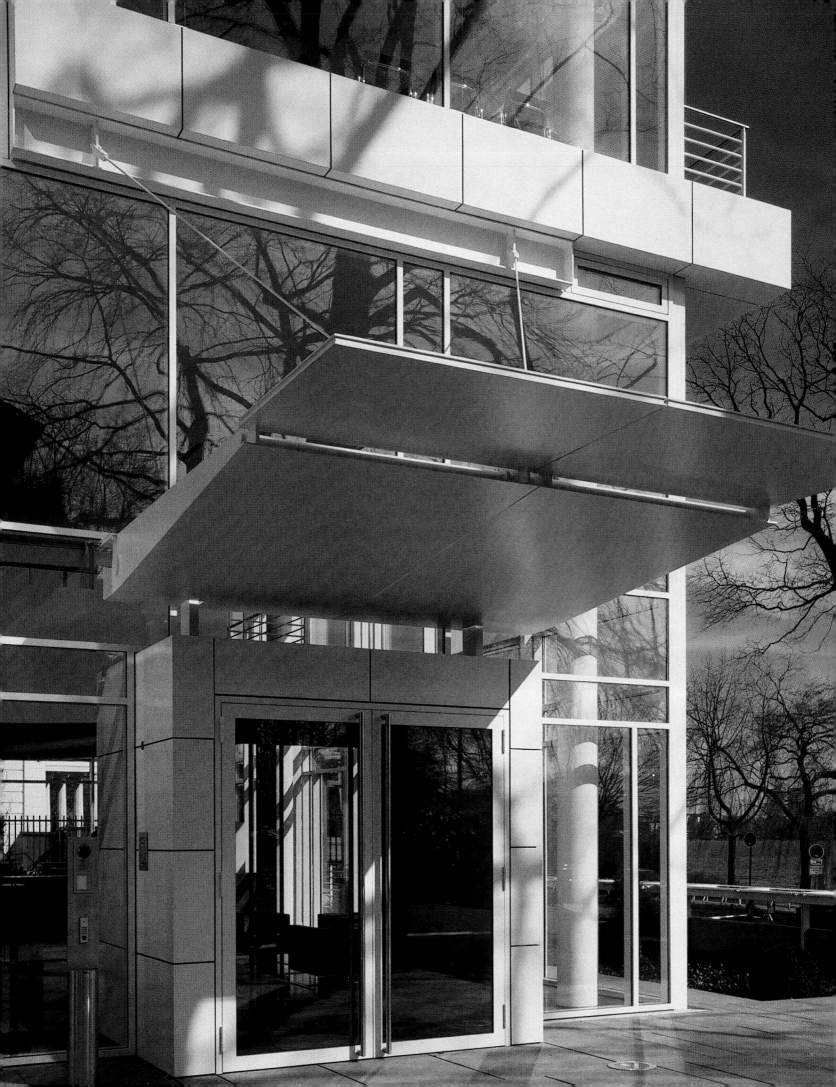

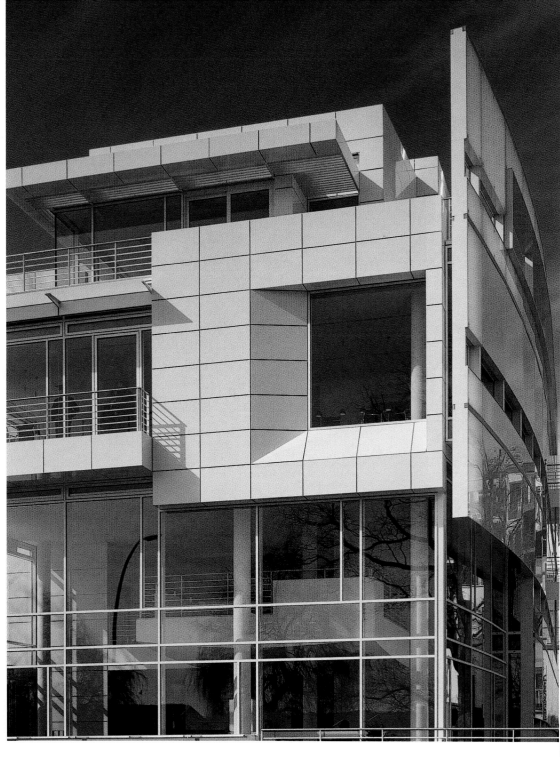

Rickmers Reederei Headquarters

ARCHITECT RICHARD MEIER PLANNED THE NEW GENERAL HEADQUARTERS OF THE NAVAL
COMPANY RICKMERS REEDEREI IN HAMBURG, GERMANY. THE NEW CONSTRUCTION OF
CLEAN, CONCISE, AND WELL-DEFINED LINES IS LOCATED BESIDE THE MAN-MADE LAKE OF
AUSSENALSTER, A LARGE LAKE THAT IS CONNECTED TO THE PORT OF HAMBURG AND IS
PART OF A NETWORK OF CANALS. THE STRIKING AND RECOGNIZABLE ARCHITECTURAL
FEATURES OF THE BUILDING ARE A REFLECTION OF AND INSPIRED BY THE SPIRIT OF THE
COMPANY.

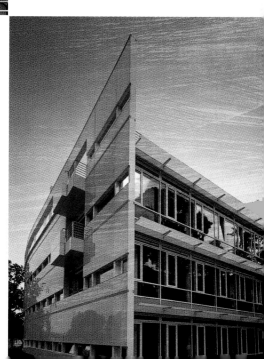

Rickmers Reederei Headquarters

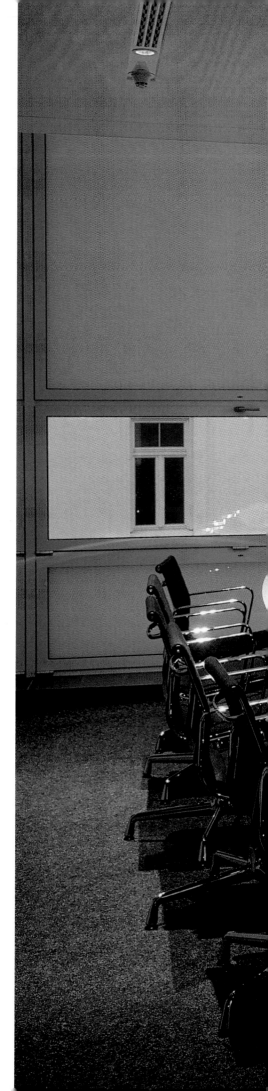

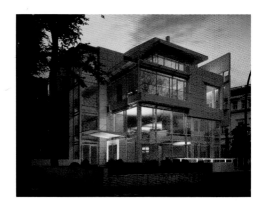

Architect: **Richard Meier & Partners**
Client: **Rickmers Reederei**
Location: **Hamburg, Germany**
Construction Date: **2000**
Photography: **Klaus Frahm, Oliver Heissner / ARTUR**

The project consists of a sober and rational space that pairs the most absolute modernism with the elegance of classicism. The main facade was made almost entirely of glass and extends above the rest of the building. The volume is slightly curved and resembles a sail propelled by the wind in the middle of the ocean. Furthermore, it seems to be suspended inside, with an exhibit of the company's model ships. The canopy and entrance door to the headquarters give way to an ample hall from which stem the different sections and areas that make up the company.

Everything in the interior of the building reflects austere spaces conceived as elements that are reminders of the maritime activities of the firm. Many construction and architectural features are references to the connection to the ocean, such as substituting wood slats with visible joints for the carpet of the offices and the meeting room, similar to the deck of a ship. The furnishings also reinforce the strict rationality of the ships that sail the oceans, where everything must be ready to ensure a pleasant and comfortable voyage. In this case, these consist of a selection of pieces of contemporary design, functional and aesthetically beautiful, which help make all activities easier.

The most revered contemporary design pieces are set in an interior of striking functionality, where the reduction of materials, furnishings, and decorative elements create a compositional unity and become the focal points, while still allowing the architecture to express itself.

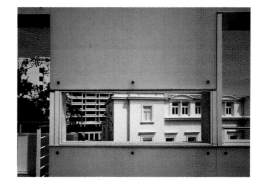

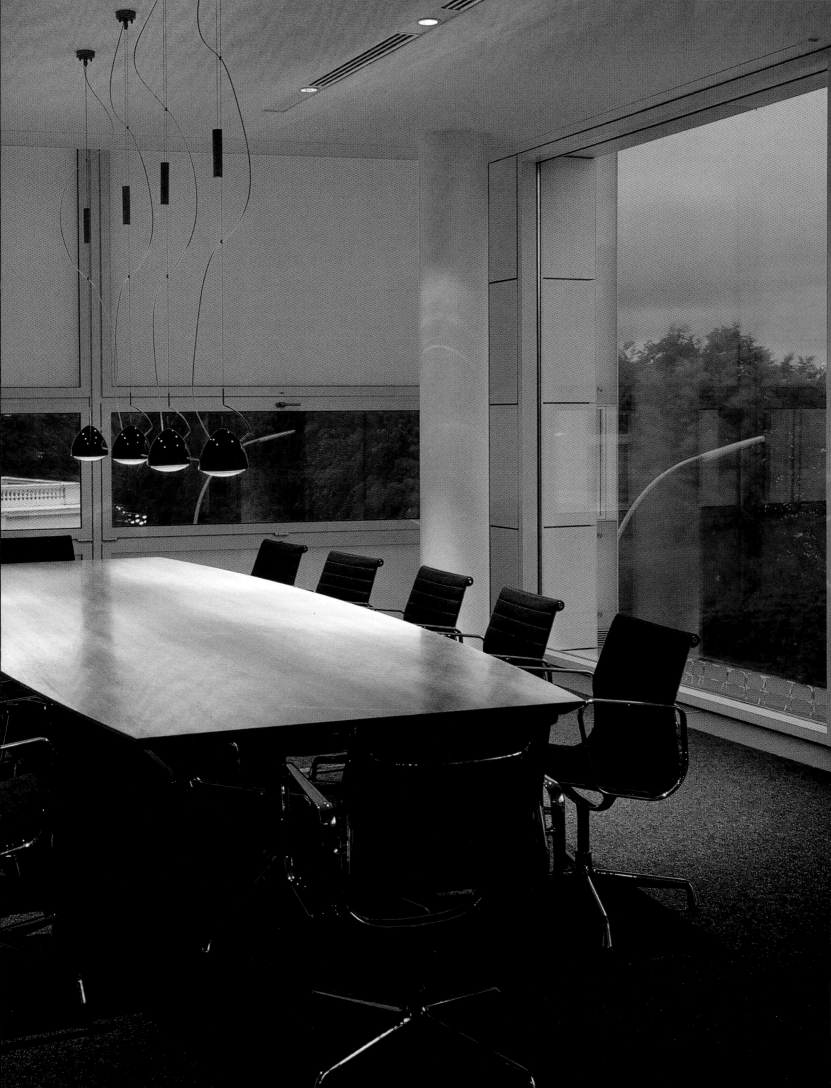

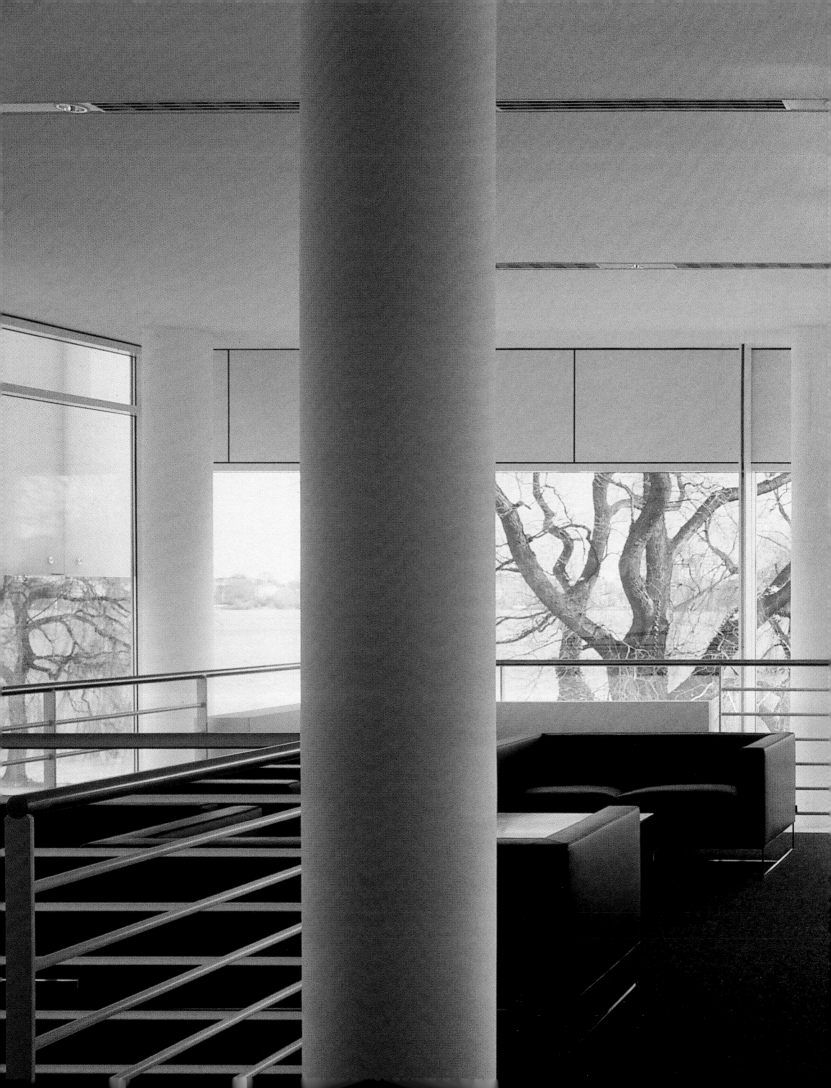

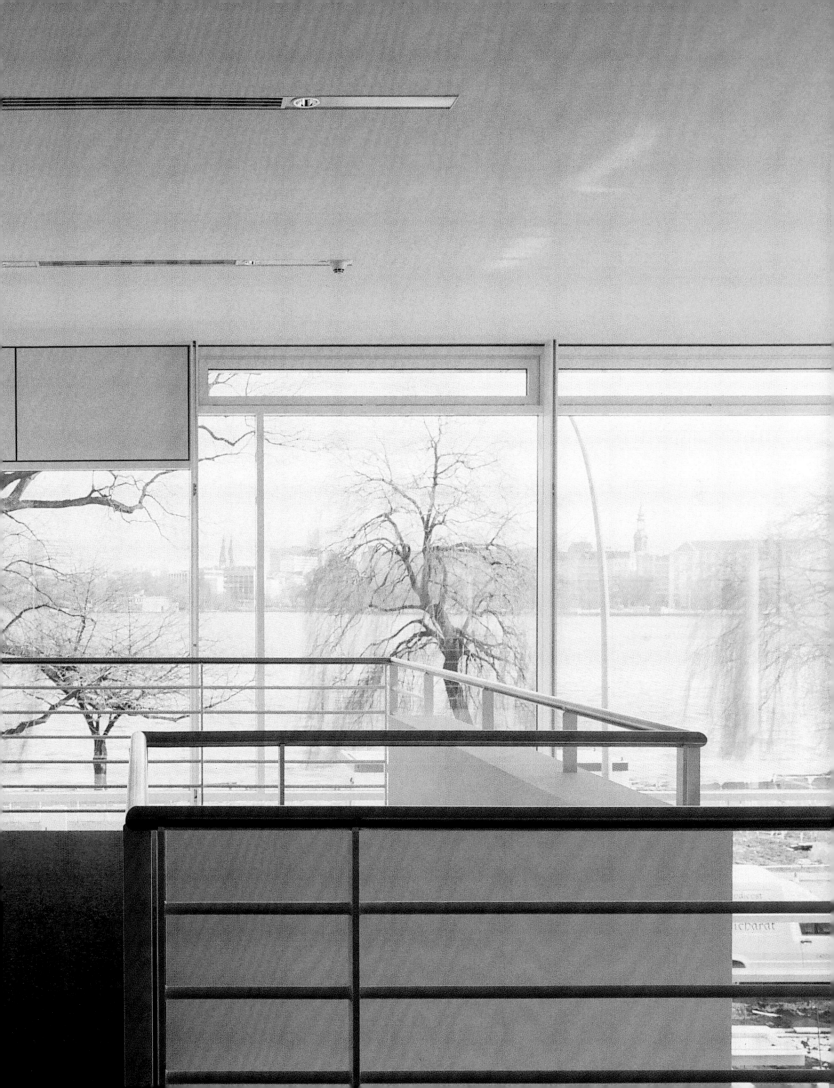

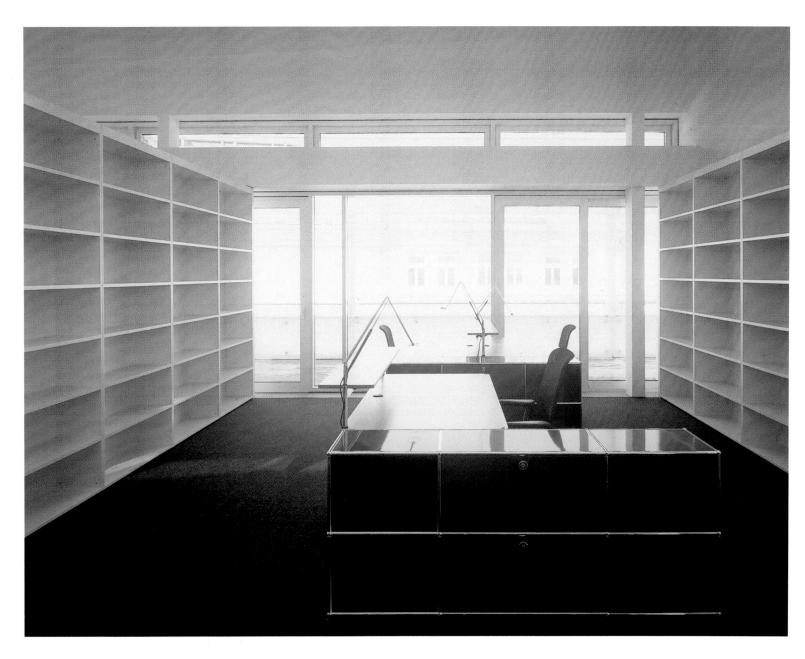

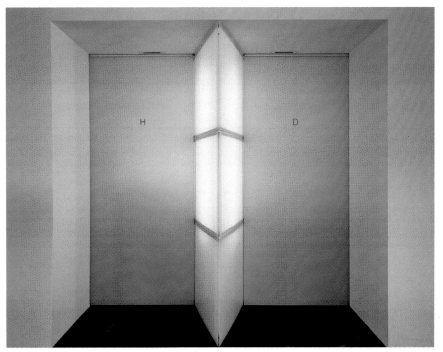

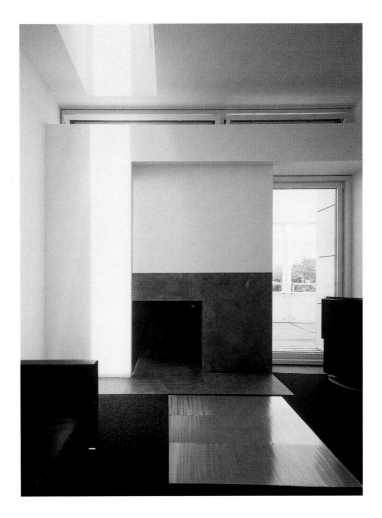

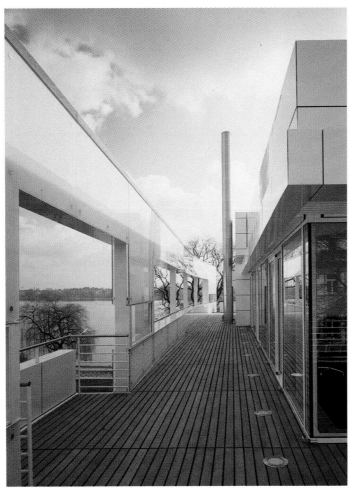

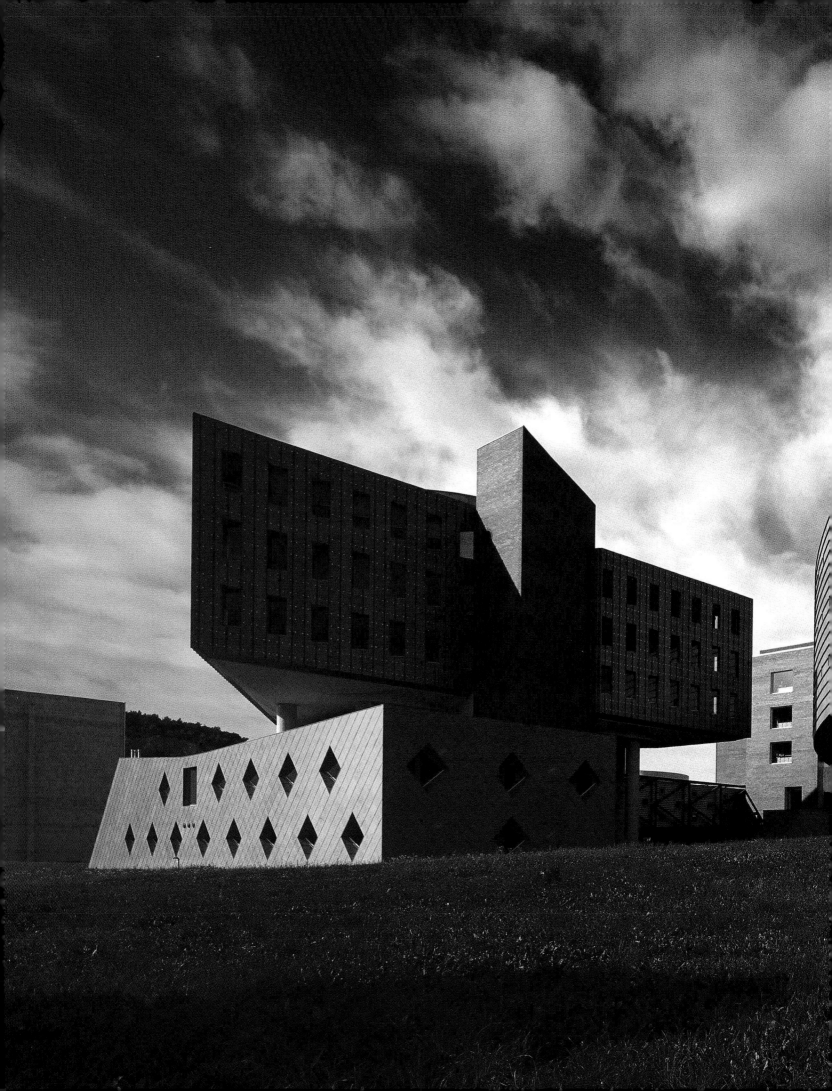

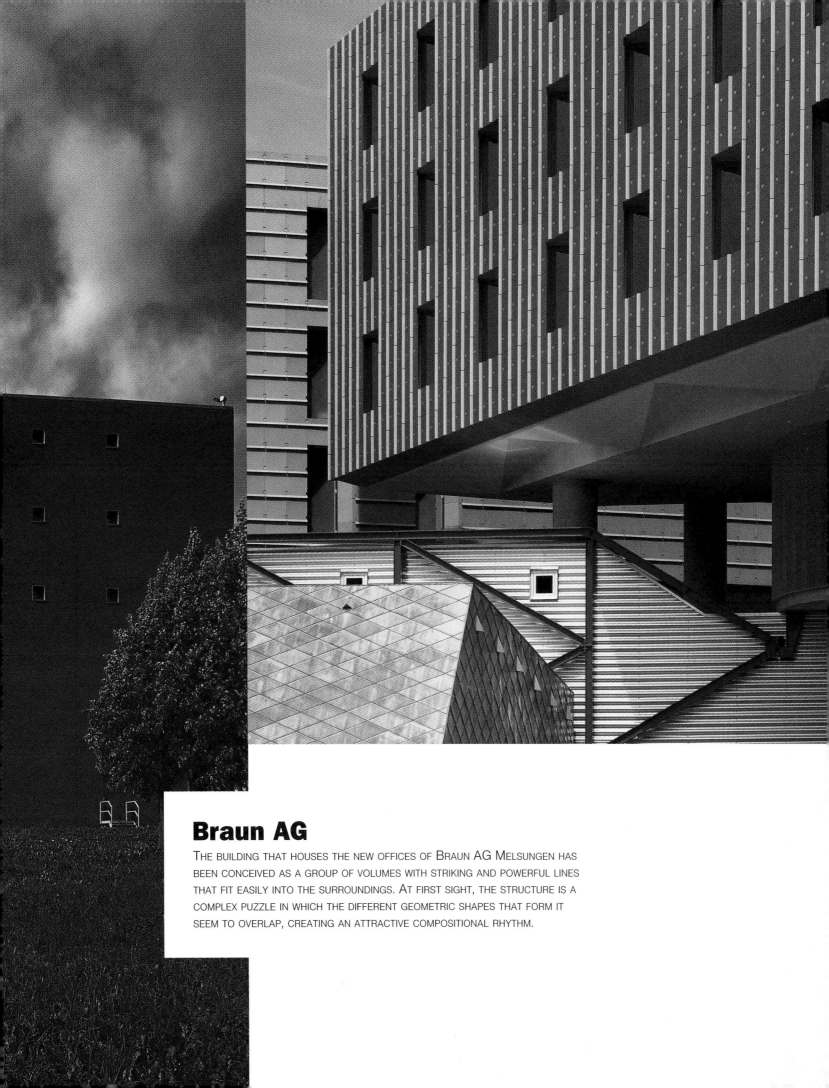

Braun AG

THE BUILDING THAT HOUSES THE NEW OFFICES OF BRAUN AG MELSUNGEN HAS
BEEN CONCEIVED AS A GROUP OF VOLUMES WITH STRIKING AND POWERFUL LINES
THAT FIT EASILY INTO THE SURROUNDINGS. AT FIRST SIGHT, THE STRUCTURE IS A
COMPLEX PUZZLE IN WHICH THE DIFFERENT GEOMETRIC SHAPES THAT FORM IT
SEEM TO OVERLAP, CREATING AN ATTRACTIVE COMPOSITIONAL RHYTHM.

Braun AG

Architect: **Wilford + Partner**
Collaborator: **Manuel Schupp**
Client: **Gelimer**
Location: **Melsungen, Germany**
Construction Date: **2001**
Photography: **Monika Nikolic / ARTUR**

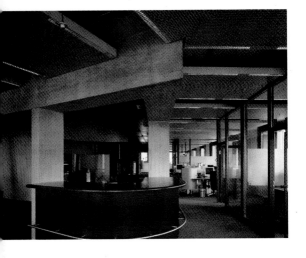

The geometric counterpoint of the volumes creates a strongly expressive building with structural coherence, a project of immeasurable conceptual clarity, extremely ordered, with great visual purity. The straight lines and impressive forms of the different multifunctional modules that share the facilities of the complex are fully integrated into the surrounding landscape. The objective was to create a self-contained space, independent from the outdoors but at the same time fitting into the landscape.

Each volume that makes up the composition is based in a geometric figure. The main entrance and main offices are located in a space with a triangular floor plan. The base of the building is a two-story rectangular structure, and the center of the composition, where the technical department is located, has a round shape.

The interiors are open and flowing, facilitating the distribution of the various practical spaces required by the company. The final result of this project, whose essence is in its imagination and substance in its sensible composition, is a building as complex as it is aesthetically striking. A true exercise of spatial mastery, the building is respectful of the landscape while establishing a truthful dialogue between background and form.

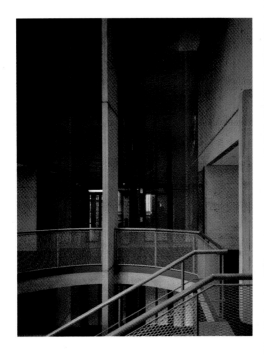

The project has purposely distanced itself from the formal and functional characteristics of traditional office buildings. The goal was to create a modern space whose distribution is based on a thoughtful and efficient internal structure. The architectural solution employed to reach it is a hybrid of open versus closed.

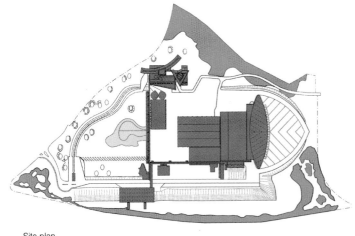

Site plan

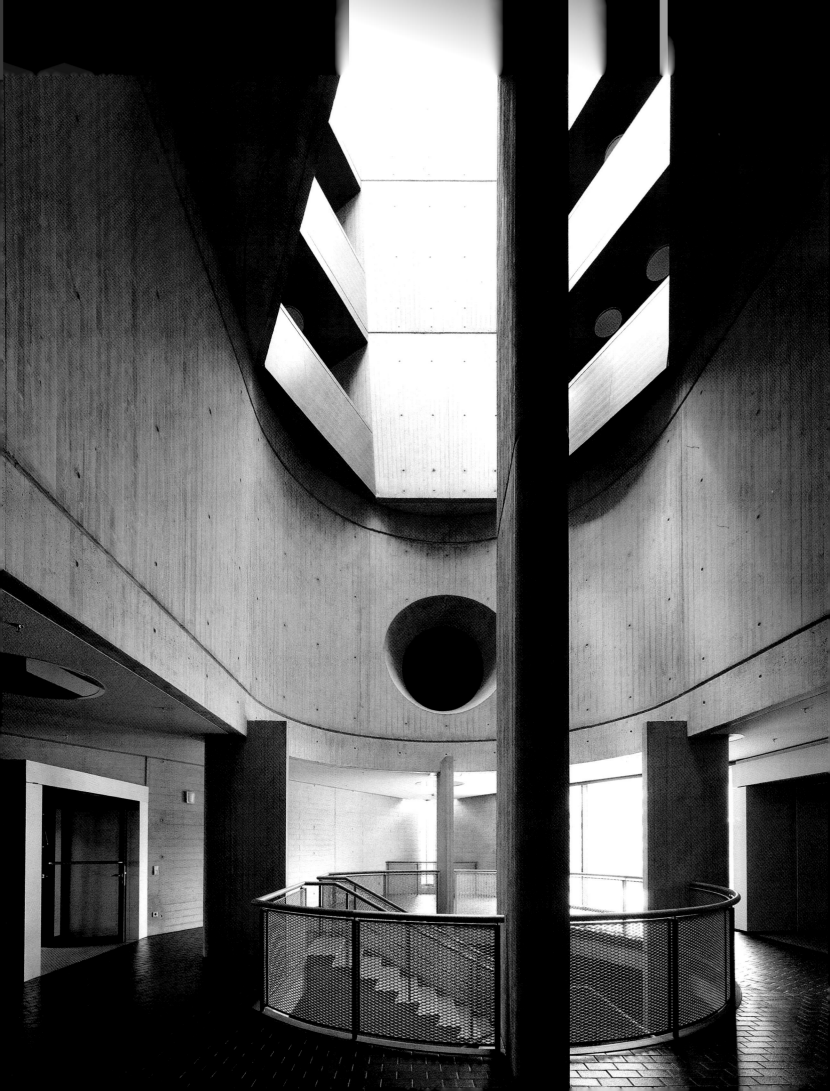

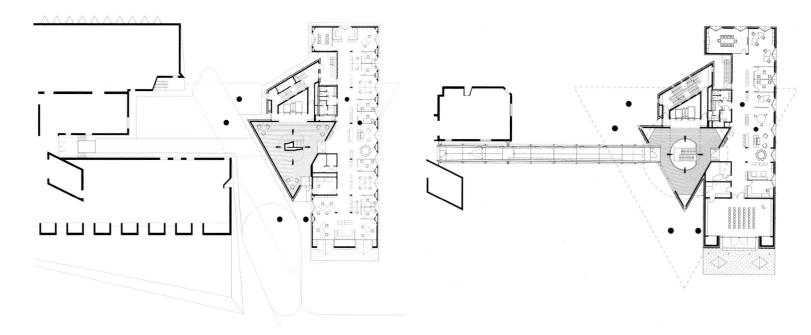

Ground floor

First floor

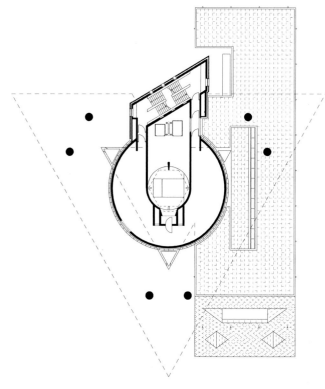

Second floor

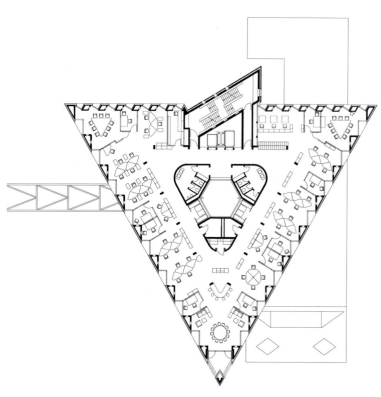

Third floor

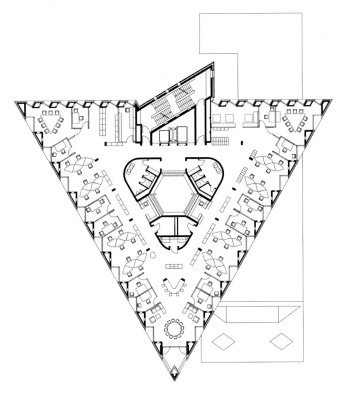

Fourth floor

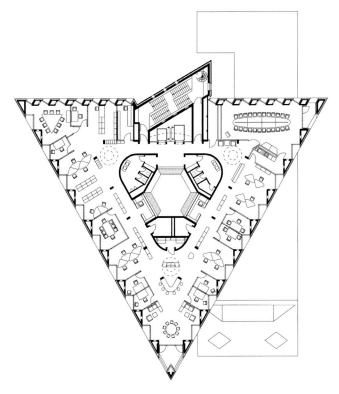

Fifth floor

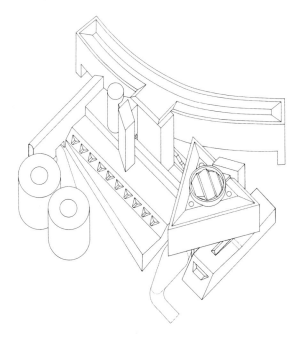

Perspective

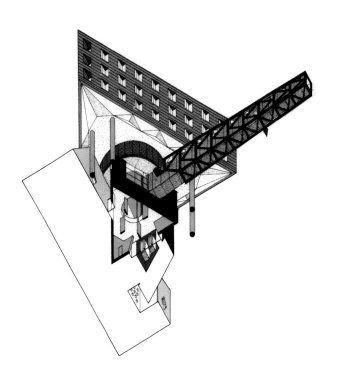

Perspective from below

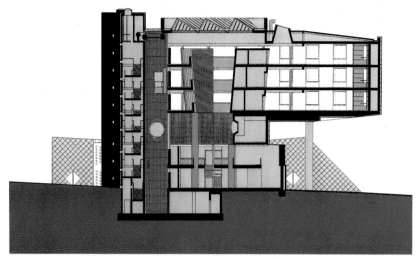

Section

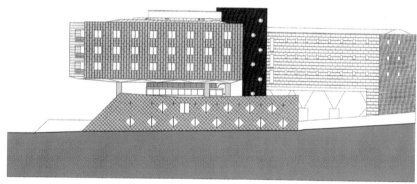

Elevation

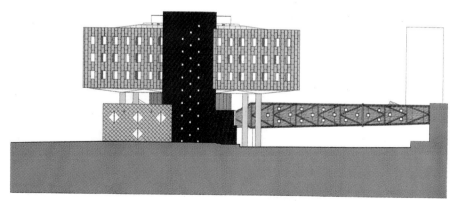

Elevation

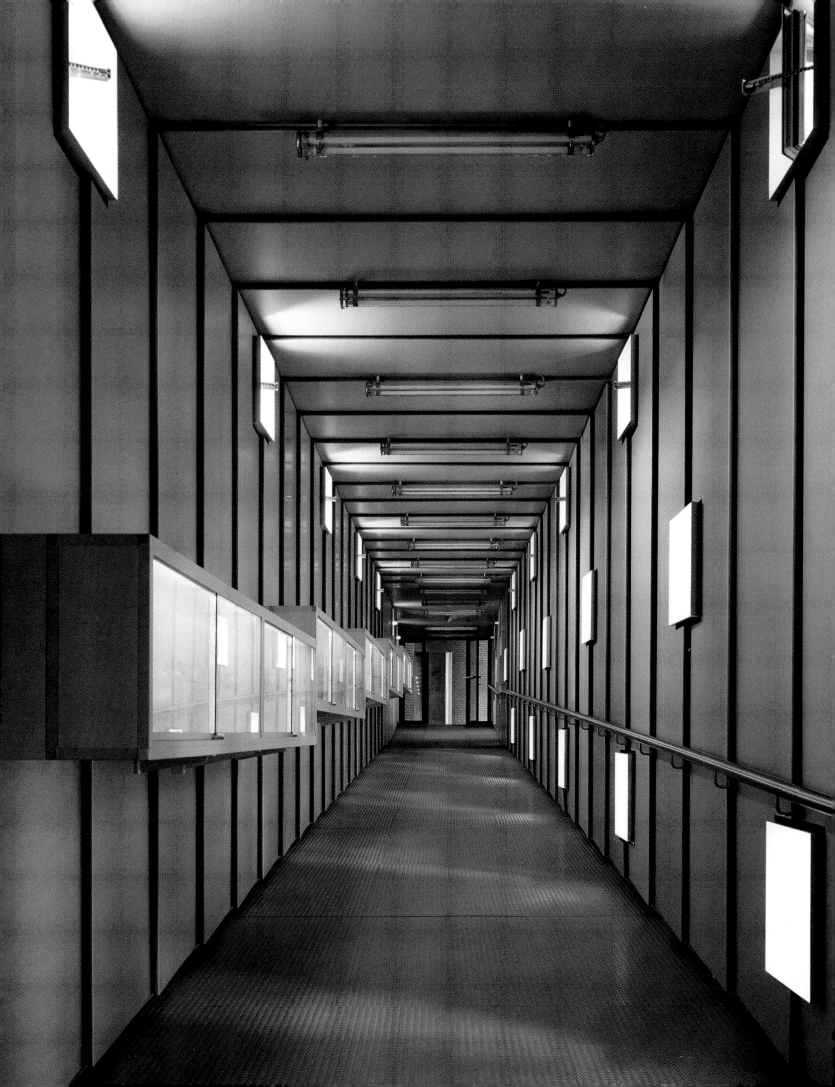

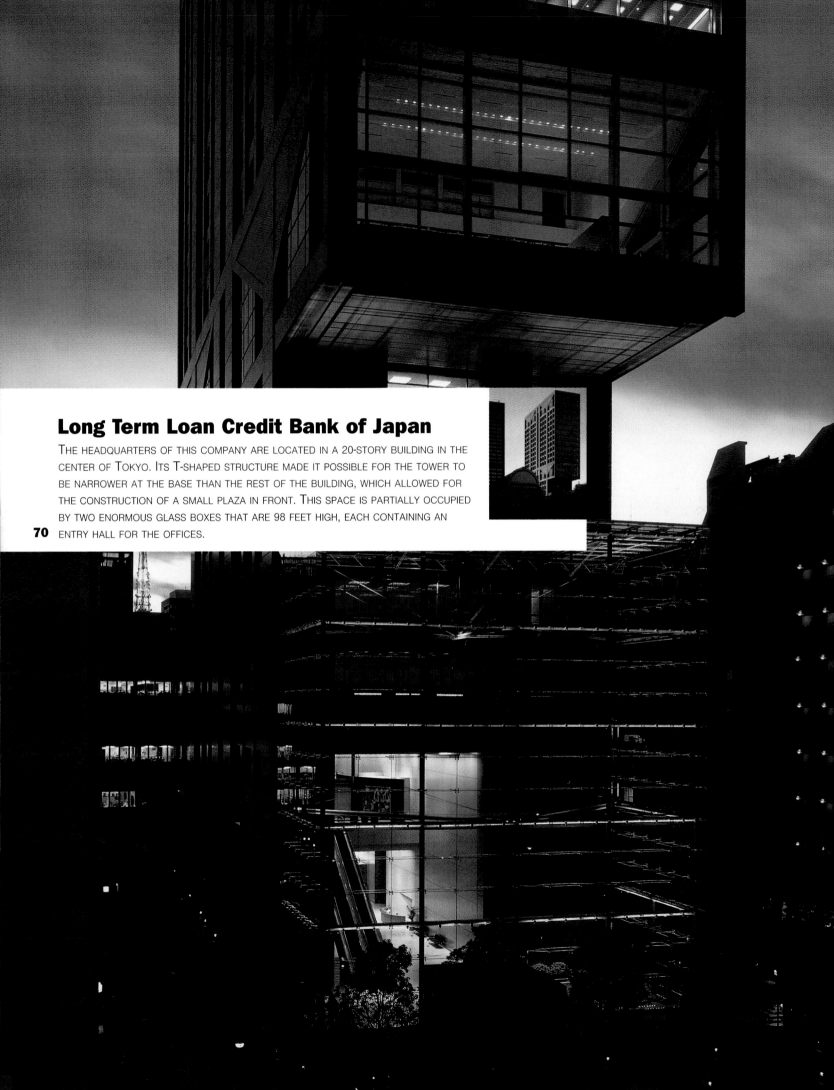

Long Term Loan Credit Bank of Japan

THE HEADQUARTERS OF THIS COMPANY ARE LOCATED IN A 20-STORY BUILDING IN THE CENTER OF TOKYO. ITS T-SHAPED STRUCTURE MADE IT POSSIBLE FOR THE TOWER TO BE NARROWER AT THE BASE THAN THE REST OF THE BUILDING, WHICH ALLOWED FOR THE CONSTRUCTION OF A SMALL PLAZA IN FRONT. THIS SPACE IS PARTIALLY OCCUPIED BY TWO ENORMOUS GLASS BOXES THAT ARE 98 FEET HIGH, EACH CONTAINING AN ENTRY HALL FOR THE OFFICES.

70

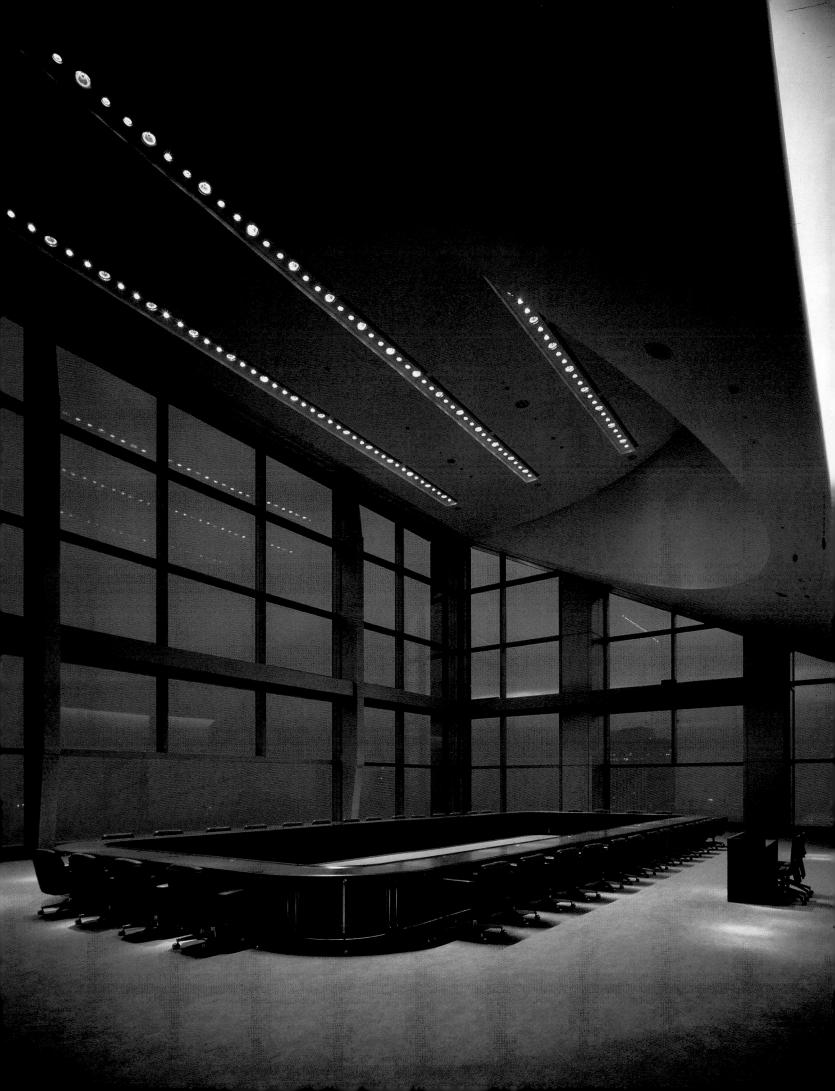

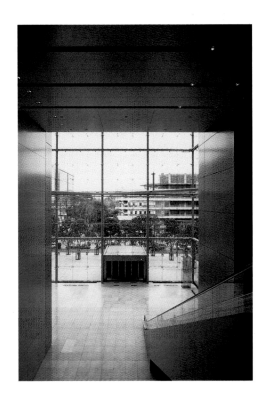

Architect: **Nikken Sekkei**
Collaborator: **Tekenaka Corporation (contractor)**
Client: **Long Term Loan Credit Bank of Japan**
Location: **Tokyo, Japan**
Construction Date: **1995**
Photography: **Nácasa & Partners**

The rhythm of the composition of the facades is governed by the building's structural system. The pillars and wrought iron are reflected on the outside by metal strips that frame the glass panes. In the large corner offices, the tilted pillars allow the use of large glass walls that, besides providing a view, bathe the interior in natural light.

The building's "T" shape is a major technical accomplishment. In fact, all public areas, including the lobby, conference room, auditorium, cafeteria, and dining room, have a representative and spectacular character. In a country accustomed to small interiors and in a city where the price-per-square-meter is very high, this building lavishly uses space. In this sense, the top floor is the most representative. The two ends of the building, which enjoy a spectacular panoramic view, house a large room for meetings and a 39-foot-tall room to welcome visitors. These generous dimensions are more in line with an opera stage than a work place. The rooms are furnished sparingly, with only a few armchairs, a table, and a rug. This decorative austerity further emphasizes the size of the spaces.

Enclosing the entire building with glass provides abundant natural light. Polished materials and smooth surfaces, like the stone on the floor and the anodized aluminum of the interior partitions in the reception area, were used to maximize the effect of reflecting and enhancing the light.

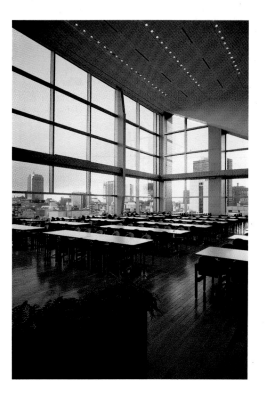

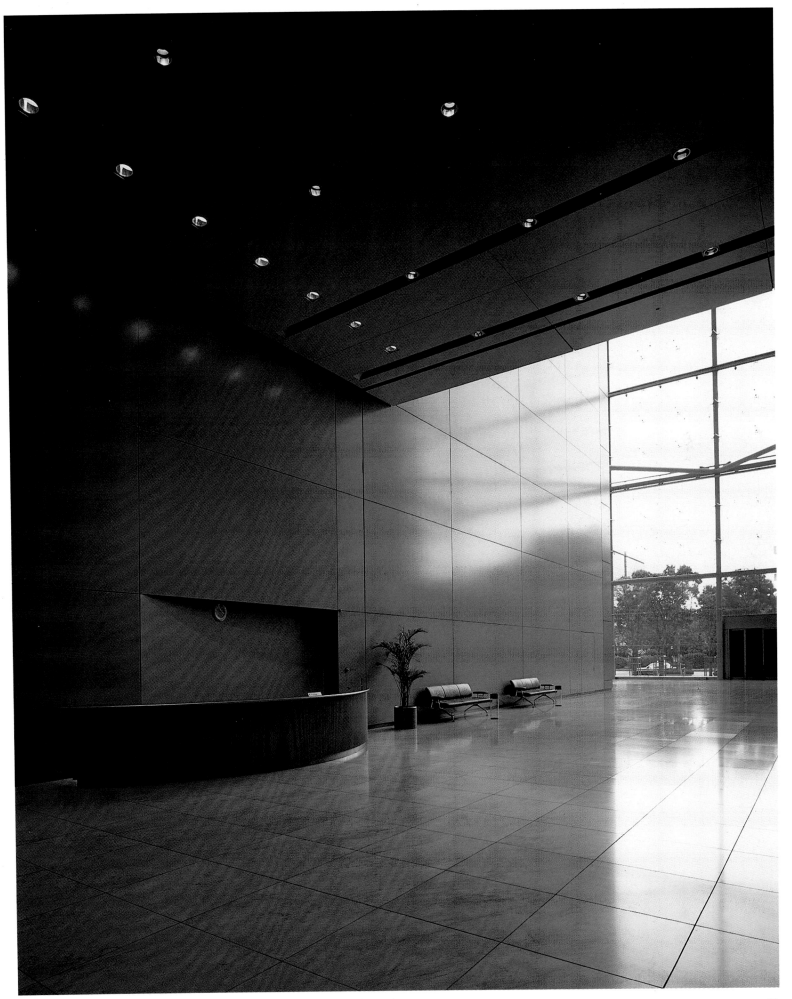

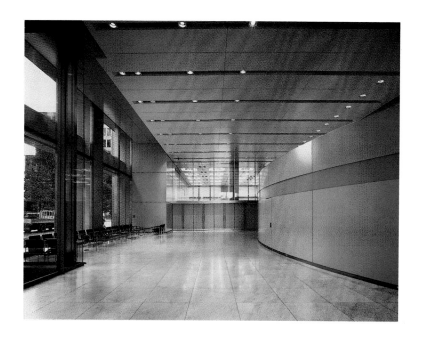

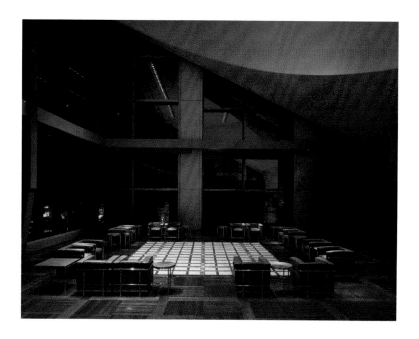

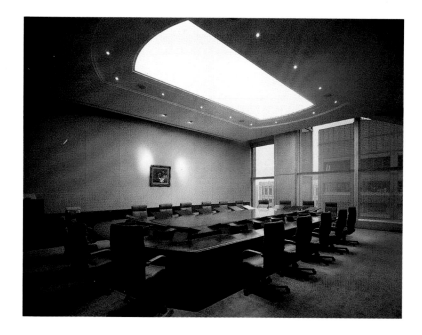

The decision to make some of the conference and meeting rooms very high was not only an architectural solution but also formed part of a meticulous corporate strategy. If a bank projects the image of opulence and confidence, it will be able to attract new clients more easily.

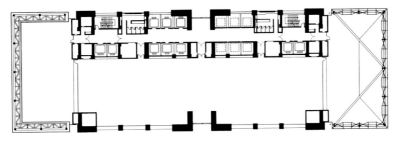

Floor plan: lower floors

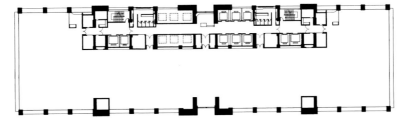

Floor plan: upper floors

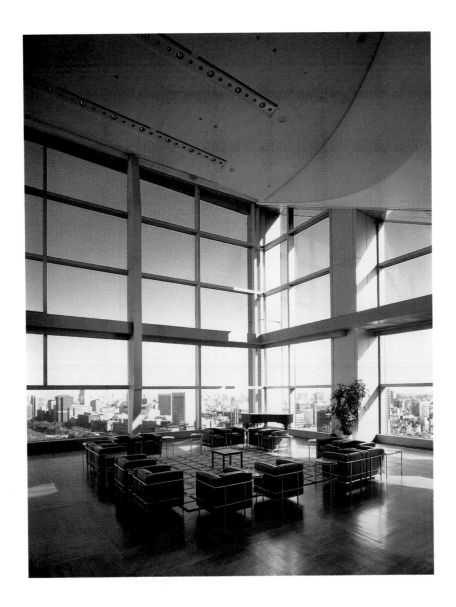

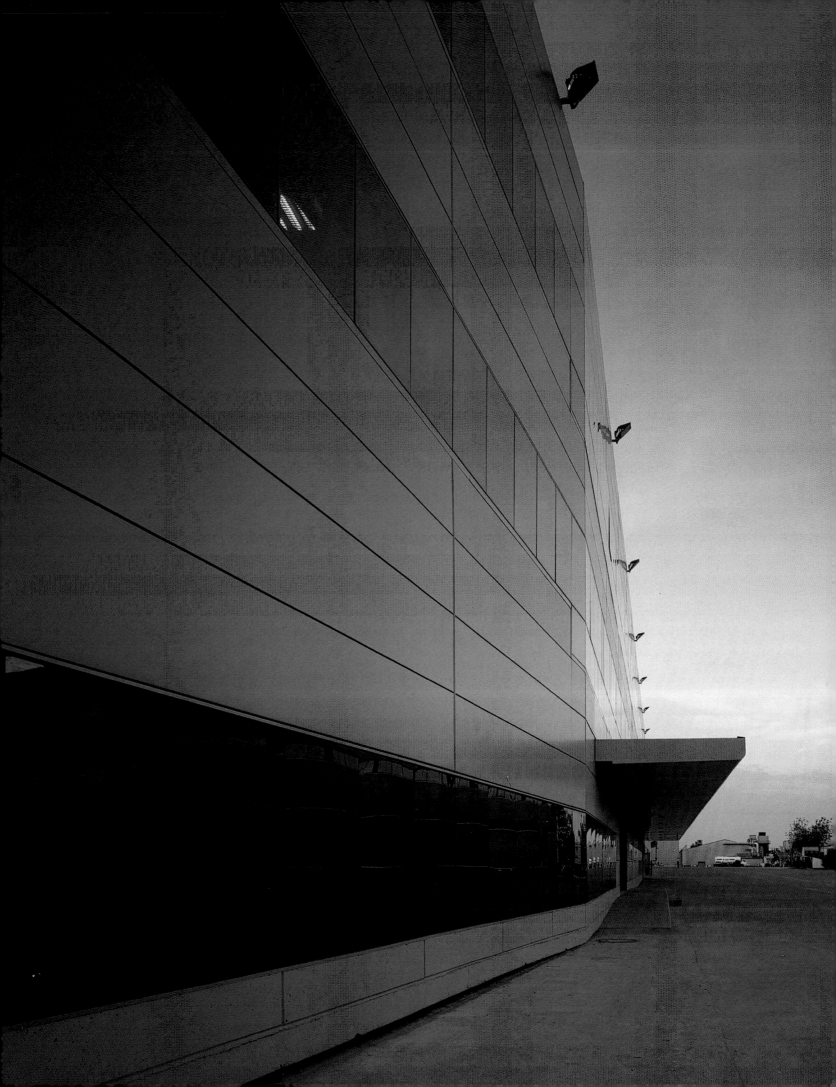

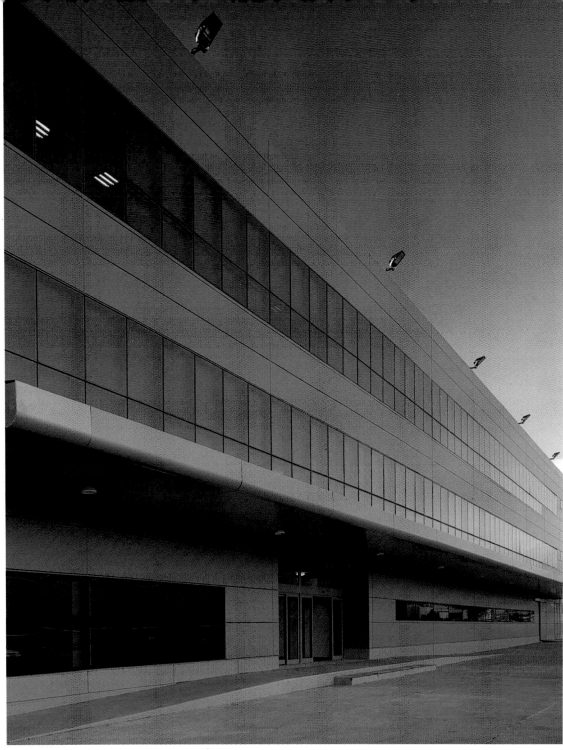

Engineering Office Building for EADS/C.A.S.A.

THE ARCHITECTURE STUDIO OF OLMOS OCHOA ARQUITECTOS, WHICH WAS RESPONSIBLE FOR PLANNING THESE OFFICES, WAS ASKED TO ENLARGE A BUILDING WHOSE DESIGN HAD TO FOLLOW THE LINES GOVERNED BY THE ACCOMPANYING STRUCTURE, YET ALSO BE VISIBLY INDEPENDENT FROM THE ALREADY EXISTING BUILDING.

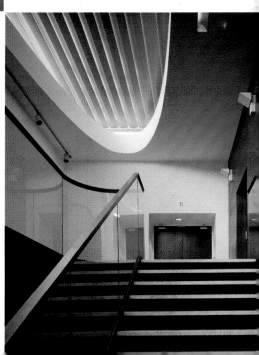

Engineering Office Building for EADS/C.A.S.A.

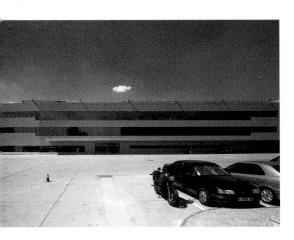

Architect: **Olmos Ochoa Arquitectos**
Collaborators: **Vázquez and Herranz, José Mª Fernández, Enrique Medina, and Ramón Sánchez-Hombre**
Client: **EADS/C.A.S.A.**
Location: **Madrid, Spain**
Construction Date: **2002**
Photography: **Ángel Baltanás**

A considerable canopy, indicating the entrance to the building and protecting it from sun and rain; a visually powerful main staircase; and a subtle and angular enclosure on the south side (a solution that allows the lines to be stylized) are the main elements that give form to the client's particular guidelines.

Divided into different levels, the building devotes the two top floors to offices and reserves the bottom level for the company's laboratories. Spatial versatility and functionality were key when planning the interiors. To this end, the main core includes the general services such as the bathrooms, rest areas, and places where various installations are centralized. Placing the main group of stairs in the interior, illuminated with natural overhead light, frees up as much space as possible at the front for the offices. From the offices, this nucleus can be seen as a large wooden box along with glass enclosures that house various services. Inside, the use of different materials (stucco, Carrara marble, metal elements, glass, and wood) and the color schemes (using red, white, and black) give the space a singular character that is full of personality and sets it apart.

The staircase has been constructed with metal parts to be able to bear the weight that the structure will carry. The stairs are located in an area defined with reinforced concrete and solid block walls. The steps are made of marble, and the banister consists of two sheets of Planilux encased in a metal frame. The glass panels are put into place without sealing in between them, leaving a seam of about 1/8 inch.

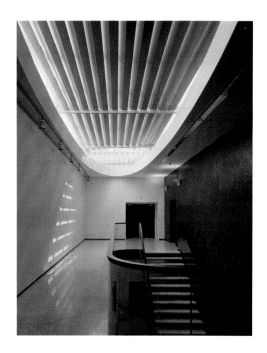

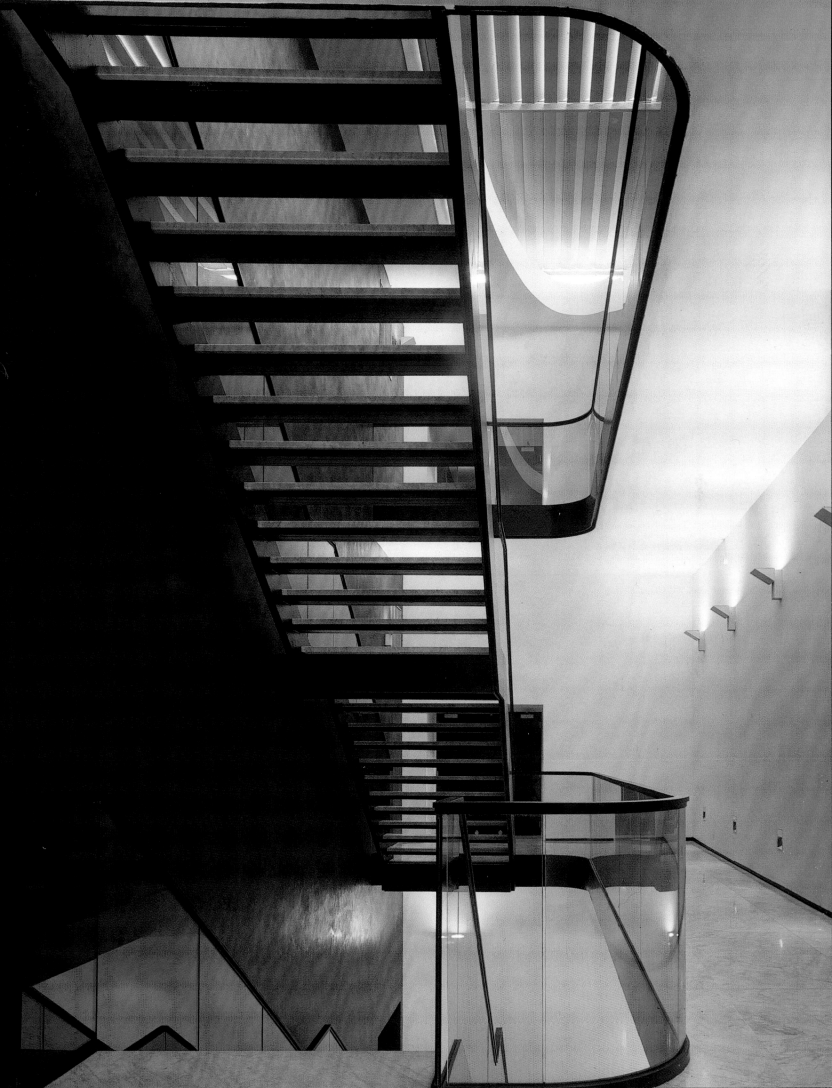

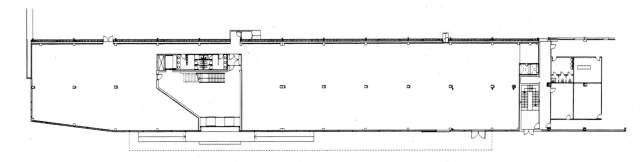

Ground floor

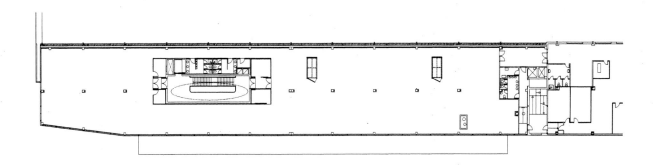

First floor

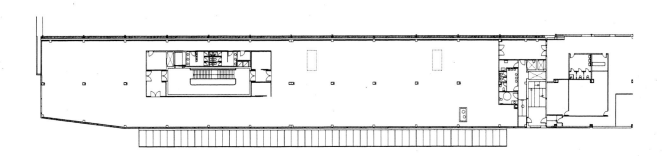

Second floor

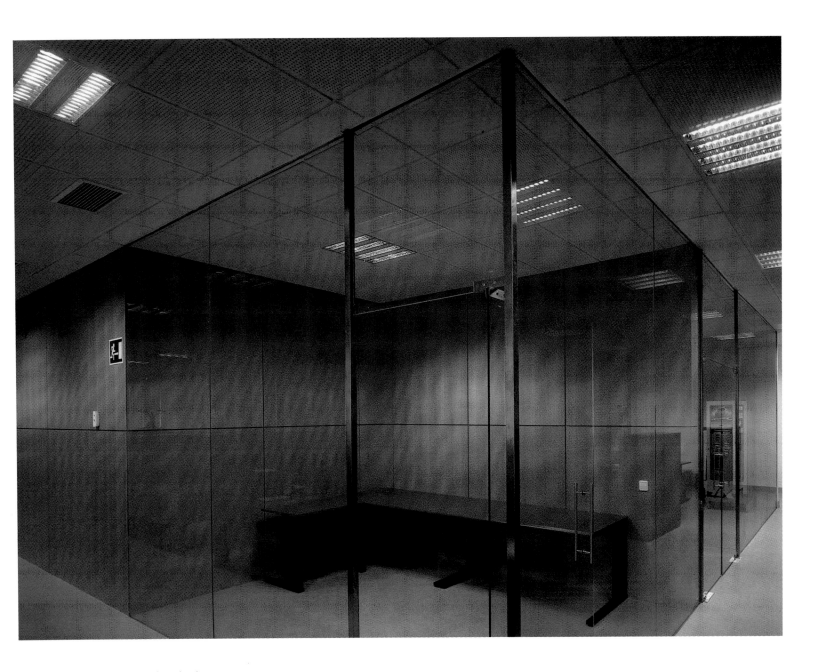

Some areas resemble large cubes of wood and glass, the interiors of which house various services. The transparency of the glass is used to capture the light as well as to connect the various areas, thus reducing visual barriers.

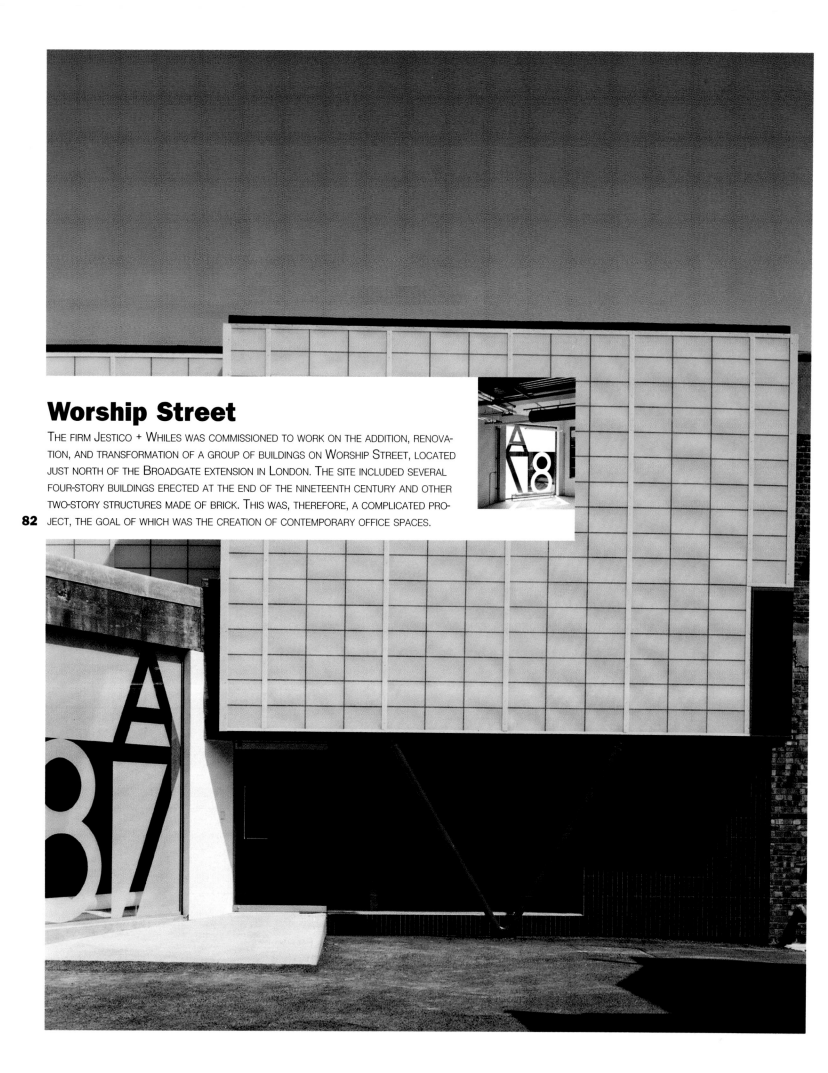

Worship Street

THE FIRM JESTICO + WHILES WAS COMMISSIONED TO WORK ON THE ADDITION, RENOVATION, AND TRANSFORMATION OF A GROUP OF BUILDINGS ON WORSHIP STREET, LOCATED JUST NORTH OF THE BROADGATE EXTENSION IN LONDON. THE SITE INCLUDED SEVERAL FOUR-STORY BUILDINGS ERECTED AT THE END OF THE NINETEENTH CENTURY AND OTHER TWO-STORY STRUCTURES MADE OF BRICK. THIS WAS, THEREFORE, A COMPLICATED PROJECT, THE GOAL OF WHICH WAS THE CREATION OF CONTEMPORARY OFFICE SPACES.

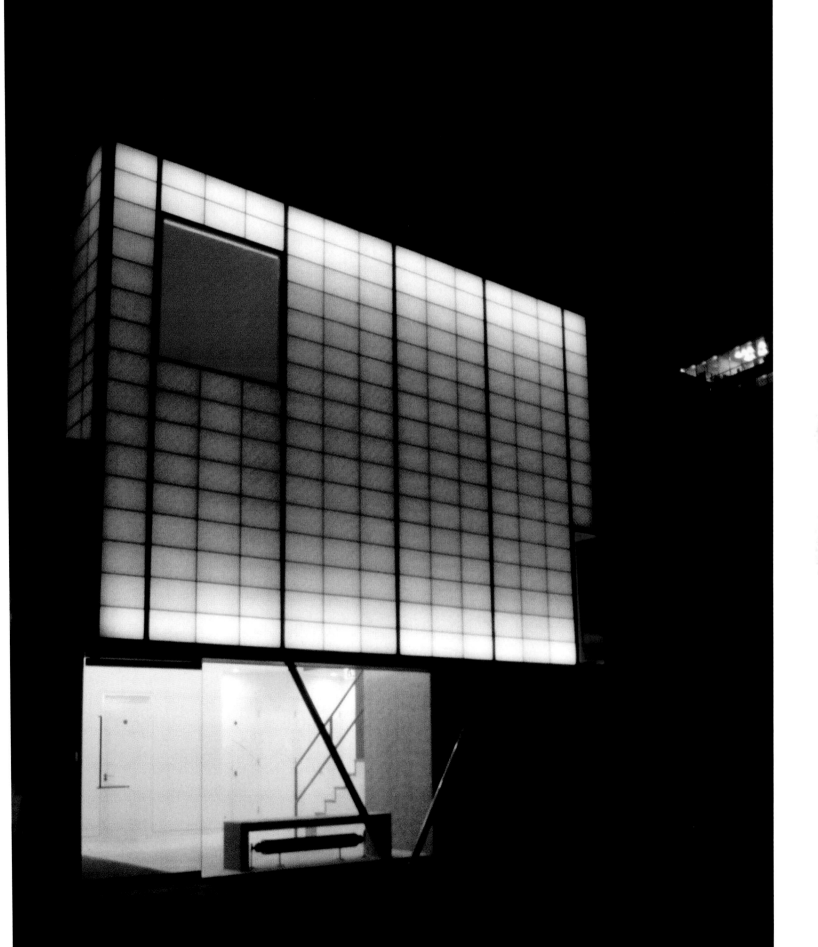

Worship Street

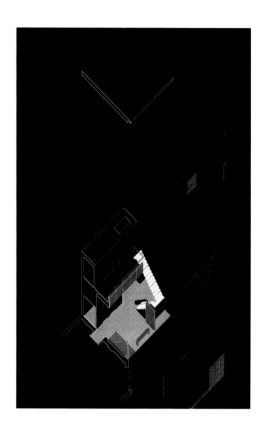

Architect: **Jestico + Whiles**
Client: **Cripplegate Foundation**
Location: **London, United Kingdom**
Construction Date: **2002**
Photography: **James Morris**

The renovation required the painstaking work of transformation to an open plan, where the office spaces had to be flexible, dynamic, and multi-functional and had to include mechanical ventilation. One of the objectives of the project was the creation of a new reception area and a small conference room on the lower level.

The new main entrance is located in an atrium painted bright orange, further enhancing the striking renovation of the building. The facade, seen from the outside, displays an enormous sign with the graphic "87 A" covering the entire window, from the entrance to the reception area, located next to the atrium. Translucent treated glass panels encased in aluminum frames cover the rest of the facade. At night, the light from these panels creates an evocative play of light that renders the building visible from quite a distance.

Inside, via the two-story ceiling of the reception area, the decorative austerity becomes obvious. The staircase rises from one side and connects with the upper level. There, three circular skylights have been opened, which bathe the interior with natural light. The use of colored glass in different areas intensifies the attractive effect that is created when light strikes them. Another accomplishment of the project was the interesting blend and contrast between materials and finishes.

The treatment used on the main facade can be clearly seen from the inside. The metal outlined glass panels replace traditional heavy walls, establishing the transition between outdoors and indoors.

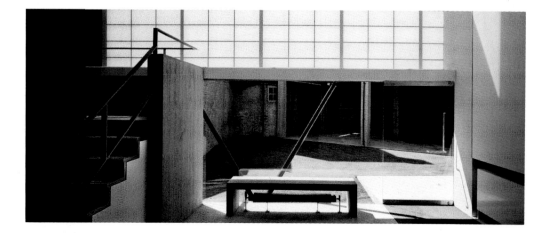

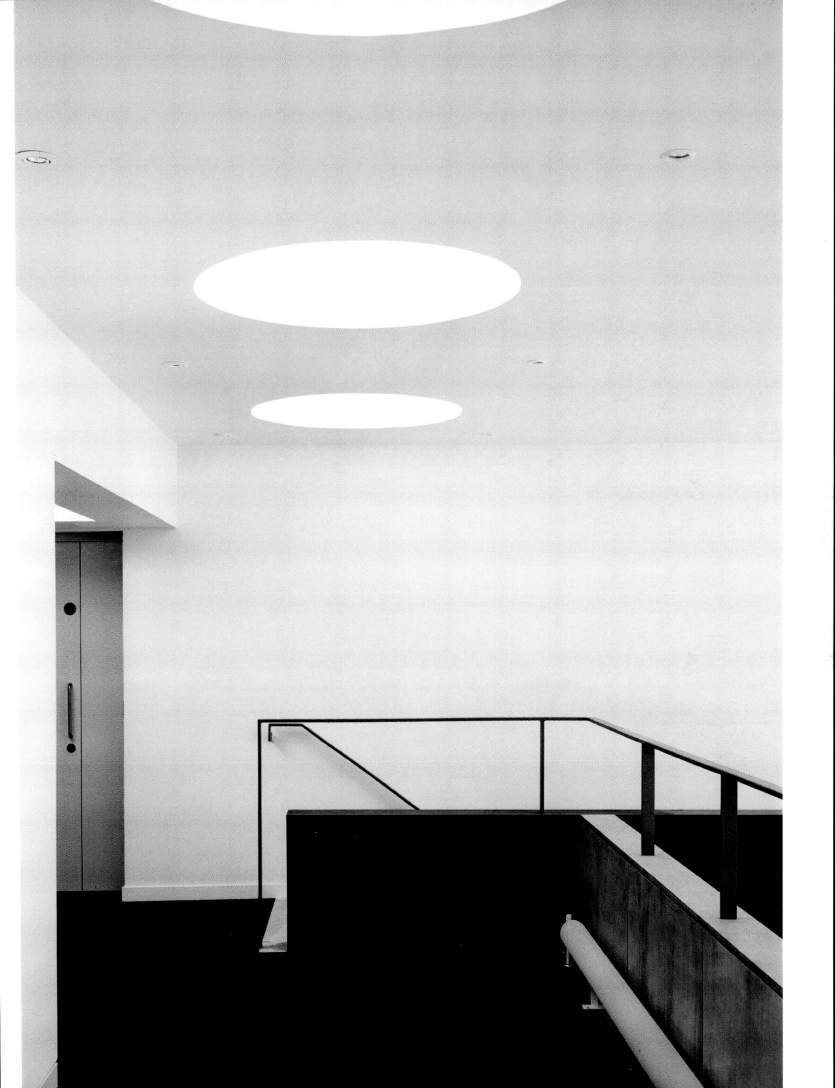

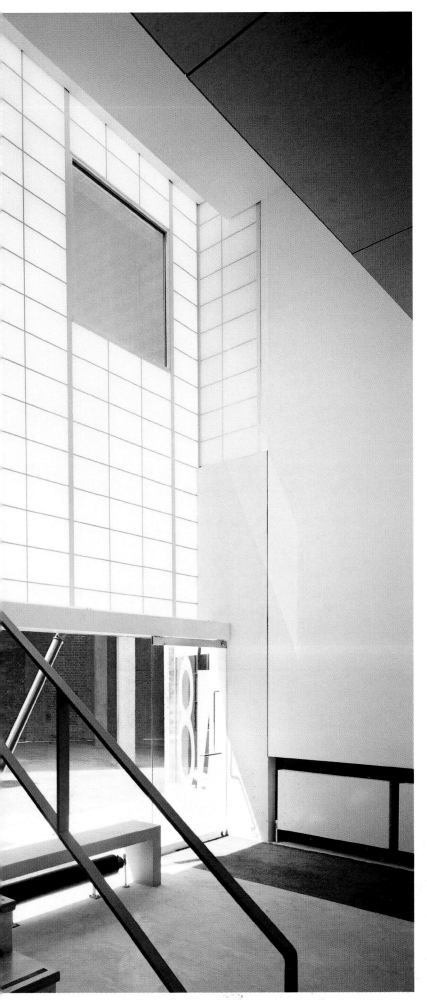
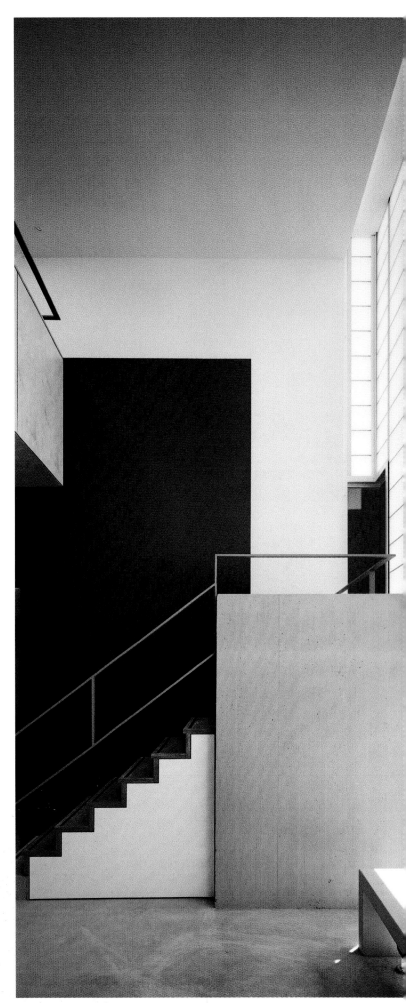

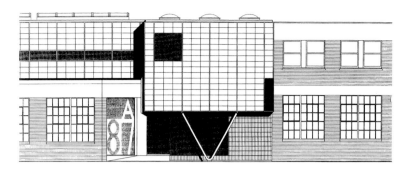

Courtyard Elevation

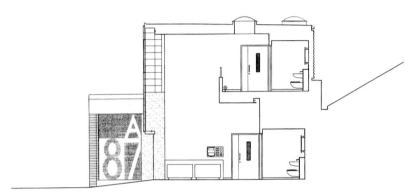

Section: courtyard reception

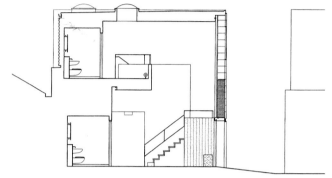

Section: courtyard reception

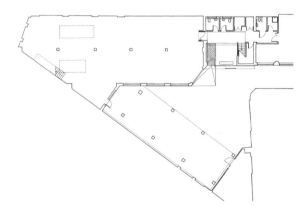

Ground floor

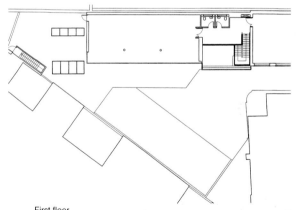

First floor

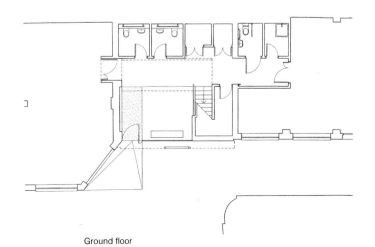

Ground floor

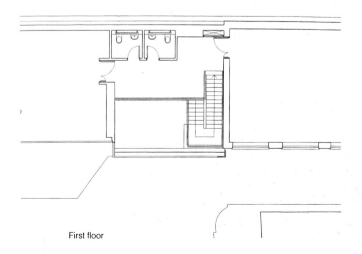

First floor

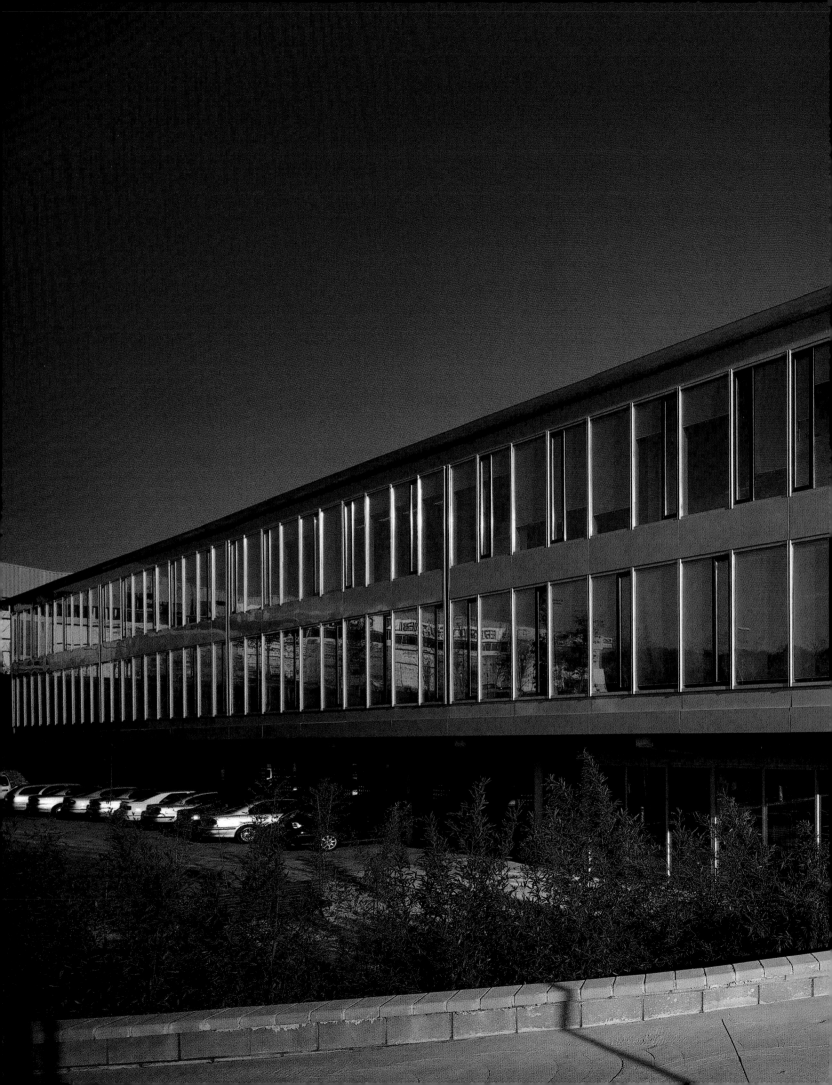

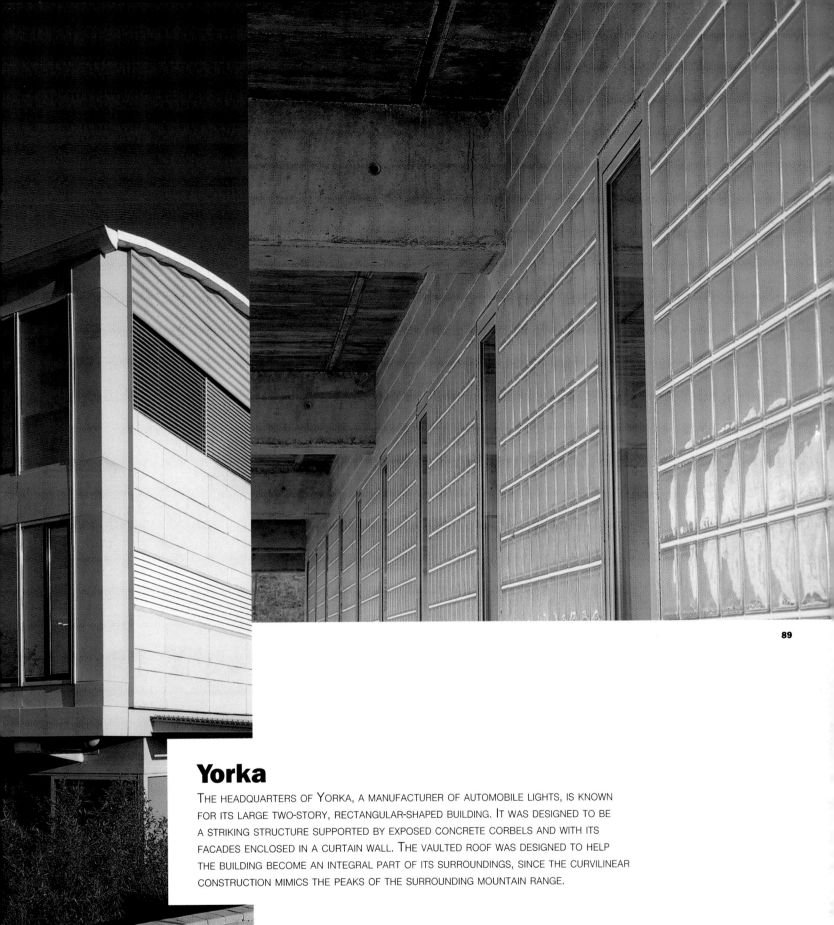

Yorka

THE HEADQUARTERS OF YORKA, A MANUFACTURER OF AUTOMOBILE LIGHTS, IS KNOWN FOR ITS LARGE TWO-STORY, RECTANGULAR-SHAPED BUILDING. IT WAS DESIGNED TO BE A STRIKING STRUCTURE SUPPORTED BY EXPOSED CONCRETE CORBELS AND WITH ITS FACADES ENCLOSED IN A CURTAIN WALL. THE VAULTED ROOF WAS DESIGNED TO HELP THE BUILDING BECOME AN INTEGRAL PART OF ITS SURROUNDINGS, SINCE THE CURVILINEAR CONSTRUCTION MIMICS THE PEAKS OF THE SURROUNDING MOUNTAIN RANGE.

Yorka

Architect: **Wortmann Bañares Moro Soucheiron**
Client: **Yorka, S.L.**
Location: **Barcelona, Spain**
Construction Date: **2001**
Photography: **Eugeni Pons**

The location of the building as well as the activities and functional needs of the company (the space had to house the administrative offices as well as the production plant) were determining factors when choosing the location, planning the construction, and also for the distribution of the interior.

The production areas, factory, labs, and workshops are located on the lower level. The top floor is devoted to offices and administrative areas. An indoor gallery illuminated with natural overhead light becomes the focal point of the project; this gallery is also the source of light for the work area.

The main entrance is located in one of the sides of the facade, and from here, one can practically predict the layout of the entire building by identifying the main elements, such as the service core for the elevators, the stairs, and the gallery.

The solid industrial image projected by the entire space, which is a reflection of the activities going on inside, is achieved in part by the building materials used. These materials are mainly the unfinished concrete, fiber-reinforced cement panels (asbestos-free) joined edge to edge, steel beams, and surface coverings, which are incorporated into an environment whose vocabulary is that of production plants, steel and concrete beams covered with corrugated sheet metal, and gypsum board. However, the resulting work areas are transparent, flexible, versatile, and well illuminated.

The administrative functions take place on the top floors. The production areas are located on the lower level, the same level as the factory, and communicate with the factory through firewall passages.

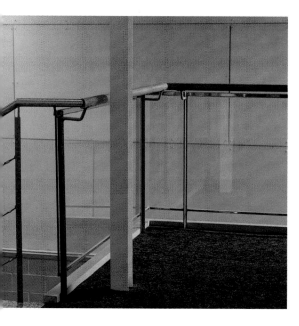

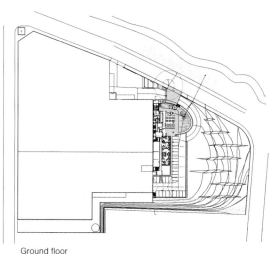

Ground floor

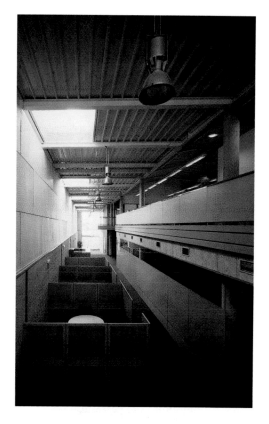

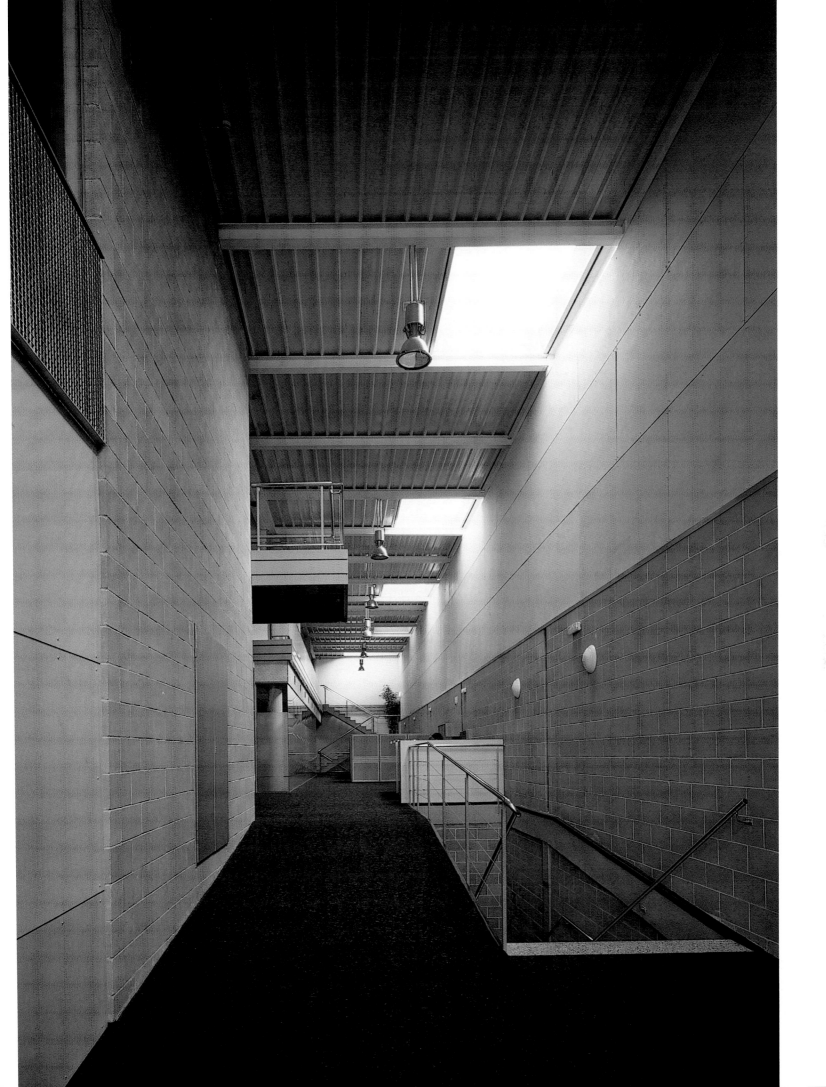

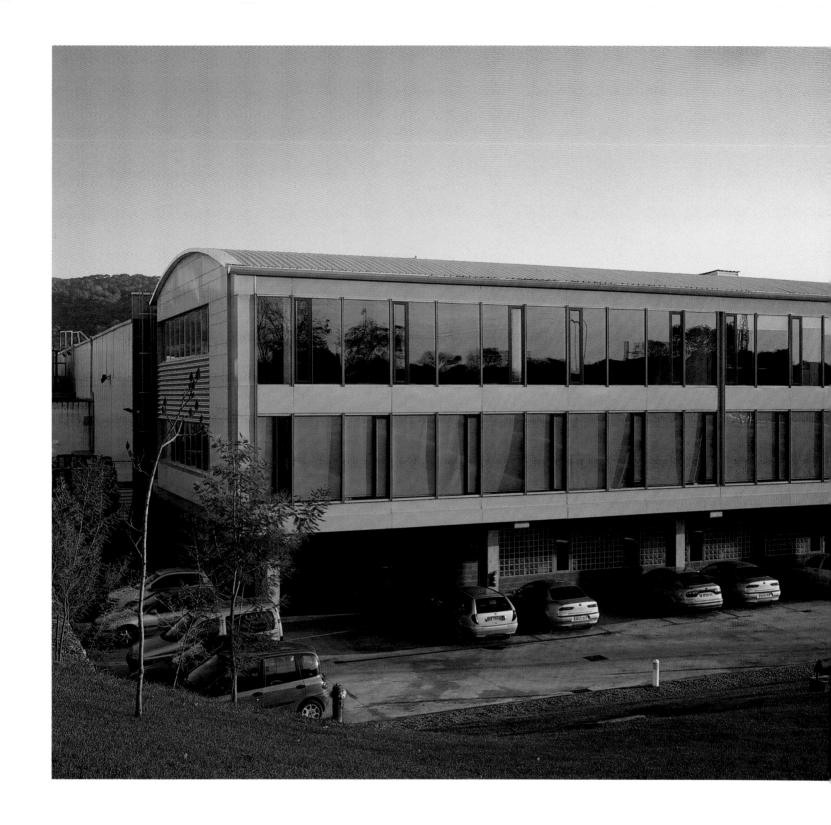

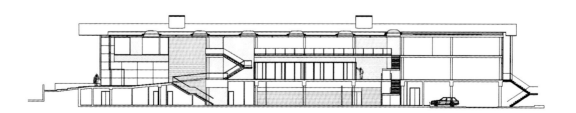

Section

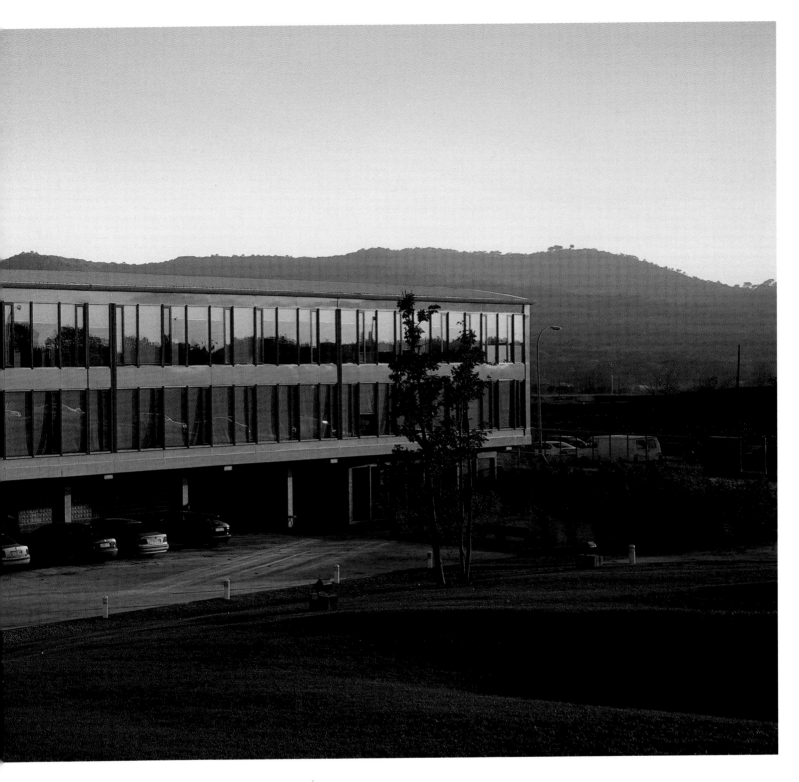

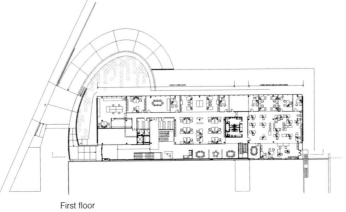

First floor

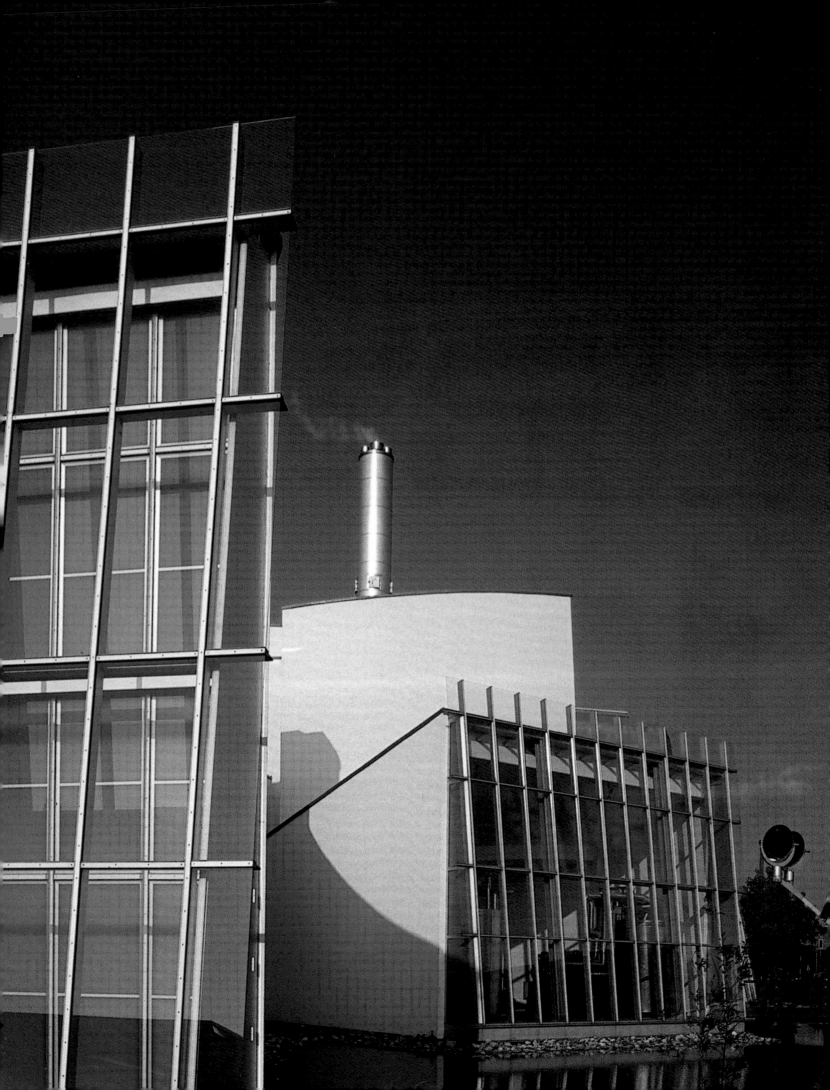

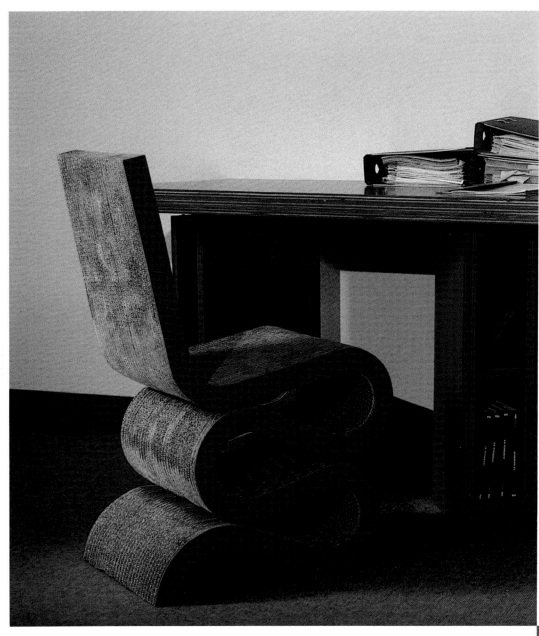

Elektrizitätswerk
Minden-Ravensberg (EMR)

MAKING USE OF THE THEATRICAL ELEMENTS OF ARCHITECTURE, ARCHITECT FRANK O. GEHRY MANIPULATES IMAGINATION AND TECHNOLOGY AT WILL TO GIVE THIS CONSTRUCTION THE EXPRESSIVE FORMS AND QUALITIES THAT DEFINE IT. THE FAMILIAR LINES APPEAR ONCE AGAIN, THIS TIME IN THIS COMPLEX BUILDING LOCATED AT B61 MINDENER STRASSE, NEAR THE HIGHWAY, WHICH CAUSES THIS CONSTRUCTION TO BE PERCEIVED AS A CONNECTING ELEMENT BETWEEN THE HIGHWAY AND THE SURROUNDINGS.

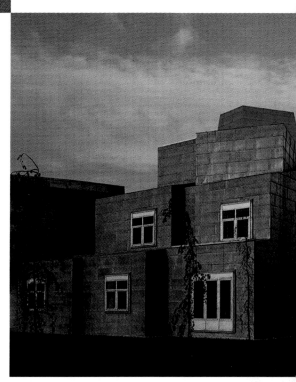

Elektrizitätswerk Minden-Ravensberg (EMR)

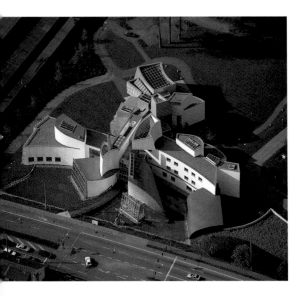

Architect: **Frank O. Gehry**
Client: **Elektrizitätswerk Minden-Ravensberg**
Location: **Bad Oeynhausen, Germany**
Construction Date: **1995**
Photography: **Thomas Mayer**

The complex, consisting of various buildings that house the different functions of the company, integrates naturally with its location. The peculiar shape of the building visually defines the space and sets physical boundaries. It is designed as a multipurpose and multifunctional space equipped to accommodate different groups of employees, depending on their activities. The spatial organization and the way the interiors were designed had to respond to the needs of the various tasks that were to be carried out. An innovative, functional, and far-from-monotonous building is the result of those requirements.

From the outside, each volume that makes up the complex, perfectly interconnected, is perceived as an independent structure that forms part of a whole. This individuality has been emphasized with a different finish for each building. The evocative geometric lines and the particular finish treatment of each volume confer a unique identity on each one of them. The result of this inspiring and invigorating architectural work is a functional complex expressed with an extraordinary exterior structure, and the intelligent exploitation and mastery of the technological resources and use of materials.

The audacity, innovation, and efficiency are also maintained in the interiors, created as multipurpose and multifunctional spaces where the talent and imagination of Gehry are proven once again.

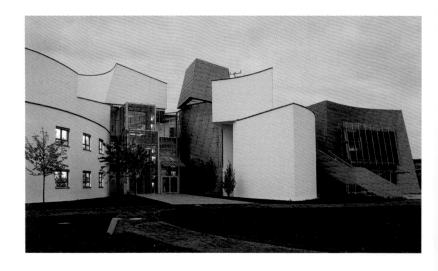

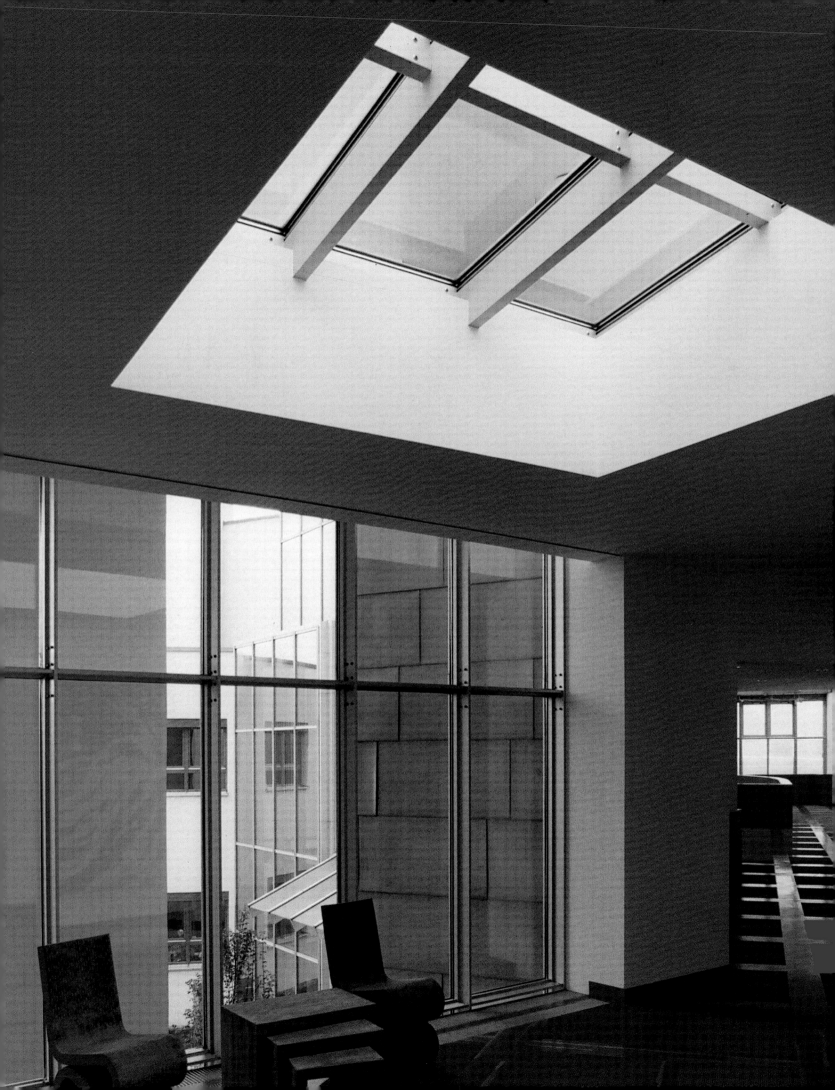

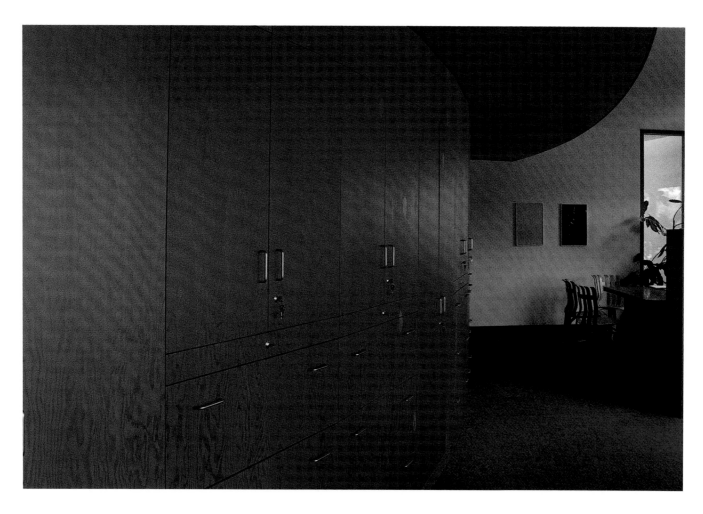

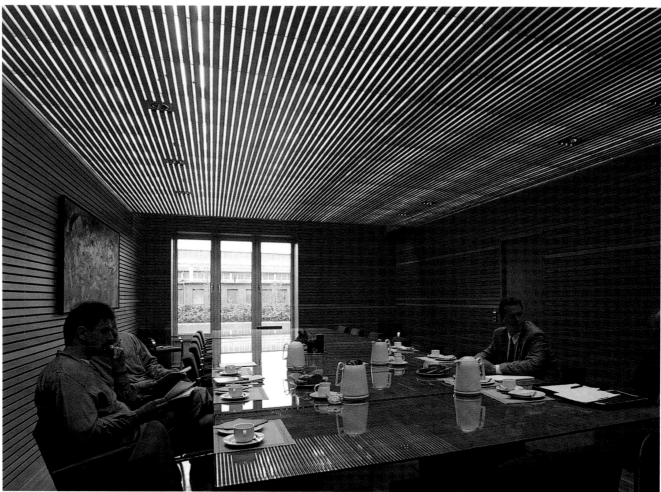

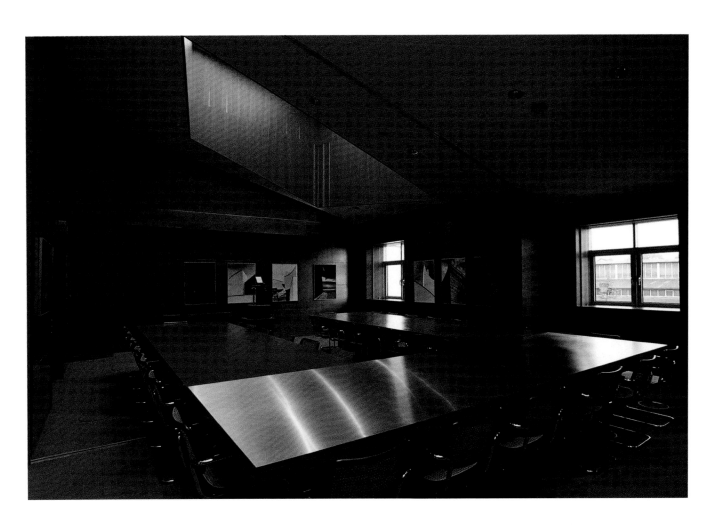

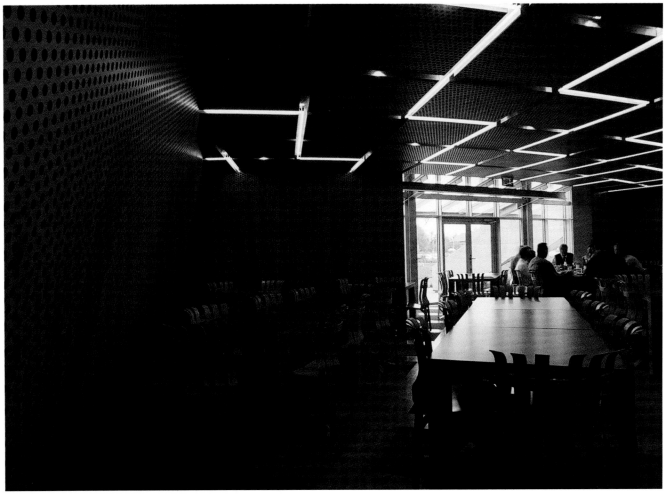

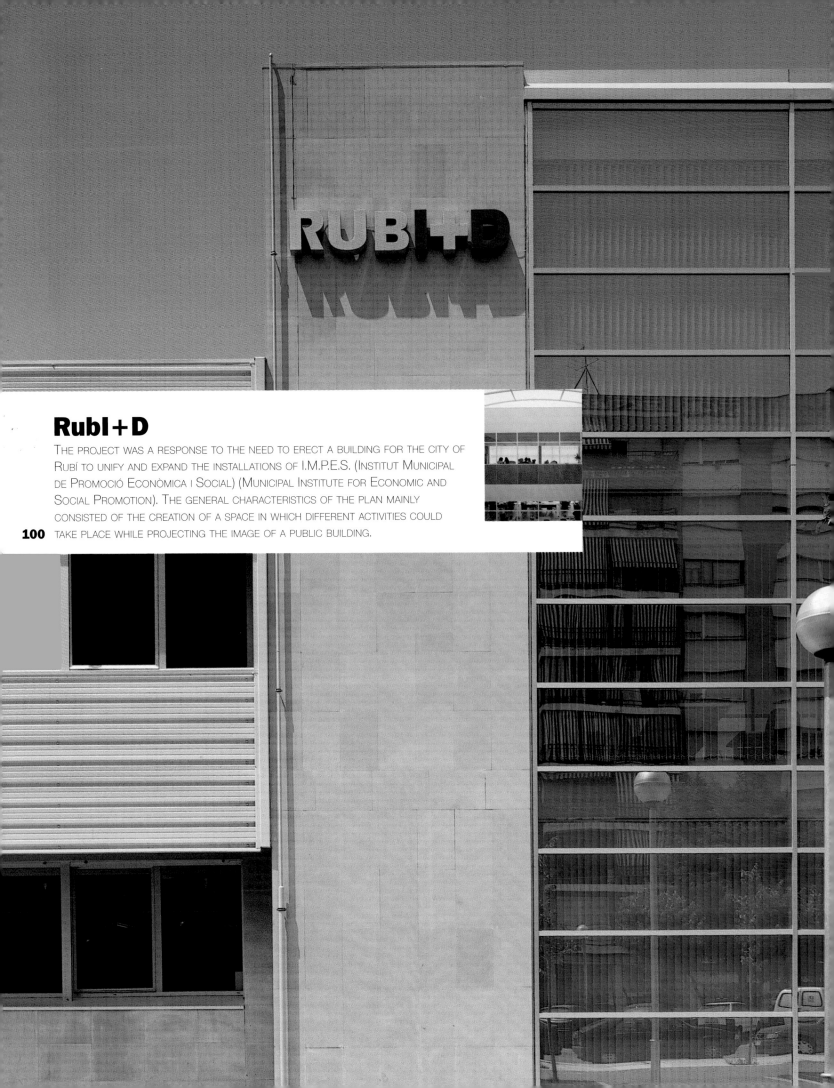

RubI + D

THE PROJECT WAS A RESPONSE TO THE NEED TO ERECT A BUILDING FOR THE CITY OF RUBÍ TO UNIFY AND EXPAND THE INSTALLATIONS OF I.M.P.E.S. (INSTITUT MUNICIPAL DE PROMOCIÓ ECONÒMICA I SOCIAL) (MUNICIPAL INSTITUTE FOR ECONOMIC AND SOCIAL PROMOTION). THE GENERAL CHARACTERISTICS OF THE PLAN MAINLY CONSISTED OF THE CREATION OF A SPACE IN WHICH DIFFERENT ACTIVITIES COULD TAKE PLACE WHILE PROJECTING THE IMAGE OF A PUBLIC BUILDING.

100

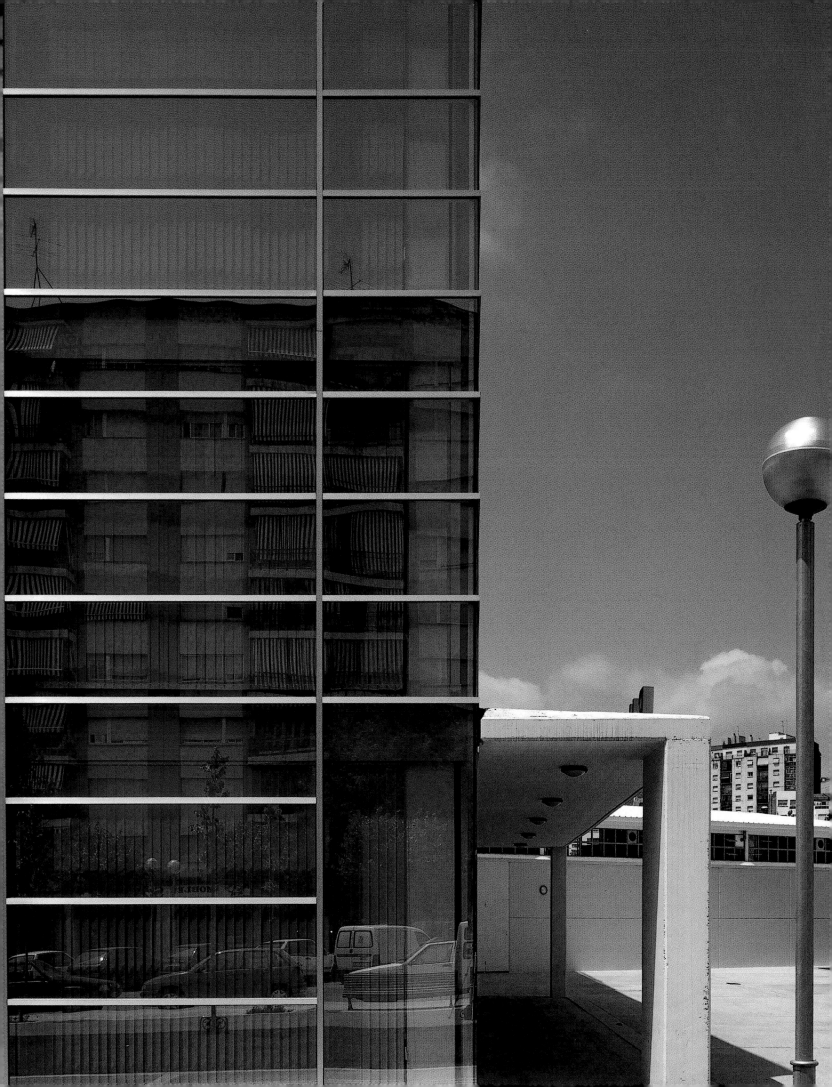

Rubí+D

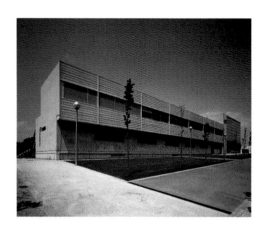

Architect: **CMT – Chico, Marco, Theilacker, Arquitectes Associats, S.L.**
Client: **I.M.P.E.S. (Institut Municipal de Promoció Econòmica i Social) of Rubí**
Location: **Rubí, Spain**
Construction Date: **1998**
Photography: **Jordi Miralles**

The construction is located in a triangular lot with a gentle slope, aspects that were kept in mind during the design process. The building is divided into three volumes that house the various functions. The general offices and services are located in the central section, which serves to define the group. The southern section houses the classrooms and corporate services, and a third section was built in the area toward the northeast. Four different entrances have been defined according to various public uses. The main access serves the administrative offices and the building in general. The two entrances on the south side are for corporate promotional services and for the companies in general, and the fourth is for the classrooms and teaching areas.

The central volume was designed in the shape of a cube and is divided into various levels for the different functions. The three floors communicate with one another through a three-story-high central atrium that is capped with a skylight. An exterior staircase in the main lobby connects the street level with the second floor, the areas with the most foot traffic. A closed interior stairway is used by employees to circulate among the three floors. A two-story, six-sided volume extends toward the south from the central structure: the lower level houses the corporate services office and eight start-up companies, and the first floor contains twelve multipurpose rooms. The north side, at a 28° angle to the main axis of the building and directly connected to the central area, contains the third section where the classrooms are located.

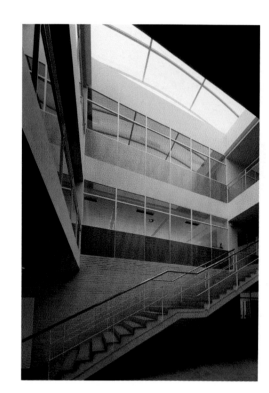

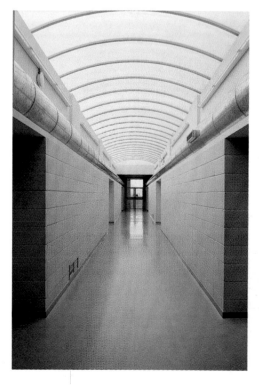

The main structure—the most used by the public—projects the image for the entire building as much through its height as with the design of the facades, which are transparent curtain walls made entirely of glass.

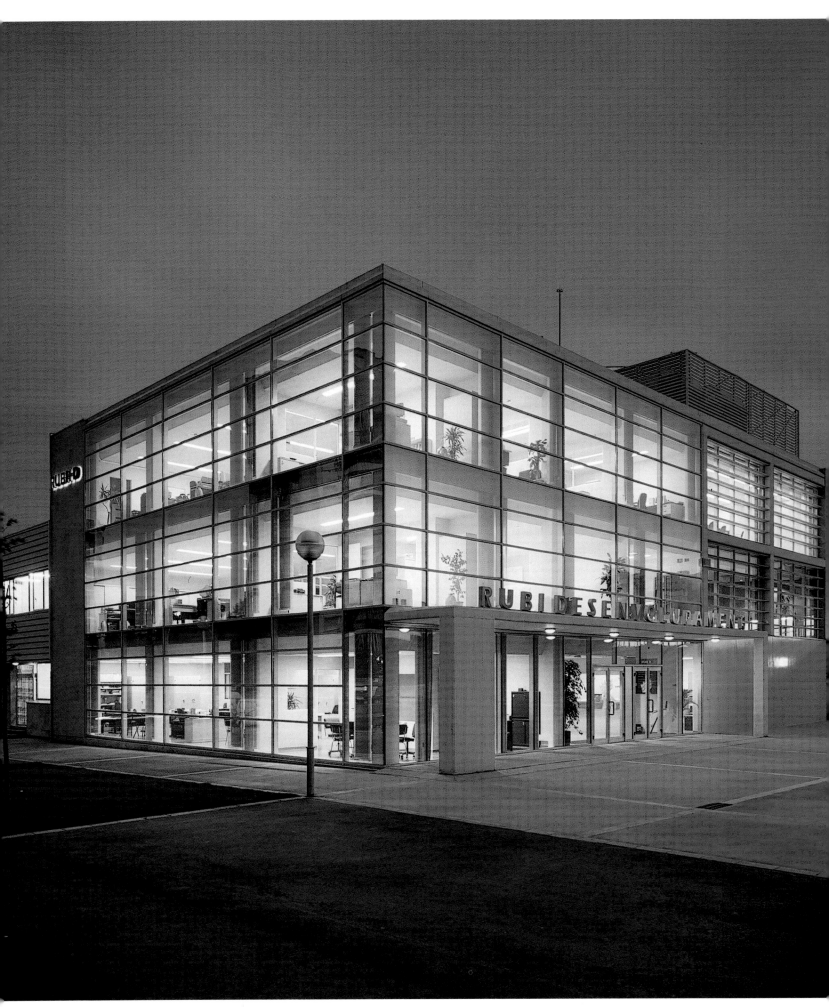

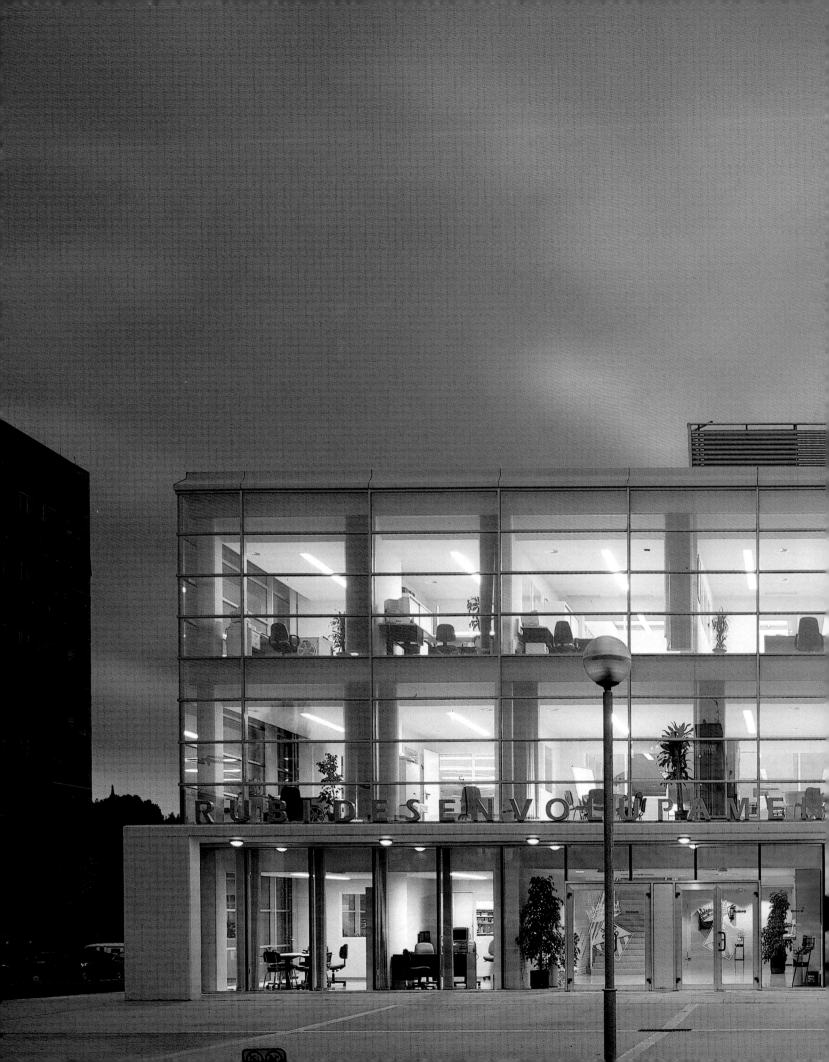

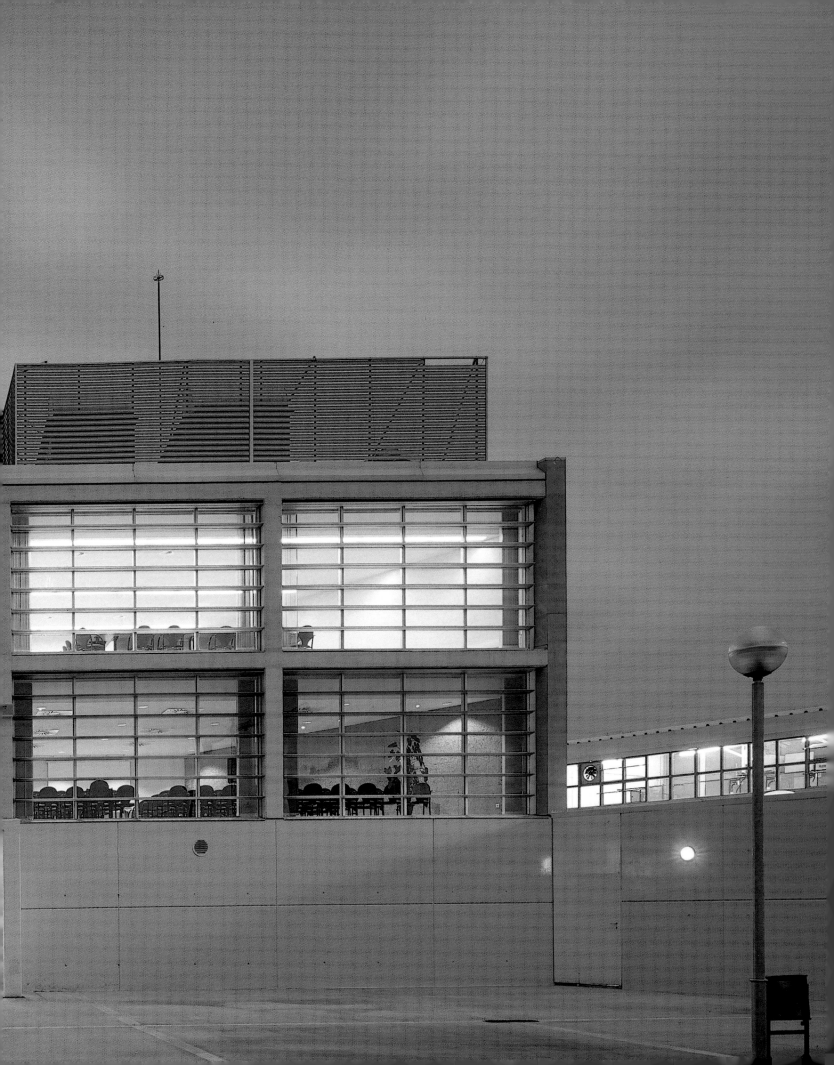

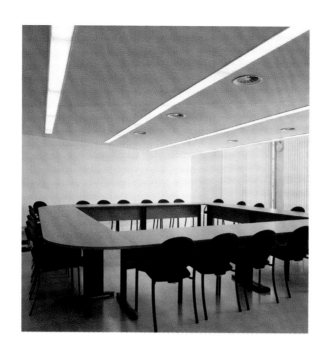

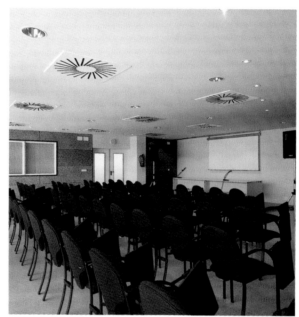

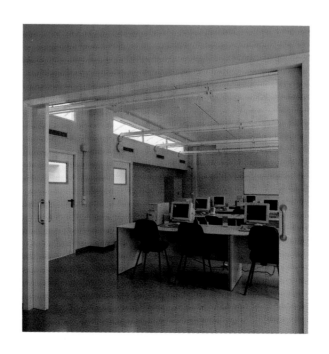

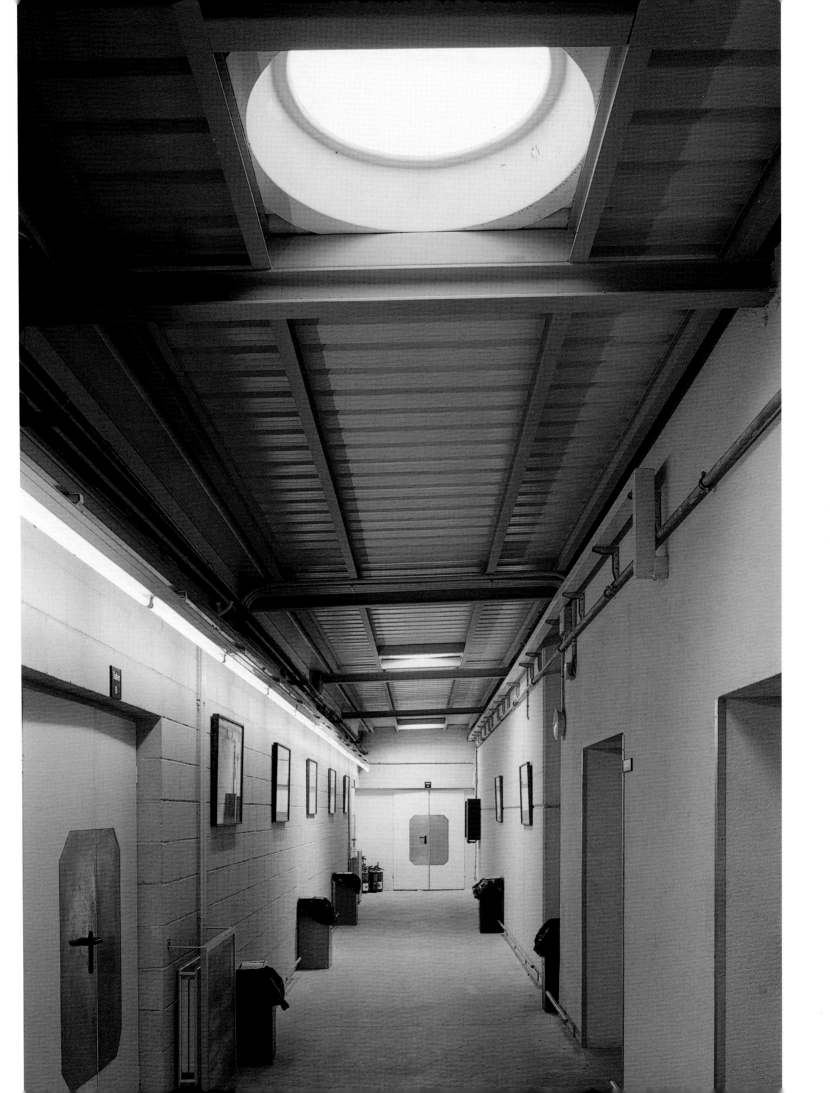

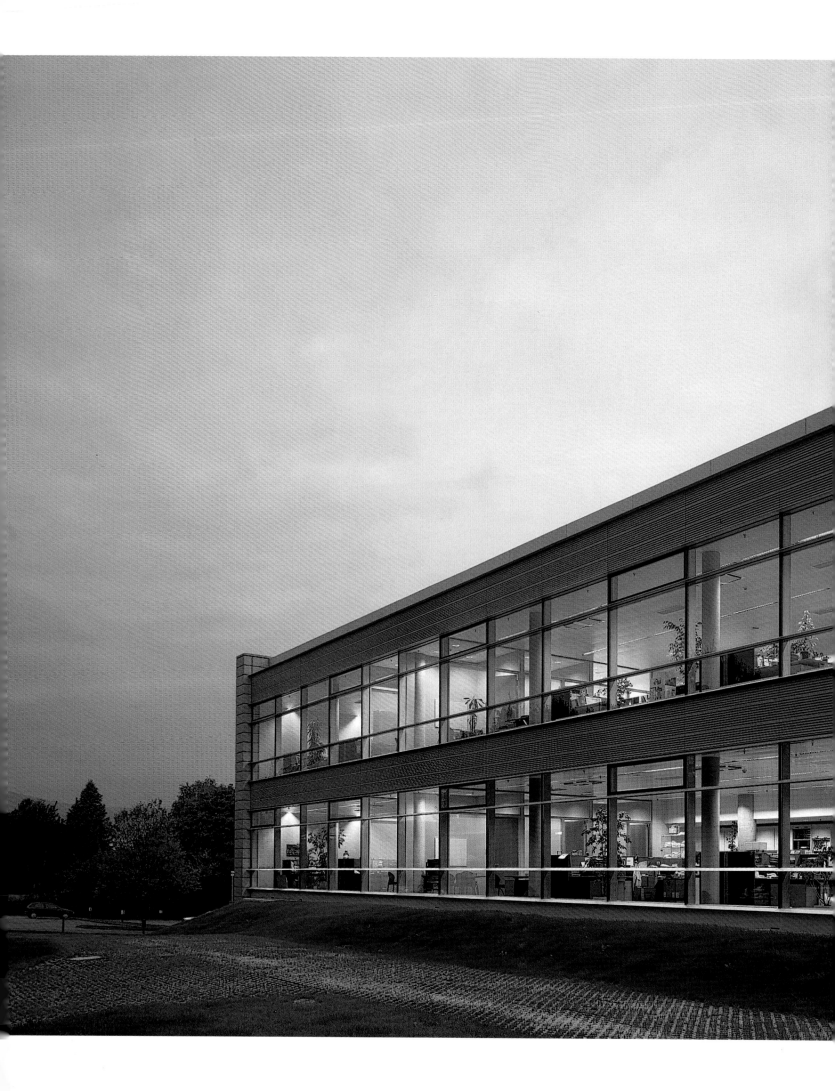

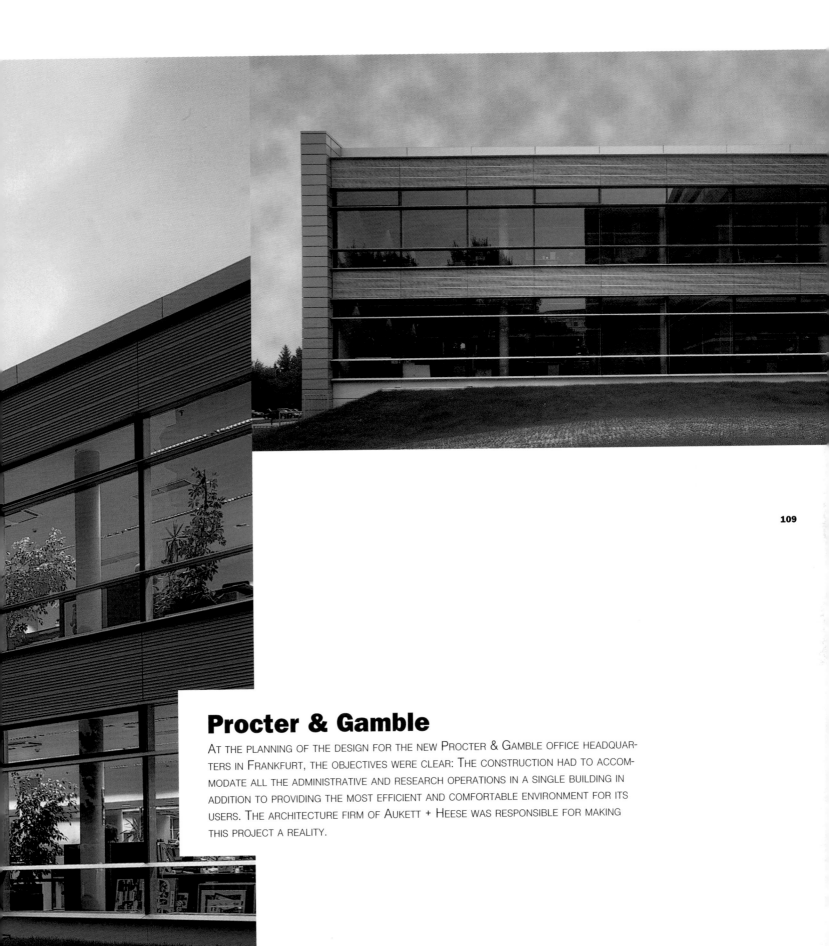

Procter & Gamble

At the planning of the design for the new Procter & Gamble office headquarters in Frankfurt, the objectives were clear: The construction had to accommodate all the administrative and research operations in a single building in addition to providing the most efficient and comfortable environment for its users. The architecture firm of Aukett + Heese was responsible for making this project a reality.

Procter & Gamble

Architect: **Aukett + Heese**
Client: **Procter & Gamble**
Location: **Frankfurt, Germany**
Construction Date: **2001**
Photography: **Werner Huthmacher / ARTUR**

The planning was guided by the client's requirements, which became essential during the design phase of the program. The client requested a flexible and dynamic distribution of the surface, capable of housing the various sectors of the organization. Also, a series of general spaces for common use had to be designed, such as a reception area, meeting rooms, conference rooms, a library, a cafeteria, and various services.

The rectangular building was divided into different levels that can be seen from the outside through the glass facades. This feature also provides excellent illumination to the interiors. The architects designed the space as a large atrium, with communicating bridges connecting the sides. These bridges cross the large indoor courtyard and create a play of light, producing a spectacular effect. This architectural solution creates infinite and effective functional possibilities.

The round, raw columns of the lobby, which can be seen from outside and appear to pierce the building vertically; the light metal stairway structures; and the original round canopy, which was given a distinguished finish, all create an aesthetically pleasing effect that contrasts and breaks with the image of discipline and geometry of the exterior architectural lines.

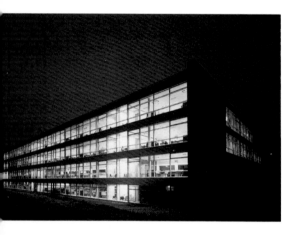

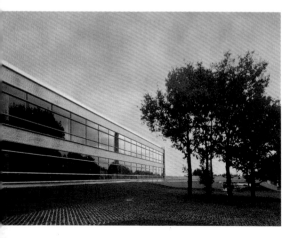

The project's objective was to create a building whose exterior conveyed a simple, modern, and technologically advanced image but whose interiors were pleasant and harmonious.

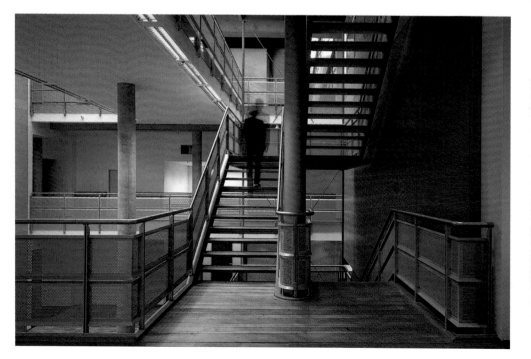

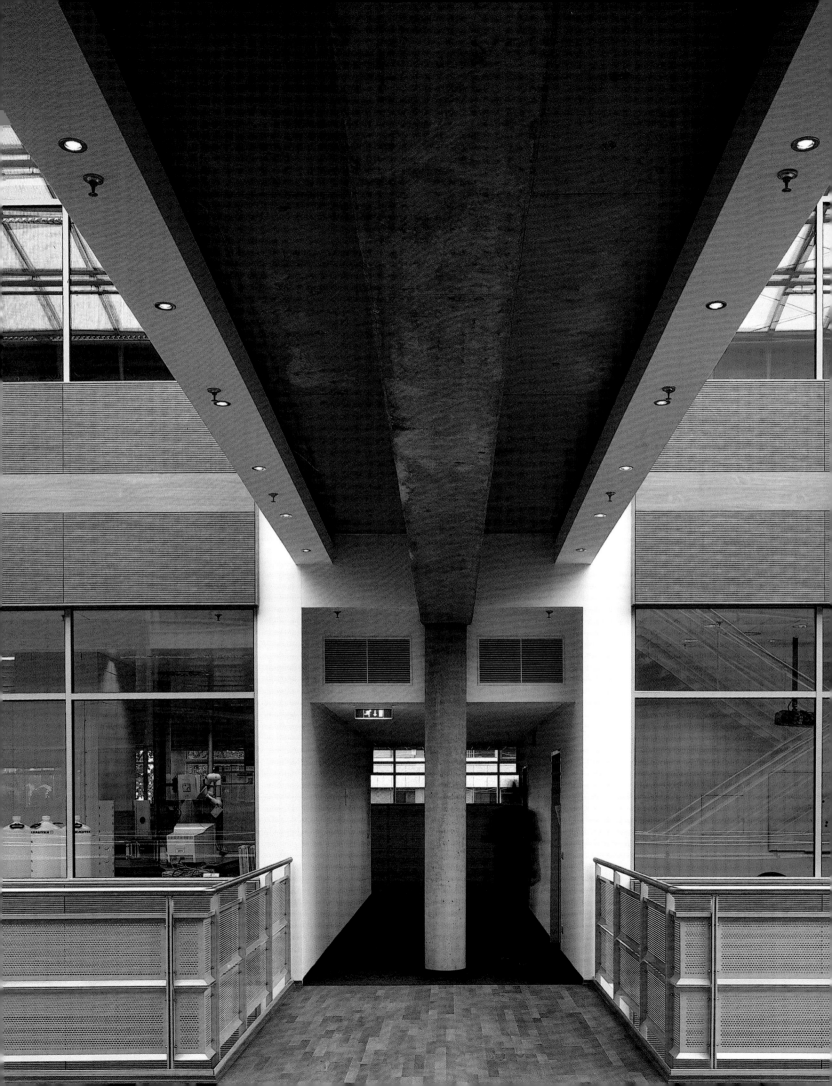

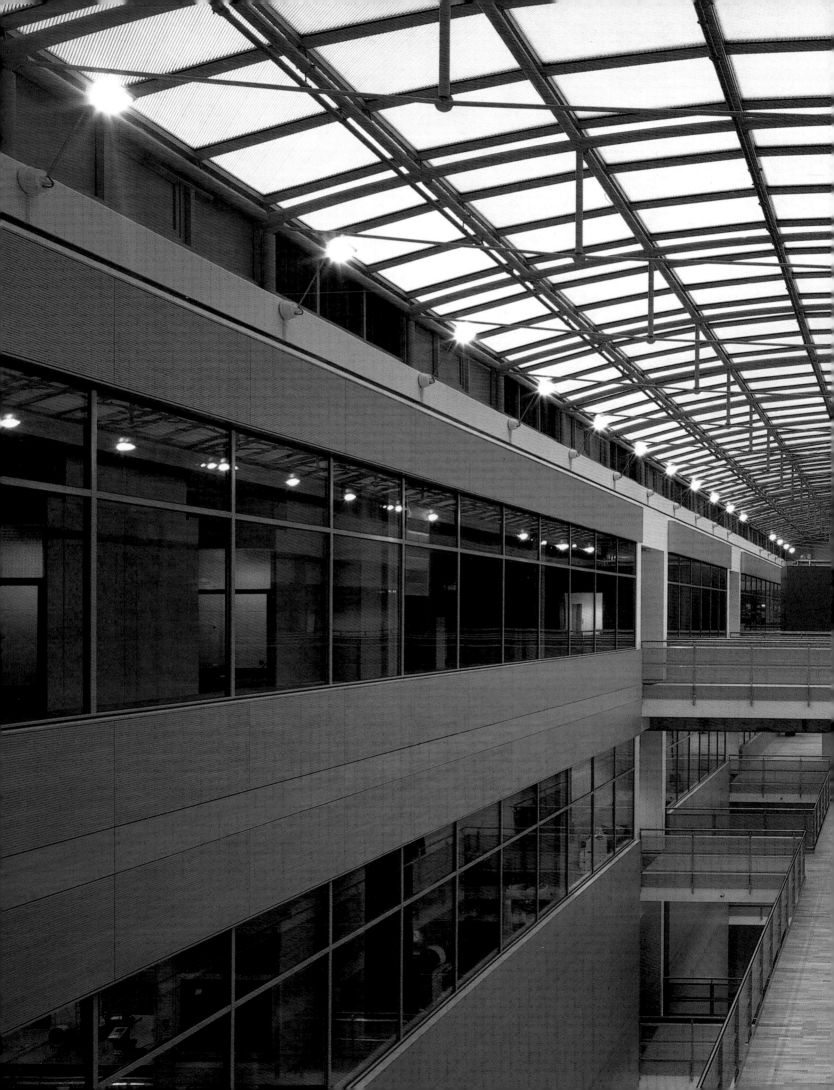

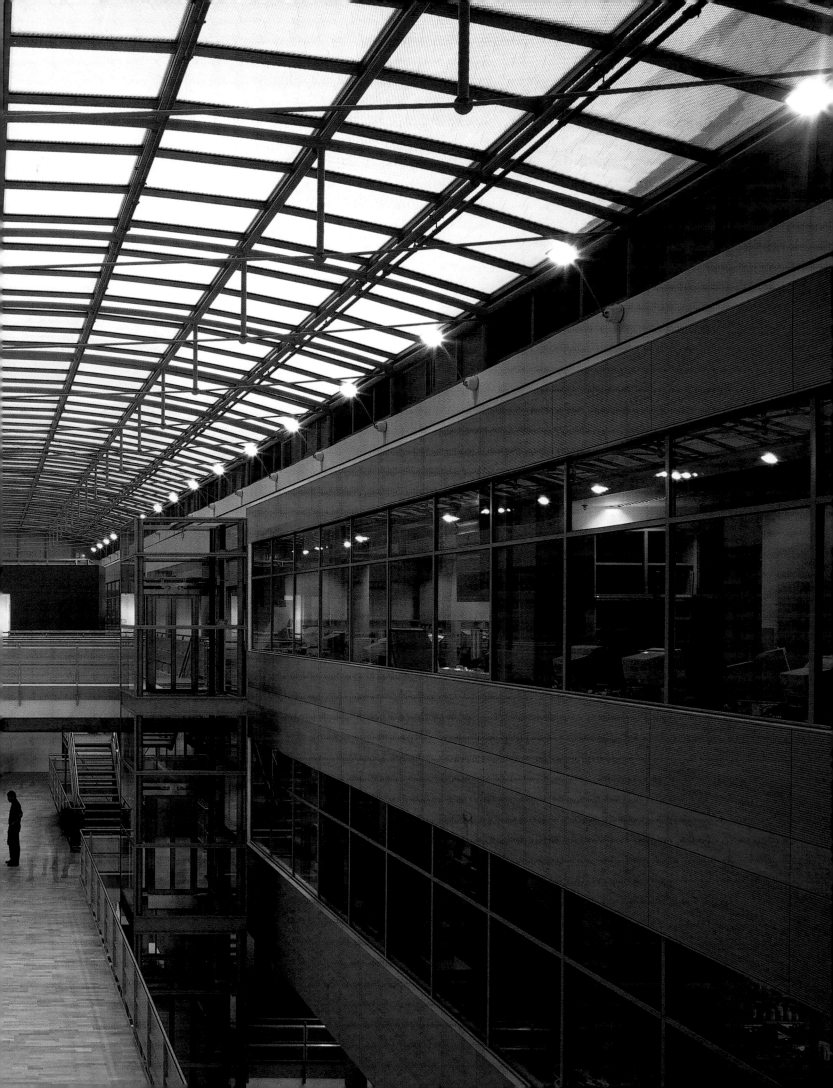

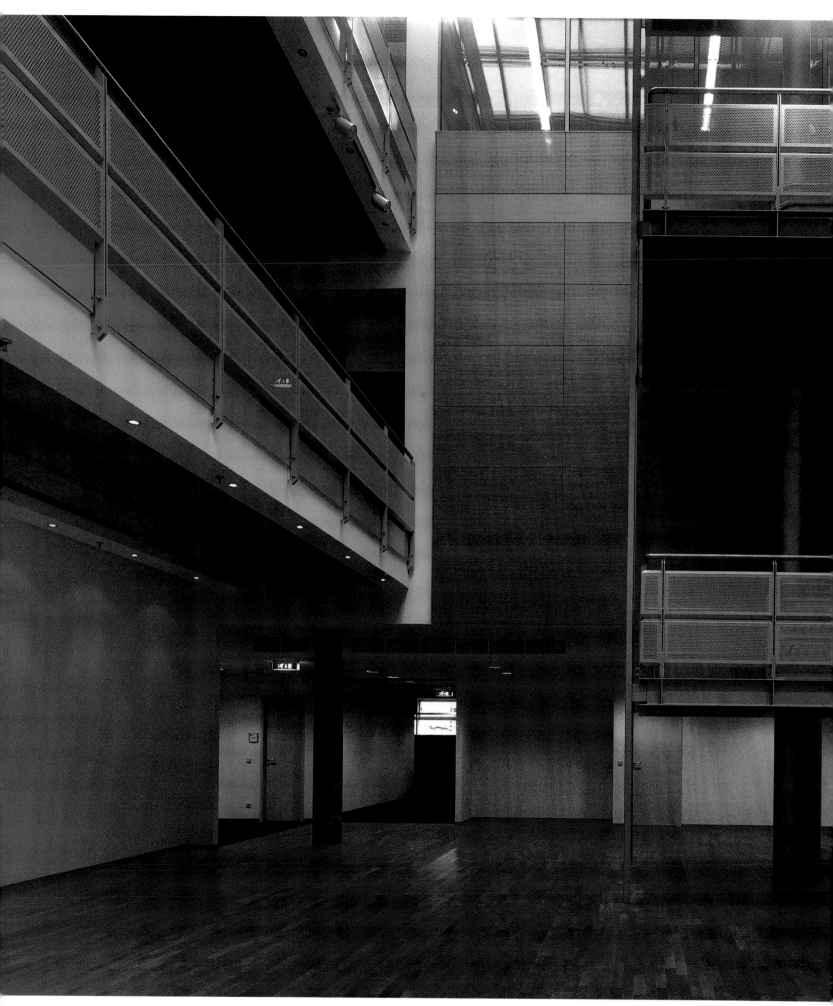

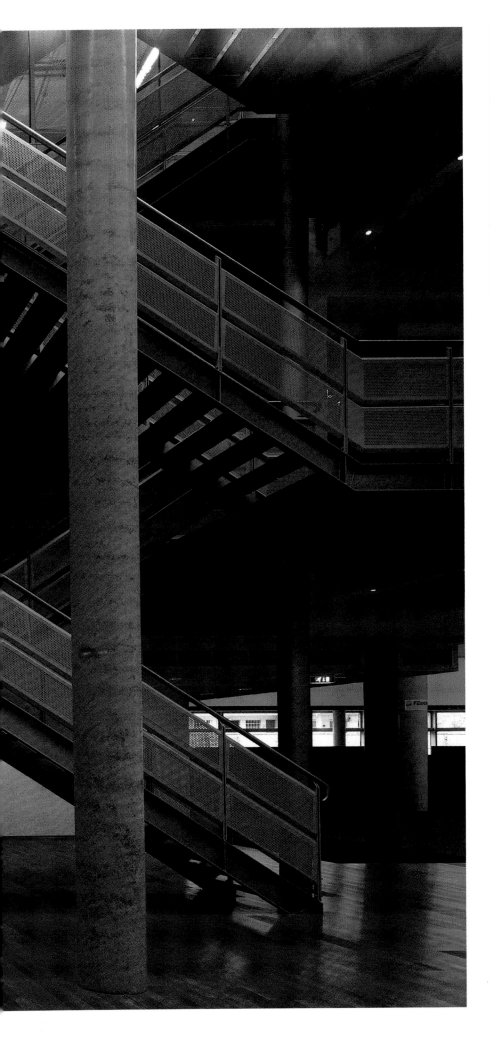

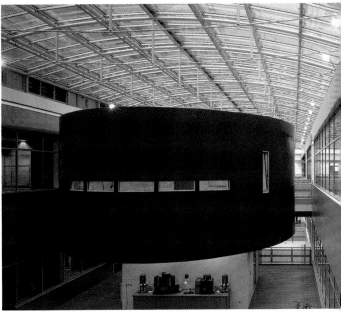

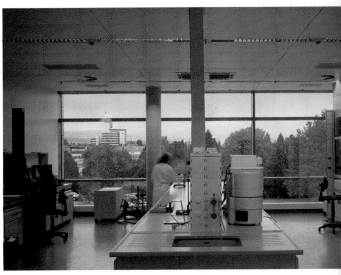

Order is always present, and the workspaces, bathed by the abundant natural light filtering through the glass that covers most of the facades, are organized according to the activities that take place there, making work much easier.

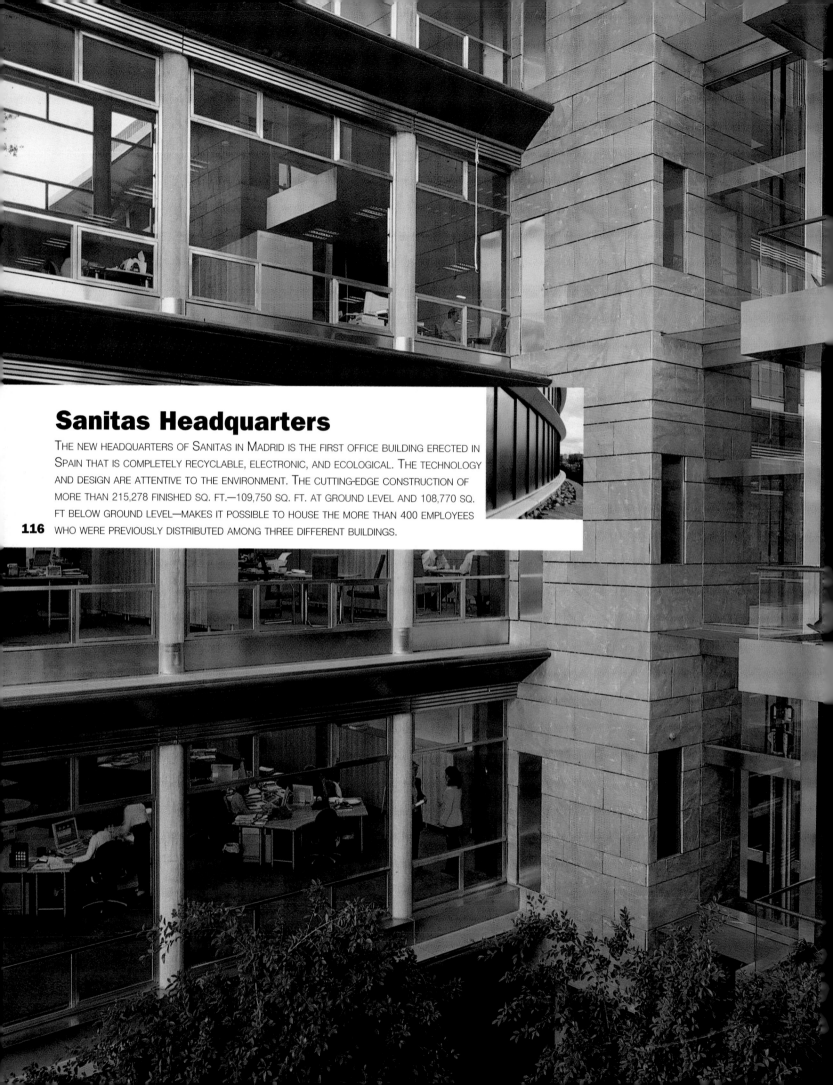

Sanitas Headquarters

THE NEW HEADQUARTERS OF SANITAS IN MADRID IS THE FIRST OFFICE BUILDING ERECTED IN SPAIN THAT IS COMPLETELY RECYCLABLE, ELECTRONIC, AND ECOLOGICAL. THE TECHNOLOGY AND DESIGN ARE ATTENTIVE TO THE ENVIRONMENT. THE CUTTING-EDGE CONSTRUCTION OF MORE THAN 215,278 FINISHED SQ. FT.—109,750 SQ. FT. AT GROUND LEVEL AND 108,770 SQ. FT BELOW GROUND LEVEL—MAKES IT POSSIBLE TO HOUSE THE MORE THAN 400 EMPLOYEES WHO WERE PREVIOUSLY DISTRIBUTED AMONG THREE DIFFERENT BUILDINGS.

116

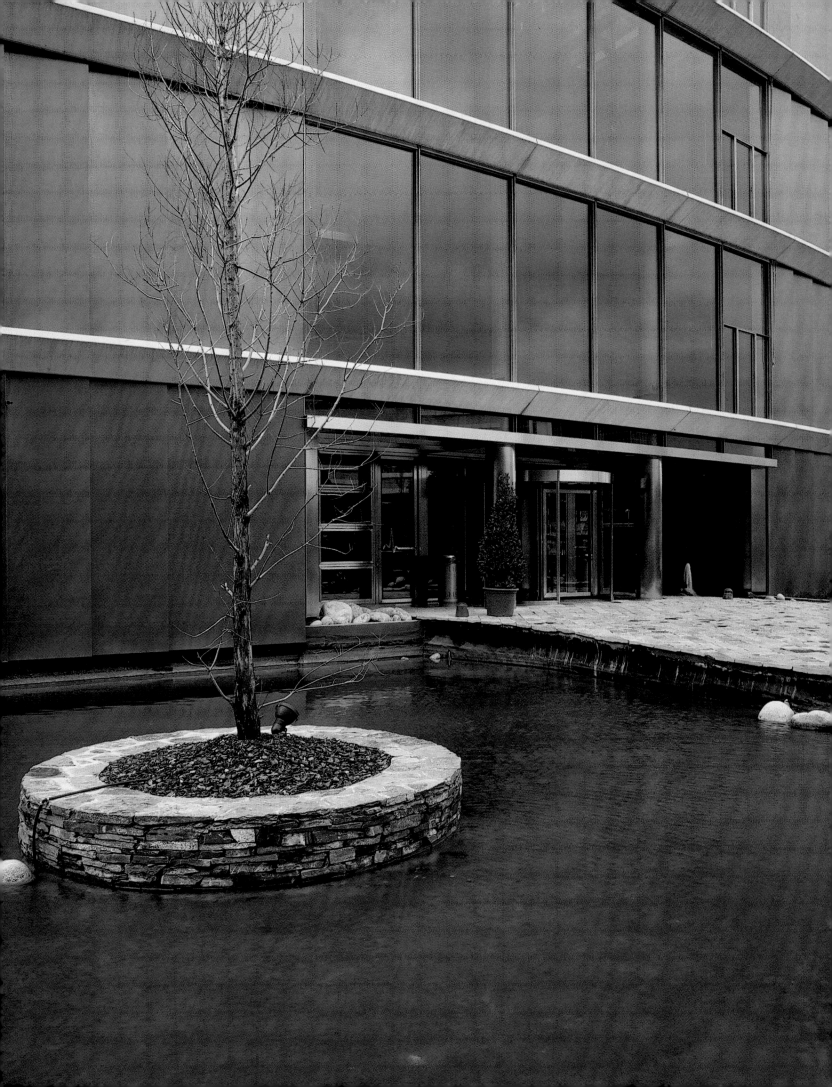

Sanitas Headquarters

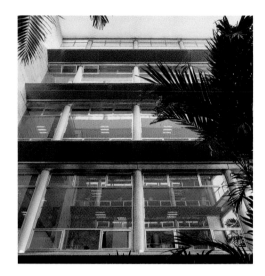

Architect: **Ortiz – León Arquitectos (Iñigo Ortiz Díez de Tortosa and Enrique León García)**
Client: **Sanitas, S.A. de Inversiones**
Location: **Madrid, Spain**
Construction Date: **2000**
Photography: **Jordi Miralles**

Two clearly identified goals guided the work of the architects responsible for carrying out this project. On the one hand, it was of the utmost importance to fully preserve the corporate image of the company. On the other hand, the idea was to create a new concept for an organic building that would be able to use outside energy sources to minimize the total use of energy. This was achieved by giving the building a north–south orientation, making optimum use of resources, increasing the use of natural energy, and guaranteeing a reduction in consumption. It is quite a challenge to combine in a single building the concern for the environment and the functionality required by an office building.

It was decided that an open structure would be designed, a factor that allowed the building to benefit from the natural elements while at the same time having the capability of enclosing itself if they are adverse. All these characteristics materialize in one building with an elliptical plan composed of three structures, where all unnecessary elements that require additional energy consumption have been eliminated.

These environmental criteria were also important when the building materials were being chosen. For example, stainless steel, glass, concrete, natural stone, or wood from managed forests were used for their low energy consumption.

In the interior, the different areas reflect a specific plan: a well-lit space with a nucleus of independent services. This solution guarantees maximum flexibility and dynamic space.

The various closed areas between floors of the building are equipped with double-waterproofed, high-density, protected fiberglass. The glass-enclosed facade, supported by a minimal stainless steel structure, guarantees proper ventilation and lighting of the interiors.

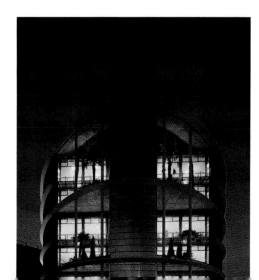

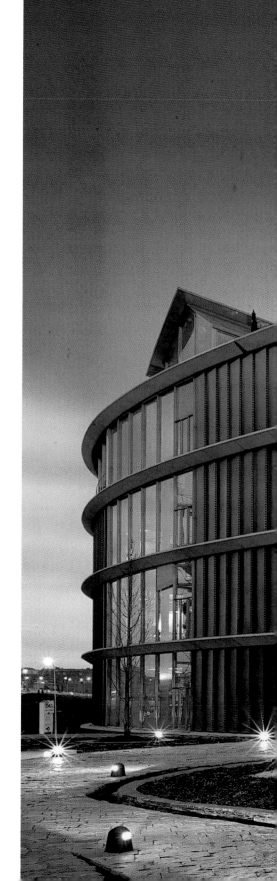

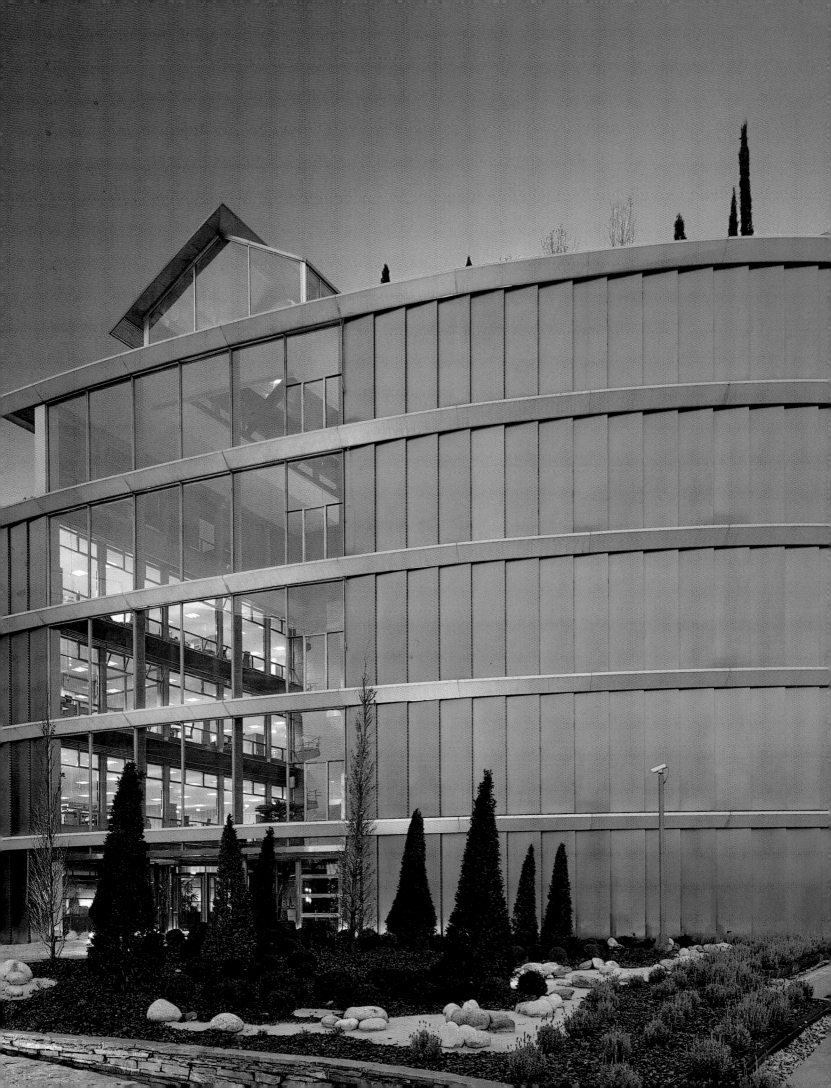

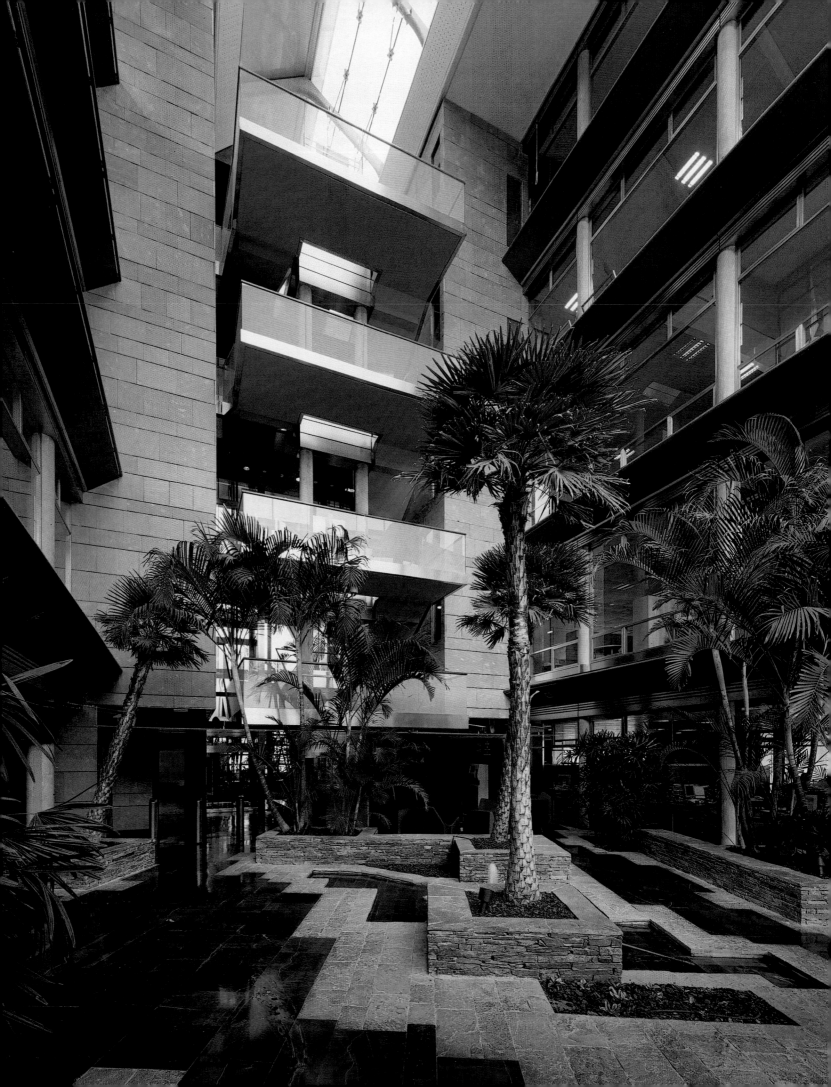

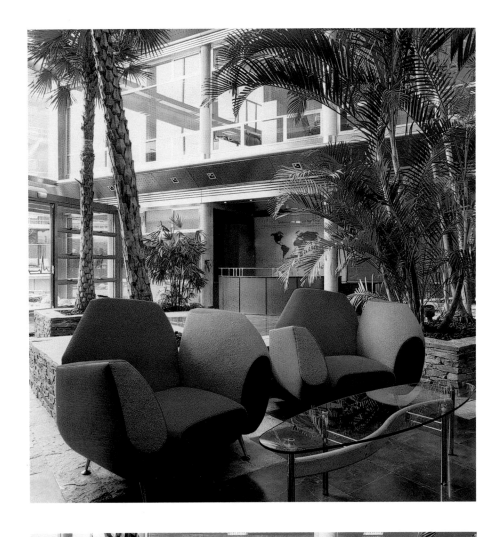

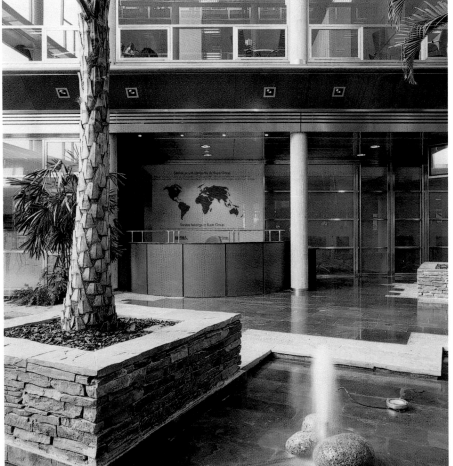

Divided by the block of vertical connecting structures, several courtyards have been designed, which cross the building from side to side. Plants and water have been included, which, in addition to aesthetically enriching the space, reduce the temperature of the air, increase the oxygen, and act as an acoustic buffer.

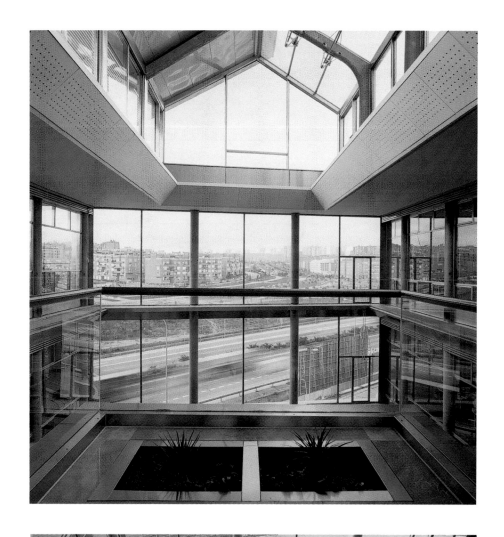

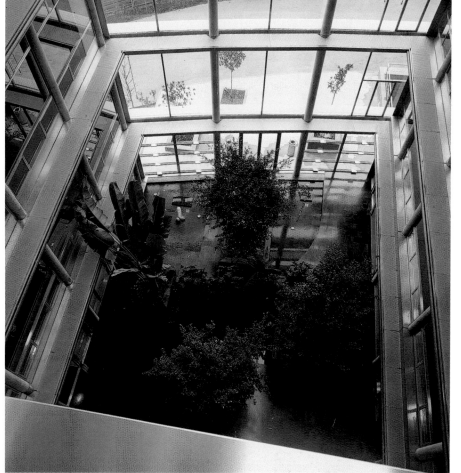

The indirect light is constant, but direct sunlight has been avoided due to the north-south orientation of the building and by using skylights and vertical windows with movable solar protection panels in the atriums of the building.

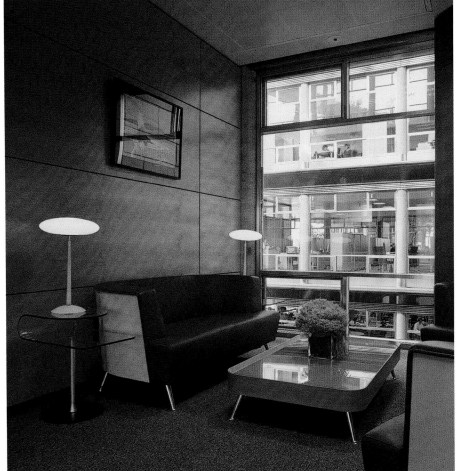

The interiors also show the same respect and discretion for the environment that characterize the building. An austere, balanced, and current décor was employed. It fits perfectly with the rational, minimalist, and environmentally friendly architecture that defines the structure.

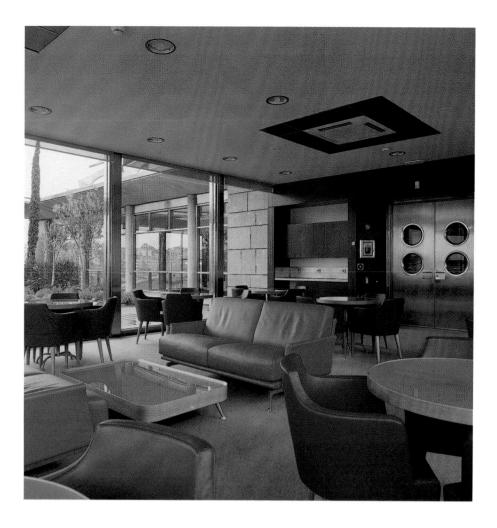

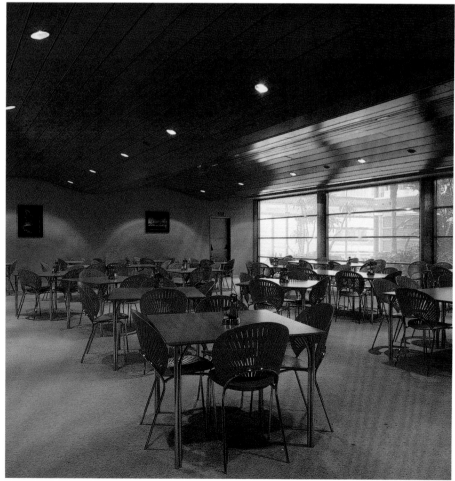

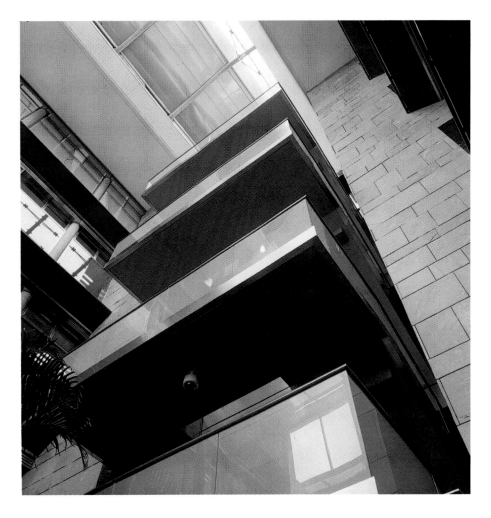

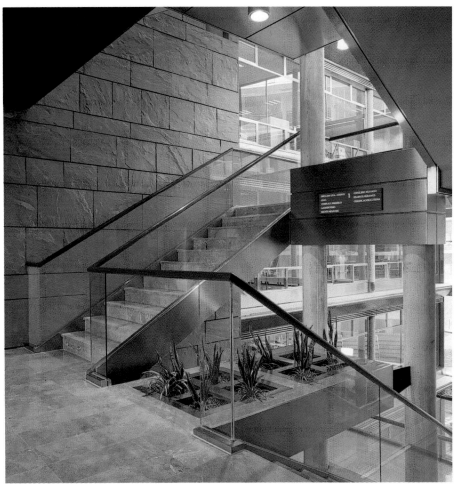

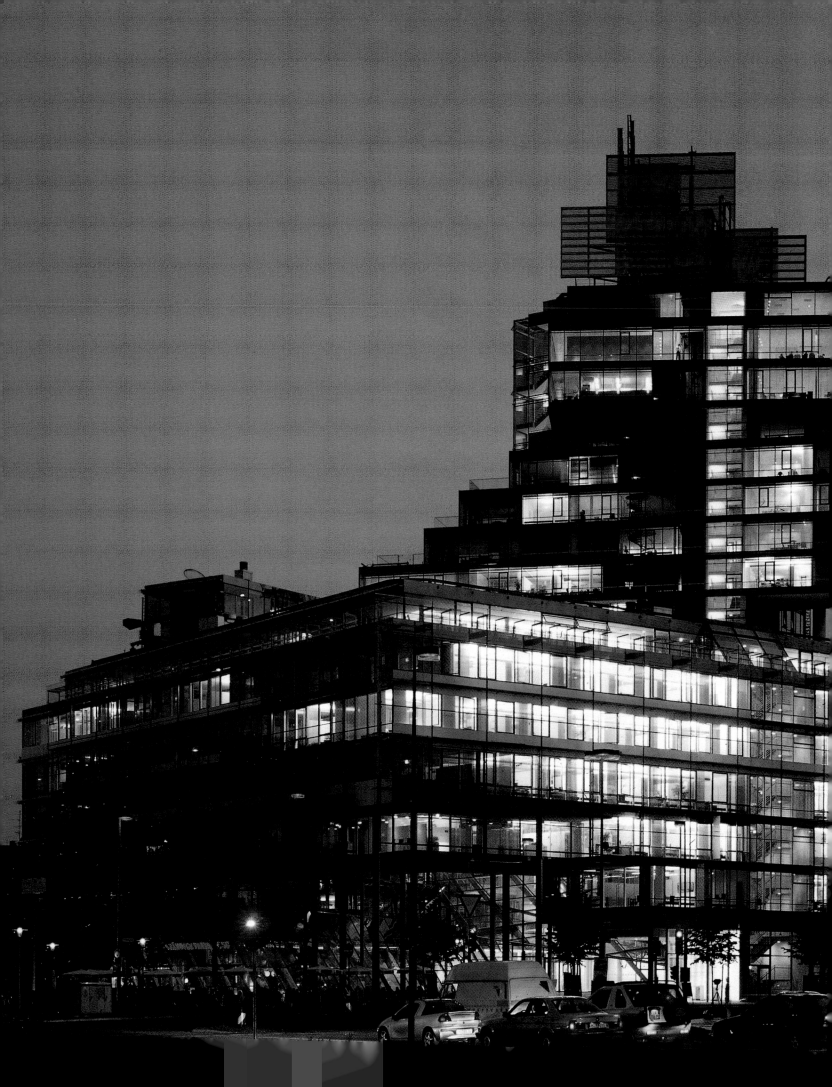

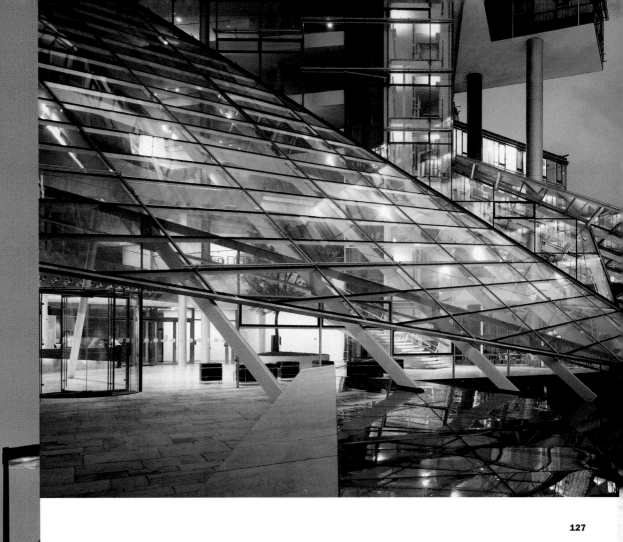

Nord LB. North German State Clearing Bank Building

NORD LB NEEDED AN ADMINISTRATION BUILDING THAT WAS ACCESSIBLE TO THE PUBLIC IN AN INTERMEDIATE AREA BETWEEN THE CITY CENTER AND THE RESIDENTIAL DISTRICT OF HANOVER. WHEN THE TIME CAME TO DESIGN THE NEW OFFICES, THE ARCHITECTS RESPONSIBLE FOR THE PROJECT LOOKED FOR A TYPE OF CONSTRUCTION THAT WOULD ADAPT TO THE SURROUNDINGS OF THE SITE AS WELL AS ESTABLISH AN EVOCATIVE RELATIONSHIP WITH THE CITY.

Nord LB. North German State Clearing Bank Building

Architect: **Behnisch, Behnisch & Partner**
Client: **Demuro Grundstücksverwaltung mbH & Co KG**
Location: **Hanover, Germany**
Construction Date: **2002**
Photography: **Christian Kandzia / B, B&P**

At first glance, the construction begins as an integral part of the surroundings and extends out from the perimeter of the central body, taking the form of a 180-foot-tall tower. It is a complex puzzle in which each piece fits perfectly. The enigmatic and unique multilevel tower, a spiral of provocative and acute angles that can be seen from a distance, is the main feature of the building. In addition to the offices, the complex includes commercial, residential, cultural, dining, and sports facilities. The objective was to create a space that was open to and accessible by the public.

The architects have designed a building that emerges from the landscape and forms an integral part of it, while the highest portion resembles an independent entity connected to the whole but perceived as a remote figure, as if it were part of the distant city. One of the main goals was to create a smart and Earth-friendly building respectful of the environment. The architects used natural resources in the construction process, requiring energy consumption and the reduction of carbon dioxide emissions to play a part in the planning of the modern and spectacular body. Windows were given priority for creating natural ventilation and providing fresh air to most of the rooms. The double outer shell helps create ventilation and, at the same time, reduces noise pollution. Also, the use of glass on the entire surface of the building makes it possible to easily control the natural light that filters through to the interiors.

This building, which houses the offices of Nord LB as well as commercial, cultural, entertainment, and sports facilities, is a self-contained complex that is open, accessible and able to meet every possible need, and is well integrated into its surroundings.

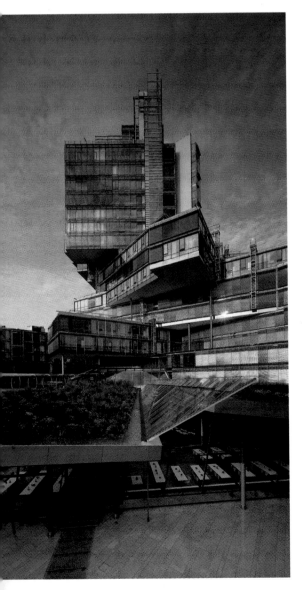

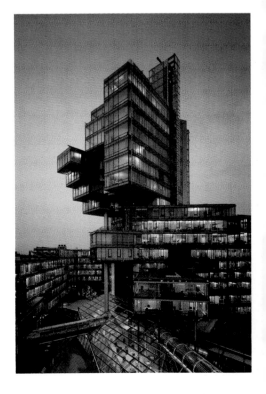

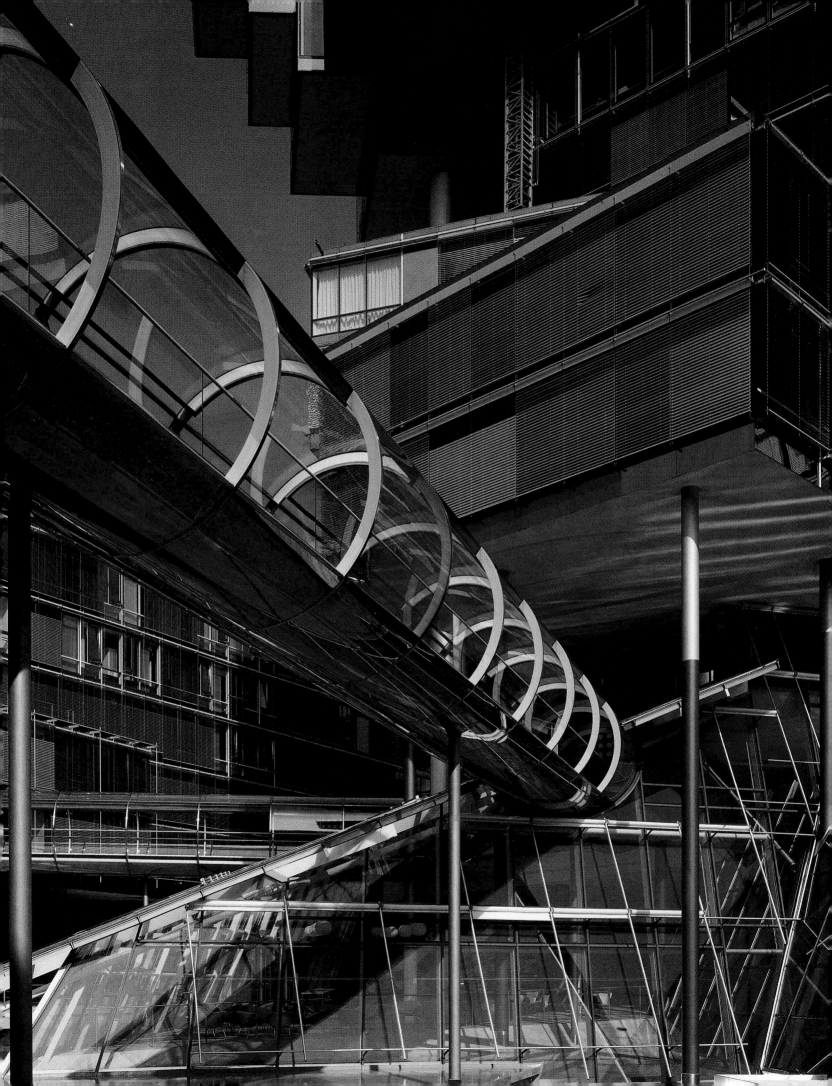

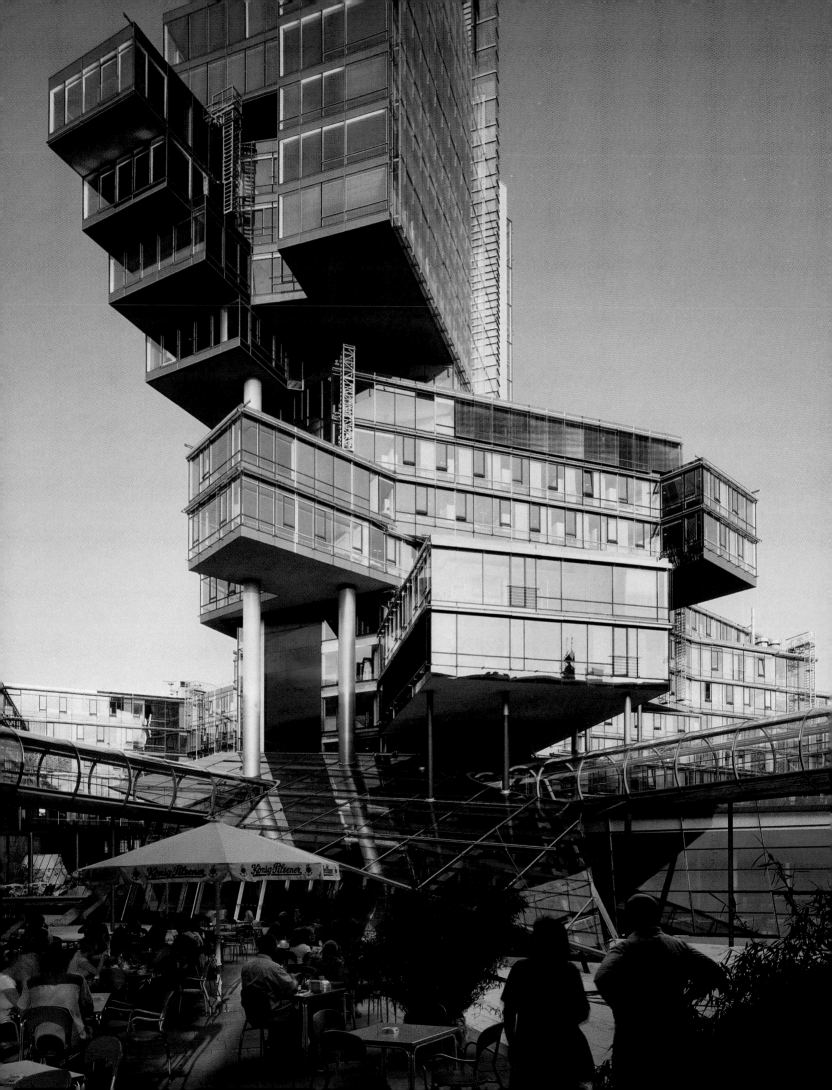

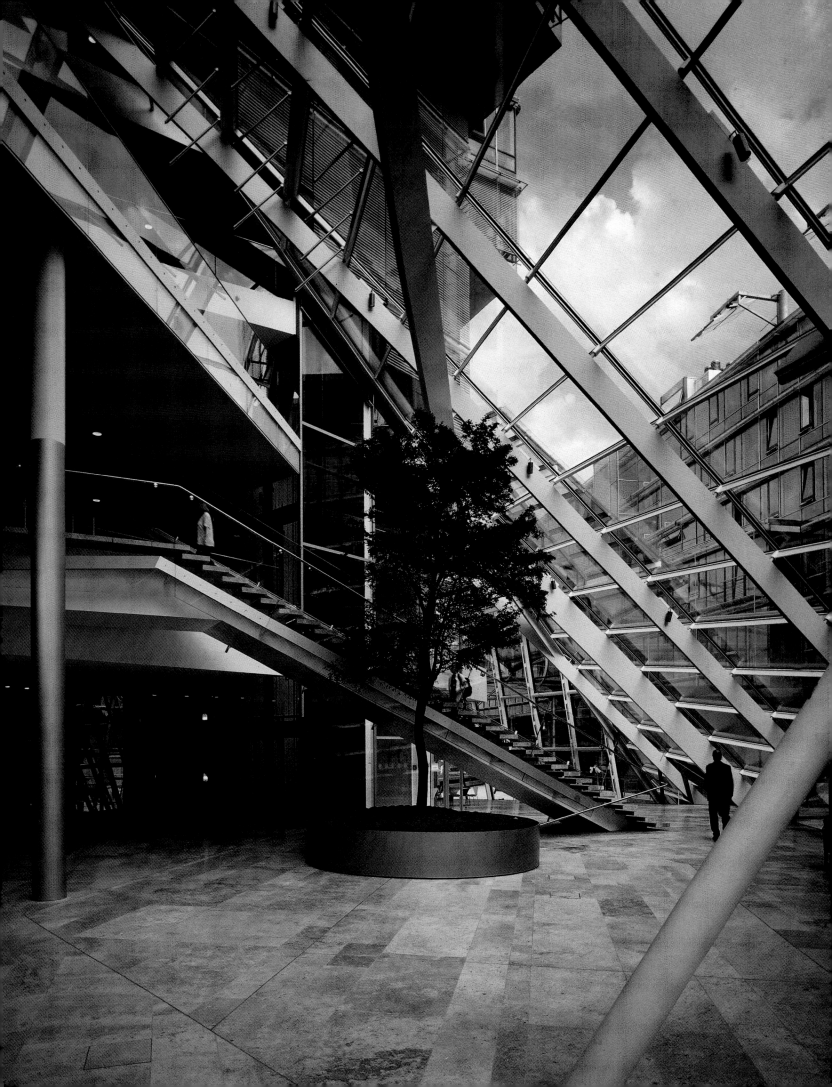

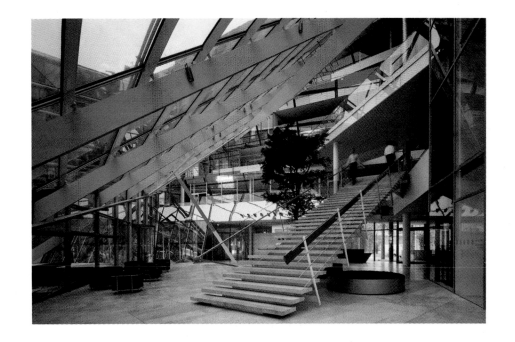

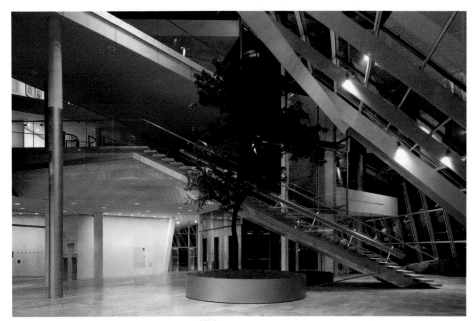

The public and common areas have been conceived as multipurpose and free-flowing open spaces. The architecture and the use of simple and functional furnishings are key elements that allow light to flood the spaces, introducing a suggestive play of light and shadow.

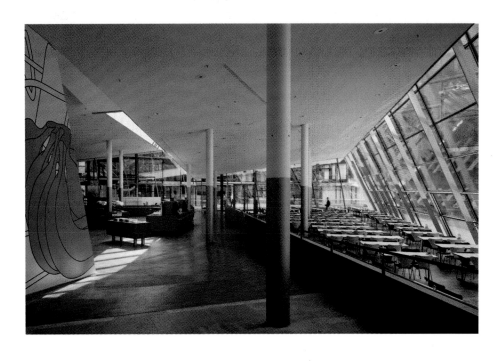

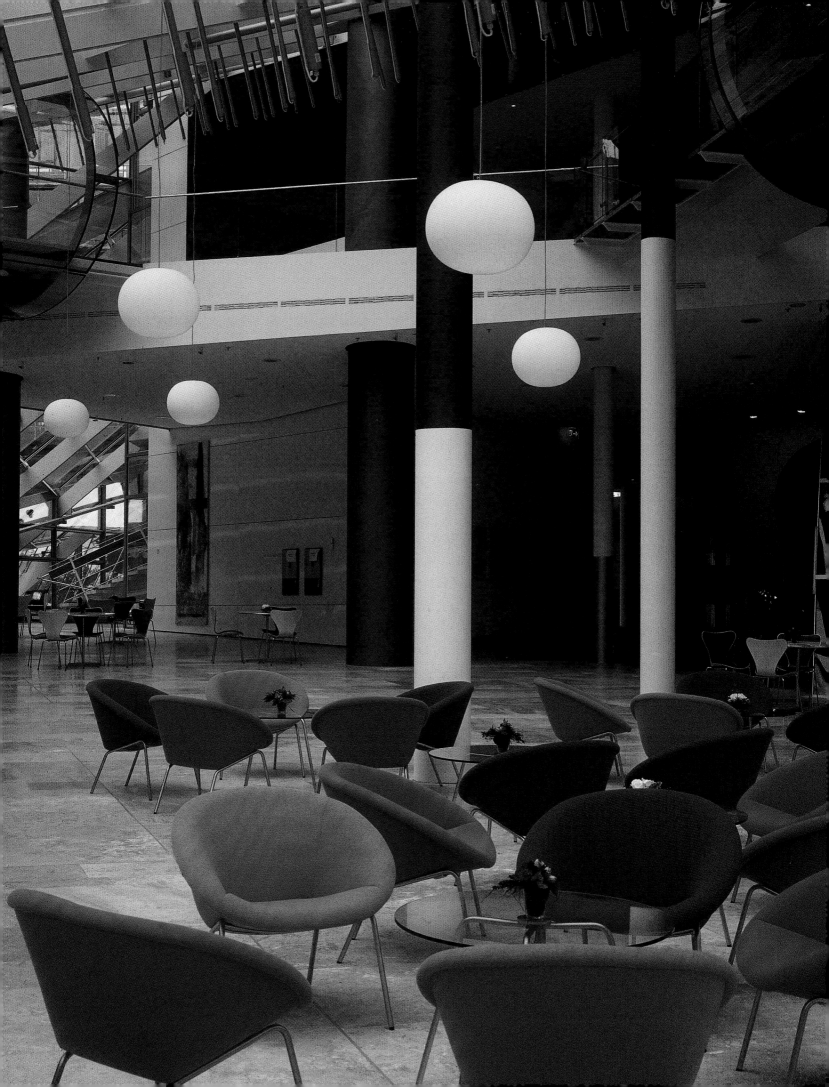

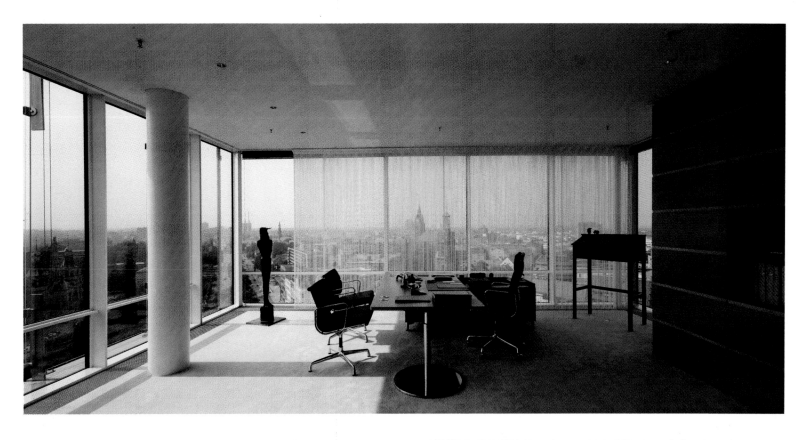

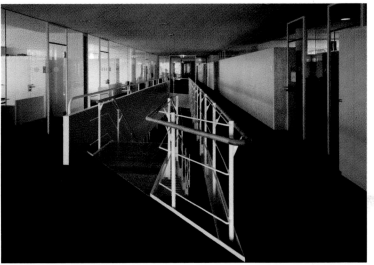

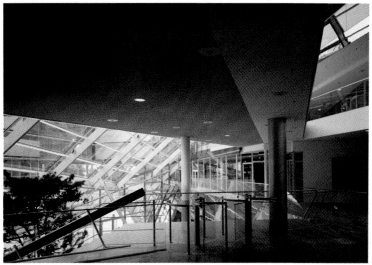

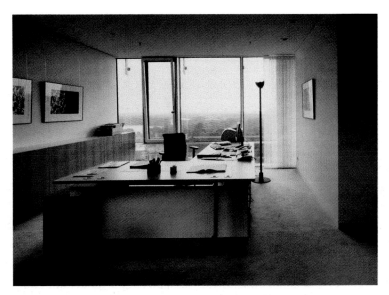

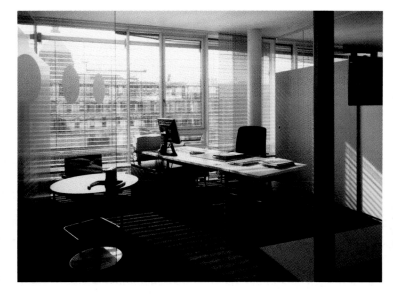

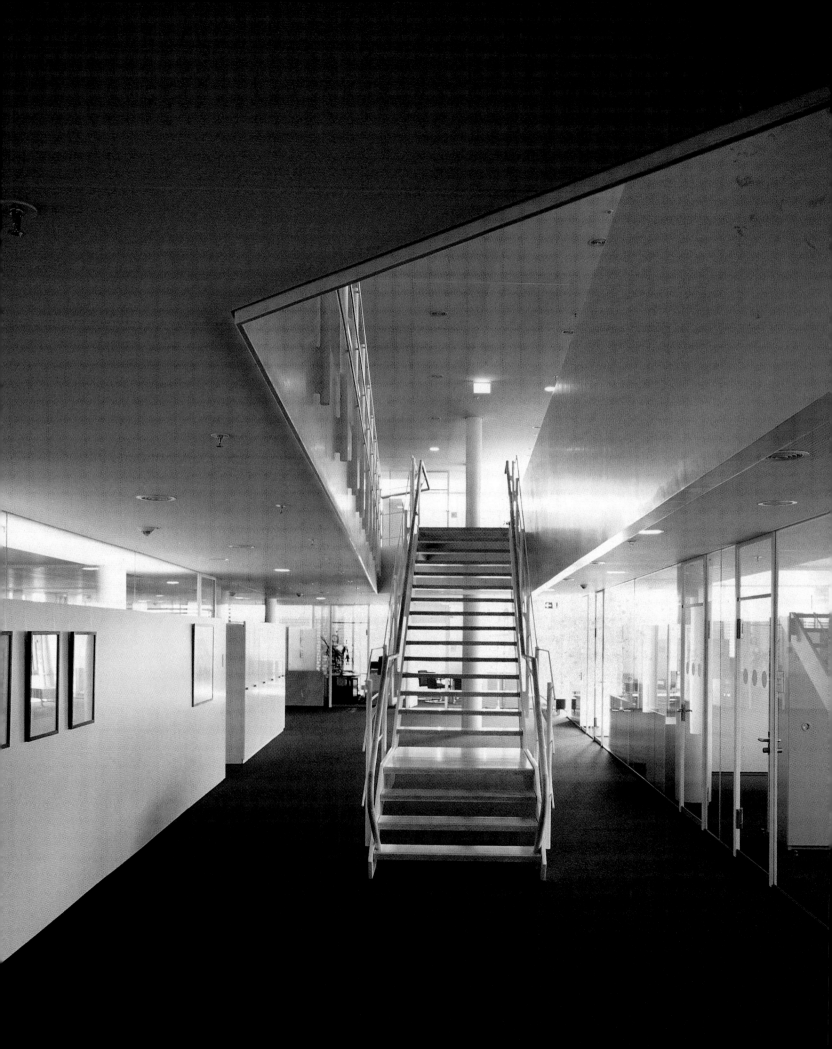

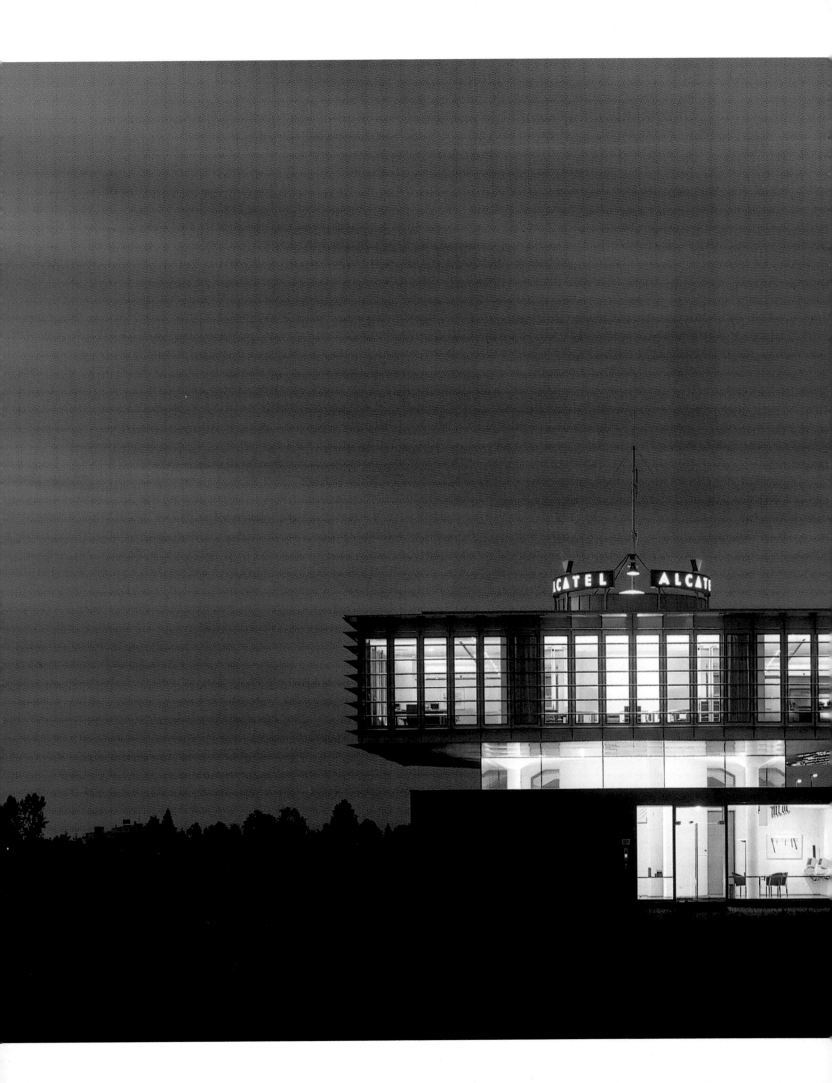

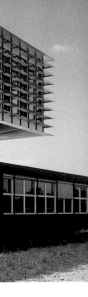

Alcatel

The important telecommunications company Alcatel commissioned the prestigious architectural firm of Baumschlager & Eberle to design their offices in Lustenau, a flourishing town in the Voralberg region in western Austria. From the beginning, clients and architects agreed on the idea of an emblematic building that, despite its small size, would stand out in the suburban enclave in which it was located.

Alcatel

Architect: **Baumschlager & Eberle**
Collaborators: **D.I. Ernst Mader (structures)**
Client: **Alcatel Austria AG**
Location: **Lustenau, Austria**
Construction Date: **1993**
Photography: **Ignacio Martínez**

The plan required a few offices, a small assembly plant, a warehouse, and a multipurpose space for meetings and public functions. Since the building was relatively small, the arrangement had to be carefully planned to maximize the functions. Through traffic was kept to a minimum, hallways were eliminated, and passageways and staircases were centralized.

The lower level includes the reception area and the equipment rooms in the front of the building. The back area houses a warehouse and a loading zone. These premises are contained within a solid block with two openings for the entrance and a line of windows on the upper section of the enclosure, which is adorned with cutouts of black tile.

A spiral staircase leads to the second floor. Here, the offices are arranged along the perimeter while a multifunctional room occupies the center. A system of four columns and a concrete cylinder that separates the staircase raises the second floor almost three feet higher than the lower level, creating the illusion of a body floating in space. This small detail becomes more prominent through the use of glass on all sides, which is protected by a series of metal slats.

The uniqueness of the volumes and the contrast of materials create a peculiar and attractive construction that is contemporary in design and has little relation to the factories of the past.

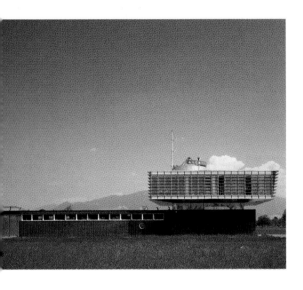

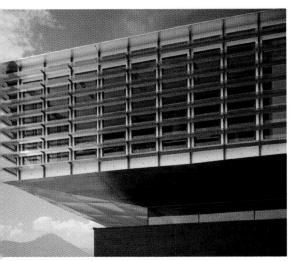

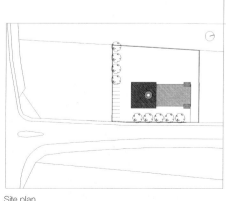

Site plan

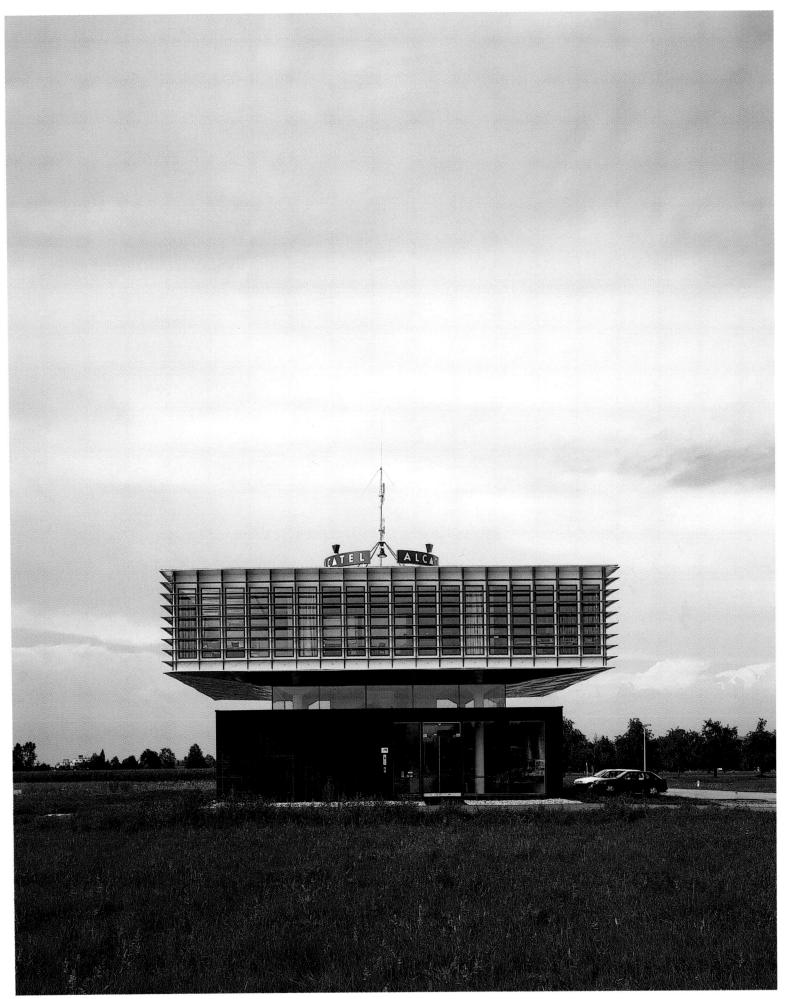

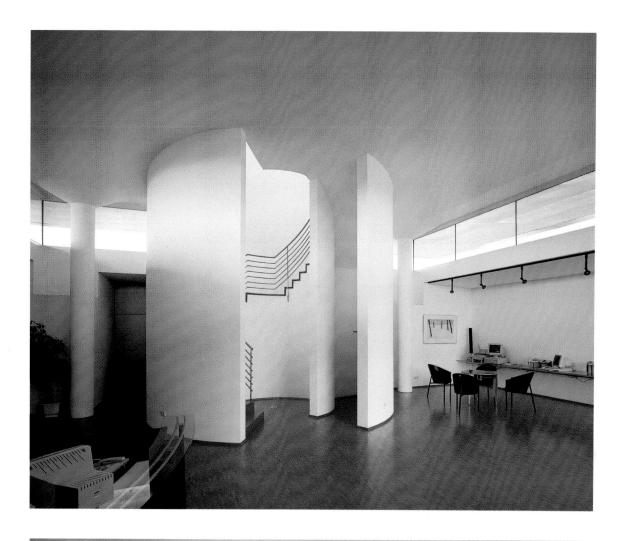

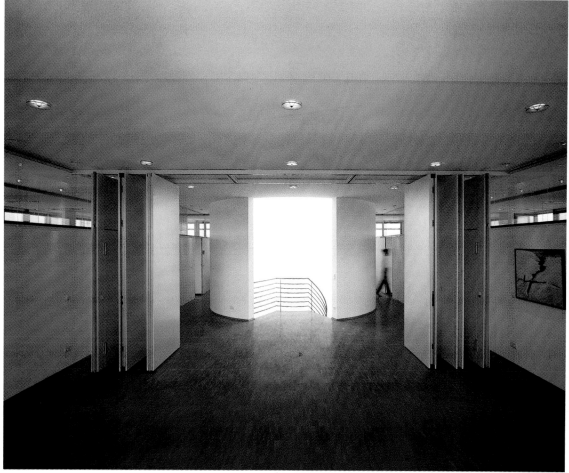

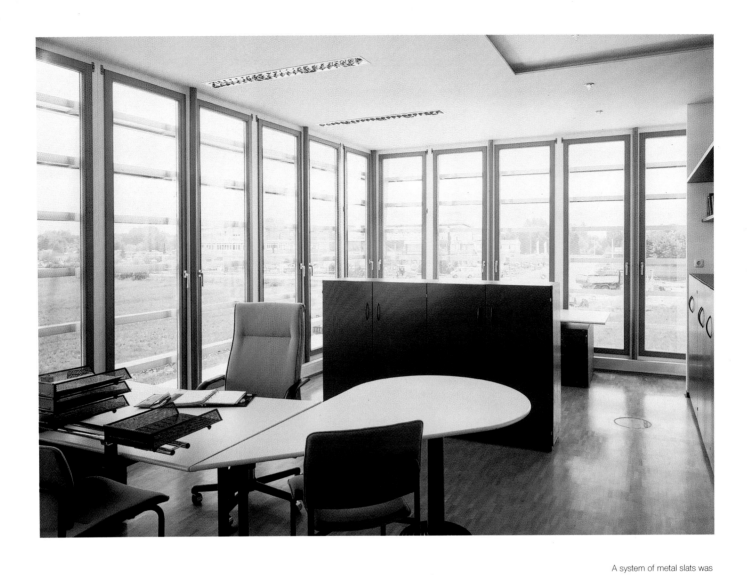

A system of metal slats was designed and placed horizontally to block direct light and to control and diffuse it as it filters through the glass walls of the top level. The sun's rays are deflected by the metal slats and are softened before entering the building.

1. Hall
2. Reception
3. Installation room
4. Bathroom
5. Technical room
6. Lockers and archive
7. Head of store
8. Store
9. Store
10. Assembly
11. Offices
12. Bathroom
13. Kitchen

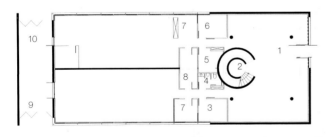

Ground floor

First floor

Section

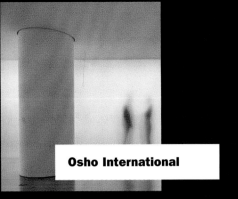

Osho International

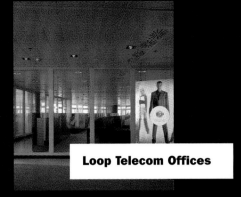

Loop Telecom Offices

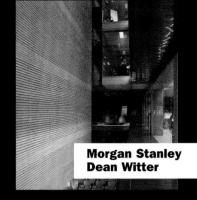

Morgan Stanley Dean Witter

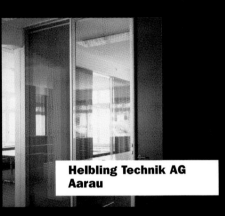

Helbling Technik AG Aarau

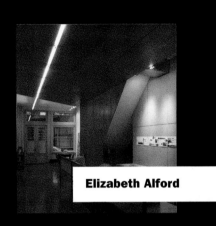

Elizabeth Alford

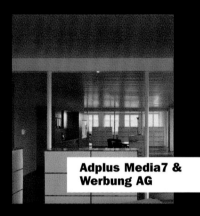

Adplus Media7 & Werbung AG

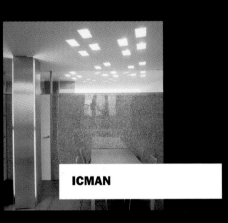

ICMAN

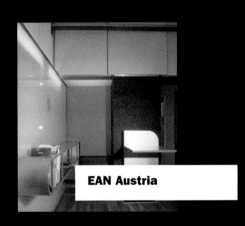

EAN Austria

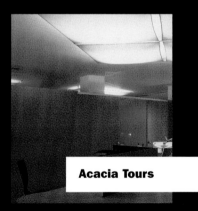

Acacia Tours

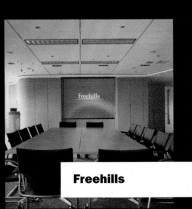

Freehills

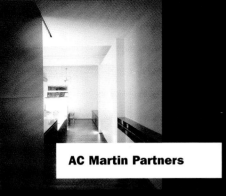

AC Martin Partners

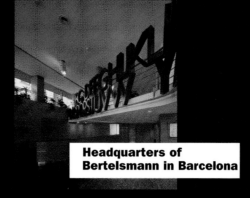

Headquarters of Bertelsmann in Barcelona

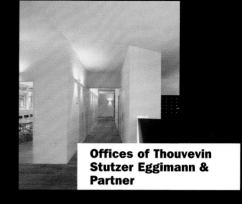

Offices of Thouvevin Stutzer Eggimann & Partner

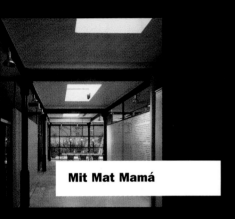

Mit Mat Mamá

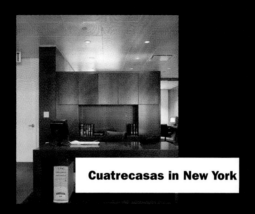

Cuatrecasas in New York

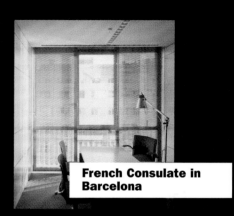

French Consulate in Barcelona

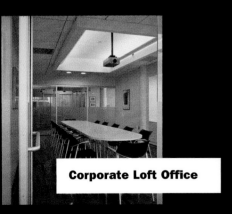

Corporate Loft Office

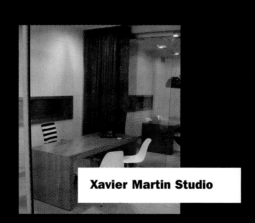

Xavier Martin Studio

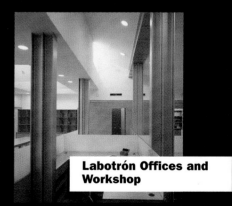

Labotrón Offices and Workshop

Interior Design

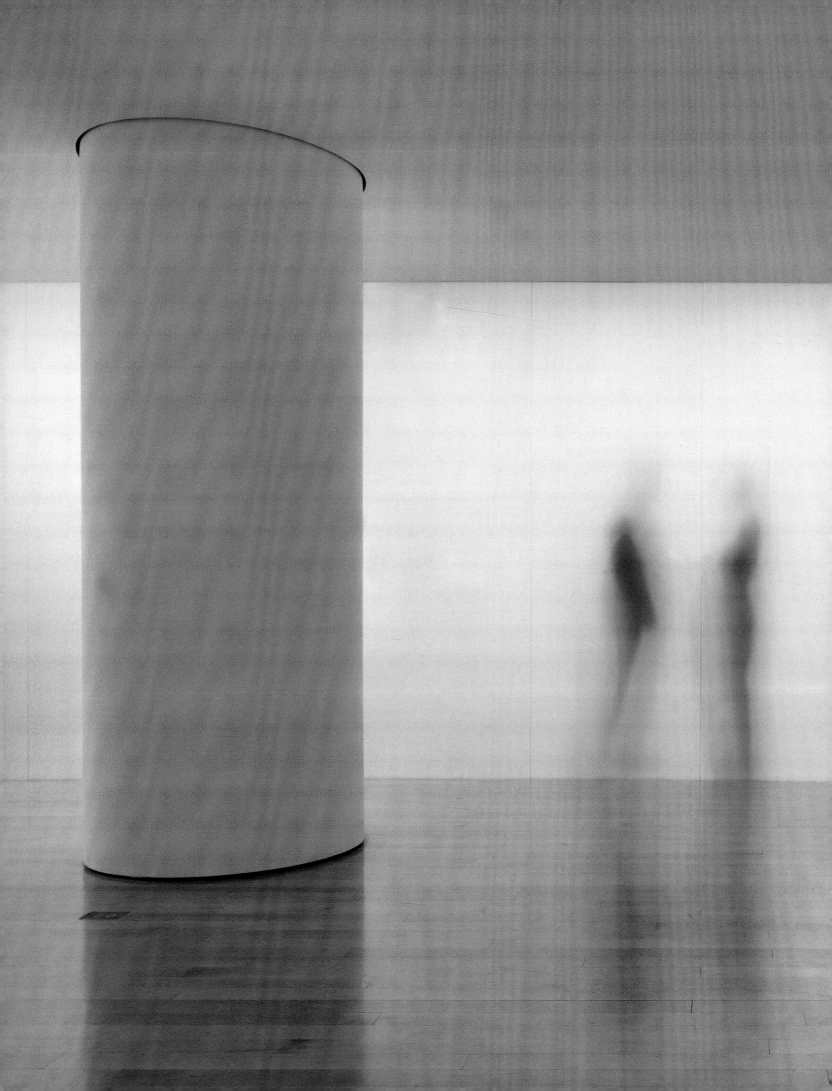

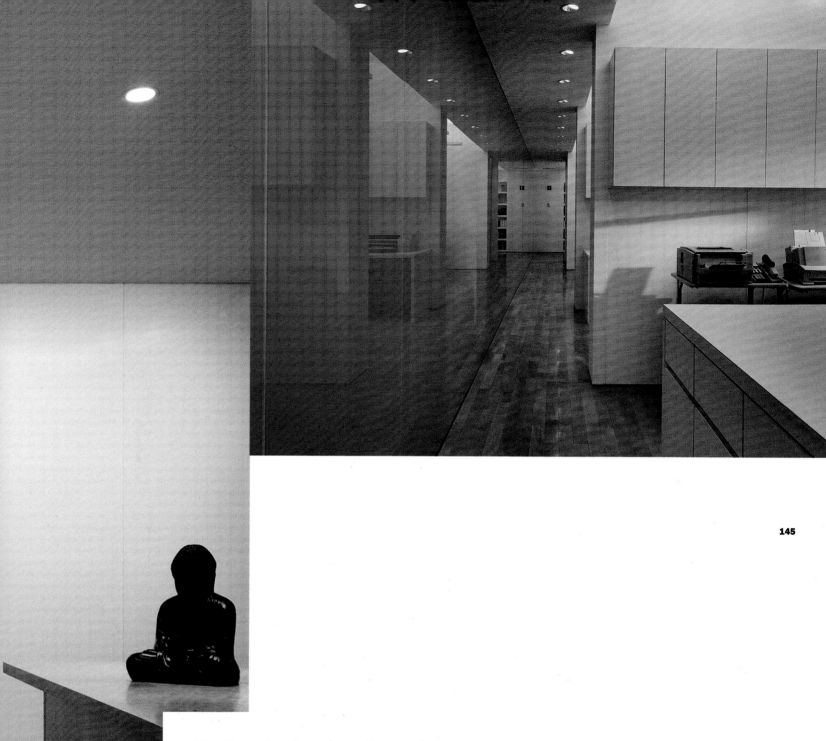

Osho International

THE NEW YORK HEADQUARTERS OF OSHO INTERNATIONAL, A PUBLISHING COMPANY SPECIALIZING IN SUBJECTS RELATED TO ZEN CULTURE AND MEDITATION, OCCUPIES THE 46TH FLOOR OF A SKYSCRAPER LOCATED ON LEXINGTON AVENUE. THIS TALL, GRACEFUL TOWER OFFERS UNUSUALLY SMALL FLOORS—ABOUT 3,067 SQ. FT.—WITH A CENTRAL NUCLEUS OF FIXTURES AND ELEVATORS ON THE SOUTH SIDE OF THE BUILDING.

Osho International

Architect: **Daniel Rowen**
Client: **Osho International**
Location: **New York City, United States**
Construction Date: **1998**
Photography: **Michael Moran**

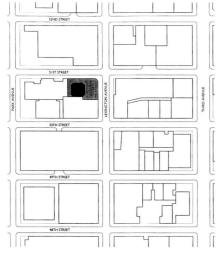

Site plan

The main purpose of the project was to create a relaxing and balanced atmosphere that reflected the spirit and personal concepts of the company and the people who are part of it. The design process was governed by the idea of unifying the entrance, reception area, and conference room into a single space. This common central space is defined on two of its sides by floor-to-ceiling storage modules. These volumes also house the communications infrastructure. On the side that faces the elevator, the space is defined by a vertical partition made of translucent glass. One of its sides is acid-etched, the other is polished. This subtle duality confers interesting perceptive qualities. Seen from the entrance, this glass screen allows a view of the movement and shadows of the spaces and the people in them. However, seen from the hallway, the surface reflects the different activities, emphasizing the privacy of the individual offices.

All decisions regarding the project—design, selection of materials, arrangement details, and construction solutions—had to be minimalist to make them coherent with each other and with the client's philosophy. The goal was to create a quiet, meditative atmosphere that would stimulate creativity and imagination while at the same time offer respite from the urban bustle of downtown Manhattan.

To better reflect the philosophy and activity of the company, a decision was made to use a neutral color palette and carefully selected materials and finishes to create a sense of austerity and spatial fluidity. All of this makes it possible to create quiet and balanced surroundings for working in harmony.

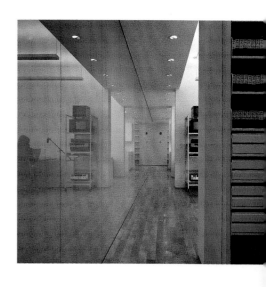

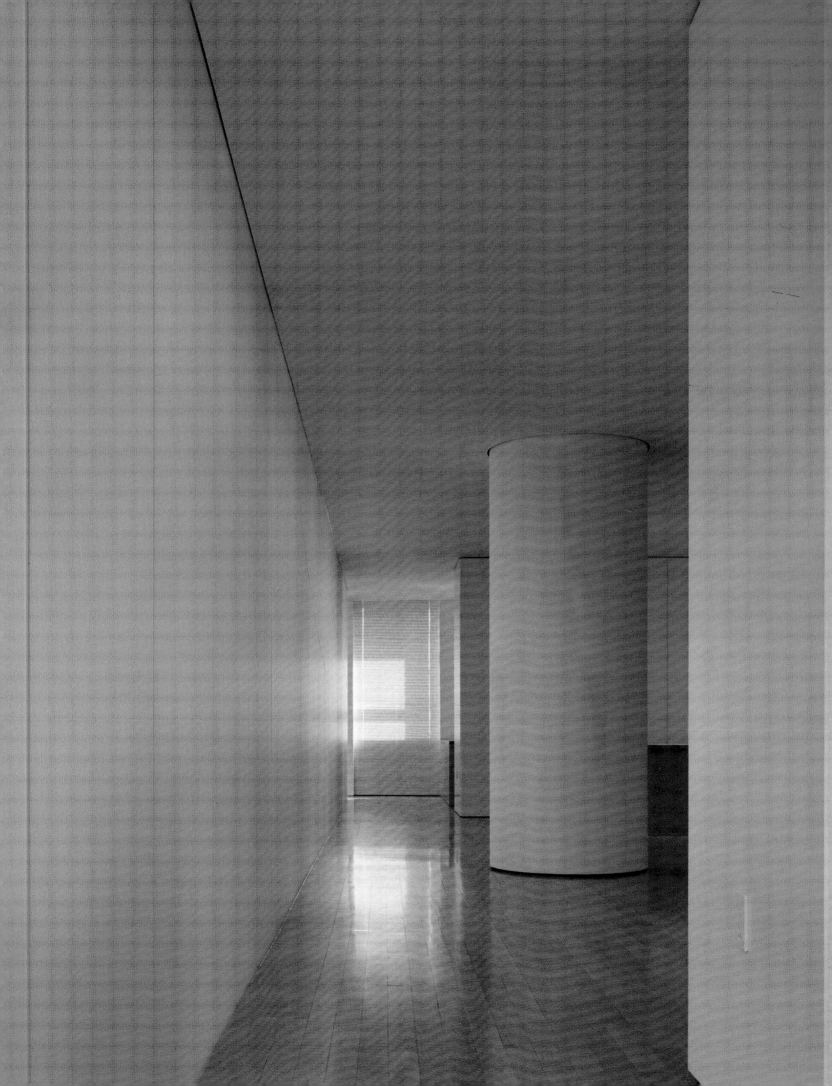

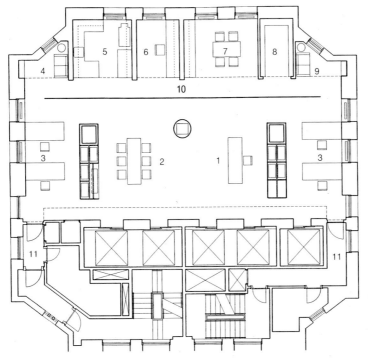

1. Reception
2. Conference room
3. Offices
4. Lounge
5. Office
6. Sound room
7. Video room
8. Archives
9. Lounge
10. Recreation room
11. Service corridor

Floor plan

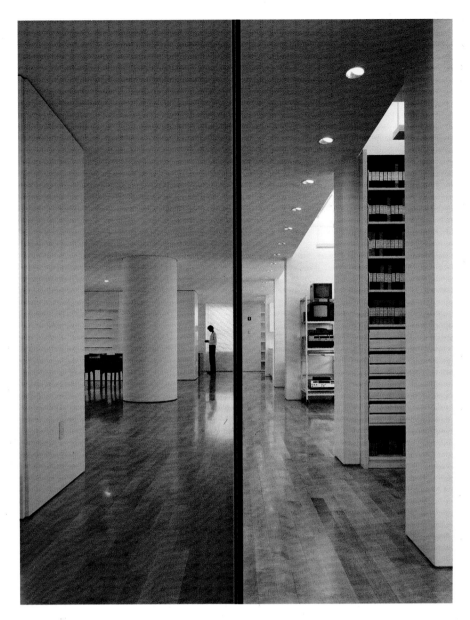

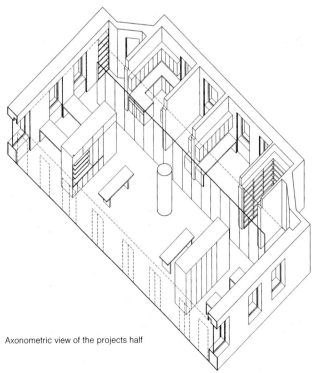

Axonometric view of the projects half

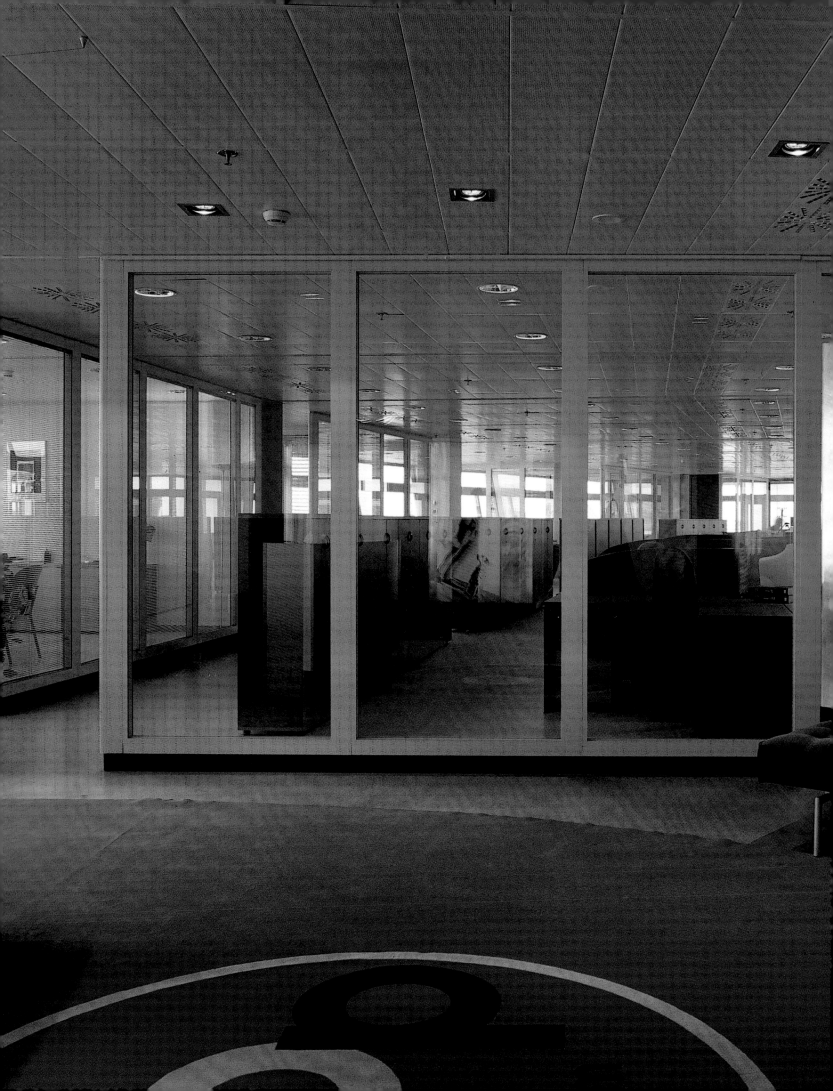

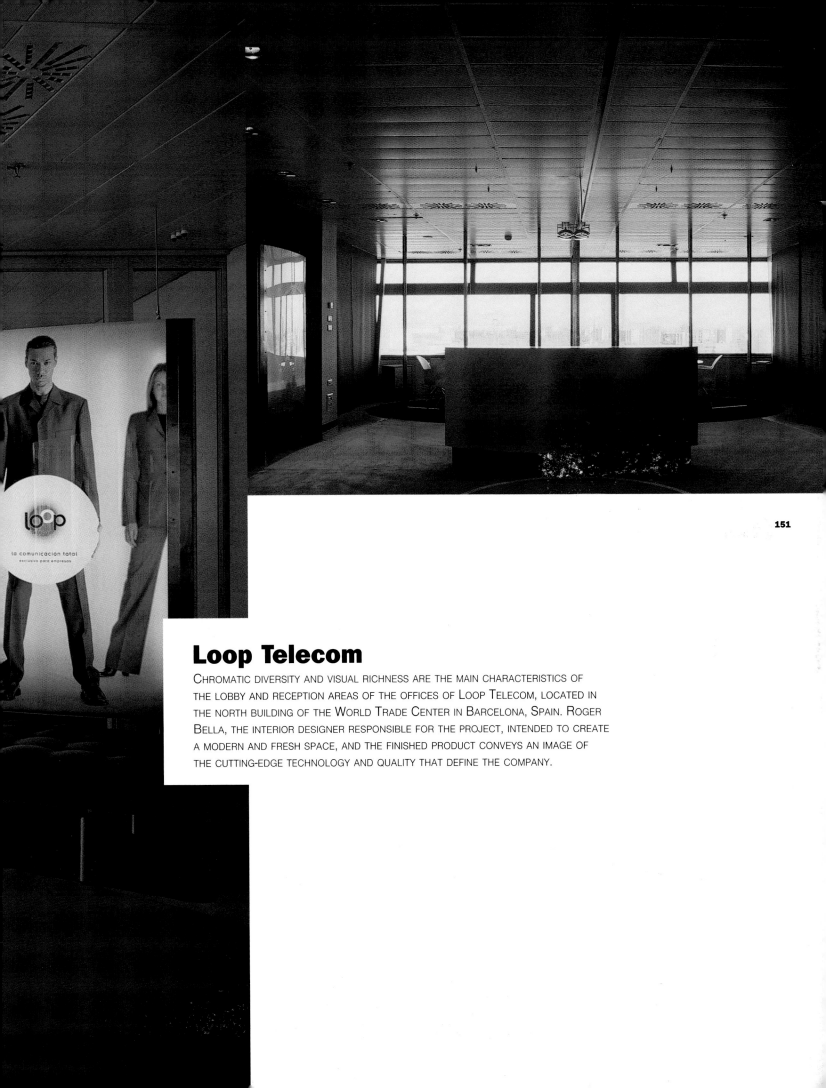

Loop Telecom

CHROMATIC DIVERSITY AND VISUAL RICHNESS ARE THE MAIN CHARACTERISTICS OF THE LOBBY AND RECEPTION AREAS OF THE OFFICES OF LOOP TELECOM, LOCATED IN THE NORTH BUILDING OF THE WORLD TRADE CENTER IN BARCELONA, SPAIN. ROGER BELLA, THE INTERIOR DESIGNER RESPONSIBLE FOR THE PROJECT, INTENDED TO CREATE A MODERN AND FRESH SPACE, AND THE FINISHED PRODUCT CONVEYS AN IMAGE OF THE CUTTING-EDGE TECHNOLOGY AND QUALITY THAT DEFINE THE COMPANY.

Loop Telecom

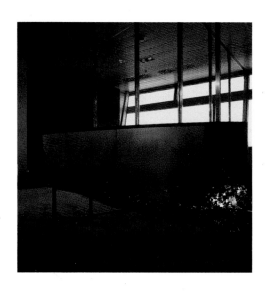

Interior Designer: **Roger Bellera**
Client: **Loop Telecom**
Location: **Barcelona, Spain**
Construction Date: **2000**
Photography: **Jordi Miralles**

Loop Telecom is a telecommunications company that specializes in corporate services. Their offices should reflect a true image of the company. In order to emphasize its graphic and corporate image, it was decided to combine materials and colors while distributing spaces into clearly distinctive areas. Blue and green, the colors in its logo, are the predominant tones, which bring a freshness and vitality to the carpet as well as to some of the furniture pieces and display units.

The access to the lobby is located at one end of the rectangular floor, which echoes the shape of the building. Two areas framed by the outlines of two intersecting ellipses divide the main space. The floor treatment—blue or green carpet, depending on the surroundings—defines each area visually as well as physically.

The reception counter, located directly across from the entrance, was constructed of wood with aluminum and corporate blue laminates. The carpet in front of the counter displays the logo of the company, while an original piece of auxiliary furniture has been placed behind. Display units have been placed at each end of the counter, and access to the offices and work areas is located on the right, through columns painted green in order to emphasize the entryway. At the far end of this reception space lie two meeting rooms and the public area, separated by open glass panels.

Aside from the tables and chairs for the meetings, the rest of the furniture was custom made to fit perfectly in the space and to adapt to the requirements of the company.

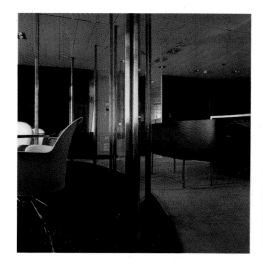

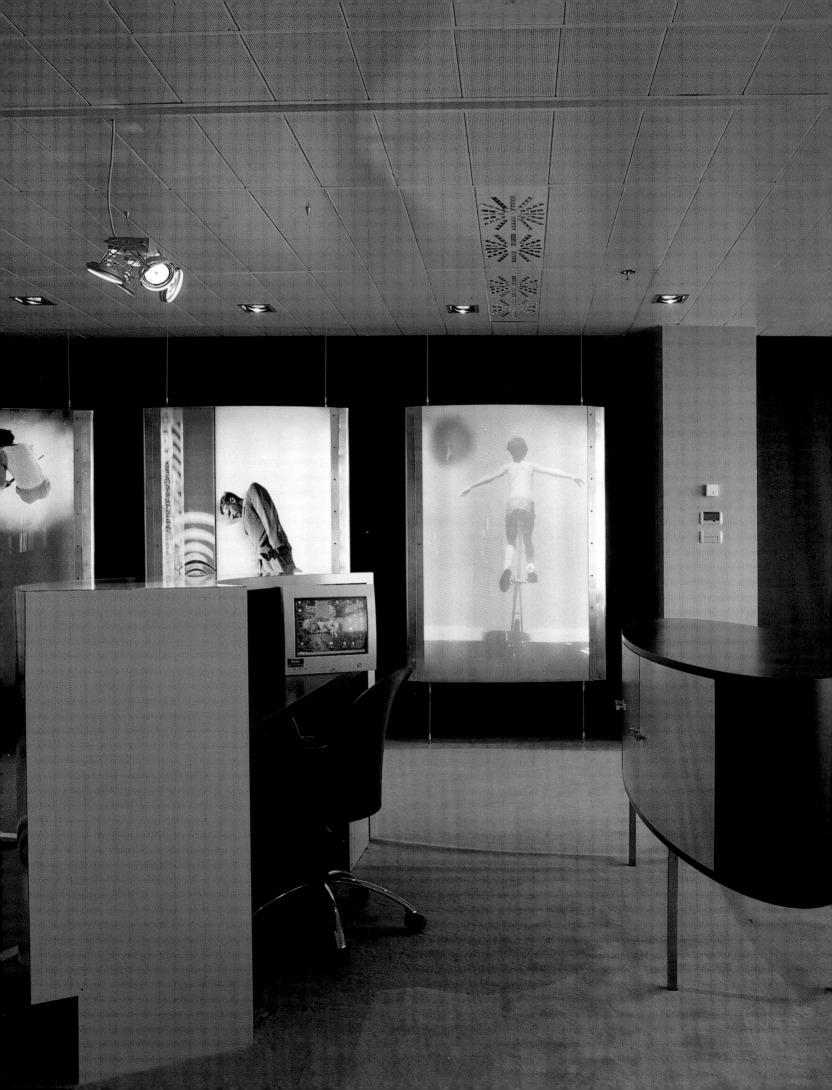

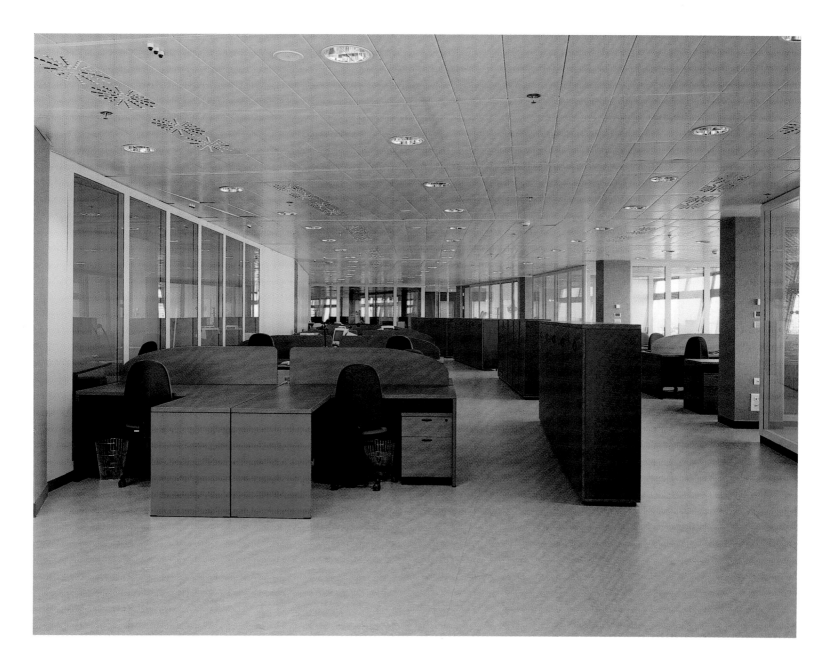

The work areas are distributed within a large room in the interior of the building. Compartmentalized spaces were created, which still communicate with one another but, despite their openness, provide sufficient privacy when it is time to work.

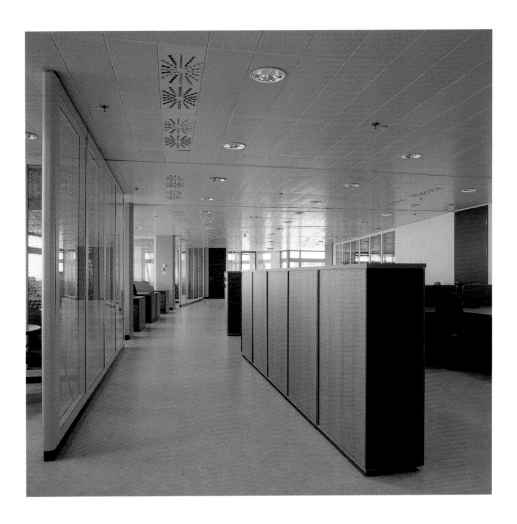

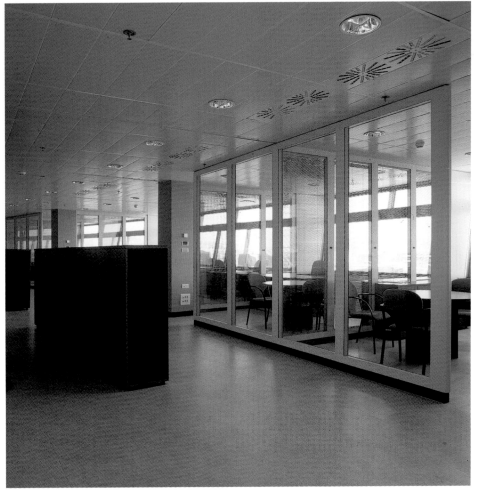

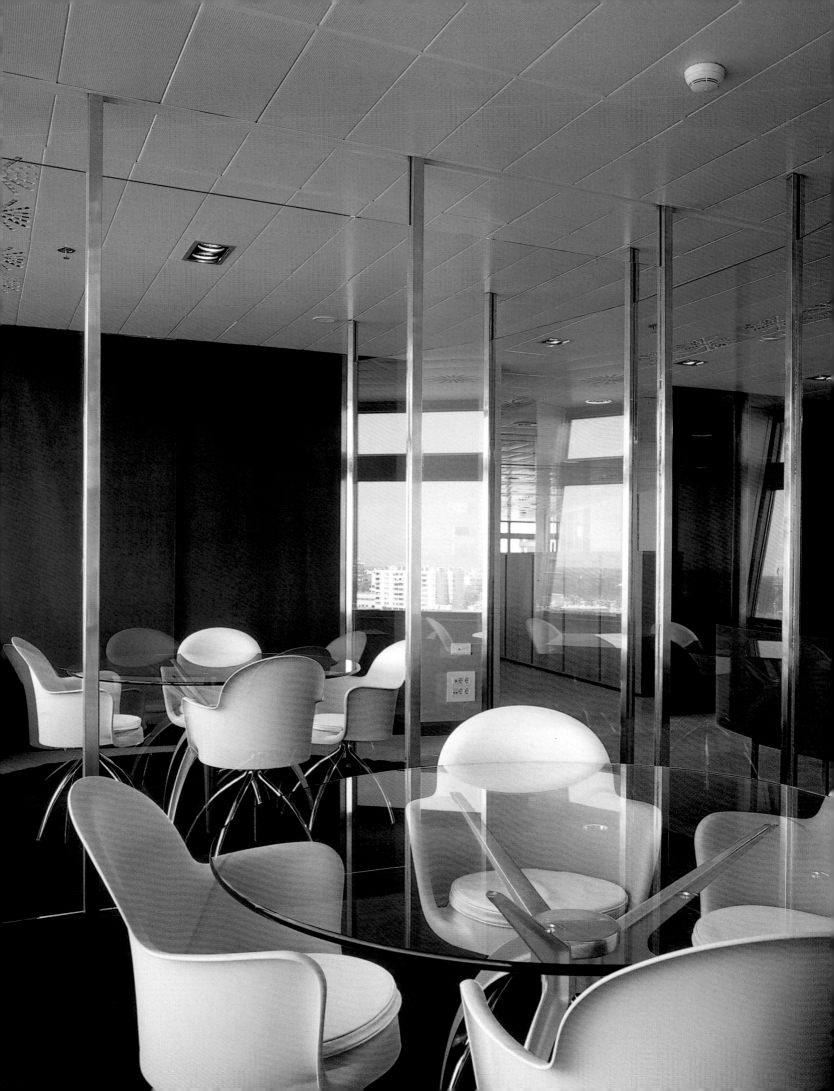

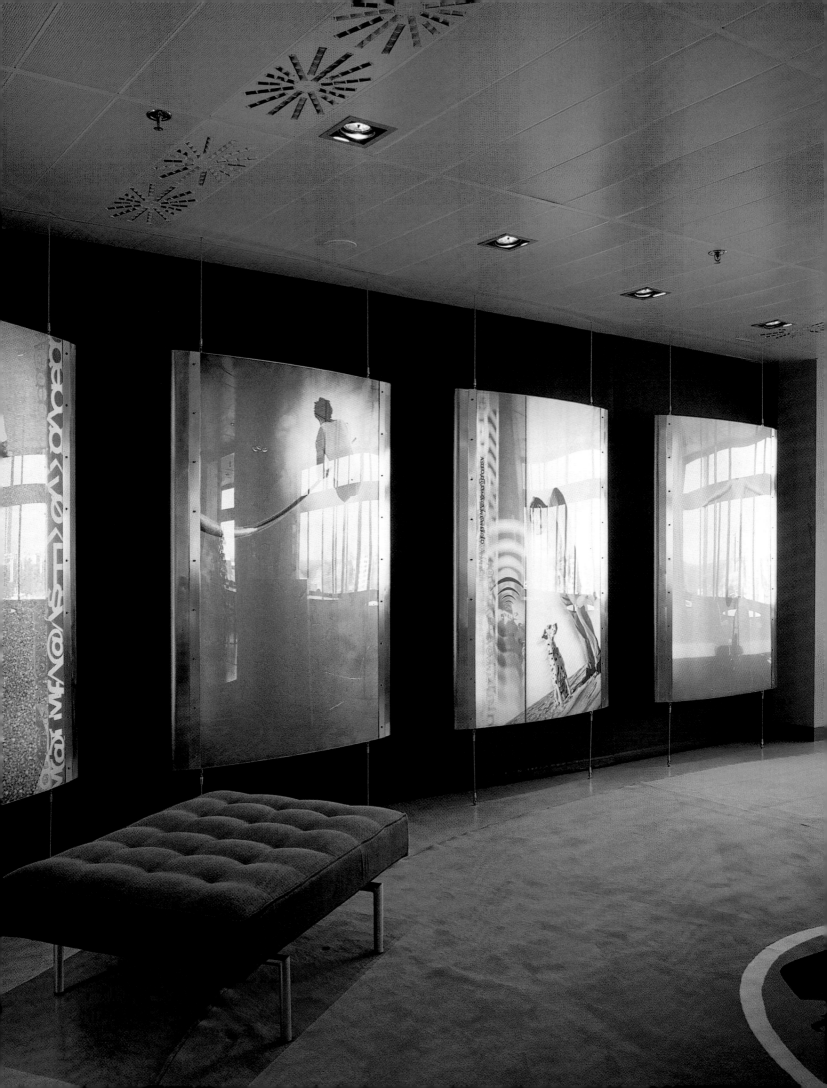

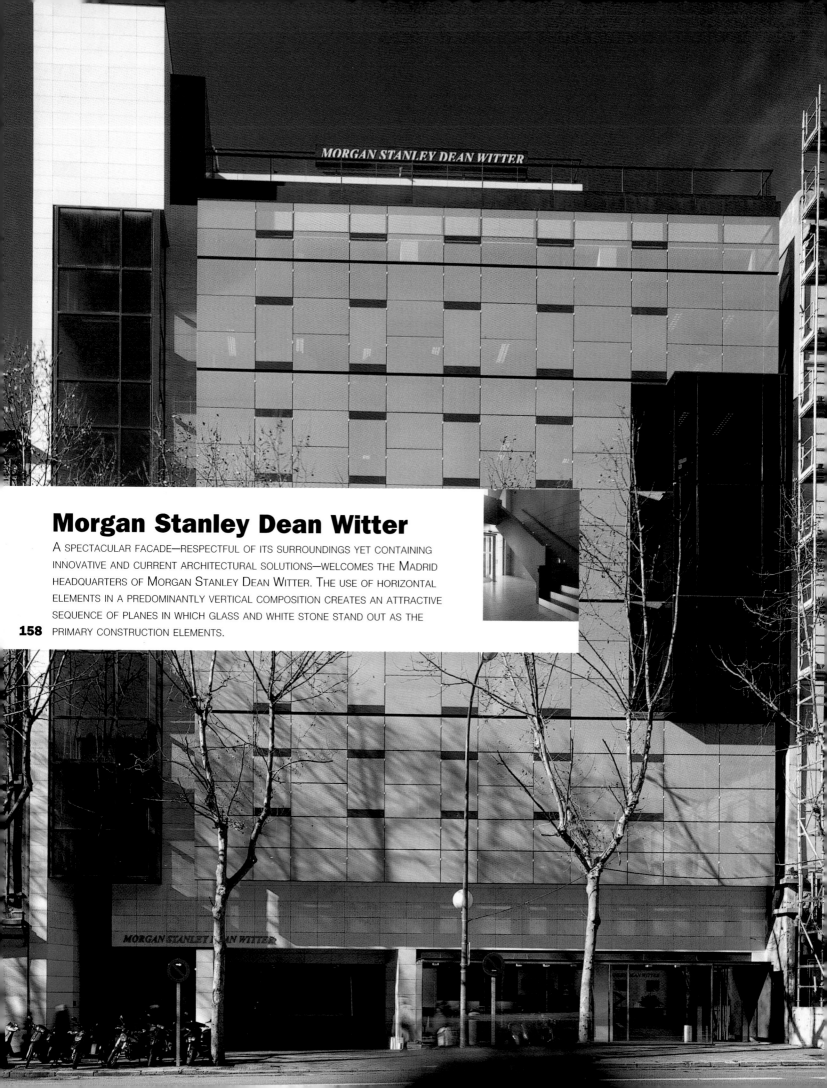

Morgan Stanley Dean Witter

A SPECTACULAR FACADE—RESPECTFUL OF ITS SURROUNDINGS YET CONTAINING
INNOVATIVE AND CURRENT ARCHITECTURAL SOLUTIONS—WELCOMES THE MADRID
HEADQUARTERS OF MORGAN STANLEY DEAN WITTER. THE USE OF HORIZONTAL
ELEMENTS IN A PREDOMINANTLY VERTICAL COMPOSITION CREATES AN ATTRACTIVE
SEQUENCE OF PLANES IN WHICH GLASS AND WHITE STONE STAND OUT AS THE
PRIMARY CONSTRUCTION ELEMENTS.

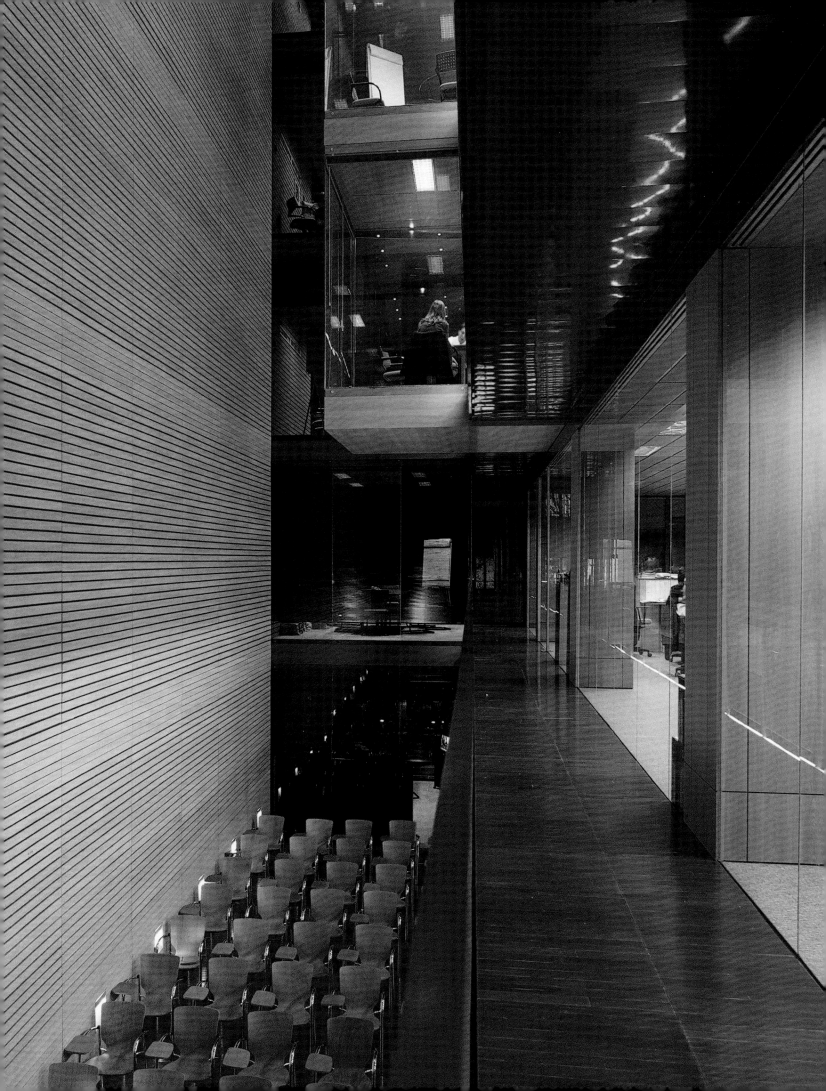

Morgan Stanley Dean Witter

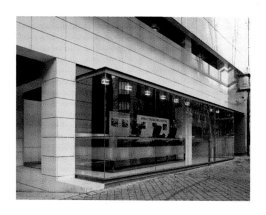

Architect: **Gabriel Allende and Ángel Serrano (Aguirre Newman Arquitectura)**
Client: **Morgan Stanley Dean Witter**
Location: **Madrid, Spain**
Construction Date: **2000**
Photography: **Jordi Miralles**

The location of the building, between two other buildings and situated on a main street in Madrid, was undoubtedly an influence at the time of its conception and planning, but that was not the only determining factor. The principal activities of the company, which specializes in financial services, also needed specific spaces that had to fulfill a series of requirements. For example, a publicity area (a storefront designed to attract clients) was provided to display the company services offered to the public, and interiors were made available in which it would be possible to work under optimum conditions.

From the outside, three clearly differentiated zones can be seen: one for pedestrian access, one for vehicles, and one for information. The interior space becomes the communication hub between the inside and the outside. This solution makes it possible to have two reception areas: one for the exterior of the building and another one for the internal flow.

The building is divided into different levels: the basement or lower one at street level; a middle zone, where a hierarchy of vertical spaces can be seen; and a top floor, which finishes the building with an attic. The interior spaces have been arranged with effectiveness and intuition. The lack of natural light, a main concern of those responsible for the project, was resolved with an interior courtyard located along the side of the building. This provision allows light to enter through a skylight that extends the length of the space from east to west.

The decision to place the meeting rooms inside two capsules suspended in space, giving them a view of the skylight while taking maximum advantage of the natural light, is one of many efficient construction solutions.

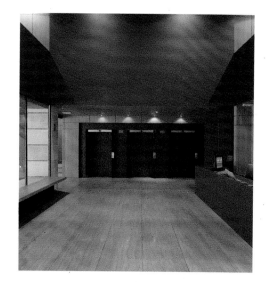

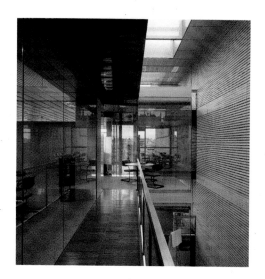

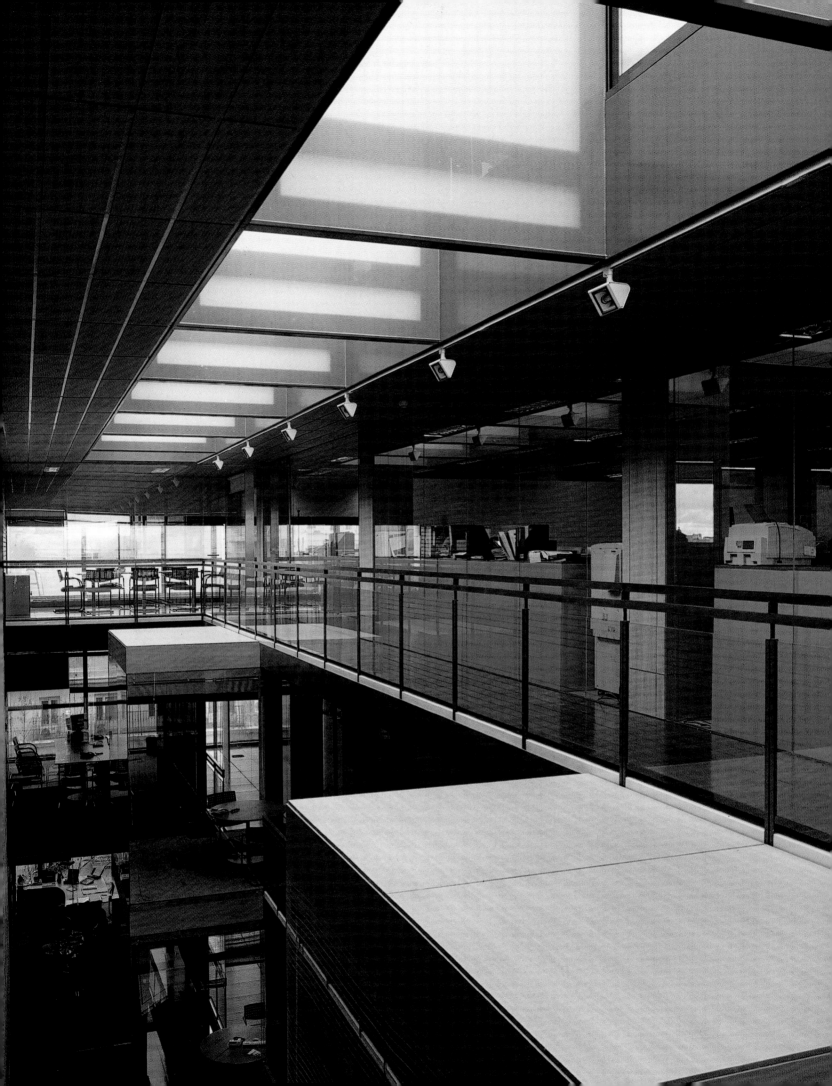

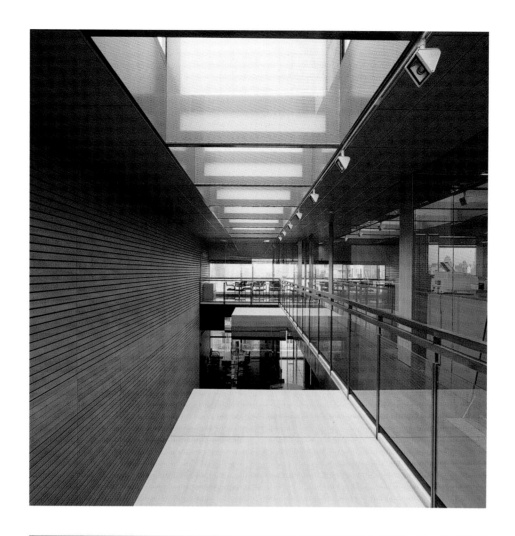

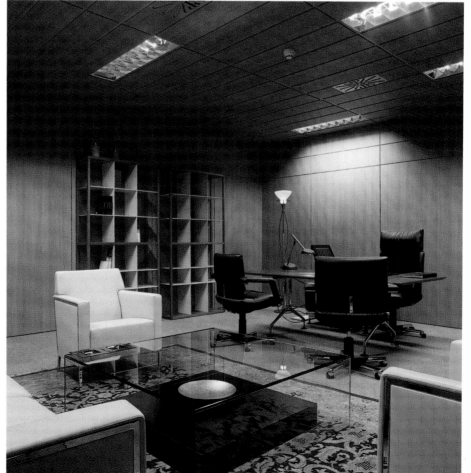

The cafeteria, located at the rear of the building, also enjoys a large amount of natural light. The glass treatment used in part of the space allows it to be visually connected to one of the meeting rooms. However, this can be blocked off with movable wood panels if necessary.

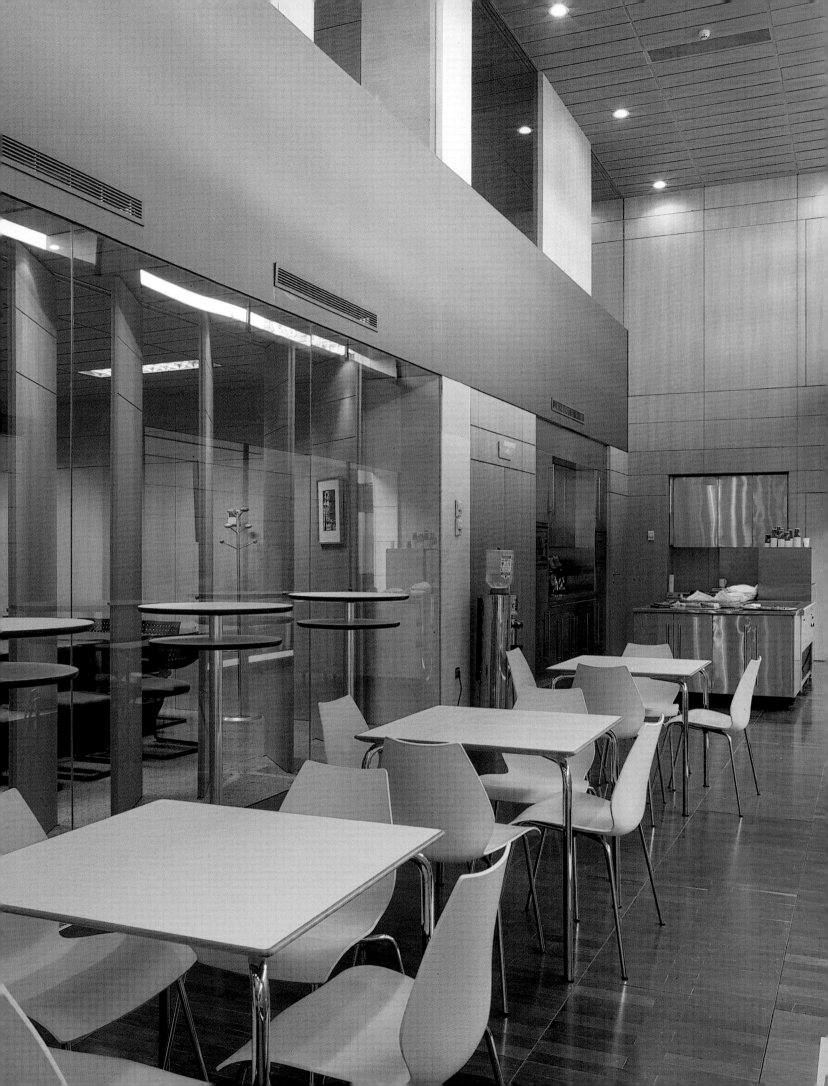

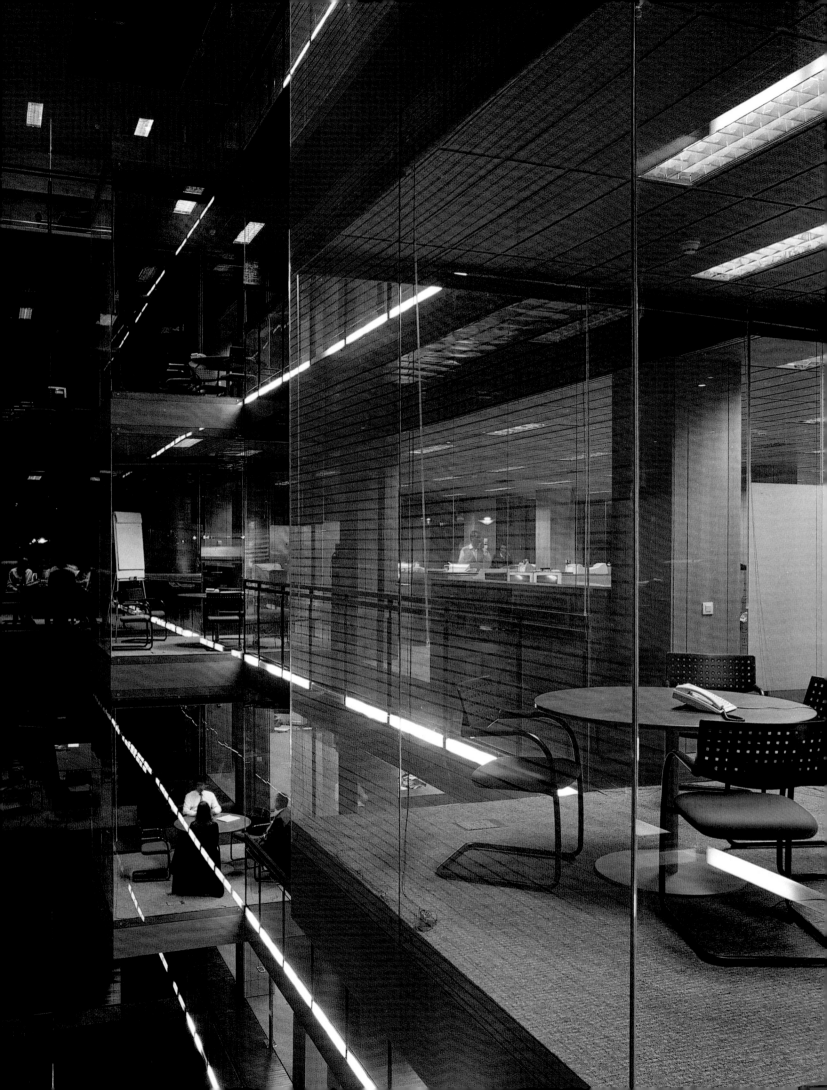

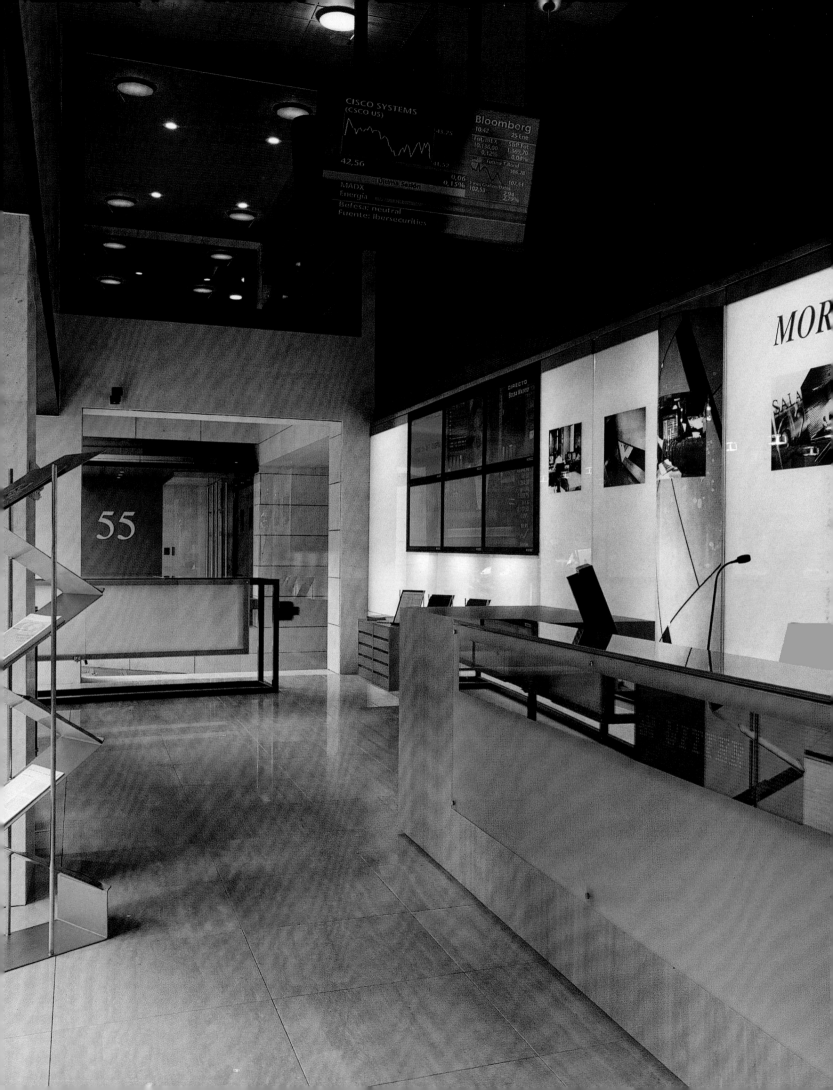

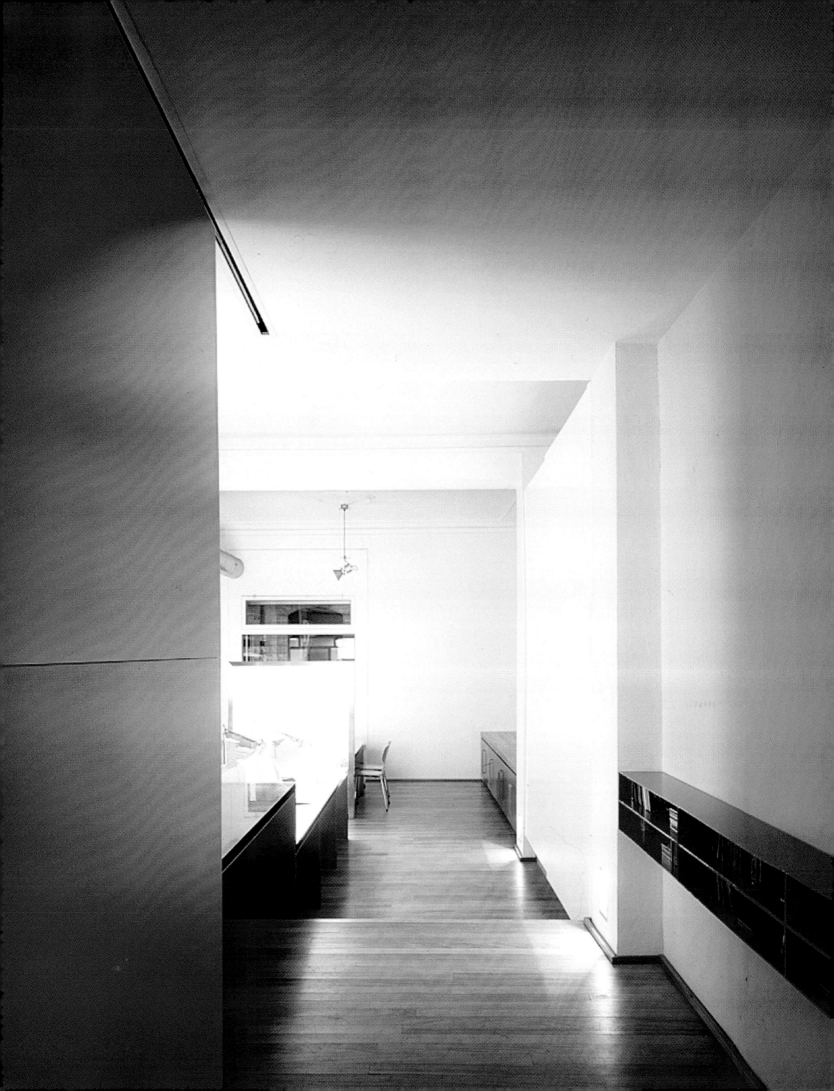

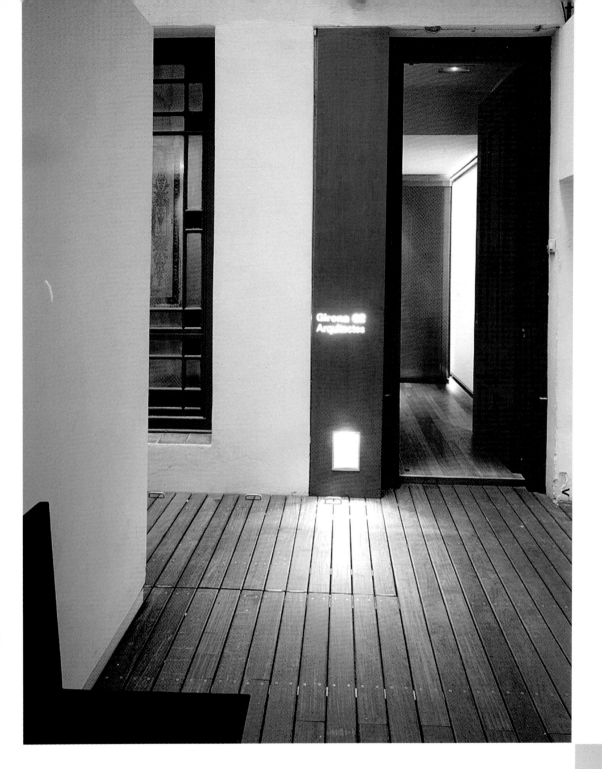

AC Martin Partners

NOTHING DEFINES THE PHILOSOPHY OF A COMPANY BETTER THAN ITS OWN WORKSPACE, ESPECIALLY IN THE CASE OF THE ARCHITECTURE STUDIO OF AC MARTIN & PARTNERS, SINCE THEY WERE IN CHARGE OF ITS PLANNING. THE INSTALLATIONS OCCUPY THE 12TH FLOOR OF AN OFFICE TOWER LOCATED IN DOWNTOWN LOS ANGELES, WHICH WAS DESIGNED BY THE ARCHITECTURE STUDIO ITSELF IN 1982.

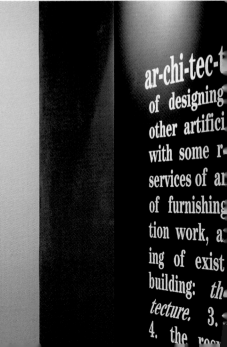

AC Martin Partners

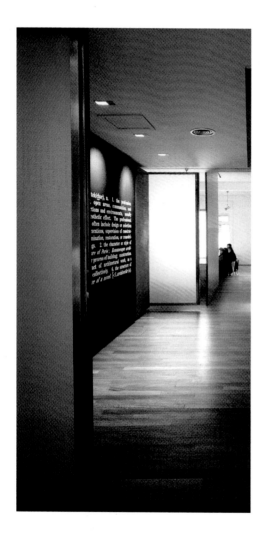

The project consisted of designing a new space capable of housing 100 employees, including architects, engineers, planning specialists, and administrative personnel. The space was finished as if it were a loft, a feeling that is highlighted by the use of concrete, wood, and glass. It has been designed as a "lab," not only for the materials and technological elements that were employed but also because those materials and systems are put to the test on a daily basis. The plan has conceived the area as an open, continuous, and flowing space where the functional needs of the different spaces, such as the conference rooms, private offices, and common areas, have been taken into account.

The reception area, sober and evocative, is the gateway to a space as engaging and attractive as it is efficient and practical. The work areas and the meeting spaces have been organized to take full advantage of space and light. The designers, engineers, and planning departments have been assigned the area around the windows, while production and meeting rooms, which require more privacy, have been accommodated in rooms that are less visible. This layout creates rational and well-defined spaces that exude sublime simplicity and a wonderful balance.

Architect: **AC Martin Partners, Inc. (ACMP)**
Client: **AC Martin Partners, Inc. (ACMP)**
Location: **Los Angeles, California, United States**
Construction Date: **2002**
Photography: **John Edward Linden**

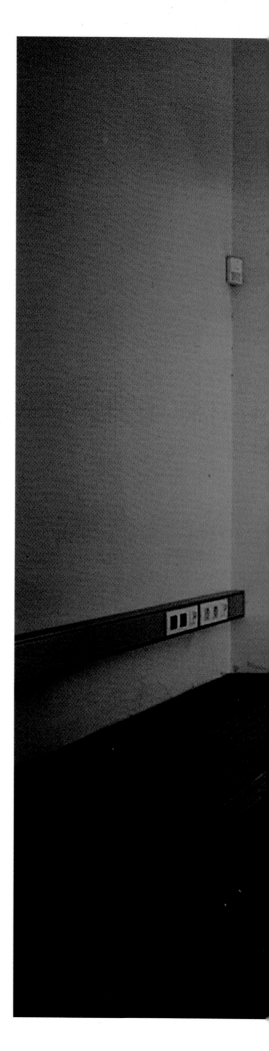

The notion of austerity is elevated through the use of specific materials (wood on the floors and in some furniture pieces, steel frames, glass, and neutral and quiet tones); well-thought-out illumination, which proves fundamental in the perception of the space and its capability for transformation; and a restrained decor.

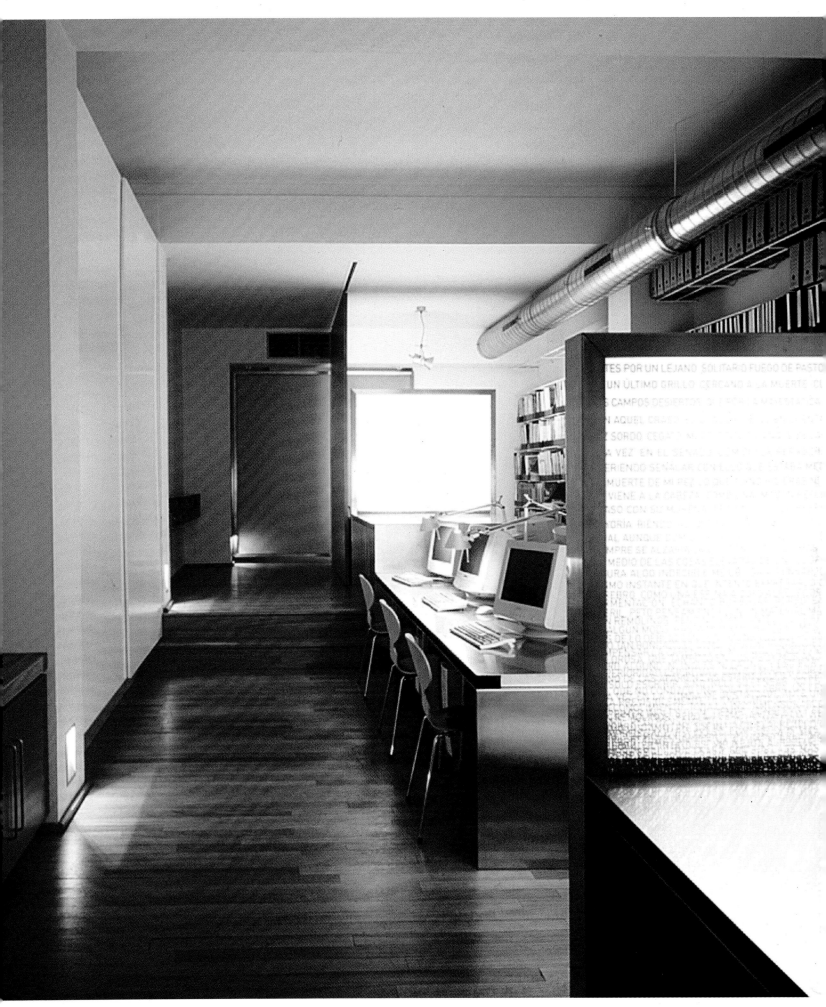

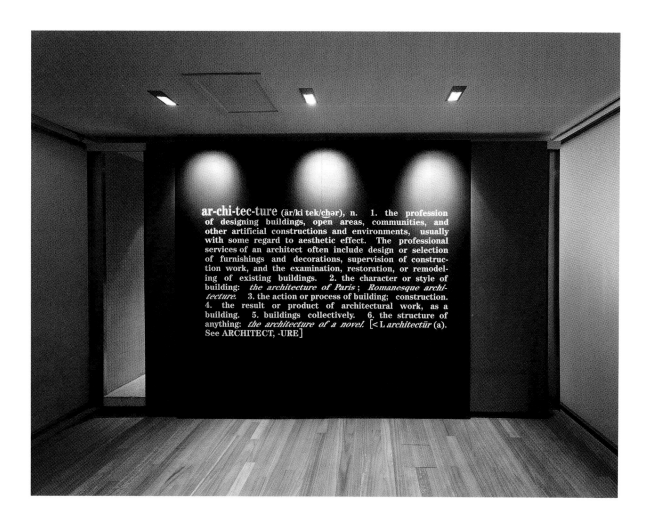

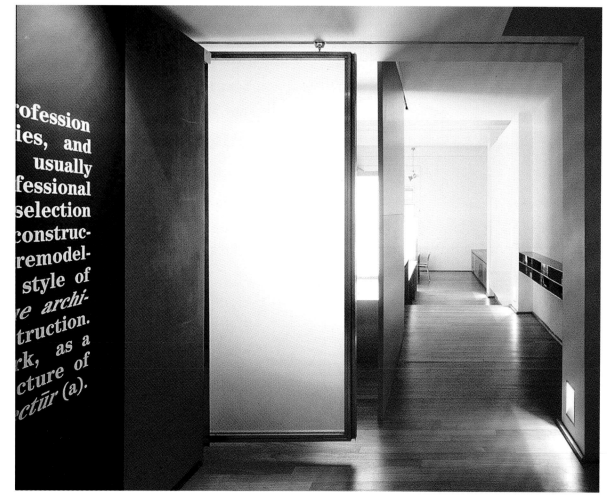

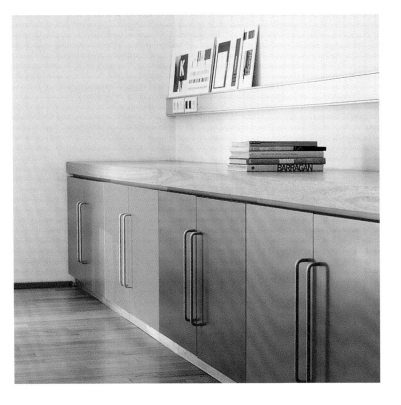

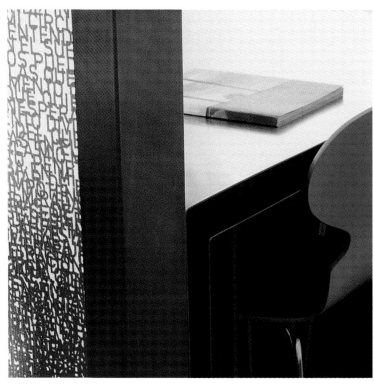

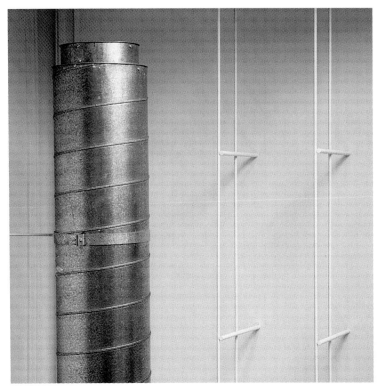

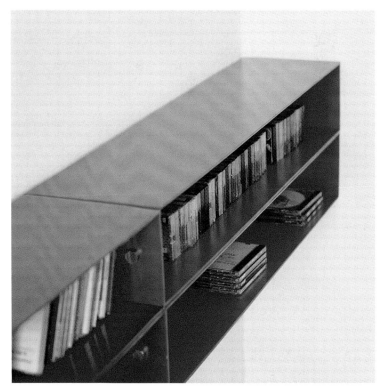

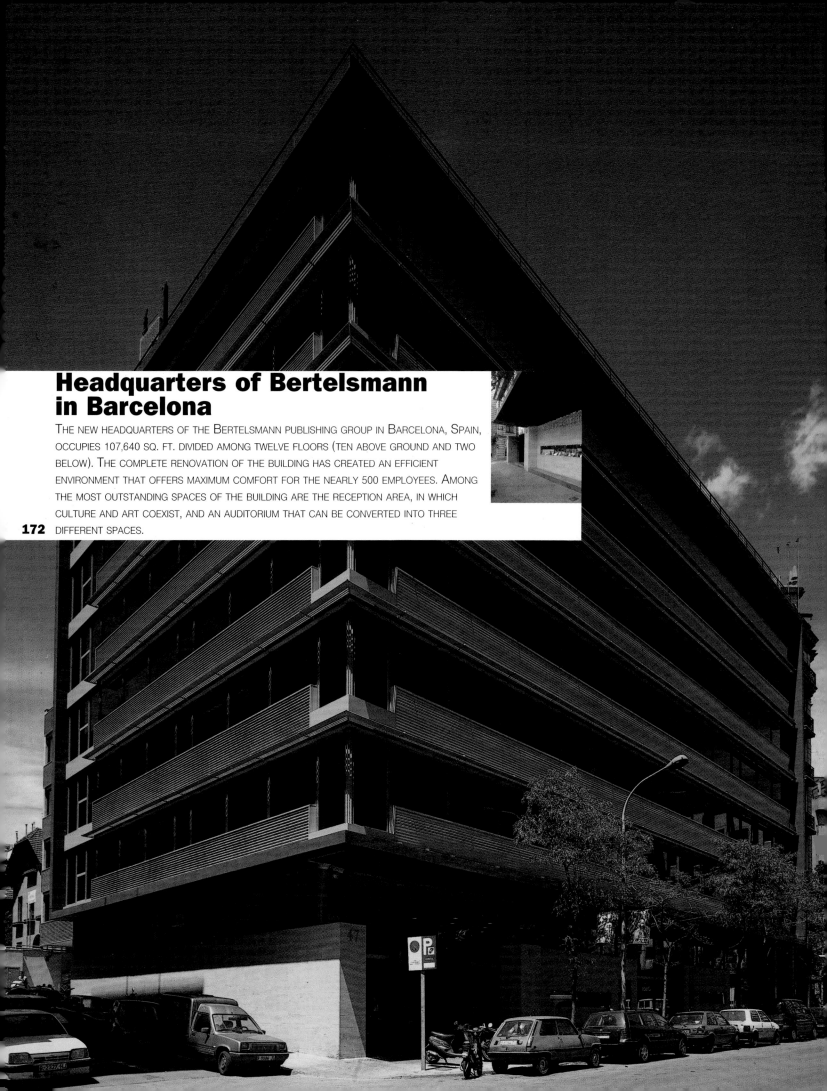

Headquarters of Bertelsmann in Barcelona

THE NEW HEADQUARTERS OF THE BERTELSMANN PUBLISHING GROUP IN BARCELONA, SPAIN, OCCUPIES 107,640 SQ. FT. DIVIDED AMONG TWELVE FLOORS (TEN ABOVE GROUND AND TWO BELOW). THE COMPLETE RENOVATION OF THE BUILDING HAS CREATED AN EFFICIENT ENVIRONMENT THAT OFFERS MAXIMUM COMFORT FOR THE NEARLY 500 EMPLOYEES. AMONG THE MOST OUTSTANDING SPACES OF THE BUILDING ARE THE RECEPTION AREA, IN WHICH CULTURE AND ART COEXIST, AND AN AUDITORIUM THAT CAN BE CONVERTED INTO THREE DIFFERENT SPACES.

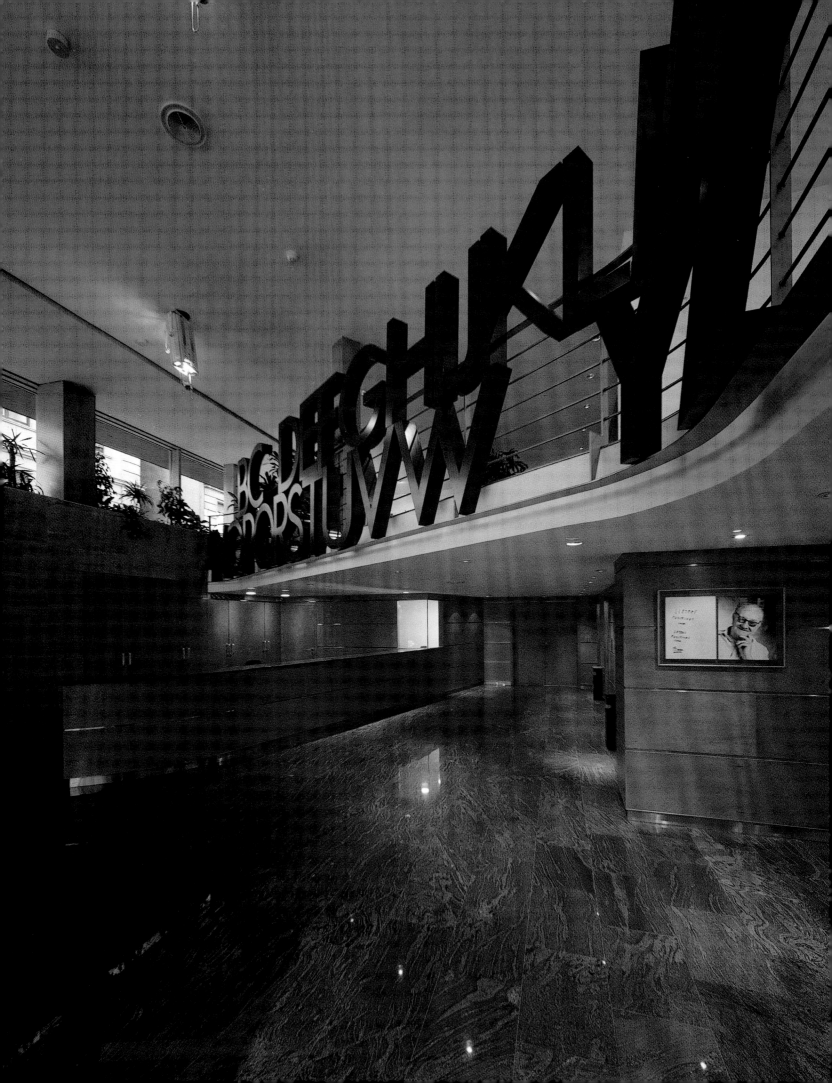

Headquarters of Bertelsmann in Barcelona

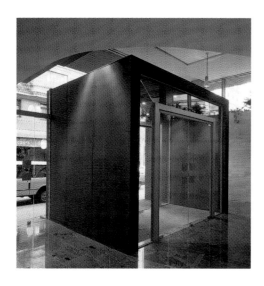

Architect: **Tekno-Bau (Lluís Arcusa and Miquel Jordà) and Martín Weischer (Technical Department of Bertelsmann)**
Client: **Bertelsmann AG**
Location: **Barcelona, Spain**
Construction Date: **1998**
Photography: **Jordi Miralles**

The painstaking renovation of the building required the modification of the original distribution, the materials used for the finishes, and the technical installations in order to make everything fit the needs of the new owner. The requirements included the creation of offices for a large number of employees (almost 500) that had to be arranged in open areas, providing a cafeteria for 250 people, a multipurpose room equipped with audiovisual installations to accommodate more than 300 people, and a lobby of generous dimensions that could be used as an area for temporary exhibits.

The project began by exposing the entire metal structure of the building and fireproofing it with sprayed vermiculite. The facade was redone in its entirety with corrugated sheeting of gray lacquered aluminum. The goal was to create a balance between an innovative, modern aesthetic and absolute functionality.

The lower level and the mezzanine house the entrance; the reception, lobby, and exhibit areas; the cafeteria, and the multipurpose space that serves as the auditorium. The idea of using movable panels to divide the areas, which were originally one space, solved the space problem. The general office floors were furnished with the equipment the employees might need to carry out their activities. Industrial flooring was installed and covered with carpet panels to provide a surface that is acoustically absorbent. Also, the suspended ceiling was constructed with gypsum board panels to create a reflective surface for optimum indirect lighting

A small area for receiving visitors was created at one end of the lobby in a contained and sober style, which is repeated throughout the spaces.

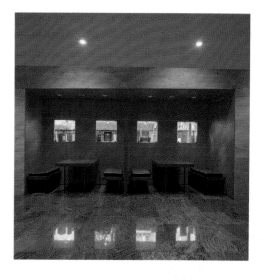

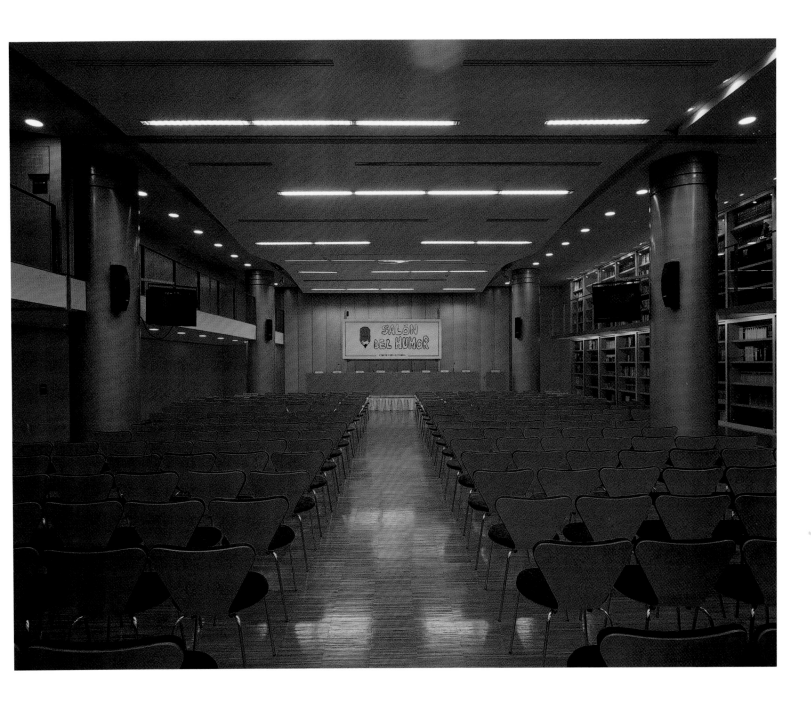

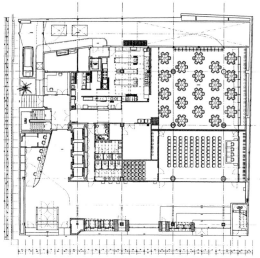

Ground floor

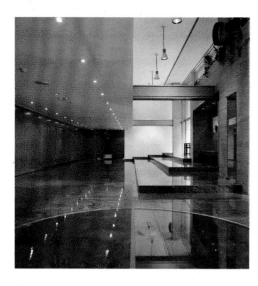

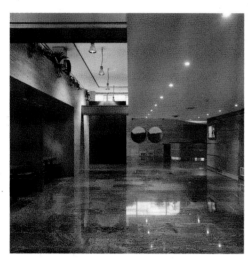

Collapsible, stationary furnishings and some movable panels, about 16 feet tall and covered with maple and birch veneers, make it possible for areas as diverse as the auditorium, the conference room, or the snack room to share the same space until the time comes to convert them into separate spaces.

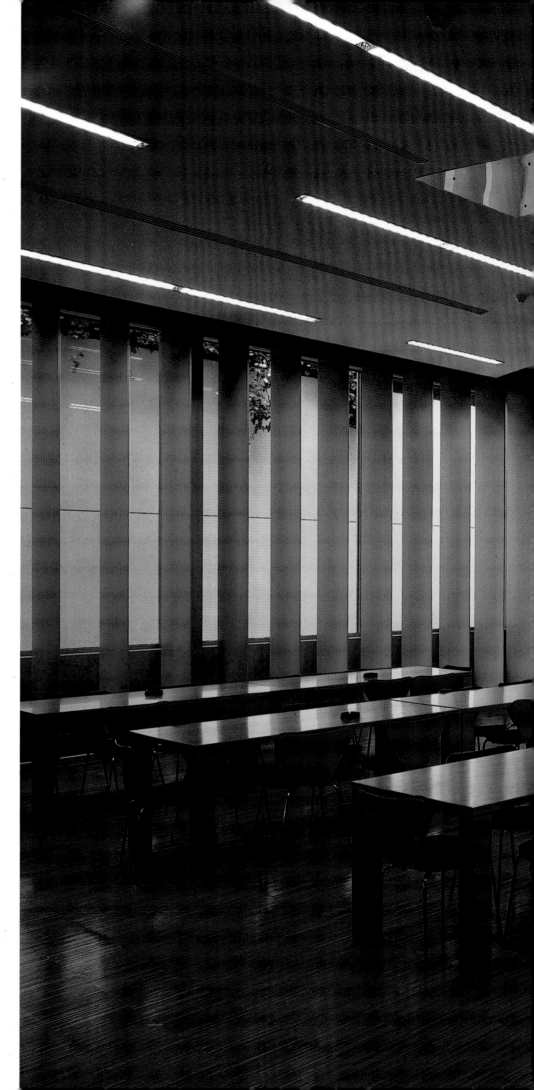

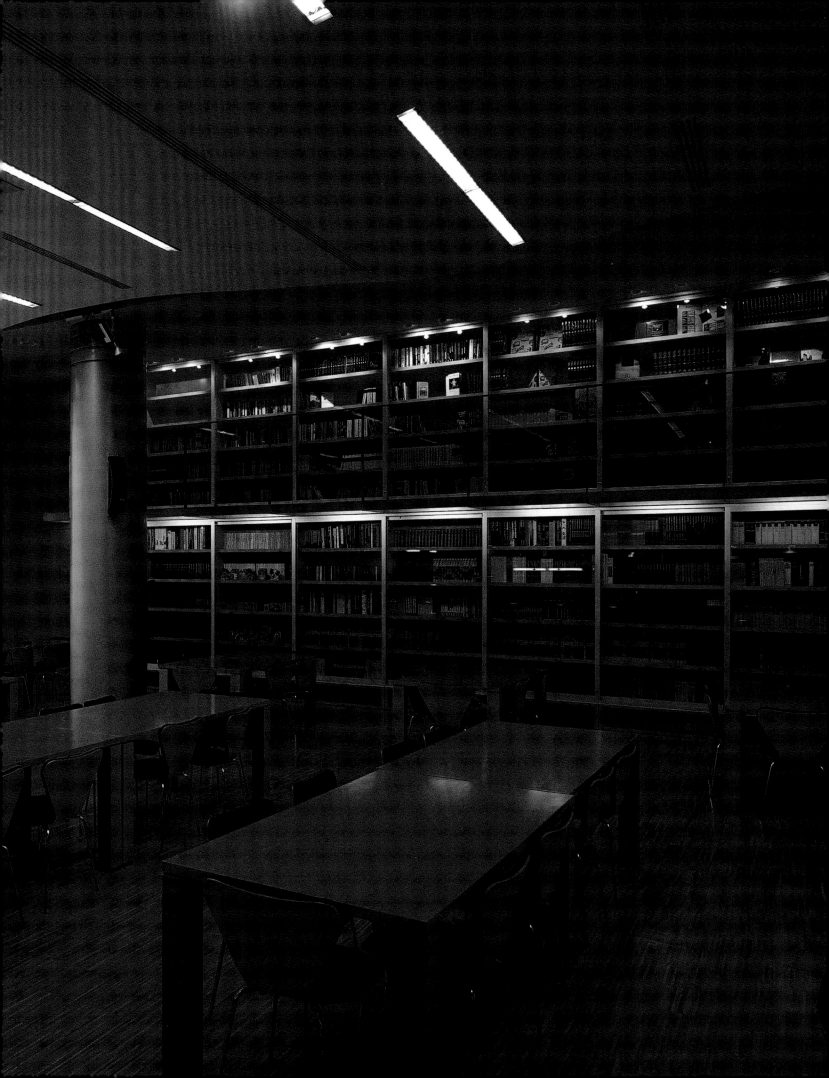

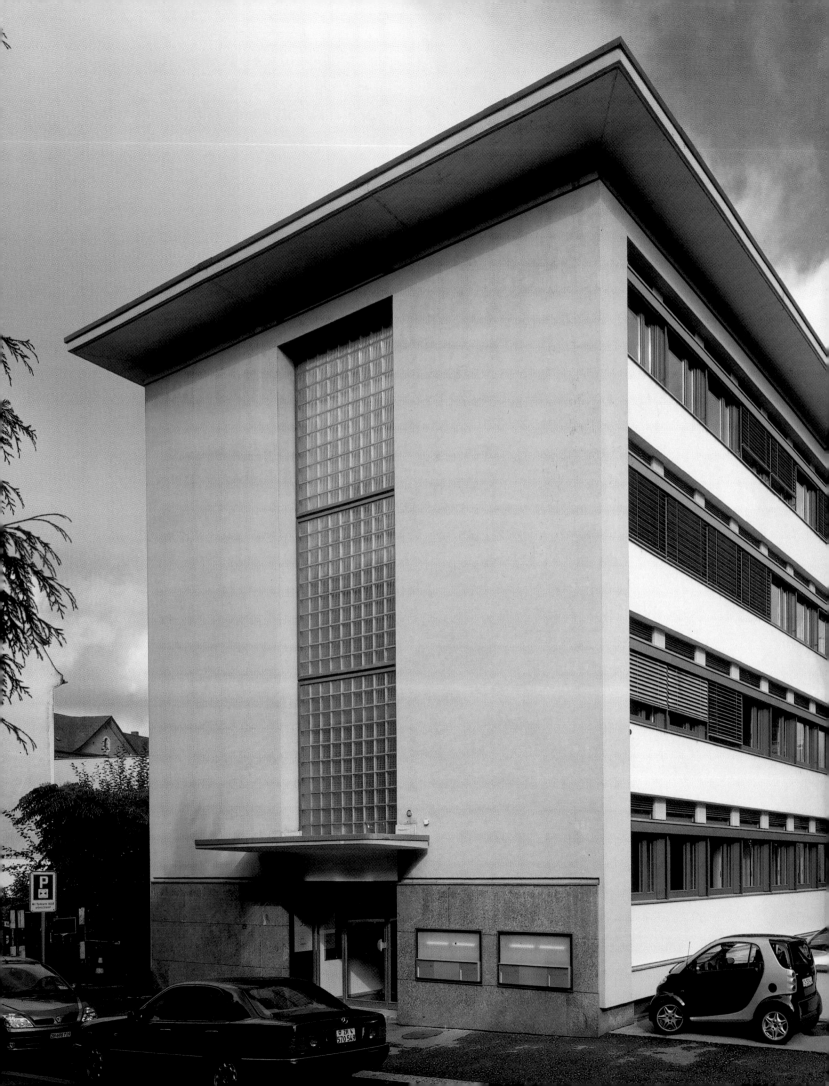

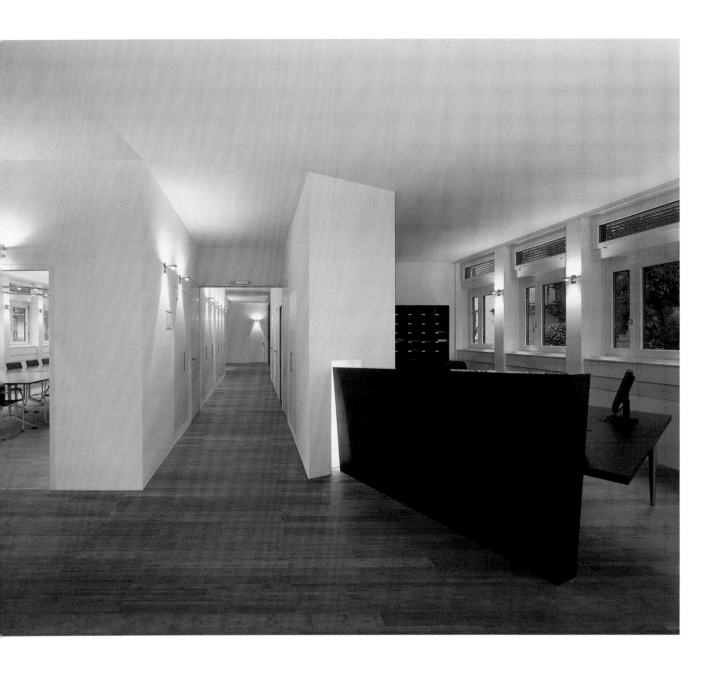

Thouvenin Stutzer Eggimann & Partner

THE ARCHITECTURE STUDIO OF HEMMI-FAYET WAS GIVEN THE RESPONSIBILITY OF DESIGNING THIS INSTALLATION, WHICH CONSISTS OF A WELL-LIT AND BALANCED SPACE WHOSE KEY ELEMENTS ARE ORDER AND AUSTERITY. THE ARCHITECTS RESPONSIBLE FOR THE PROJECT TOOK THEIR INSPIRATION FROM RATIONALISM, GEOMETRY, AND MINIMALISM, BALANCING SOBRIETY AND AVANT-GARDE AESTHETICS. THEIR SUCCESSFUL COMPOSITION VISUALLY MOTIVATES AND SHAPES INTERIORS THAT ARE FRESH, FUNCTIONAL, AND FULL OF PERSONALITY.

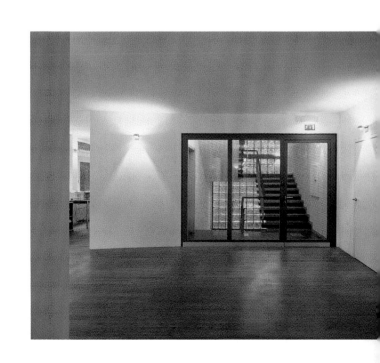

Thouvenin Stutzer Eggimann & Partner

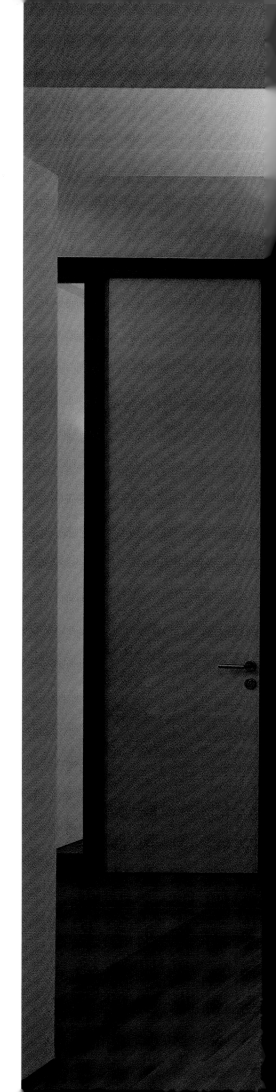

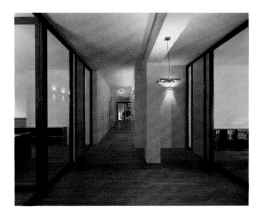

Architect: **Hemmi-Fayet Architects**
Client: **Thouvenin Stutzer Eggimann & Partner**
Location: **Zurich, Switzerland**
Construction Date: **2001**
Photography: **Hannes Henz**

The concept of austerity was a key element in the design of these law offices. This restraint is present in the color, or lack thereof, as well as in the use of materials. It takes control of the space, creating powerful interiors that generate a singular visual effect, resulting in an office that is current and efficient.

The design was developed in different levels, and the plan distributed the various functions of the company according to the activities that take place. Each space flows naturally and without interference, creating orderly surroundings in which everything has its place and where work can be done efficiently. The interior was painted completely white to maximize the light and make the space appear larger. This absence of color in the walls, floors, and ceiling provides a stark contrast to some of the dark furnishings and compositional elements. The appropriate lighting and the efficiency of the decorative scheme—the functional, multipurpose, and flexible furnishings—create spaces that are well balanced, serene, and easy to work in.

Certain work areas are located inside spaces that are only partially enclosed, since part of these rooms is visible. With the exception of the two doors that flank each side, the rest of the wall is made of glass, creating a way to link the areas, enlarge the space, and take advantage of the natural light.

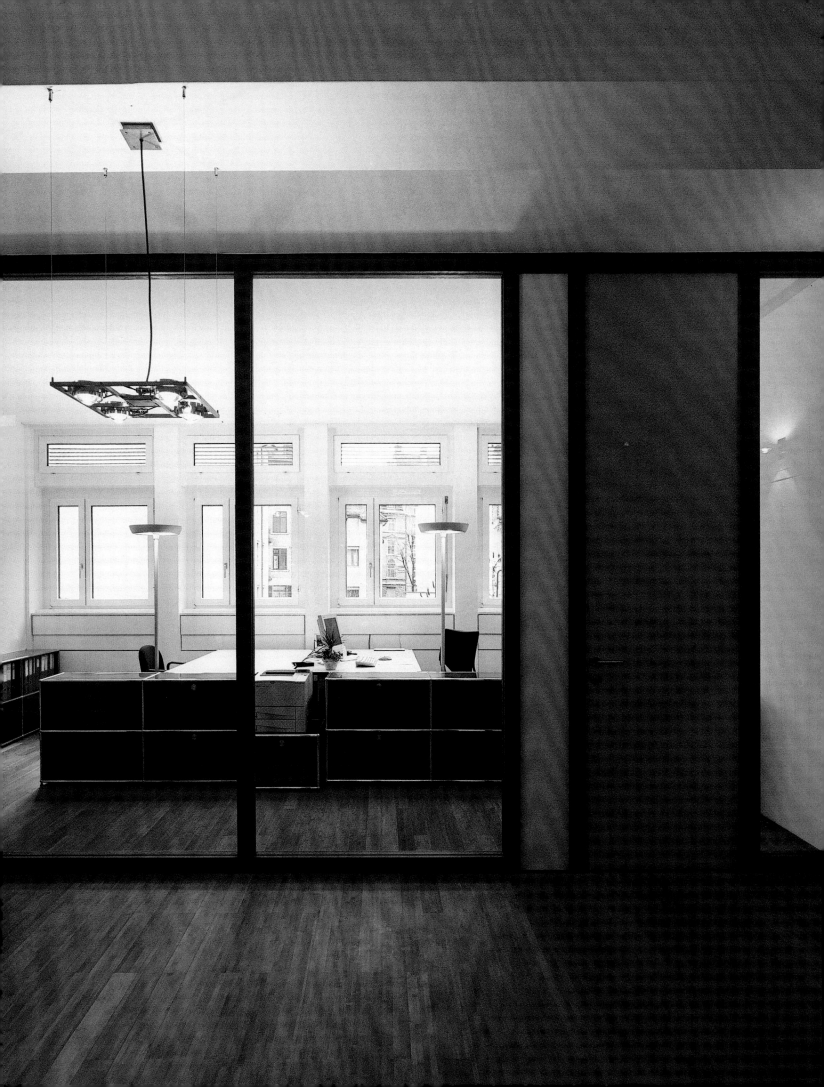

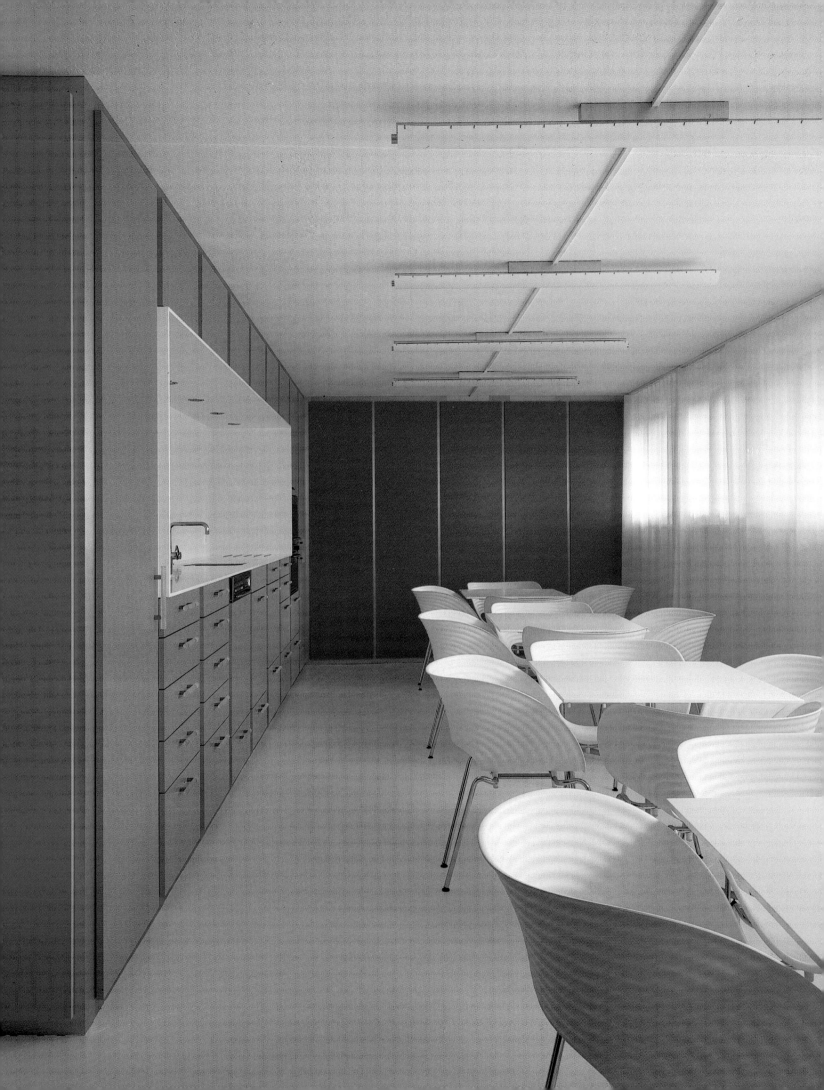

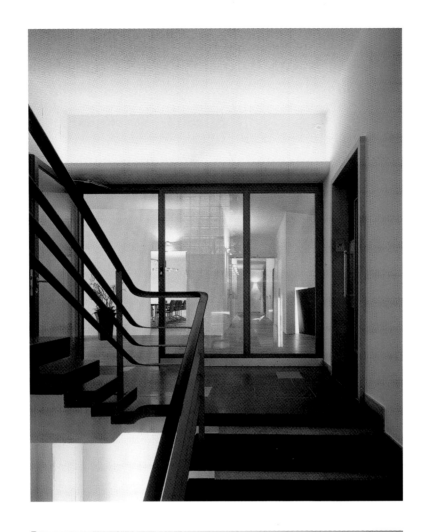

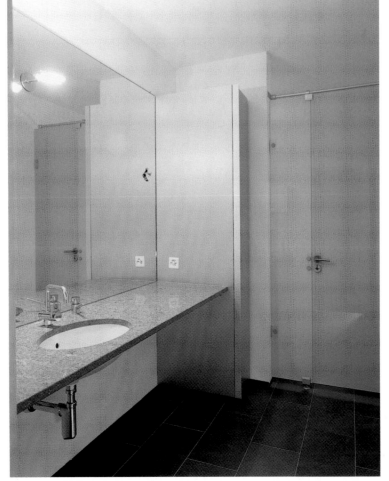

The austerity and order present in the décor are also maintained within common areas including the restrooms and the kitchen/dining room. In these areas, strokes of color break the purity of the white and create spaces that are fresh, happy, and full of vitality, without preventing functionality.

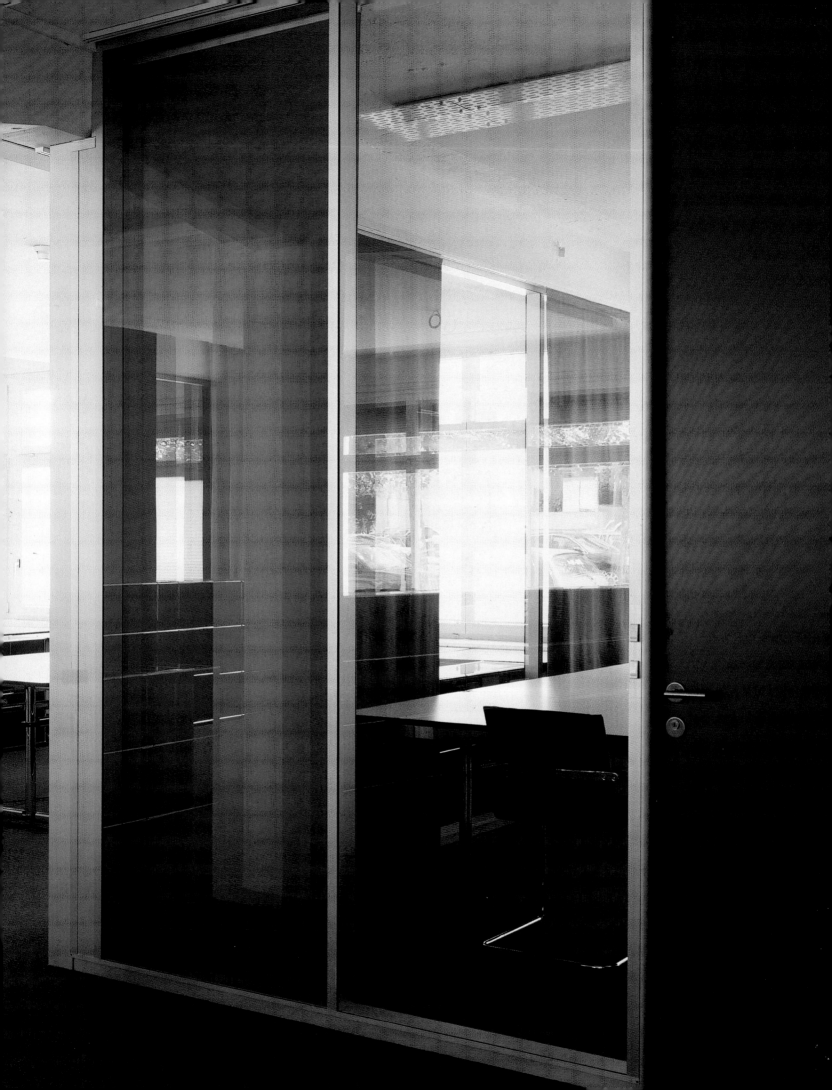

Helbling Technik AG Aarau

IN THESE OFFICES, THE FUNCTIONALITY HAS ONLY BEEN SURPASSED BY THE SCHEMATIC RATIONALISTIC VISION THAT IS FOUND IN EACH AND EVERY CORNER. HEMMI-FAYET WAS THE FIRM RESPONSIBLE FOR THIS ORGANIZED, PRISTINE, AND WELL-PROPORTIONED SPACE WHERE LIGHT AND FLUIDITY ABOUND. RESTRAINT AND SOBRIETY WERE USED WHEN SELECTING THE MATERIALS AND COLORS, ALTERED ONLY BY EVOCATIVE BRUSHSTROKES THAT BREAK THE BLACK-AND-WHITE COMBINATION.

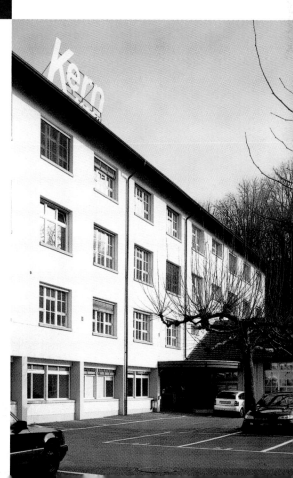

Helbling Technik AG Aarau

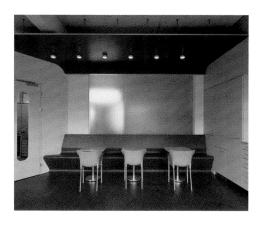

Architect: **Hemmi-Fayet Architects**
Client: **Helbling Technik AG Aarau**
Location: **Munich, Germany**
Construction Date: **1999**
Photography: **Hannes Henz**

The space was planned as a big container, where each room (common and individual offices, work areas, and meeting rooms) occupies a specific place. Order rules in this project, and the spatial organization was given careful consideration to get the most out of it.

The bearing columns that support the upper floors distribute and define the spaces naturally. The work areas have been placed to one side of them, taking full advantage of the natural window light. The meeting rooms and the individual offices are located opposite these columns and behind metal and glass dividers.

Cutting-edge furniture, clean and straight lines, lacquer, transparency, and a carefully studied color combination that plays with the juxtaposition of black and white, occasionally broken with color brushstrokes, turn the floors into spaces ready for the most varied activities. From the work areas, planned as open spaces, to the dining-cafeteria, the meeting rooms, and the other zones, everything has an austere, modern, and relaxed feeling that denotes personality.

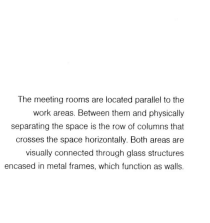

The meeting rooms are located parallel to the work areas. Between them and physically separating the space is the row of columns that crosses the space horizontally. Both areas are visually connected through glass structures encased in metal frames, which function as walls.

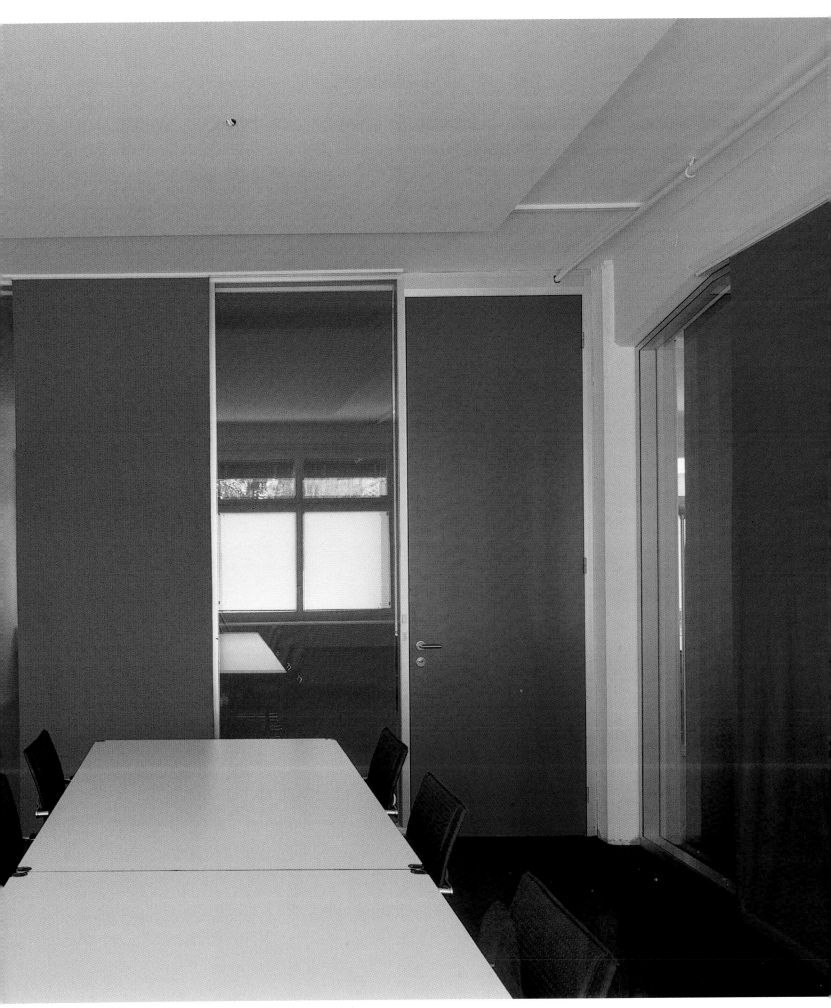

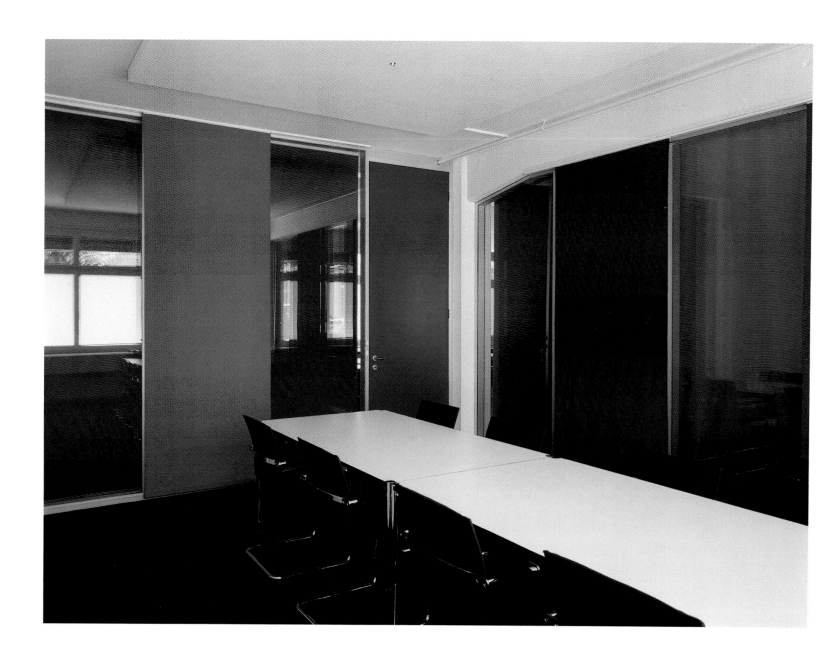

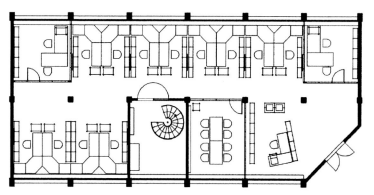

Ground floor

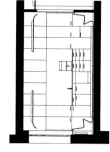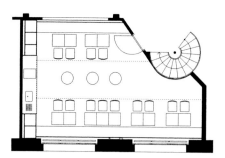

Cafeteria

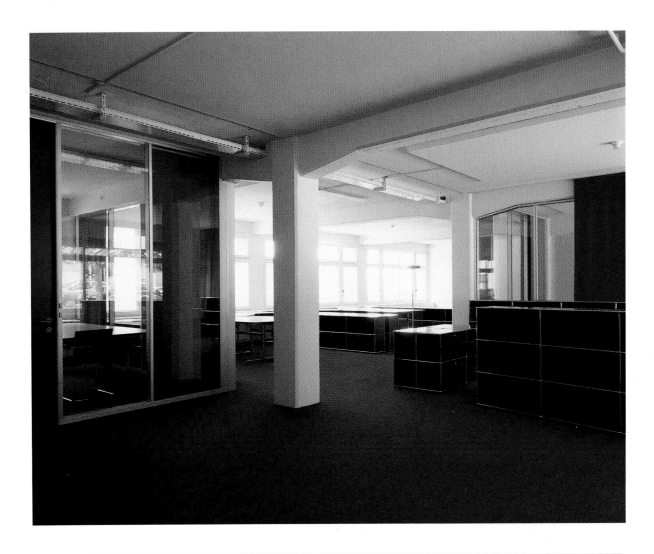

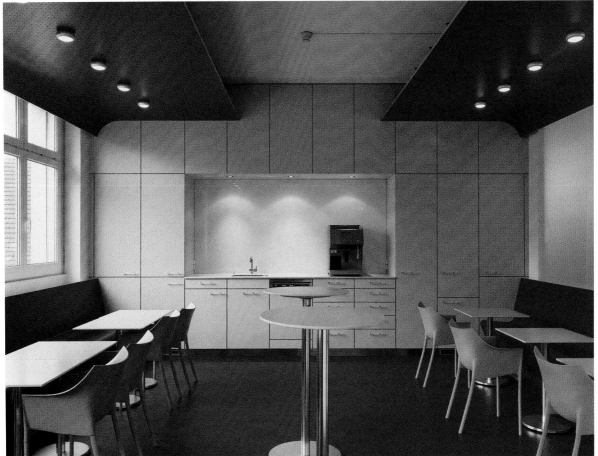

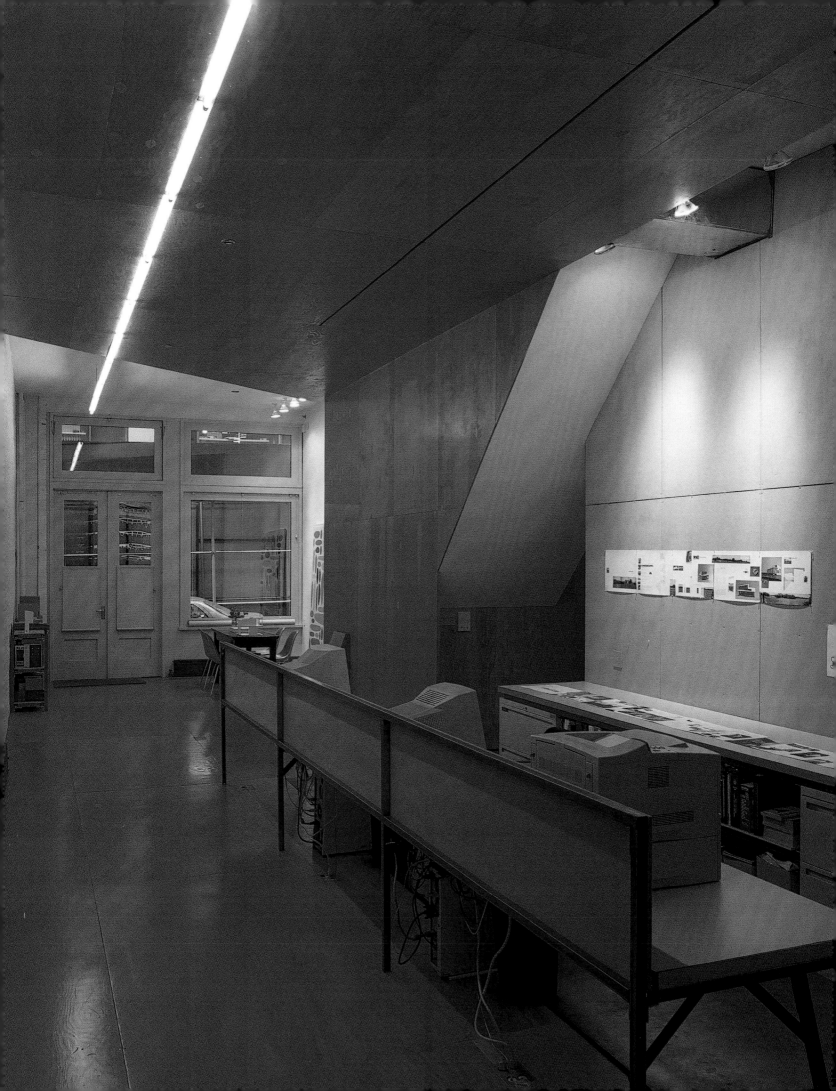

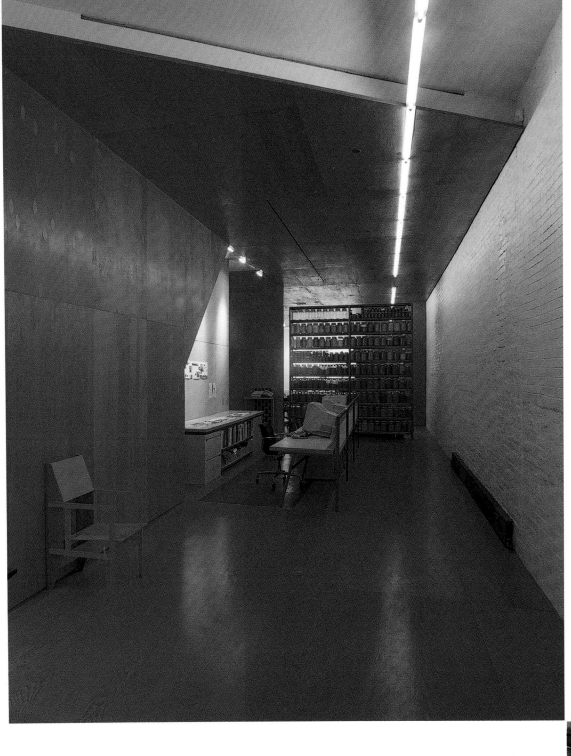

Elizabeth Alford

THE PAINTER AND ARCHITECT ELIZABETH ALFORD NEEDED A SPACE WHERE SHE COULD PRACTICE BOTH ACTIVITIES. THE STRATEGY WAS TO CREATE A MORE CONDENSED, ACTIVE, AND DYNAMIC WORKSPACE. THE RESULT IS A FRESH ENVIRONMENT INSPIRED BY THE IDEA OF A WAREHOUSE, WHERE THE AREAS ARE DIVIDED ACCORDING TO THE ACTIVITIES THAT TAKE PLACE IN THEM, BUT THAT ARE STILL PERFECTLY INTEGRATED.

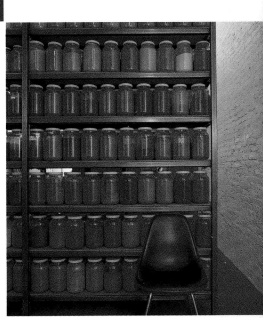

Elizabeth Alford

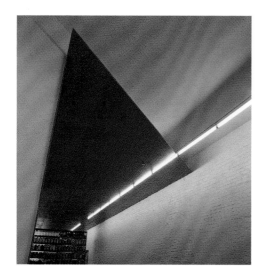

Architect: **Elizabeth Alford**
Client: **Elizabeth Alford**
Location: **New York City, United States**
Construction Date: **2001**
Photography: **Jordi Miralles**

The plan was designed in such a way that both spaces are physically separated. This division is defined by a long fluorescent tube that runs through them and by the placement of furniture pieces. A shelf unit, full of jars of sand that the artist uses for her work, functions as the visual partition between both spaces. It is an industrial steel structure that serves as an organizer, yet at the same time, it is a decorative element of great visual power in the space. The steel used for the organizer is repeated in the long desk and shelves in the area devoted to the office. Wood paneling ties the ceiling and floors together. The use of noble materials, such as wood, and the evocative color palette give the space the exquisite warmth that characterizes it.

The project, designed by Elizabeth Alford herself, pays as much attention to the decoration of the interiors as to the environment created. It relies on functional design, straight lines softened by touches of color (nothing loud and all within the same range) that are distributed through the space, and a close relationship between materials. These textures and a sound aesthetic sense have created a pleasant and contemporary place where work can be carried out freely and in harmony.

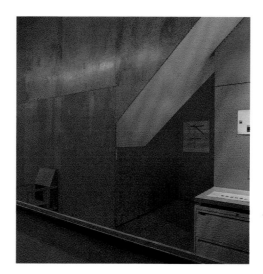

In the office area, austerity is the main feature. Sober and functional furnishings, bare walls, and the predominance of wood reinforce the idea of discretion and restraint. At the end of this area, on the other side of the steel structure that doubles as a shelf unit and a screen, is where the painting studio is located. Here, color has a key role because it reflects the activity that takes place in this area.

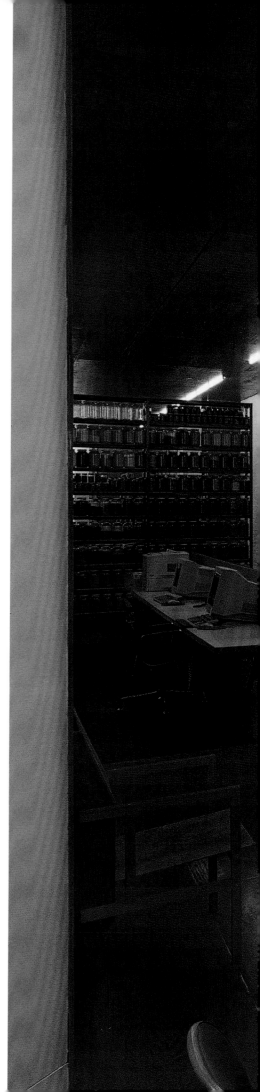

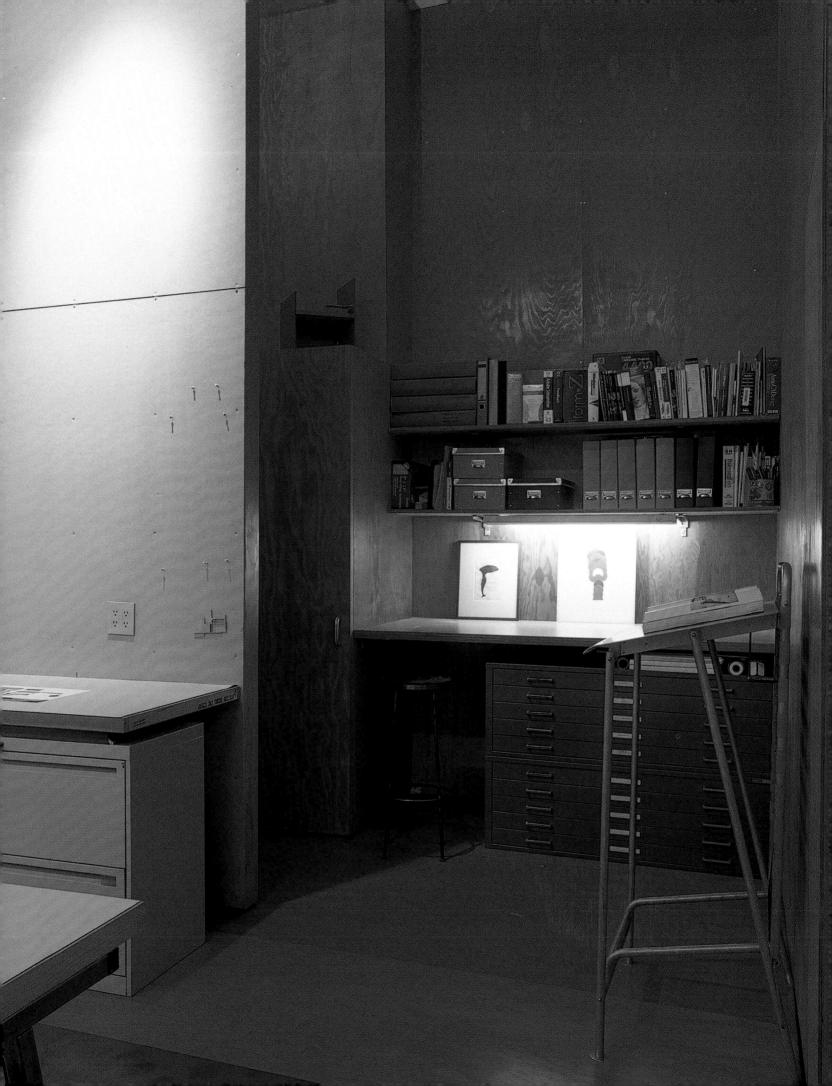

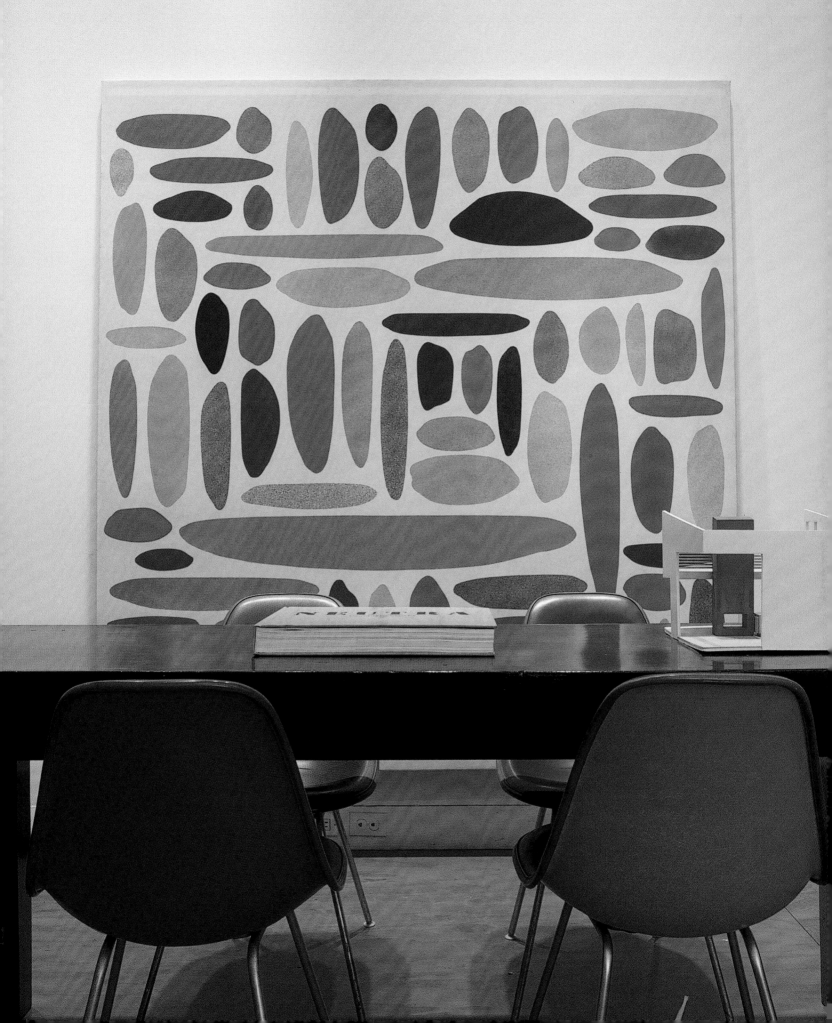

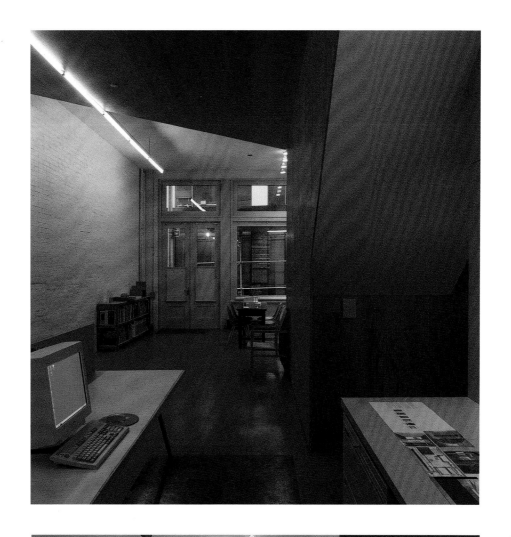

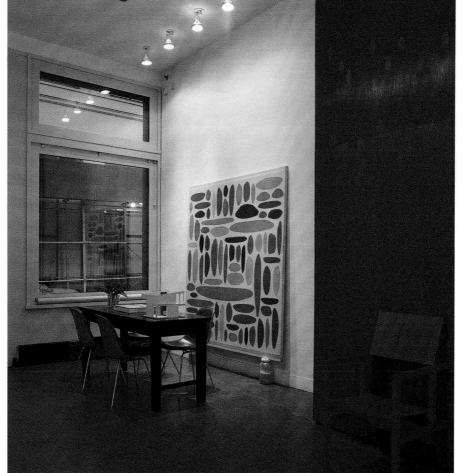

The space is not very large; therefore, in order to take full advantage of it, it was decided to create a versatile, open, and light-filled floor plan where the different areas flow naturally with structure and order.

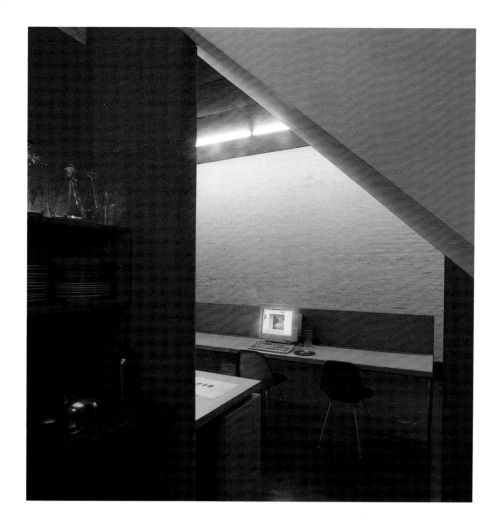

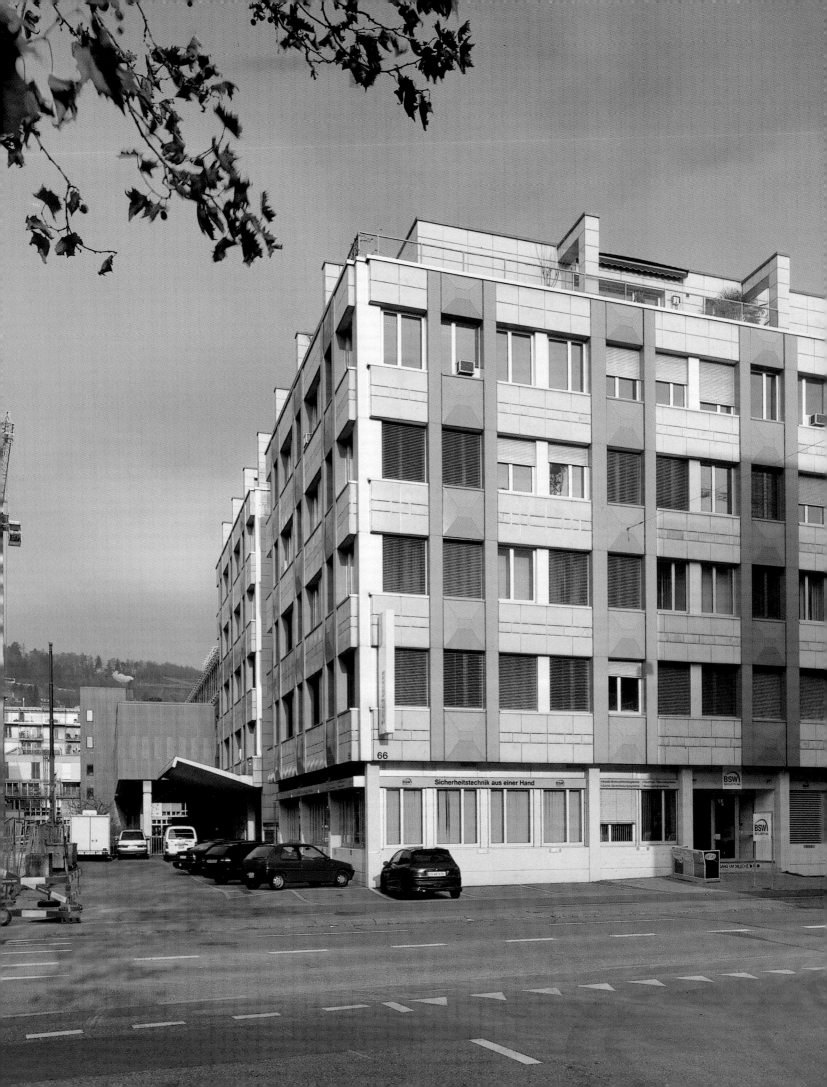

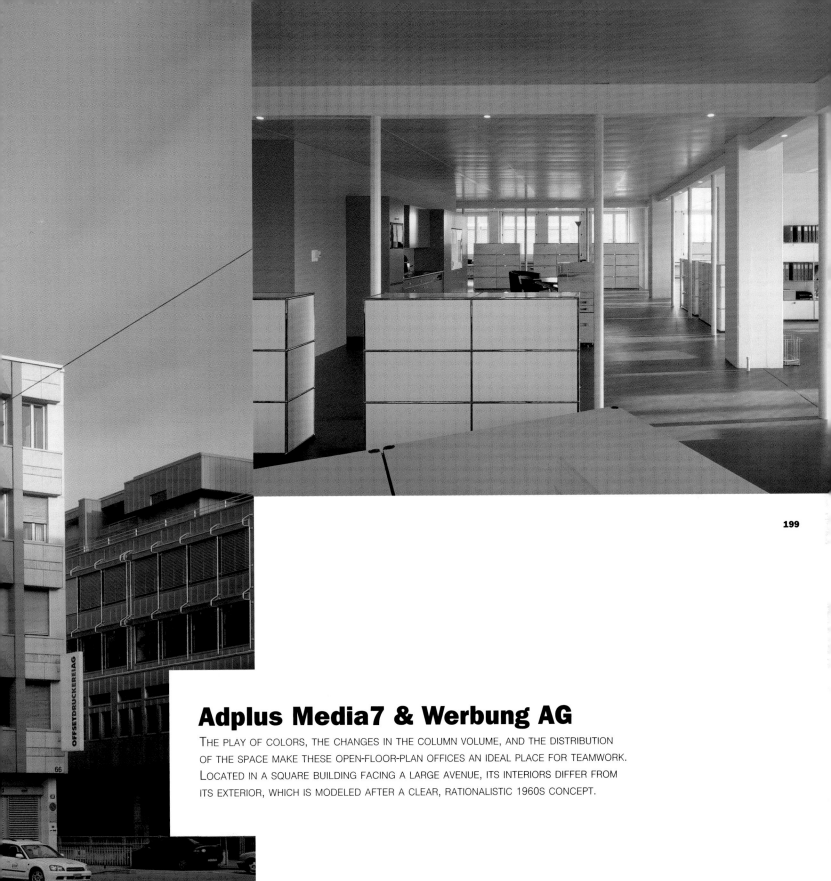

Adplus Media7 & Werbung AG

THE PLAY OF COLORS, THE CHANGES IN THE COLUMN VOLUME, AND THE DISTRIBUTION OF THE SPACE MAKE THESE OPEN-FLOOR-PLAN OFFICES AN IDEAL PLACE FOR TEAMWORK. LOCATED IN A SQUARE BUILDING FACING A LARGE AVENUE, ITS INTERIORS DIFFER FROM ITS EXTERIOR, WHICH IS MODELED AFTER A CLEAR, RATIONALISTIC 1960S CONCEPT.

Adplus Media7 & Werbung AG

Architect: **Hemmi-Fayet Architects**
Client: **Adplus Media7 & Werbung AG**
Location: **Zurich, Switzerland**
Construction Date: **2001**
Photography: **Hannes Henz**

The architectural firm of Hemmi-Fayet was asked to design these multifunctional, transparent, avant-garde, and bright spaces that defy the conventional image of the office by making them fresh, happy, and full of vitality while not being at odds with functionality. White is the main hue, and it acts as a blank canvas with brushstrokes of color included. Using white basically fulfills two purposes: to make the space appear larger and to project the reflected light onto every corner of the room.

The new design only affects one floor, which has mostly regular proportions. The layout allows natural and flowing transitions between spaces without losing the sense of order at any time. The choice of floors, the immaculate purity of the whites, or the soft color of the partition furniture pieces define the spaces devoted to different functions. Everything is open and transparent, although entryways and rooms are defined and outlined naturally. The entry to the meeting room is through a door of wide-lacquered panels located in a partition wall that separates private and public areas. The view has only been partially concealed in the main areas; it is glimpsed and lost sight of in an attractively subtle way.

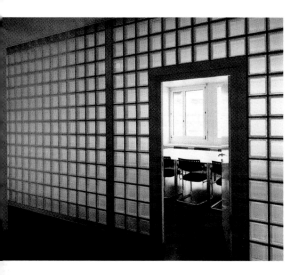

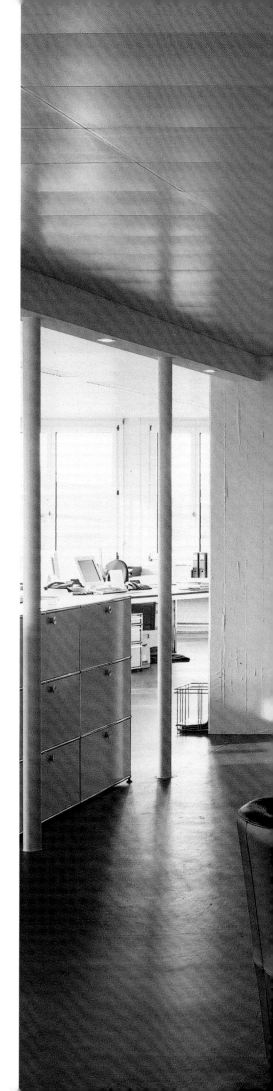

The distribution of the space is a complete compositional success that is visually motivating and that molds it into interiors that are multifunctional, dynamic, flexible, and full of personality. The architectural elements—like the columns—and the furniture pieces placed around the area establish divisions that do not physically exist because the space is open and transparent.

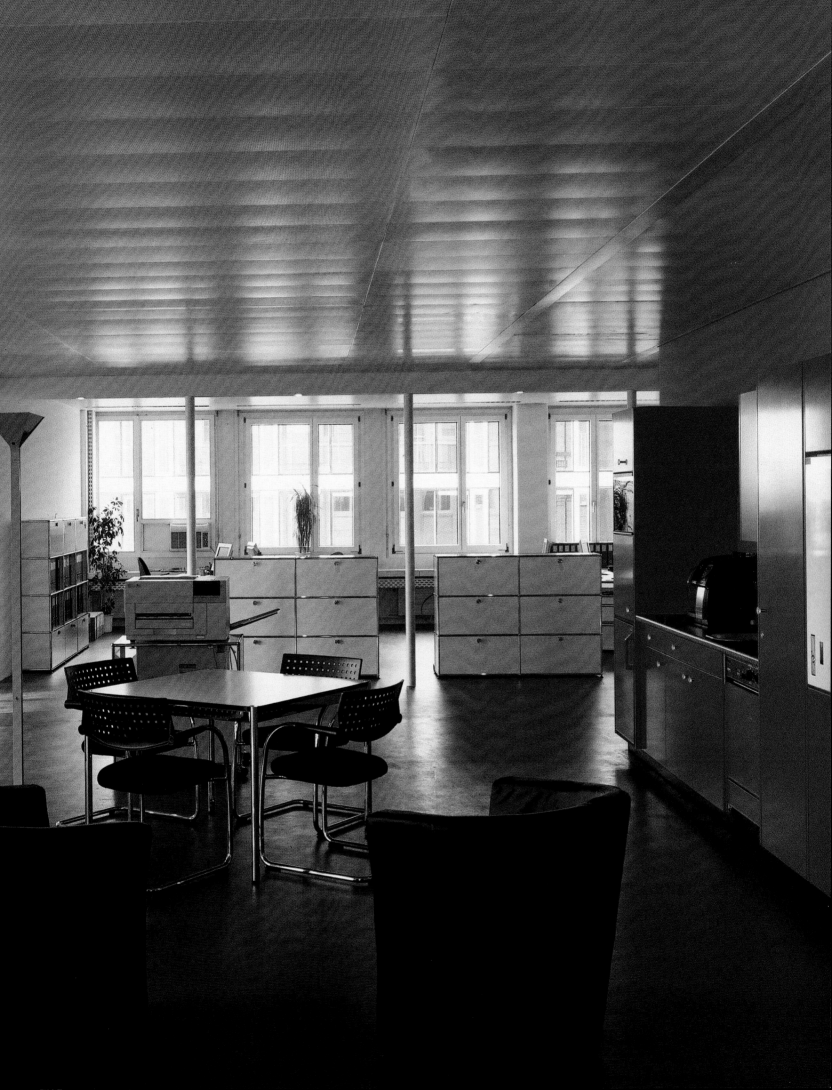

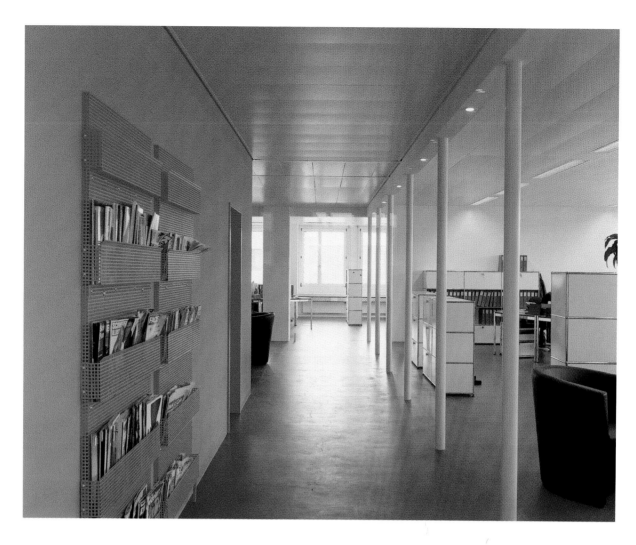

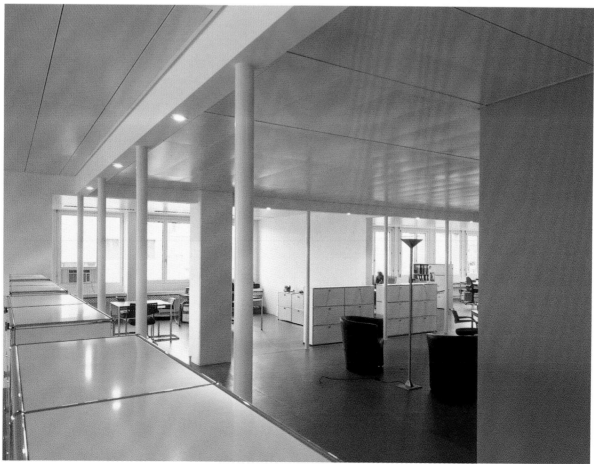

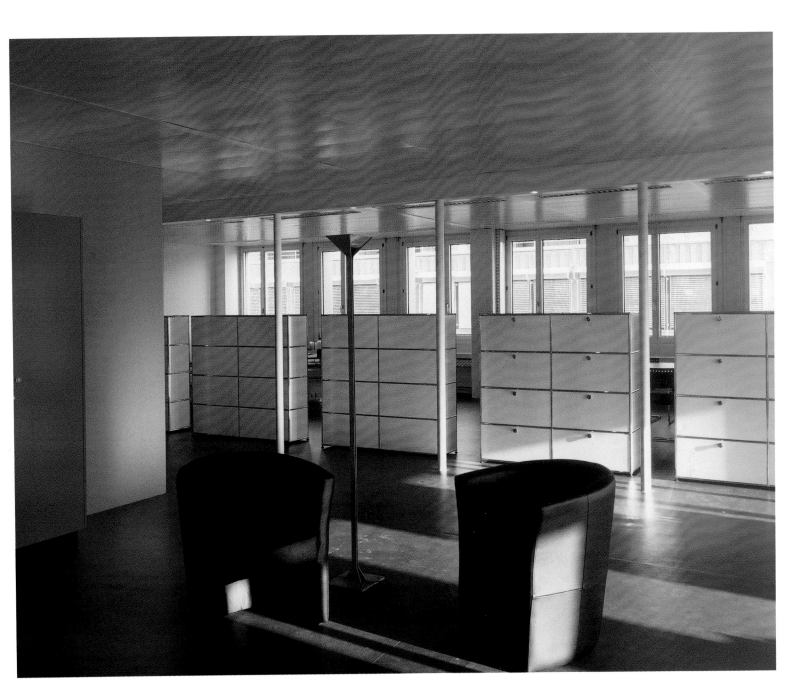

The absence of color on the walls, the columns, and the numerous furniture pieces is in contrast with the chromatic alternative used on the floors, on some walls, and on decorative elements—a successful combination that produces an original visual play in an office that is modern and imaginative.

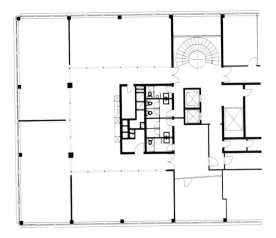

Floor plan

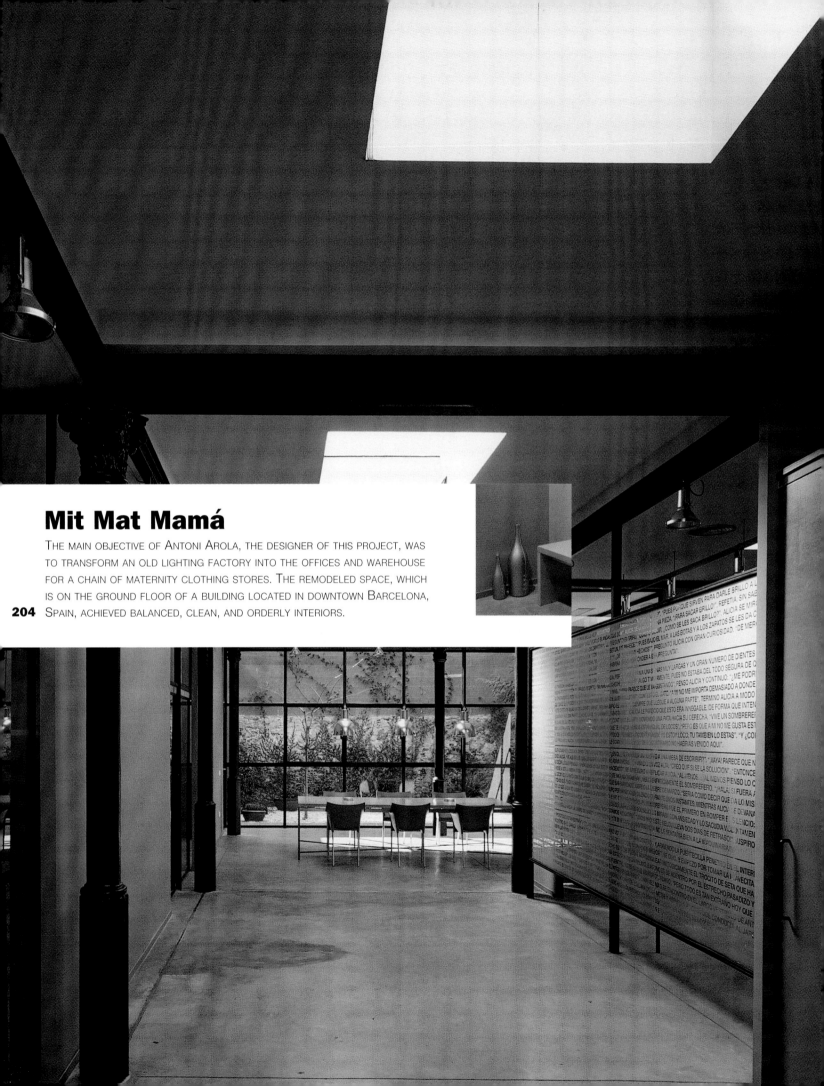

Mit Mat Mamá

The main objective of Antoni Arola, the designer of this project, was to transform an old lighting factory into the offices and warehouse for a chain of maternity clothing stores. The remodeled space, which is on the ground floor of a building located in downtown Barcelona, Spain, achieved balanced, clean, and orderly interiors.

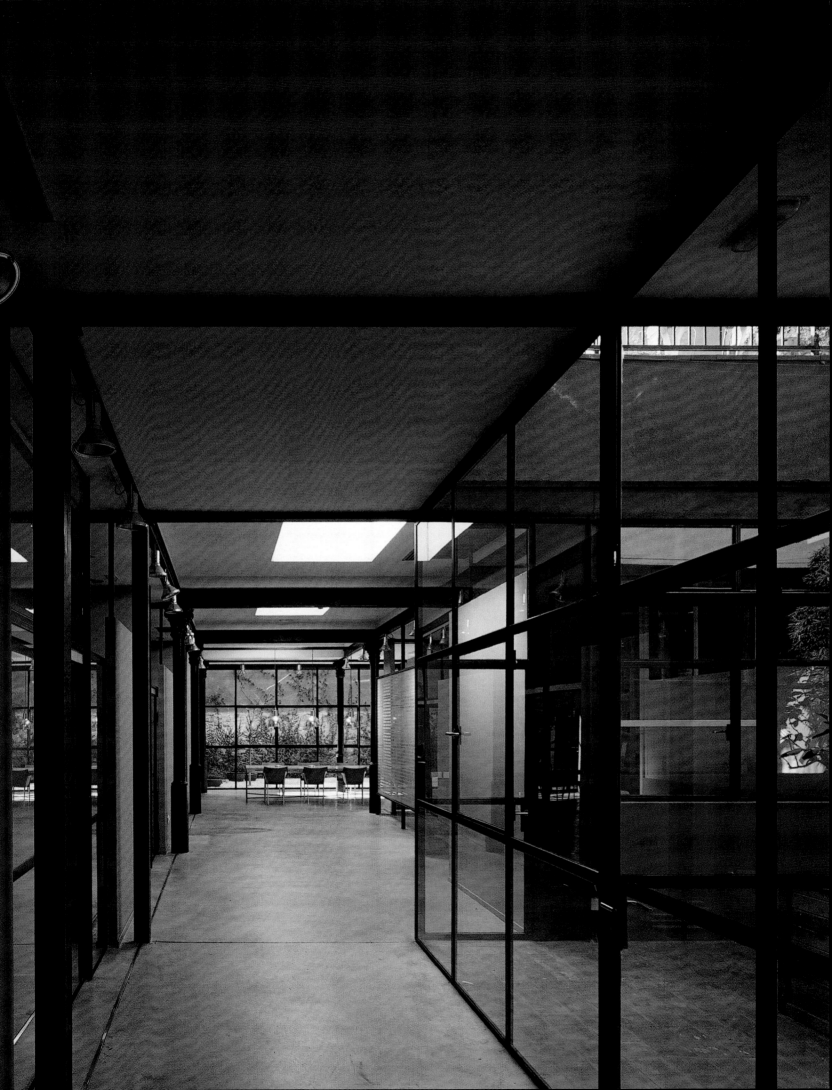

Mit Mat Mamá

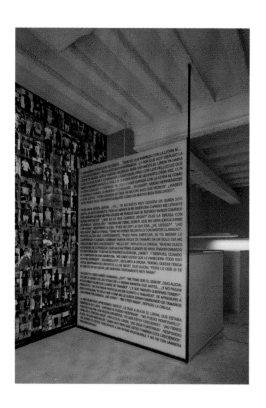

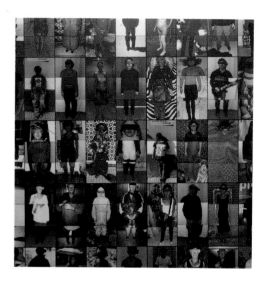

The space consisted of an elongated floor plan that was transformed into an interior corridor connecting the street with an indoor patio that has been decorated with a Mediterranean flair. This central passageway gives access to all the rooms on the floor: reception, offices, restrooms, design studio, and management.

The space has been given the atmosphere of an industrial loft. The original cast-iron columns have been preserved, and order and flexibility are the primary components. The use of these resources results in interiors that are bright, open, and multifunctional, bathed with natural light.

The pattern of the iron framework of the interior and exterior walls becomes very relevant. The coolness of the iron is combined indoors with warm gray walls that do not quite reach the ceiling, concrete floors, sliding wooden doors, acid-etched panes of glass with orange tones, and applied graphics. The result is an evocative space marked by the purity and simplicity of the lines, along with the exquisite warmth and an elegant avant-garde touch. This is a dynamic, graceful, and flexible space in constant movement, which transforms according to the situations and activities as required.

Interior Designer: **Antoni Arola**
Collaborators: **Sylvain Carlet and Jordi Tamayo**
Client: **Mit Mat Mamá**
Location: **Barcelona, Spain**
Construction Date: **2000**
Photography: **Eugeni Pons**

Sober interiors with an industrial flair are achieved through the use of materials and textures. Sublime functionality and a well-understood minimalism fit perfectly with the elegance of the whole project. The power of austerity and the elimination of anything unnecessary create a multipurpose space that is very functional.

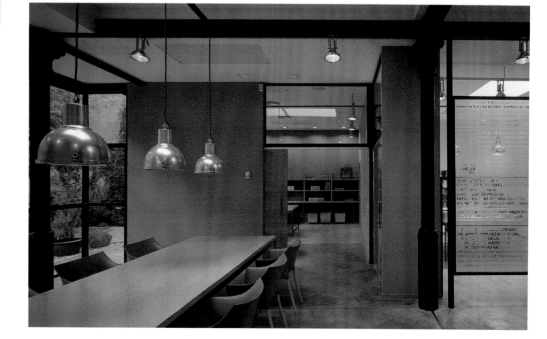

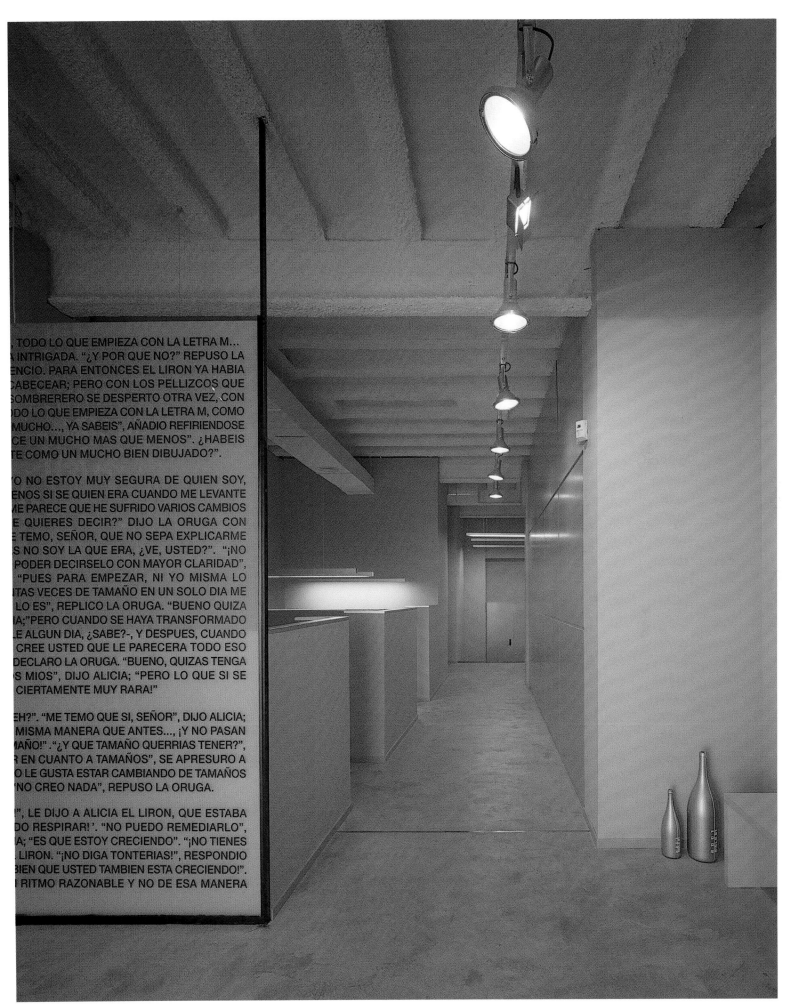

TODO LO QUE EMPIEZA CON LA LETRA M...
INTRIGADA. "¿Y POR QUE NO?" REPUSO LA
ENCIO. PARA ENTONCES EL LIRON YA HABIA
CABECEAR; PERO CON LOS PELLIZCOS QUE
SOMBRERERO SE DESPERTO OTRA VEZ, CON
DO LO QUE EMPIEZA CON LA LETRA M, COMO
MUCHO..., YA SABEIS", AÑADIO REFIRIENDOSE
CE UN MUCHO MAS QUE MENOS". ¿HABEIS
TE COMO UN MUCHO BIEN DIBUJADO?".

O NO ESTOY MUY SEGURA DE QUIEN SOY,
ENOS SI SE QUIEN ERA CUANDO ME LEVANTE
ME PARECE QUE HE SUFRIDO VARIOS CAMBIOS
E QUIERES DECIR?" DIJO LA ORUGA CON
E TEMO, SEÑOR, QUE NO SEPA EXPLICARME
S NO SOY LA QUE ERA, ¿VE, USTED?". "¡NO
PODER DECIRSELO CON MAYOR CLARIDAD",
"PUES PARA EMPEZAR, NI YO MISMA LO
ITAS VECES DE TAMAÑO EN UN SOLO DIA ME
LO ES", REPLICO LA ORUGA. "BUENO QUIZA
IA;"PERO CUANDO SE HAYA TRANSFORMADO
LE ALGUN DIA, ¿SABE?-, Y DESPUES, CUANDO
CREE USTED QUE LE PARECERA TODO ESO
DECLARO LA ORUGA. "BUENO, QUIZAS TENGA
S MIOS", DIJO ALICIA; "PERO LO QUE SI SE
CIERTAMENTE MUY RARA!"

EH?". "ME TEMO QUE SI, SEÑOR", DIJO ALICIA;
MISMA MANERA QUE ANTES..., ¡Y NO PASAN
MAÑO!" ."¿Y QUE TAMAÑO QUERRIAS TENER?",
R EN CUANTO A TAMAÑOS", SE APRESURO A
O LE GUSTA ESTAR CAMBIANDO DE TAMAÑOS
"NO CREO NADA", REPUSO LA ORUGA.

", LE DIJO A ALICIA EL LIRON, QUE ESTABA
DO RESPIRAR!'". "NO PUEDO REMEDIARLO",
A; "ES QUE ESTOY CRECIENDO". "¡NO TIENES
LIRON. "¡NO DIGA TONTERIAS!", RESPONDIO
BIEN QUE USTED TAMBIEN ESTA CRECIENDO!".
RITMO RAZONABLE Y NO DE ESA MANERA

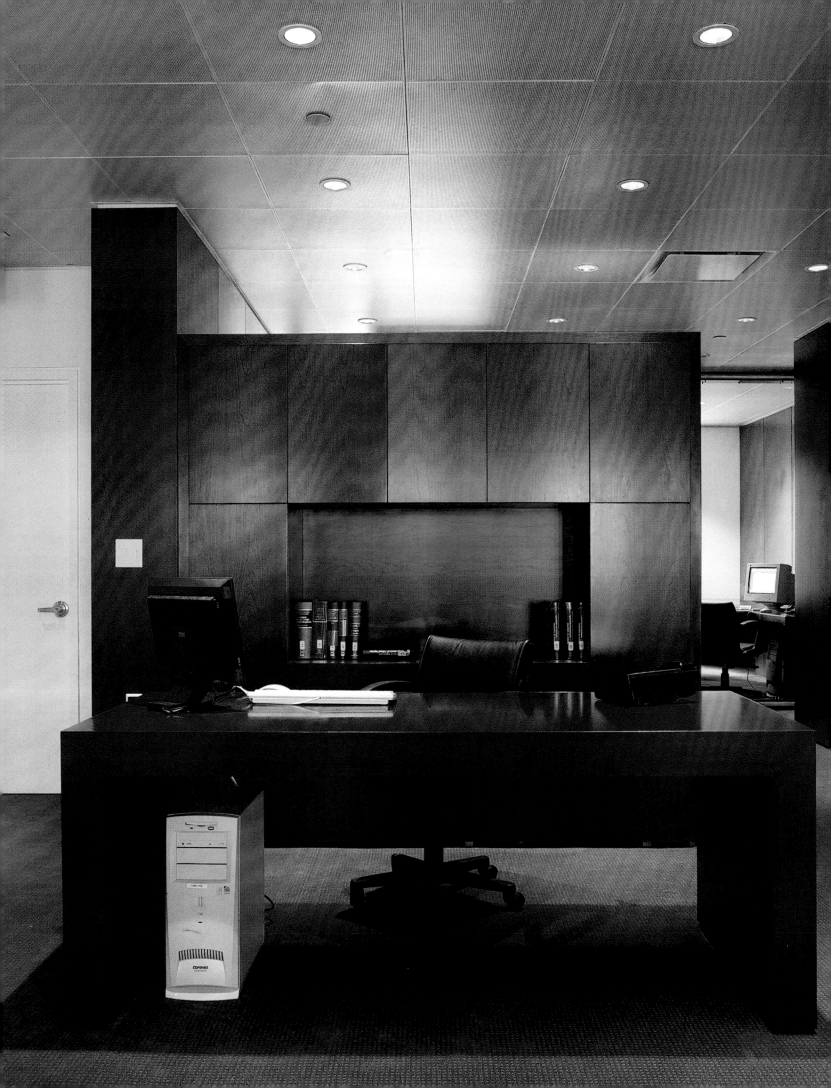

Cuatrecasas in New York

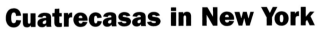

THE PROJECT CONSISTED OF ARRANGING THE NEW YORK OFFICES OF THIS LAW FIRM TO MAKE THE NEW SPACE AS FUNCTIONAL AS NEEDED TO CARRY OUT WORK WITH MAXIMUM COMFORT. THE ARCHITECTS IN CHARGE OF THE PROJECT CREATED A WORKING ENVIRONMENT THAT IS SOBER, FUNCTIONAL, CONFIDENTIAL, AND MODERN—VERY MUCH IN LINE WITH THE ACTIVITY THAT TAKES PLACE IN IT—AND WERE ABLE TO CONVEY A SINGULAR AND PERSONALIZED CORPORATE IMAGE TO THE SPACE.

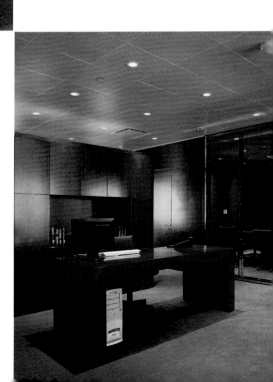

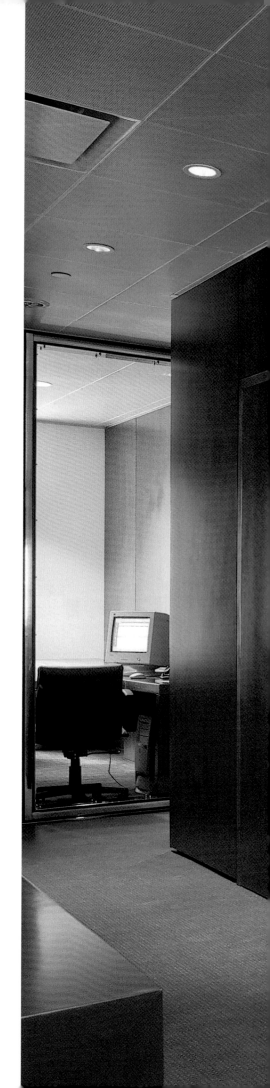

Cuatrecasas in New York

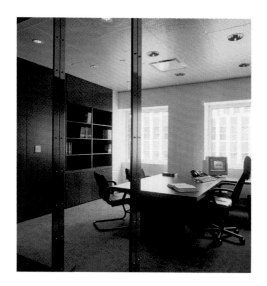

Architect: **GCA Aquitectos**
Client: **Cuatrecasas, Gonçalves Pereira,
Castelo Branco and Associates**
Location: **New York City, United States**
Construction Date: **2002**
Photography: **Jordi Miralles**

One of the main objectives of the project was to create a modern environment that was a faithful reflection of the law firm Cuatrecasas. A thorough organization of the space was required in order to layout the different areas in the best possible way. Consistency and a sense of unity were the constant goals of the arrangement.

The space was treated as a whole to make sure that each clearly defined and individual zone in which the various functions and departments of the company are located form part of a unified whole. The workspace is functional, elegant, and easily identifiable, and this is delivered in the brightly lit and organized interiors that are the perfect frame for the activities that are carried out there. These spaces are created with simplicity and efficiency. Also, visual relationships and spatial communications have been addressed.

The materials, mainly wood, and the color palette chosen are limited to few elements. The furnishings used in the decoration consisted of discreet and elegant lines and reinforced the idea of balance, practicality, and elegance already outlined by the architectural features. The result is an efficiently equipped workspace with a serene atmosphere, where the workers feel completely supported in carrying out their work.

Parting from the premise that the work environment had to be neutral, balanced, and serene, an effective program was conceived in which the unity and continuity of space is crucial. One of the elements that created this effect was the replacement of several doors or walls with glass counterparts to create the optical illusion of larger space, while at the same time connecting areas devoted to different functions, such as the meeting room and reception area.

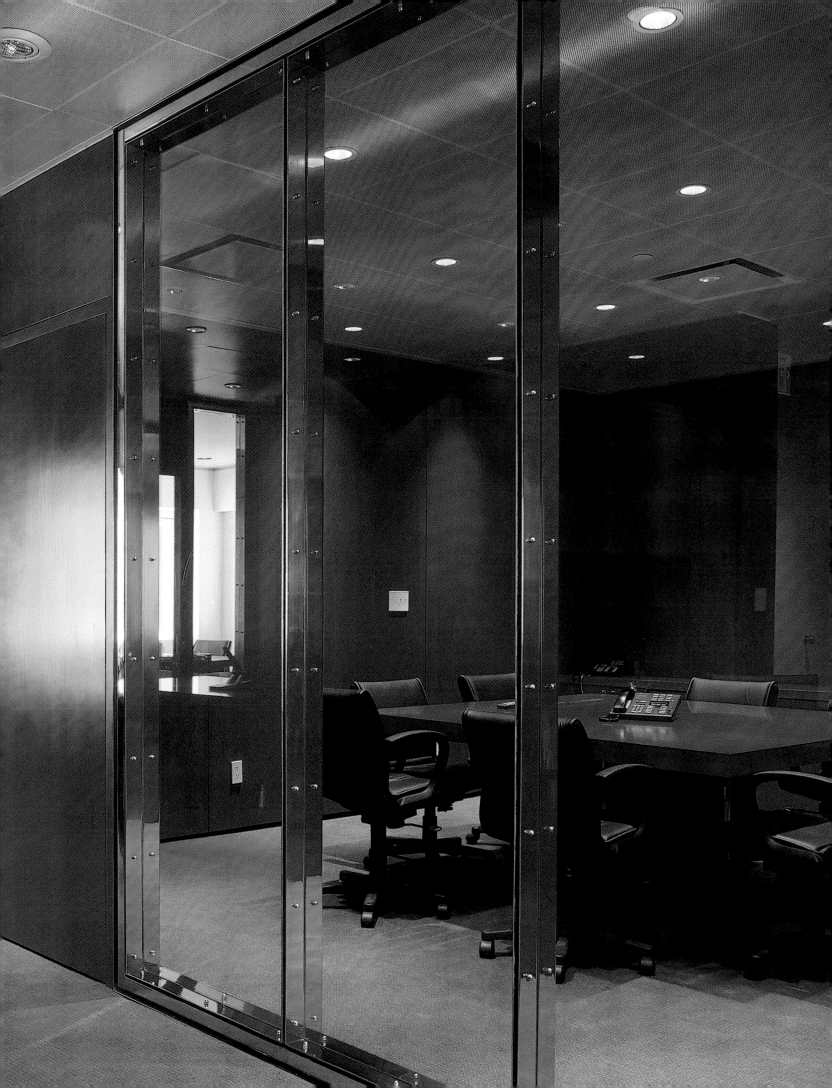

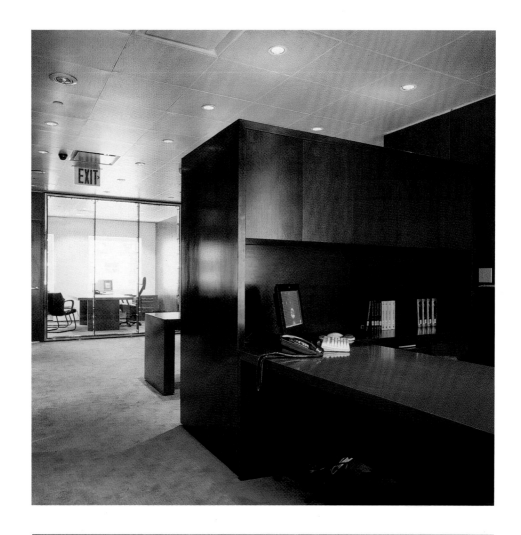

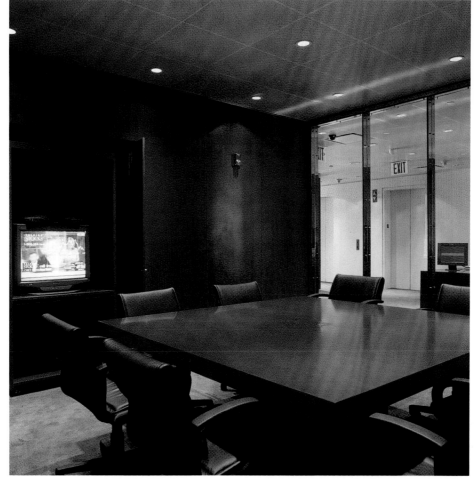

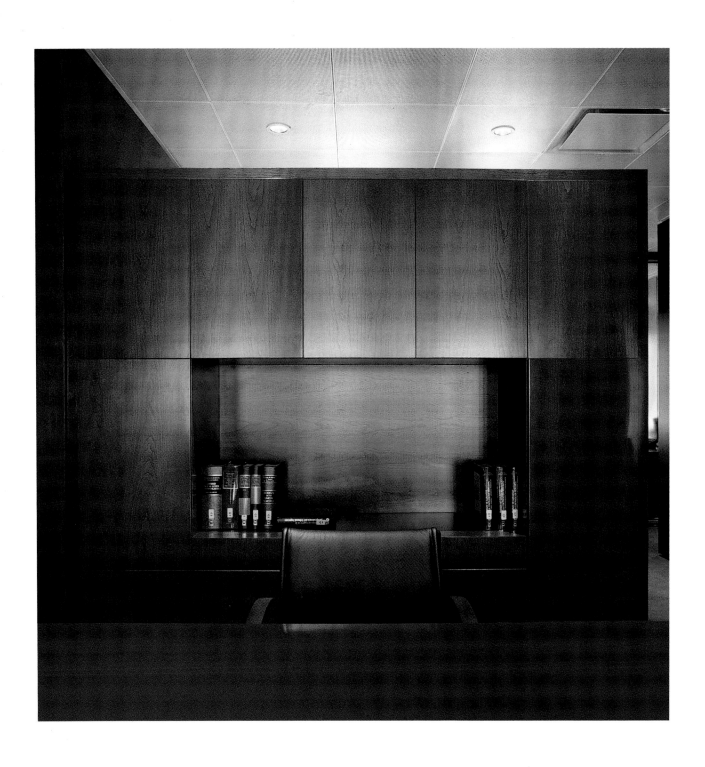

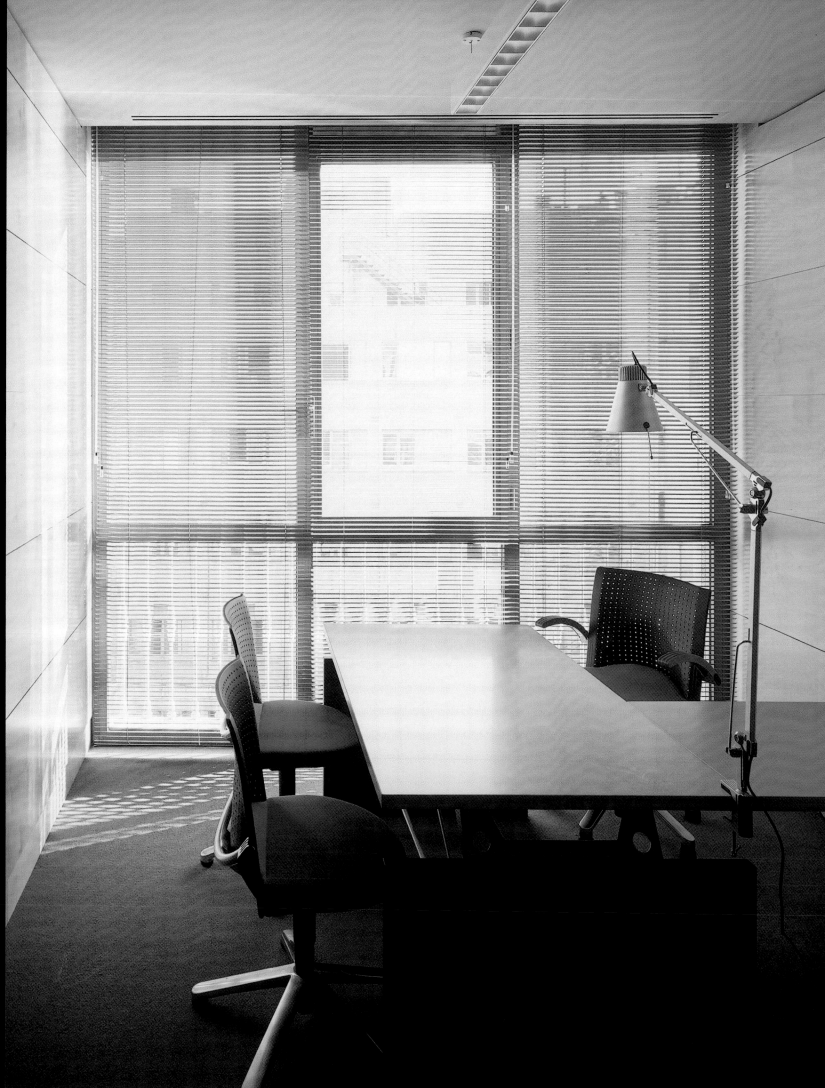

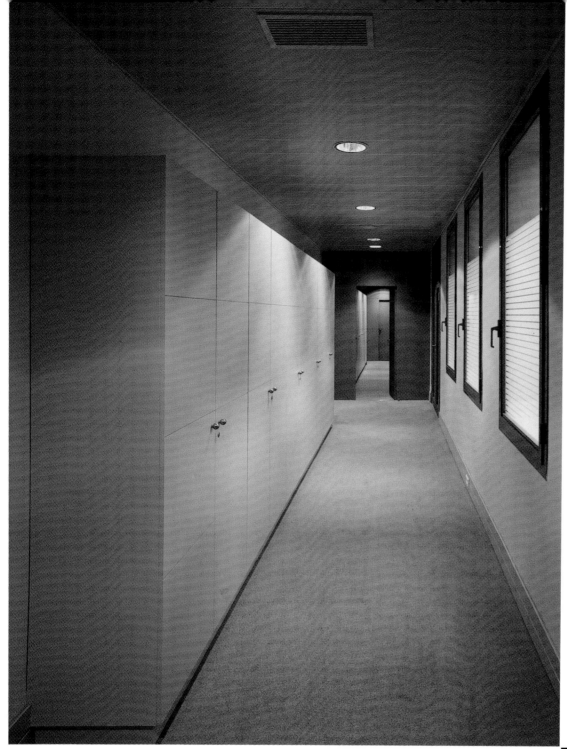

French Consulate in Barcelona

THE OFFICES OF THE CONSULATE GENERAL OF FRANCE IN BARCELONA, SPAIN, ARE LO-
CATED IN CENTER OF THE CITY IN A CORNER BUILDING THAT HAS A COURTYARD. THESE
CHARACTERISTICS WERE TAKEN INTO CONSIDERATION WHEN ARRANGING THE DISTRIBUTION.
THE OFFICES WERE ORGANIZED IN THREE DISTINCT TIERS ACCORDING TO THEIR FUNCTION.
EACH ONE HAS BEEN TREATED DIFFERENTLY, DEPENDING ON THE REQUIREMENTS OF THEIR
USE AND IMPORTANCE.

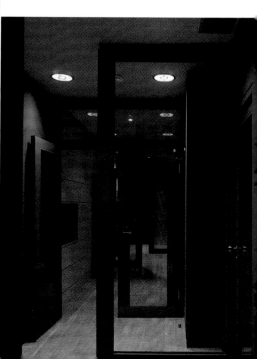

French Consulate in Barcelona

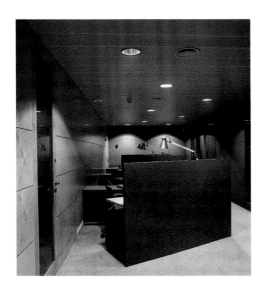

Architect: **Espinet / Ubach Arquitectos**
Client: **Consulate General of France**
Location: **Barcelona, Spain**
Construction Date: **1996**
Photography: **Eugeni Pons**

The criteria for the building renovation were security, functional use and traffic patterns, flexibility in the distribution of the interiors, and controlled acoustics. The project involved only one 7,534-square-foot level, where the various areas that make up the installations were distributed according to their use. Therefore, the control for the entrances, surveillance, thefts, visas, files, computing, etc., were placed in the middle tier of the building. The area that opens to the courtyard was reserved for the service to the public, notary, social assistance, and civil registry. The services and the offices of the consul, vice-consul, documentation, and press were located in a third area.

The southern side, where the services with the most public traffic are located, were planned as a space with predominantly light colors, the warmth of sycamore wood, and the austerity of the gray steel construction. The floor was covered with a highly resistant carpet to endure foot traffic. The furniture combines light wood with a gray-green color, which is also repeated in the upholstery to make it consistent. In the central area, which has more restricted traffic and is under surveillance, a lot of gray-painted metal elements and acid-etched, ornamental transparent glass abound. The floor in this area has been covered with travertine. In the main offices, colors get darker, the wood acquires a leather-like tone, blue is substituted for the green of the furnishings and upholstery of the other areas, and merbau wood is used for the floors.

The functional requirements expected of the space were combined with the introduction of peripheral materials, colors, textures, furnishings, and lighting, which conveys a feeling of comfort and balance.

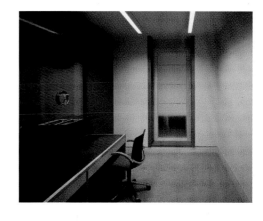

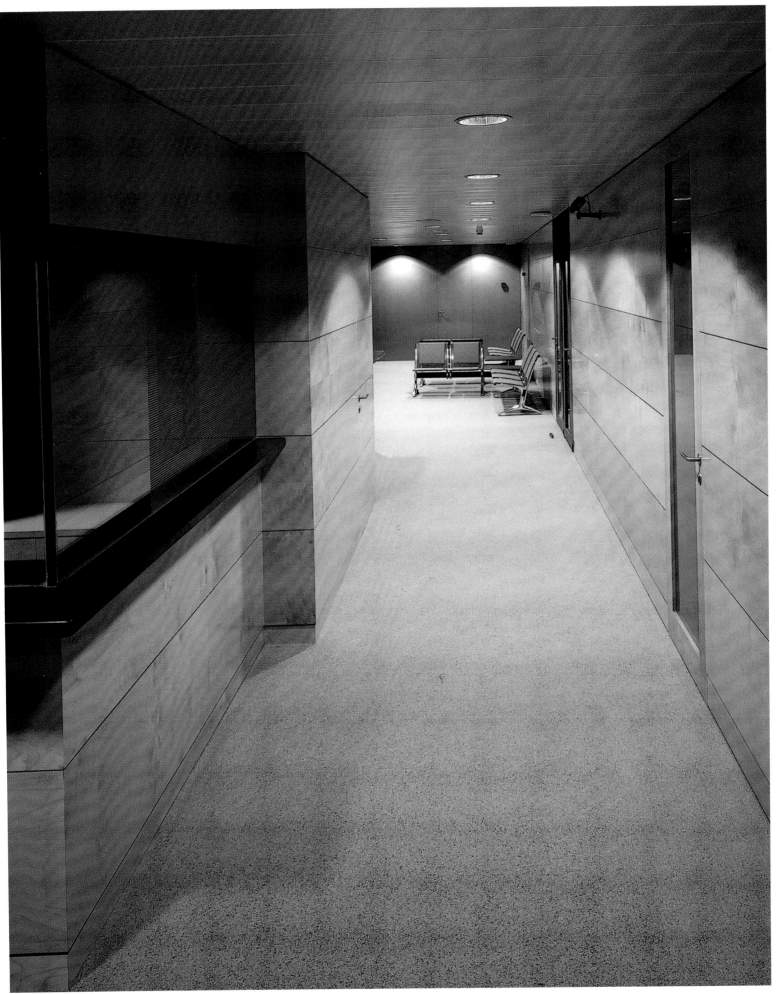

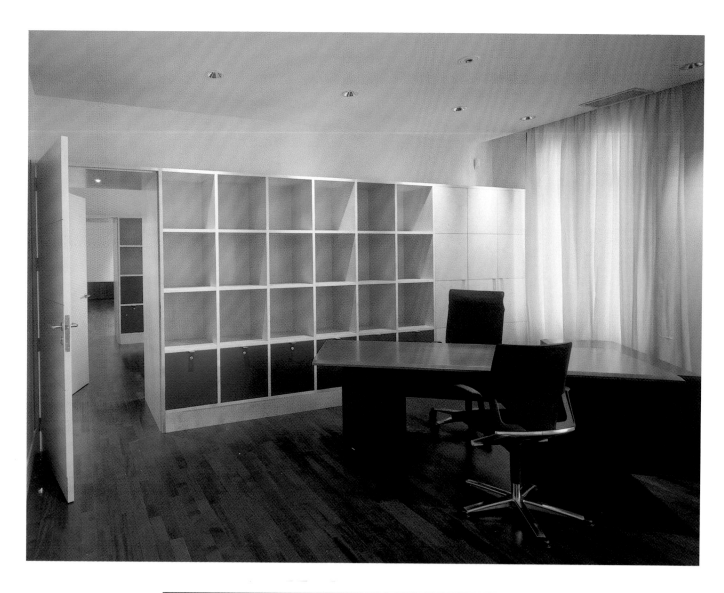

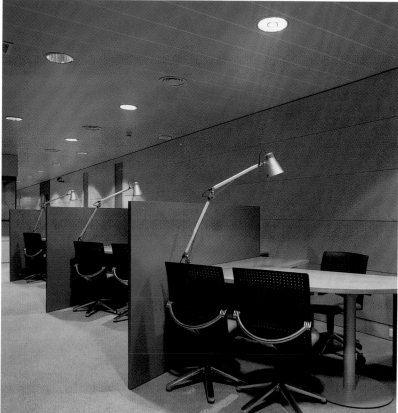

The furnishings chosen for the interiors—contemporary design pieces—are the elements that provide a touch of personality and color to the interiors dominated by brightness, the charm of simplicity, and functionality.

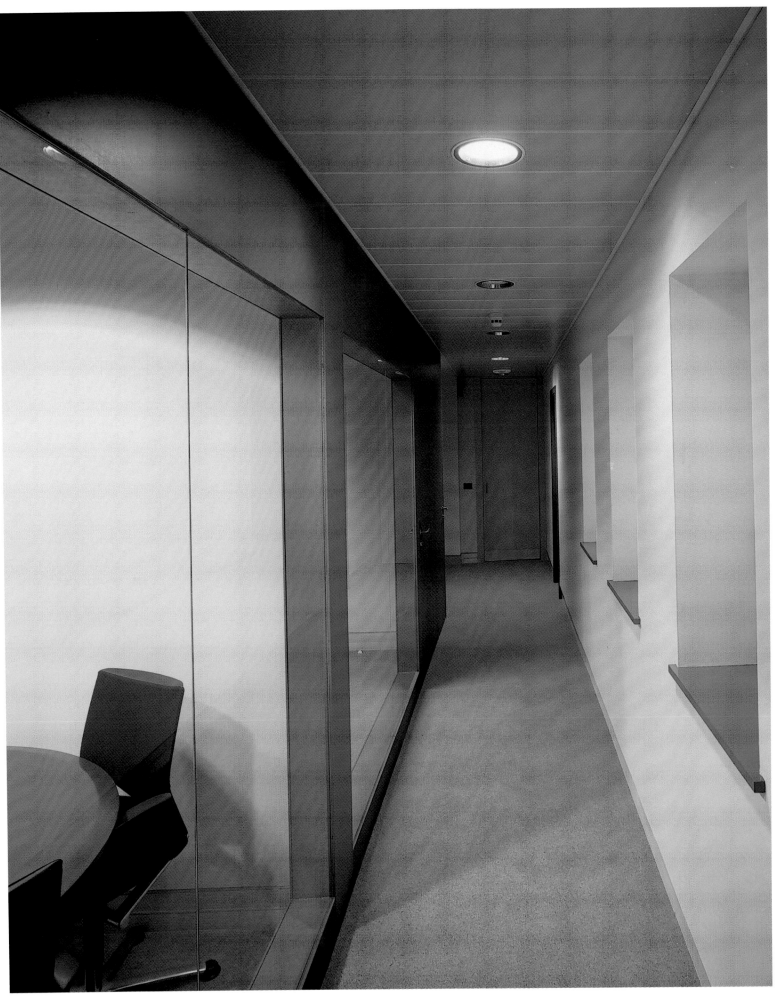

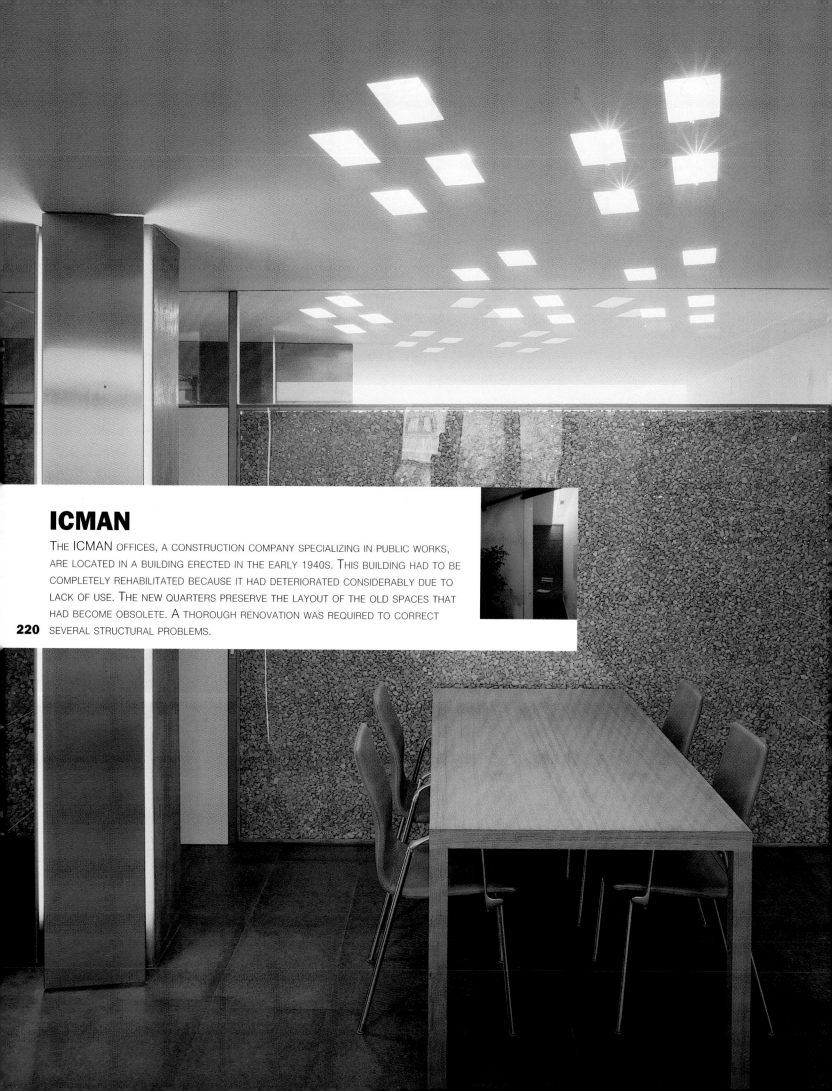

ICMAN

THE ICMAN OFFICES, A CONSTRUCTION COMPANY SPECIALIZING IN PUBLIC WORKS, ARE LOCATED IN A BUILDING ERECTED IN THE EARLY 1940S. THIS BUILDING HAD TO BE COMPLETELY REHABILITATED BECAUSE IT HAD DETERIORATED CONSIDERABLY DUE TO LACK OF USE. THE NEW QUARTERS PRESERVE THE LAYOUT OF THE OLD SPACES THAT HAD BECOME OBSOLETE. A THOROUGH RENOVATION WAS REQUIRED TO CORRECT SEVERAL STRUCTURAL PROBLEMS.

220

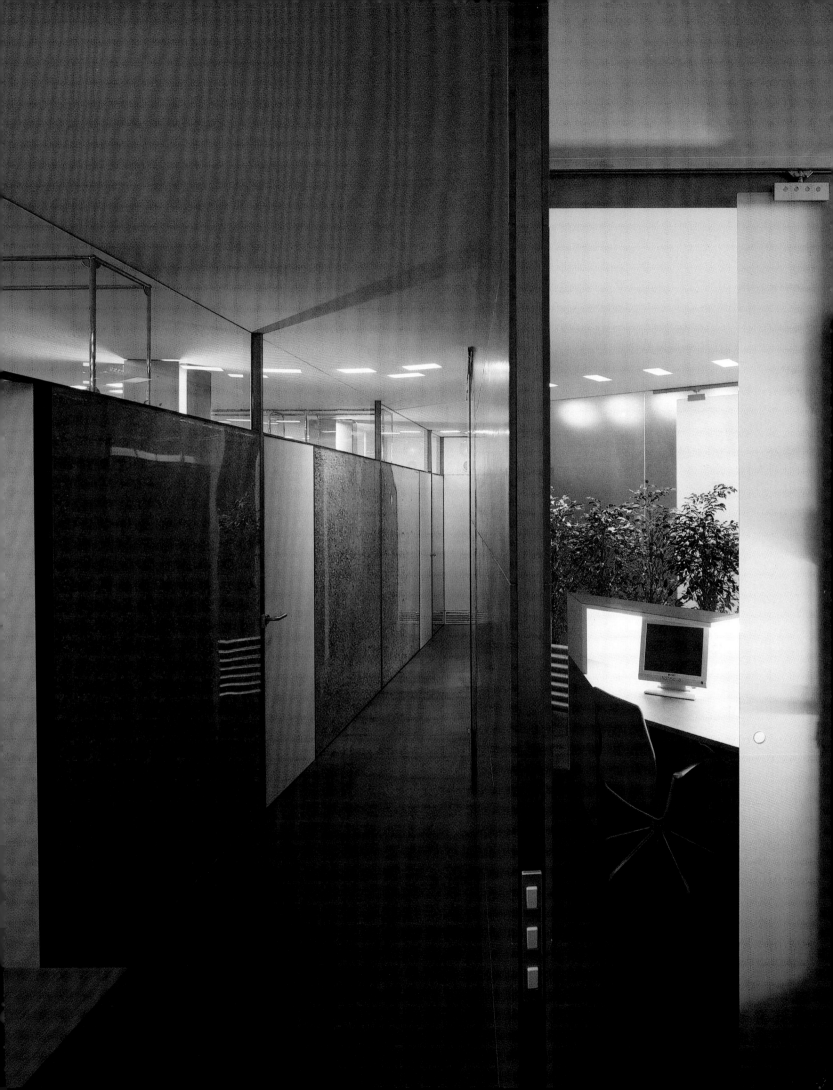

ICMAN

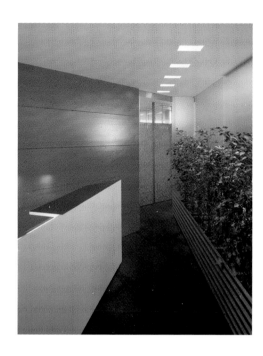

Interior Designer: **Agustí Costa, Design Studio**
Client: **ICMAN**
Location: **Barcelona, Spain**
Construction Date: **2001**
Photography: **David Cardelús**

The assignment involved planning the offices from scratch on a rectangular plan of about 1,345 square feet, with uneven and insufficient natural lighting. There were only four windows in the facade, and it was not possible for light to come in any other way. Therefore, the main challenge was to devise spaces that were flexible and that allowed light to enter without sacrificing the privacy the owners required for the management offices. In conjunction with the desire to lightly define zones for different uses and to encourage interaction, this took the form of subtle solutions with an unassuming and transparent presence using degrees of translucency, reflection, and opacity that would be transformed with the passing of time and be subject to the effects of variations of color and the direction and intensity of the light on the surfaces. This meant designing a series of flexible spaces open to a variety of forms of communication. Each area—reception, waiting room, secretarial spaces, and main offices—can be isolated to establish varying levels of communication by simply sliding panels of translucent glass. All of these architectural solutions are reinforced by the choice of materials, which also allude to the activities of the company.

To prevent the loss of the formal characteristics of the original building, the windows and the paneled wood entrance door were conserve, and the floor plan was faithfully replicated to avoid altering the overall composition of the building. Problems were resolved in a natural and spontaneous way, and aesthetics occupied an important place in the decision-making process.

Inside the offices, divisions of space were made using translucent and opaque materials, the latter being light yellow to introduce a bright accent and at the same time to enhance the light from the windows. The spaces are enclosed with permanent walls and unframed sliding glass panels that are translucent with some transparent areas.

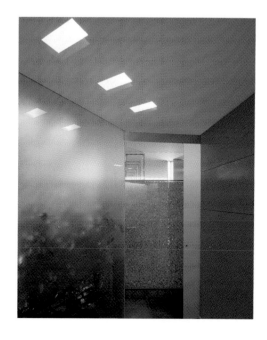

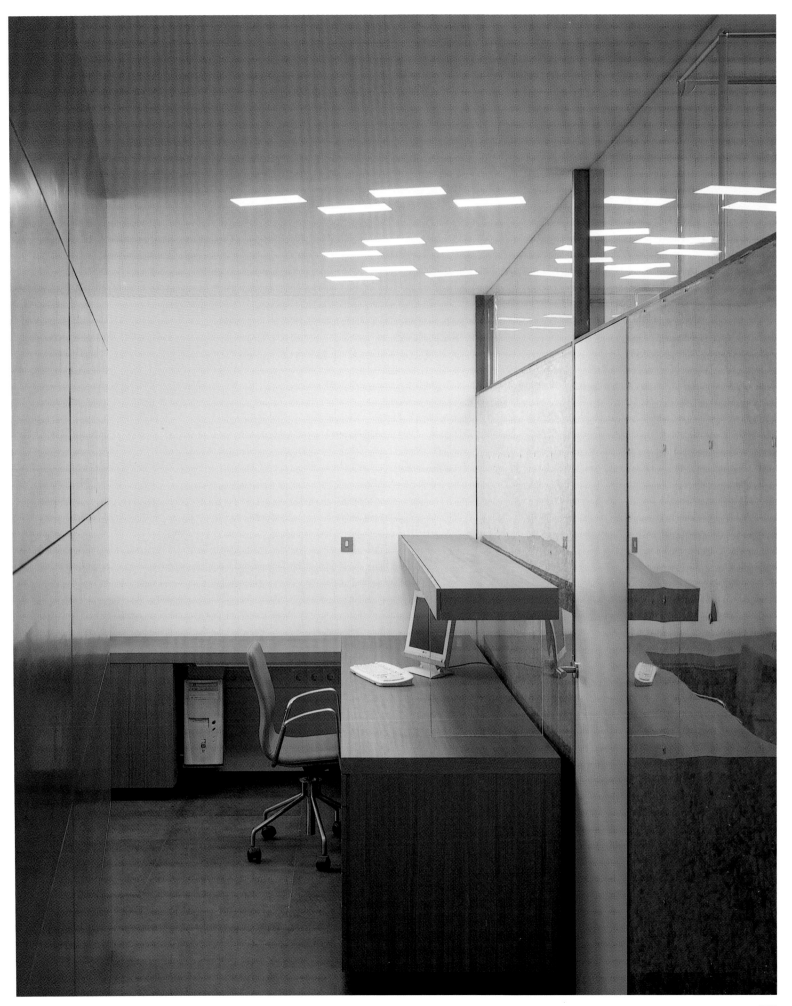

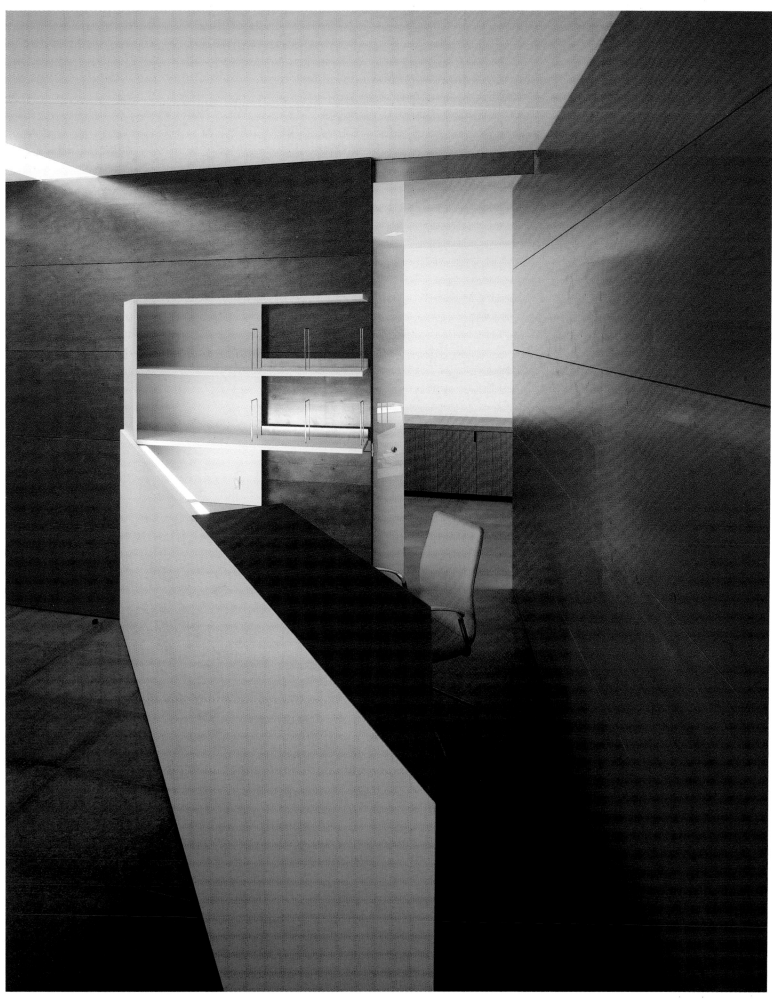

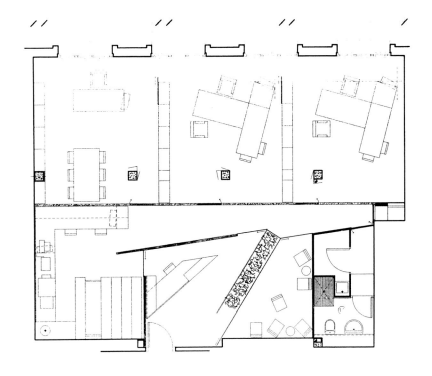

Floor plan

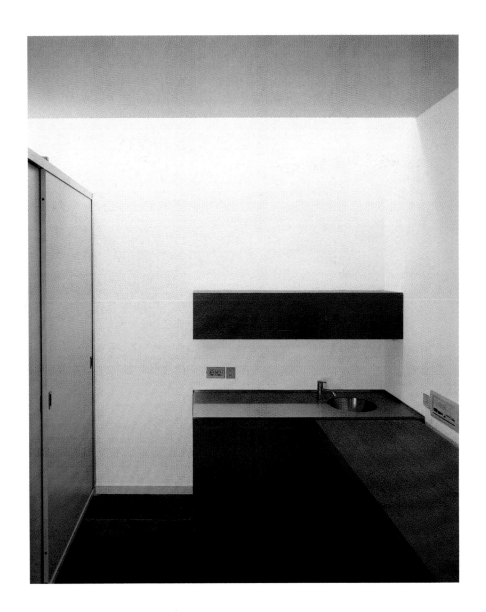

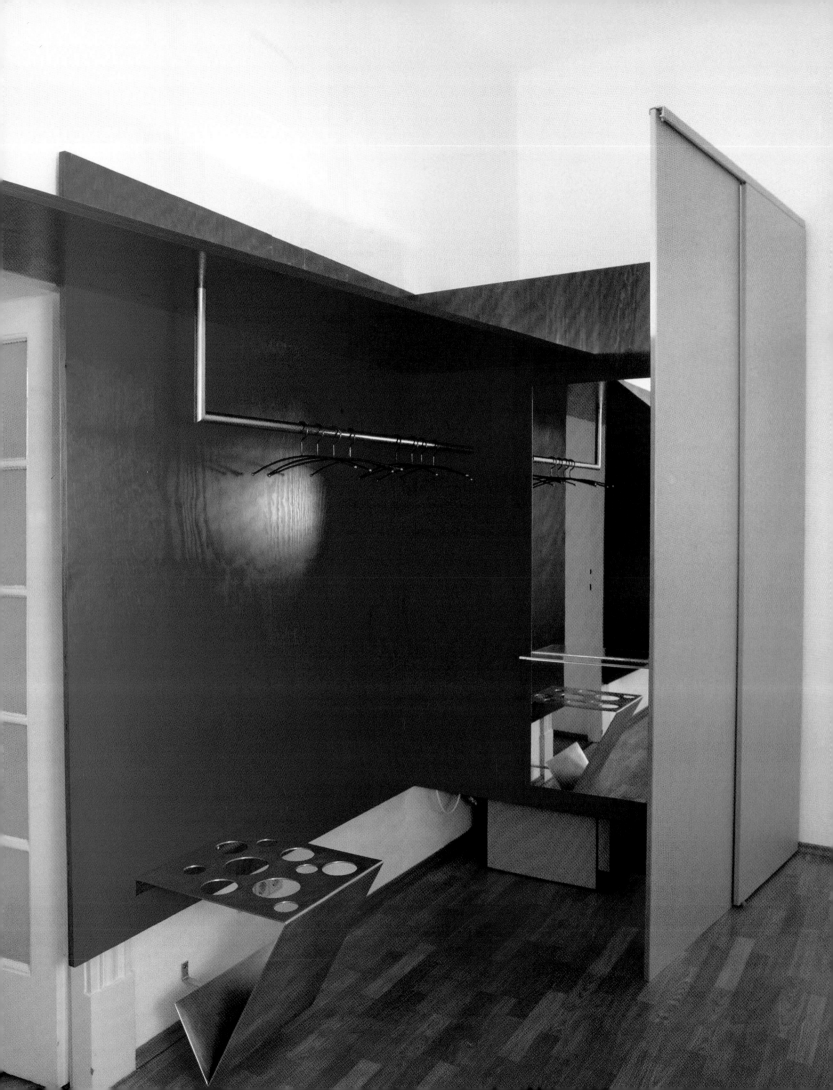

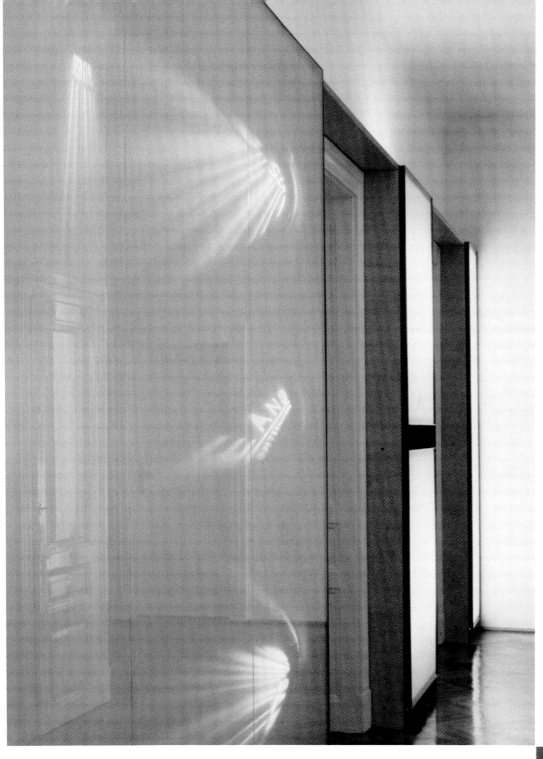

EAN Austria

SET IN AN ORIGINAL CONSTRUCTION WHOSE INTERIORS ARE ARCHITECTURALLY ATTRACTIVE,
IT WAS DECIDED TO PRESERVE SOME OF THE ELEMENTS OF THE BUILDING, MIXING THEM
WITH OTHER ELEMENTS FAR MORE INNOVATIVE AND MODERN. THE END RESULT IS A
SUGGESTIVE PLAY OF STYLES, WHERE PAST AND PRESENT COEXIST AND ENRICH ONE
ANOTHER. THE OBJECTIVE OF THIS PROJECT WAS TO CREATE A NEW, FLEXIBLE, DYNAMIC,
AND MULTIFUNCTIONAL SPACE.

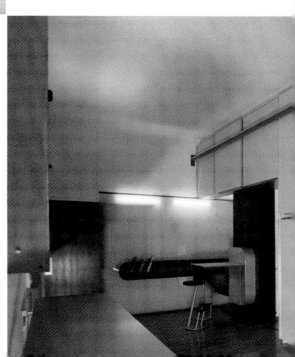

EAN Austria

Architect: **Rataplan**
Client: **EAN Austria**
Location: **Vienna, Austria**
Construction Date: **2001**
Photography: **Markus Tomaselli**

The Austrian architecture studio Rataplan conceived the design for the renovation. The project required the creation of a smooth transition between the areas that make it up, which must accommodate different functions within the company. Each area had to be perfectly defined and prepared for the particular activity that would take place in it, so the spaces had to be multipurpose and functional.

One of the main objectives was to equip the space with the necessary details and accessories, but with the least possible changes to the already existing areas in the original building.

The space is captivating because of its decorative content, where personal minimalism mixes with elegant classicism. Anything superficial and unnecessary was eliminated, but some ornamental elements that saturate the place with an inspirational avant-garde flair were combined.

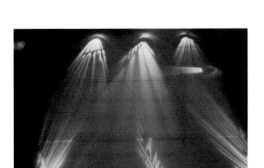

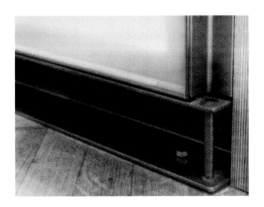

The floor plan, quite regular and geometric, allows an efficient distribution of the space. The choice of materials and textures as well as the color palette have been carefully monitored. The meeting rooms have been placed in spaces where the old ceilings and floors were preserved. Sober and restrained colors, like white and blue, and noble materials, such as wood, have been chosen for these rooms. The new areas, on the other hand, have been treated with brighter colors, glass, and metal. Movable panels and sliding doors have been used here, not only allowing more freedom of movement between the different spaces but also keeping costs down.

The mixture of tendencies and styles are the best introduction to the space. The carefully selected lighting for the areas, the successful combination of materials, and the suggestive color palette create a space that is current, comfortable, and functional.

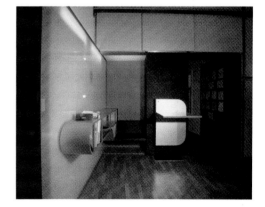

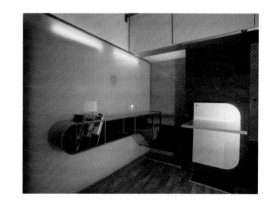

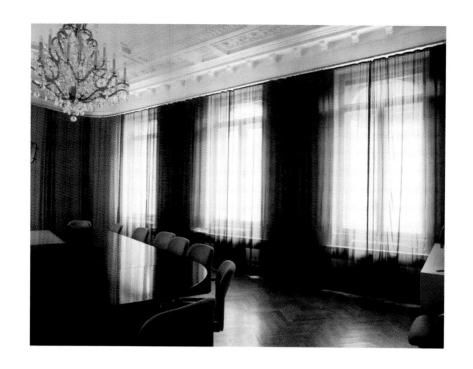

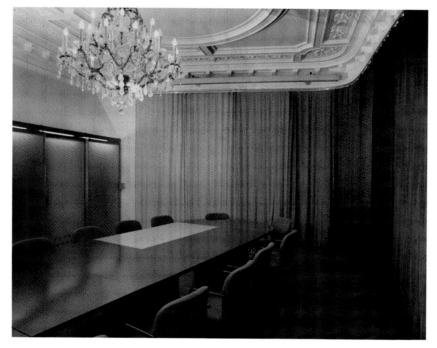

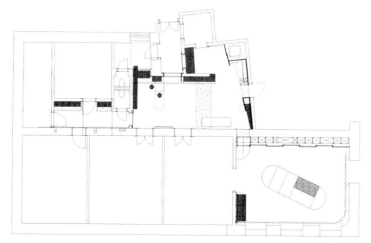

Floor plan

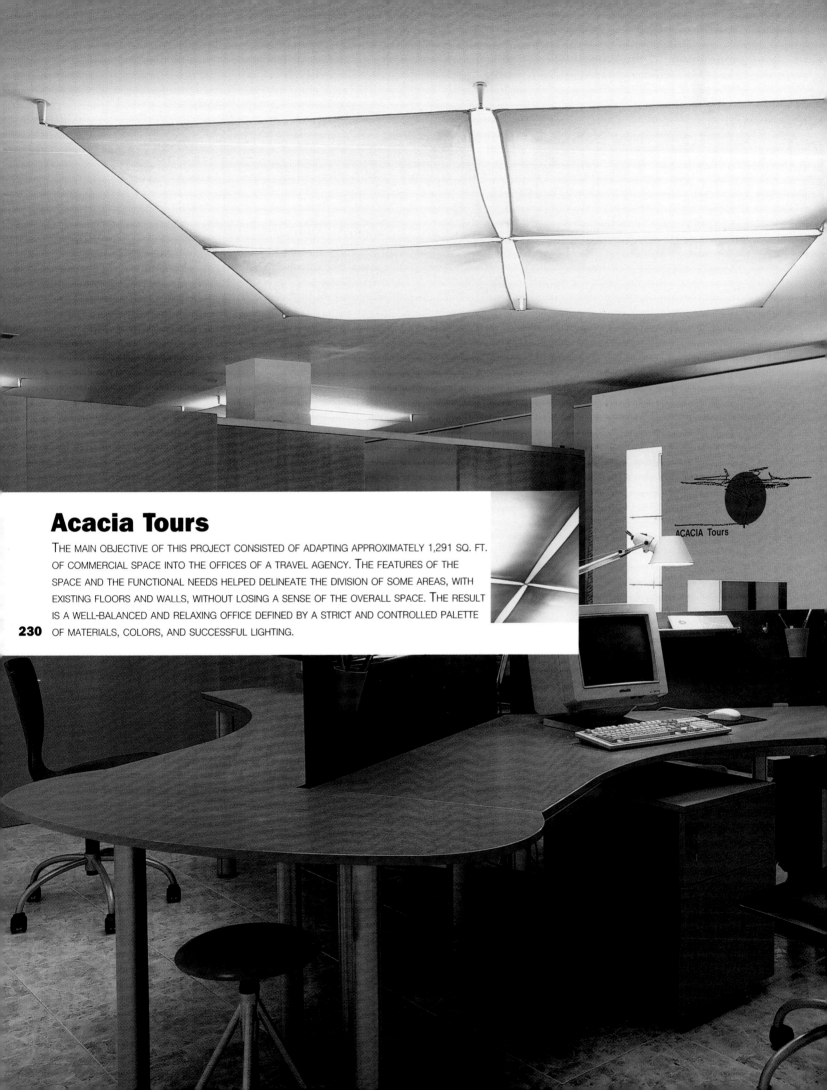

Acacia Tours

THE MAIN OBJECTIVE OF THIS PROJECT CONSISTED OF ADAPTING APPROXIMATELY 1,291 SQ. FT. OF COMMERCIAL SPACE INTO THE OFFICES OF A TRAVEL AGENCY. THE FEATURES OF THE SPACE AND THE FUNCTIONAL NEEDS HELPED DELINEATE THE DIVISION OF SOME AREAS, WITH EXISTING FLOORS AND WALLS, WITHOUT LOSING A SENSE OF THE OVERALL SPACE. THE RESULT IS A WELL-BALANCED AND RELAXING OFFICE DEFINED BY A STRICT AND CONTROLLED PALETTE OF MATERIALS, COLORS, AND SUCCESSFUL LIGHTING.

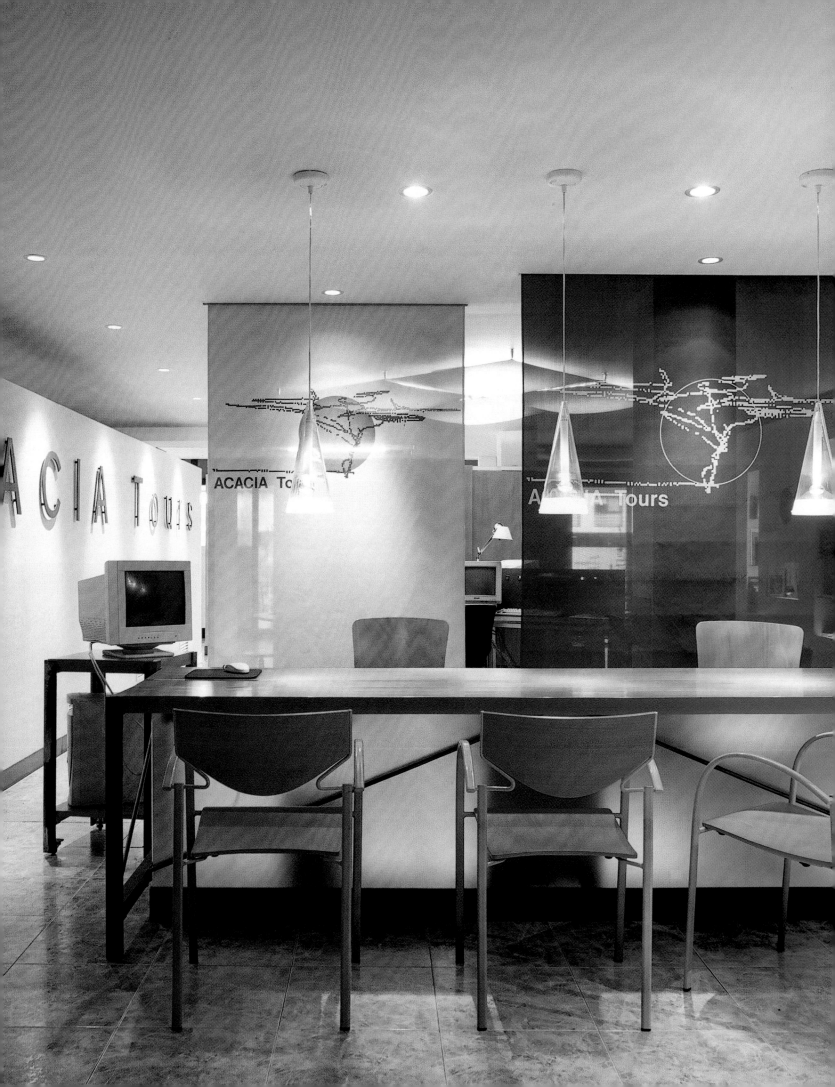

Acacia Tours

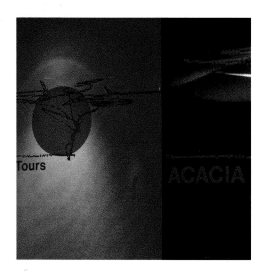

Interior Designer: **Marta Ortega Batlle**
Client: **Acacia Tours**
Location: **Girona, Spain**
Construction Date: **1998**
Photography: **Eugeni Pons**

Interior designer Marta Ortega Batlle planned the creation of a neutral and perfectly organized space, where the independent vertical planes made of wood, plasterboard and screen define the different functions of the agency, such as the administrative areas, customer service, storage, and offices.

In the lobby, two large screen panels bearing the logo of the agency welcome visitors. They are located behind a large counter whose height allows a view of the inside activity. The depth of the space is defined by a wall of plasterboard, where the name of the agency is spelled in steel letters, visually limiting the access to the more private areas of the office. This structure conceals the administrative area. The goal was to isolate this section from the exterior while not losing the light, creating points of reference between what is inside and what lays outside of the space, between what can be seen and what is hidden. This is achieved by using movable dividers and display panels that modify the perception of the space by being open or closed. Lacquered steel, maple wood, and translucent laminated glass are the materials used to make the customer service counter.

All the applied resources contributed to a balanced, restrained, and highly functional space where visitors go to plan dream vacations and where employees carry out their activities efficiently.

The customer service counter as well as the display panels, dividers, and the rest of the steel, wood, and glass elements—all designed by the interior designer—create a relaxing, balanced, and basic space in which there are no superfluous elements that interfere with the neutrality and functionality of the atmosphere.

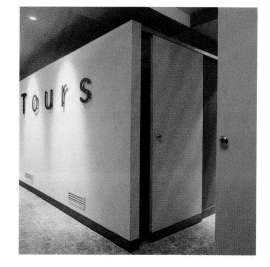

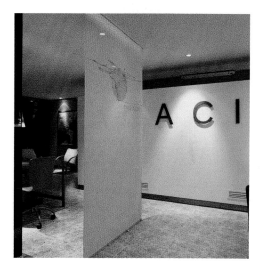

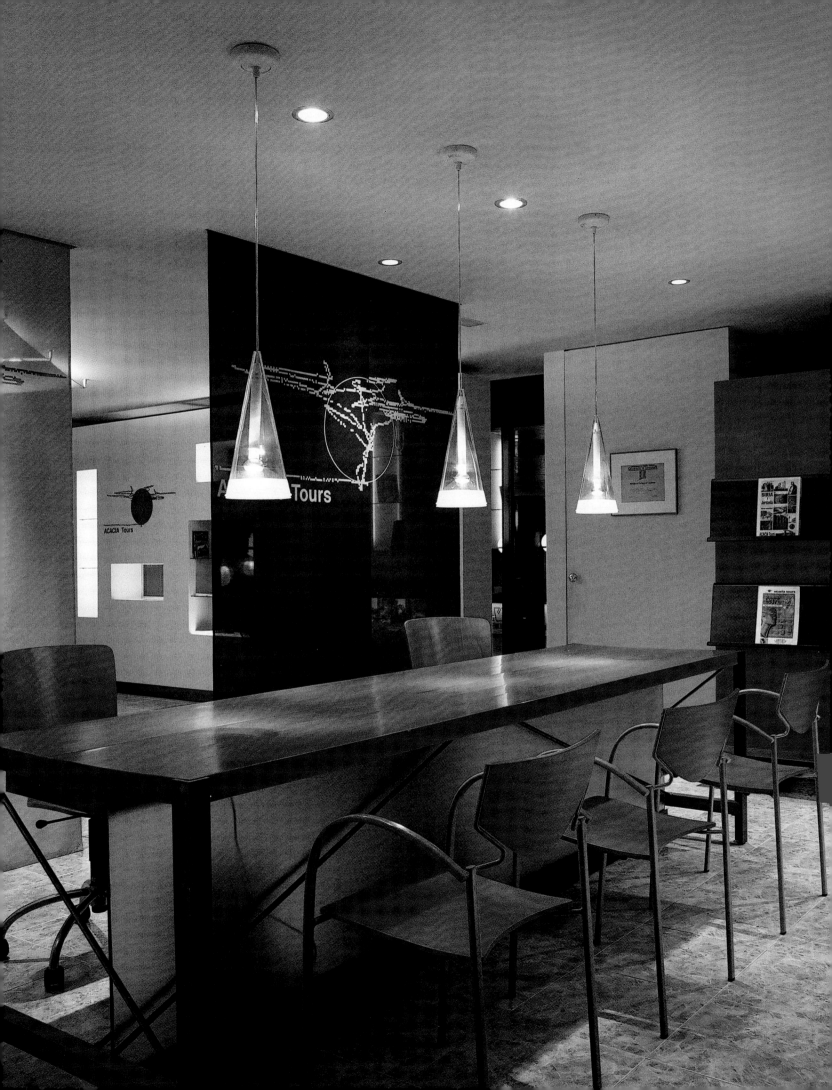

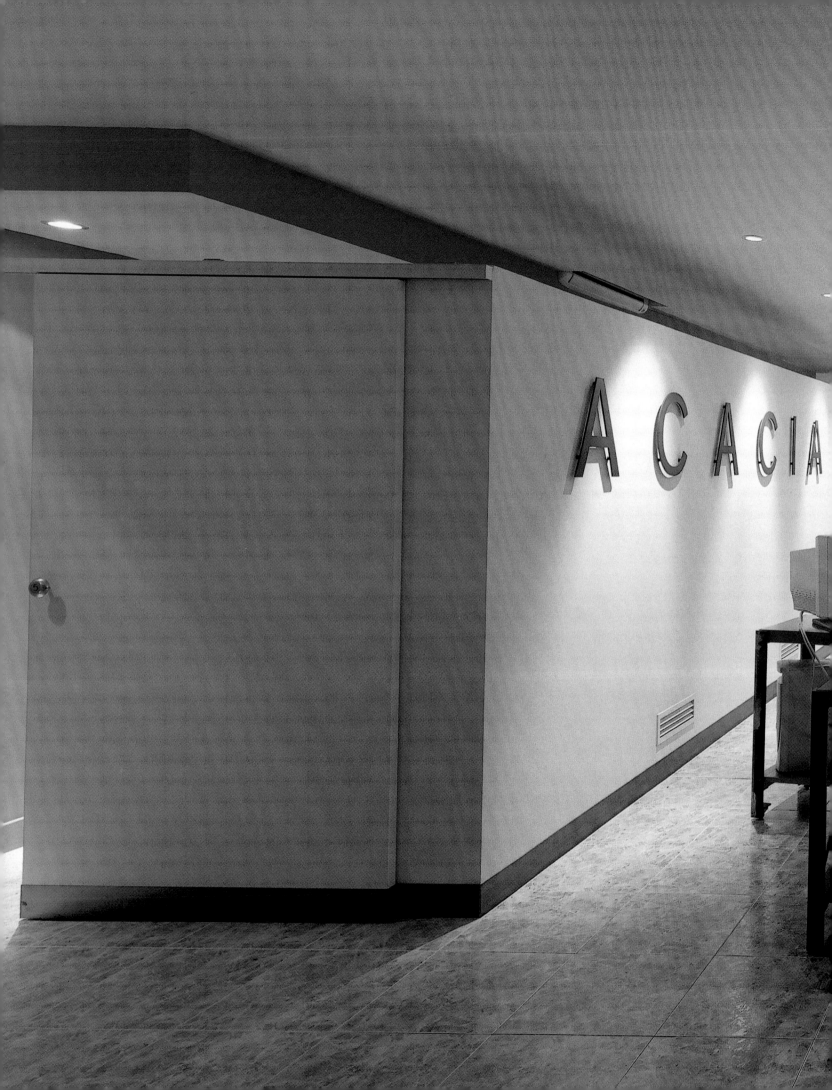

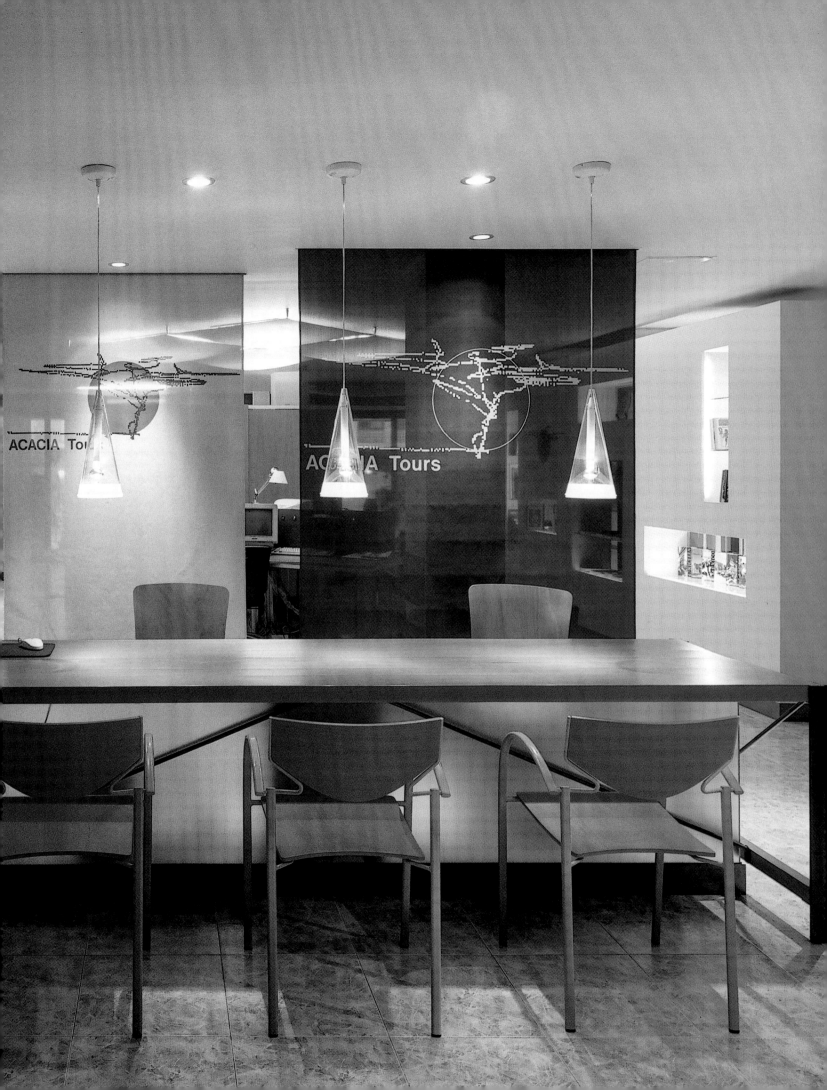

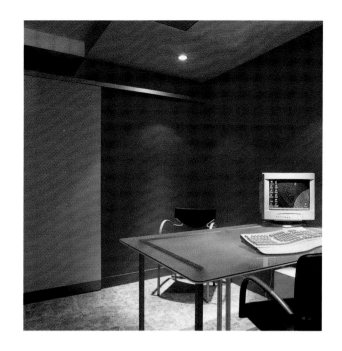

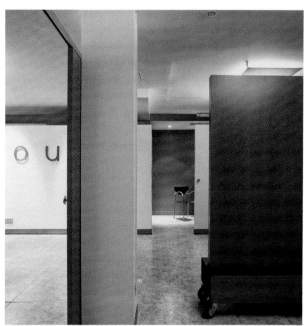

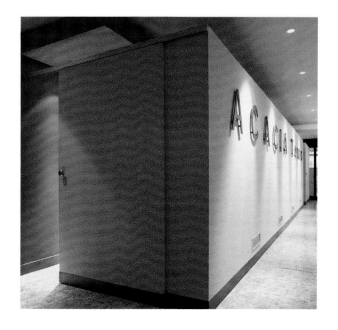

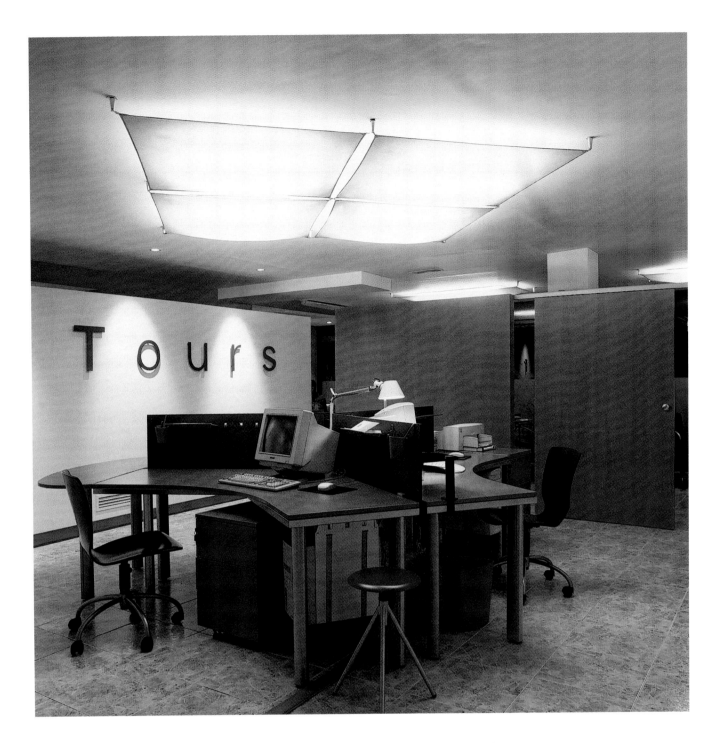

A neutral space where homogeneity and
simplicity are the dominant elements was created.
The strict and controlled palette of materials
(wood, steel, plasterboard, and glass) as well as
the treatment of the light contribute to the main
objective of the project—balance and pragmatism.

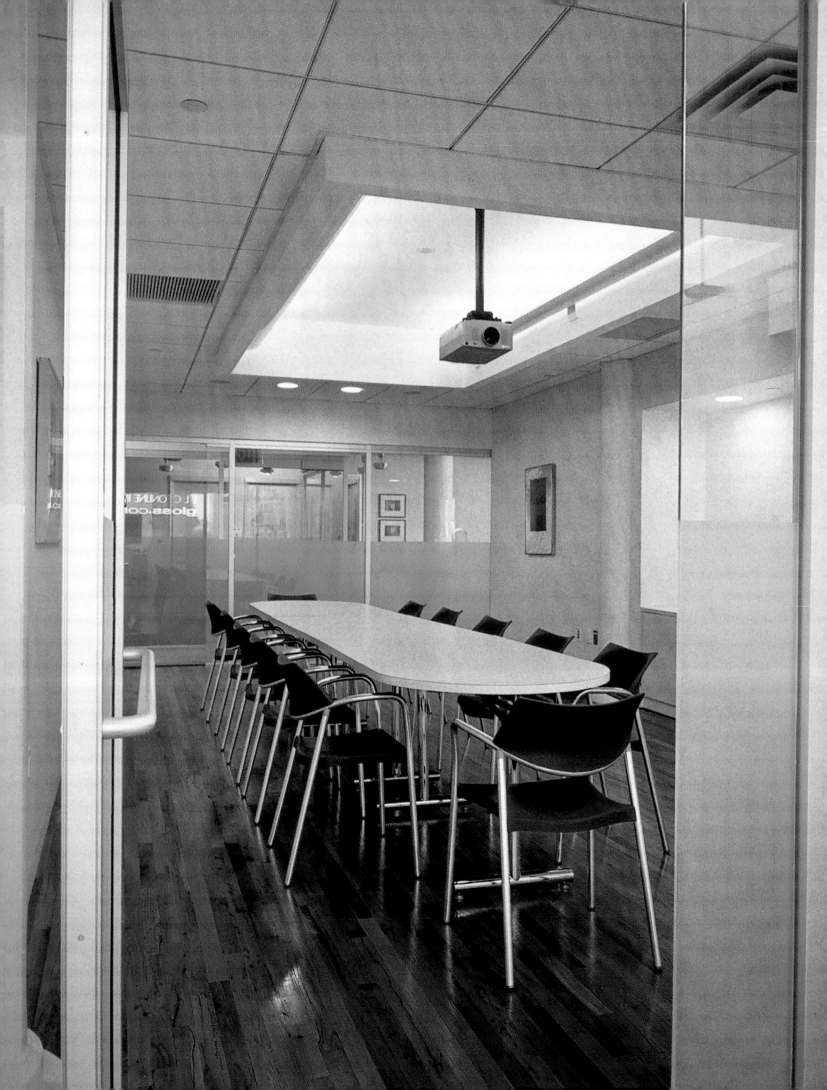

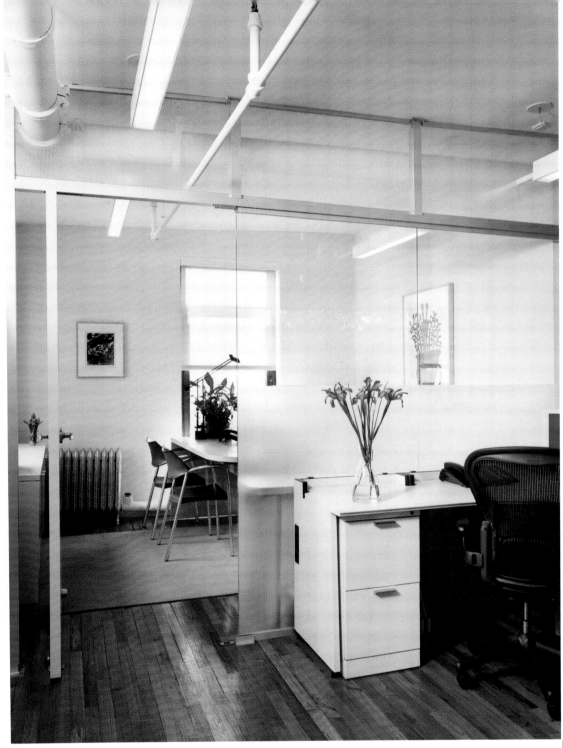

Corporate Loft Office

Fox & Fowle Architects designed the offices located on the 30th floor of an historic building in downtown Manhattan, which was designed by Louis Sullivan. The space was conceived as a neutral and flexible floor plan capable of housing the different uses that the client required. To achieve that fluidity and dynamism, the space has been treated as a loft.

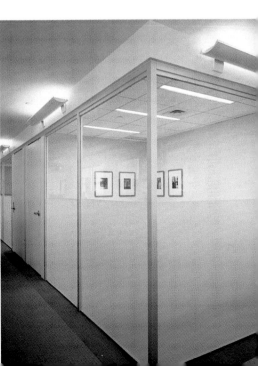

Corporate Loft Office

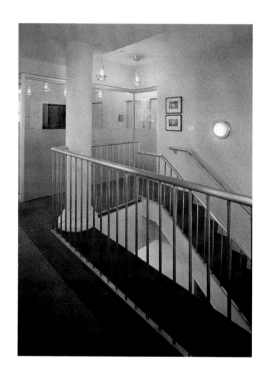

The team of architects was able to maximize the space despite the 7,500-square-foot size. A circular traffic area was created, which follows the perimeter of the floor, taking full advantage of the surrounding windows. Also, the existing columns distributed throughout the space are left exposed and are emphasized with the lighting. The perfectly organized work areas are defined with a system of knockdown partitions. The meeting and conference rooms were also placed within spaces enclosed with panels that allow the areas to be reconfigured. Both the materials and the furnishings are used as elements for separating the space. Lighting, whether natural or artificial, is defined differently depending on the function, so the amount needed to ensure an optimum level of illumination can be controlled. All these solutions work together in the design of rigorous, geometrically ordered, and open spaces for maximum comfort and the fulfillment of the client's needs.

The client plans to occupy more floors of the same building, so the treatment of the space, the selected materials, and the finishes that were used will be the same as the new installations to create a homogenous and coherent image.

Architect: **Fox & Fowle Architects, PC**
Client: **Withheld by request**
Location: **New York City, United States**
Construction Date: **2000**
Photography: **Lydia Gould Bessler**

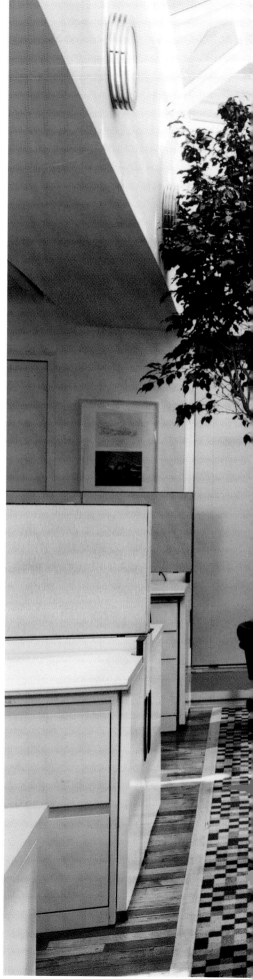

It was decided to create welcoming interiors and environments that at times resemble domestic spaces more than work areas, since color is used very playfully, blatantly, and expressively in some areas, and warm textures and materials are used together with comfortable and functional furnishings.

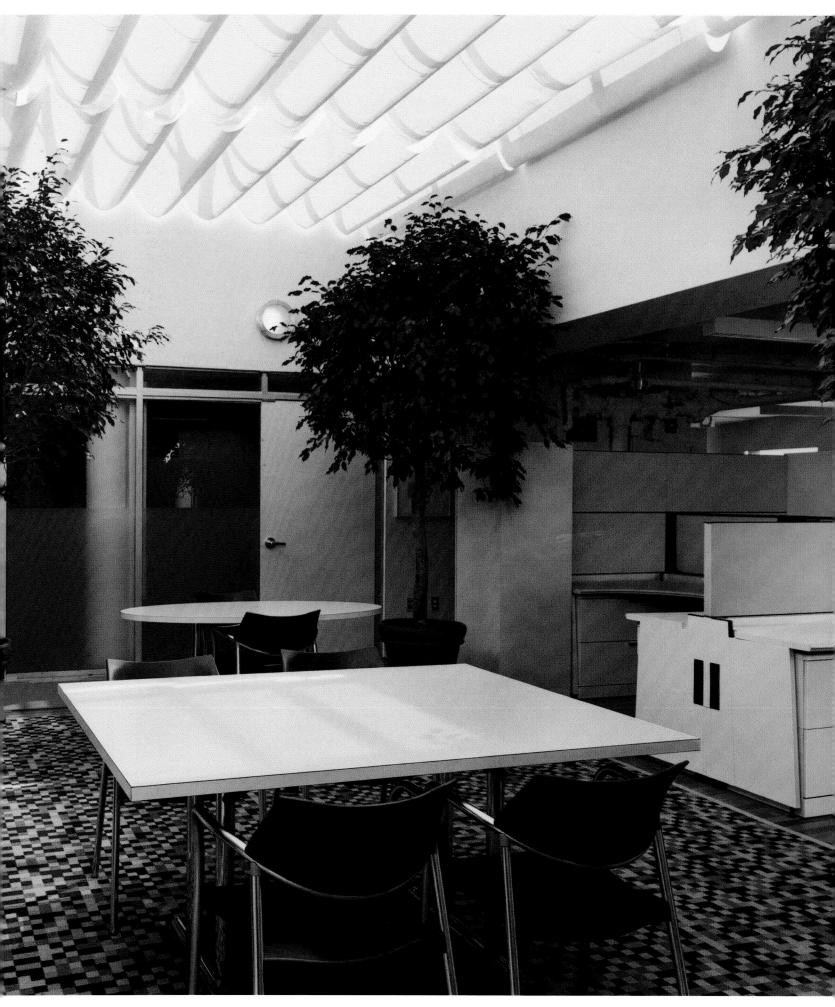

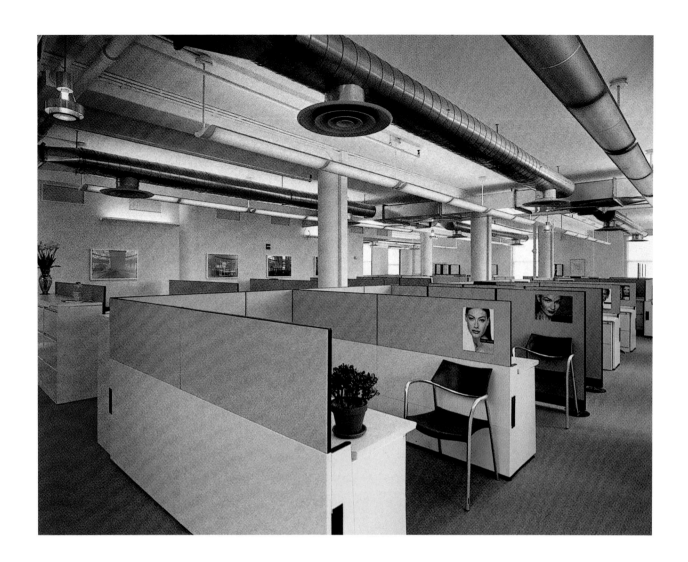

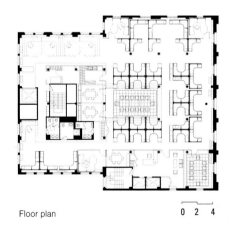

Floor plan

0 2 4

The limitations of the space are downplayed with effective architectural and decorative solutions, including the careful lighting, the successful organization of the space, the use of neutral and light colors in some areas, or the absence of unnecessary elements.

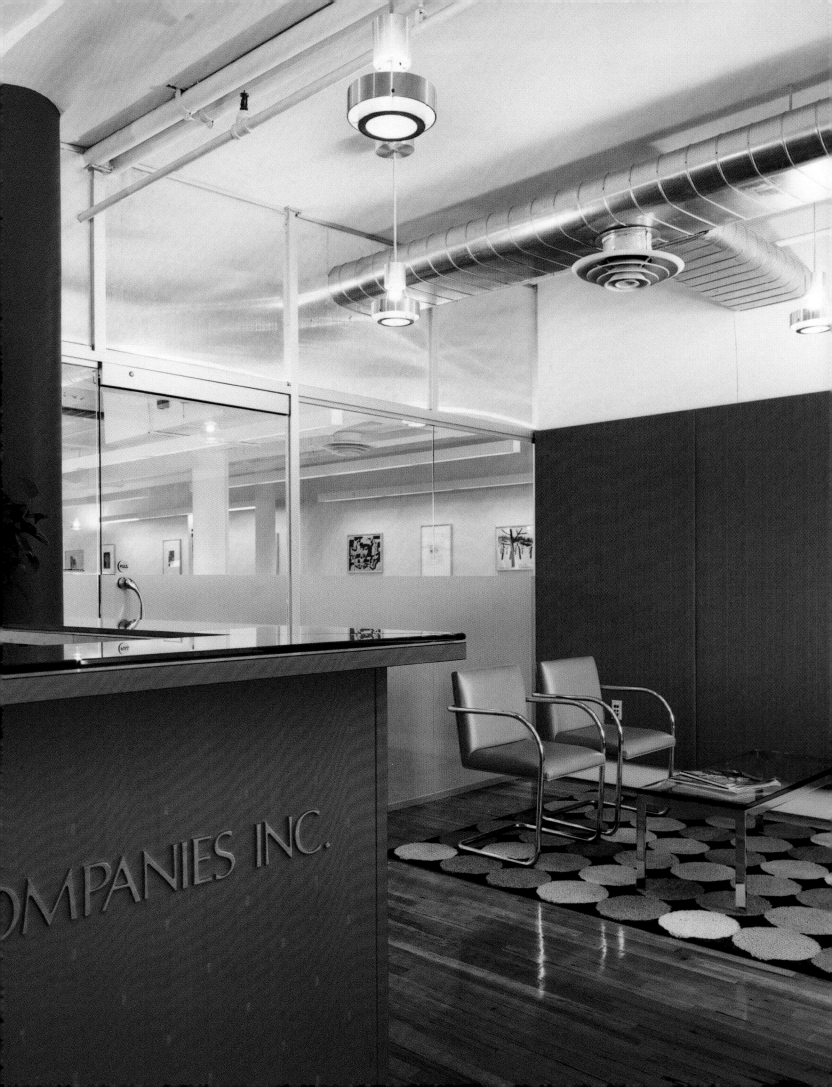

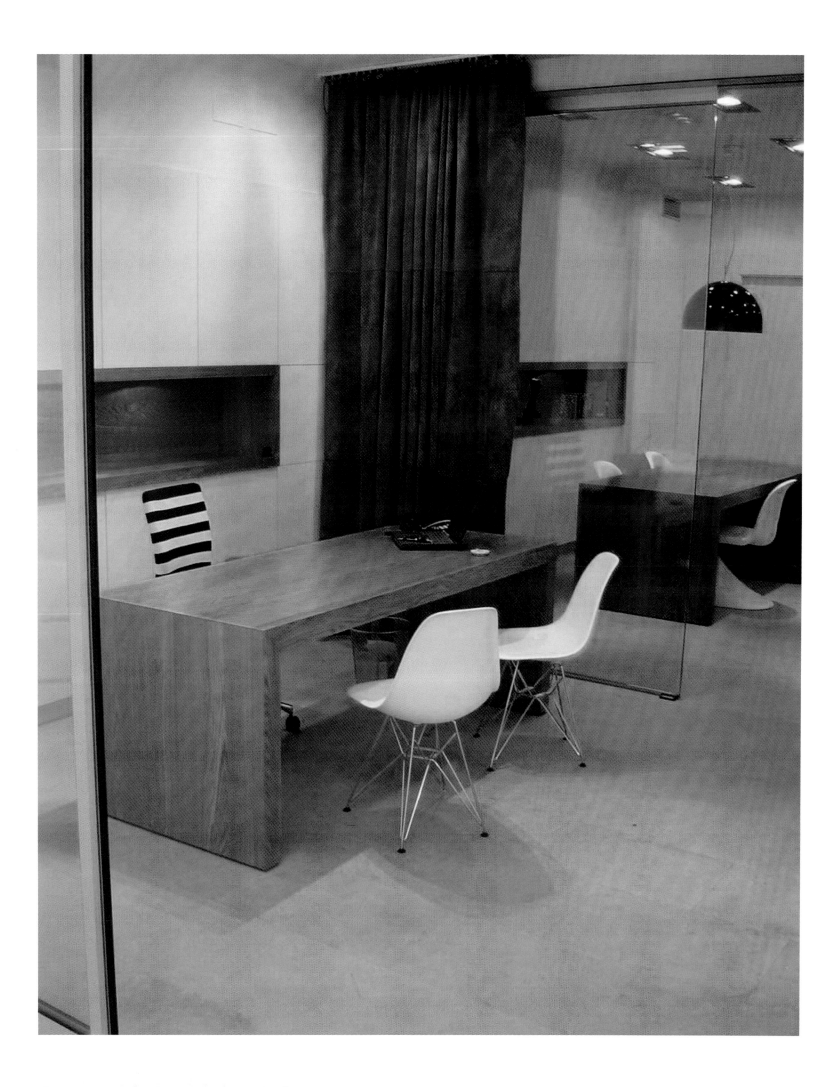

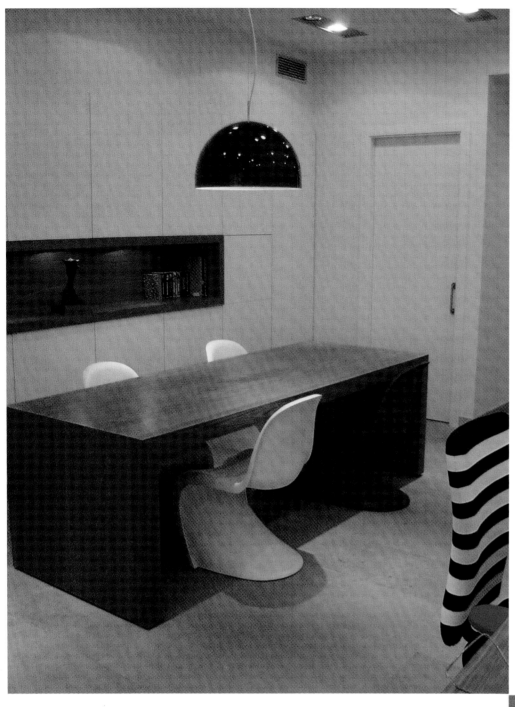

Xavier Martin Studio

CONVENIENTLY LOCATED ON ONE OF THE MOST CENTRAL STREETS IN MATARÓ, SPAIN, A CITY NEAR BARCELONA, THE NEW XAVIER MARTÍN STUDIO IS A MULTIFUNCTIONAL SPACE THAT OCCUPIES APPROXIMATELY 969 SQ. FT. OF THE LOWER LEVEL OF AN EARLY TWEN-TIETH-CENTURY BUILDING. BETWEEN TWO OTHER BUILDINGS, THIS SITE FORMERLY HOUSED A SMALL TEXTILE FACTORY.

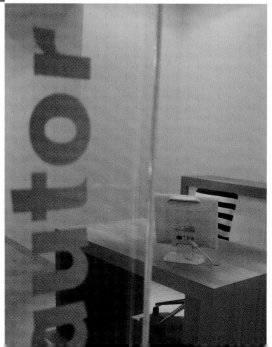

Xavier Martin Studio

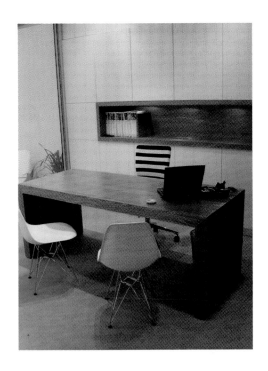

The goal of the remodeling project was to remove the partition walls to create a larger fluid space without visual interruptions. One of the main priorities of the project was to open up the space by eliminating all the obstacles, visual and physical, to turn the studio, which specializes in architecture, interior design, and furniture design, into a loft with minimalist tendencies and Mediterranean connotations. Access to the space is gained through a stainless steel door almost 10 feet tall, with the logo of the company painted on it. The facade boasts a window in which displays are changed periodically.

An oak table designed by the studio, the sinuous Panton chairs, and the file cabinet with simple lines and no pulls welcome the visitor into the space. A table in the shape of a Z rising approximately 12 inches from the floor, where flyers, magazines, or cards are on display, is the element that unifies the various functions of the space. Order and neutrality are the main features, and the fluidity of the space, the austerity, and the selection of well-known contemporary furniture are the focal points. All the work areas share the space, except a private office enclosed in glass with an automatic door, which can be quickly closed from view when necessary. The patio, located at the rear of the space, has been renovated and incorporated into the interior.

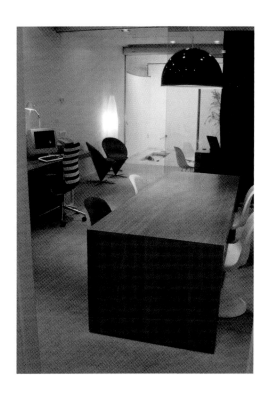

The project focused on creating spatial fluidity and order. Following the guidelines used for traditional lofts, a single space was created where the different areas were defined by the distribution of furnishings.

Interior Designer: **Xavier Martín**
Client: **Xavier Martín Studio**
Location: **Barcelona, Spain**
Construction Date: **2002**
Photography: **Xavier Martín**

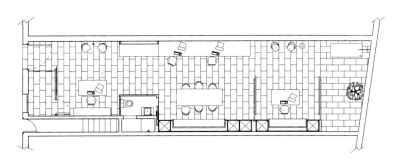

Floor plan

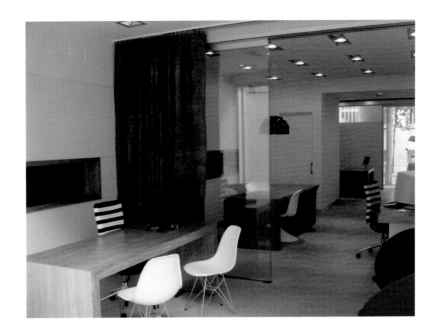

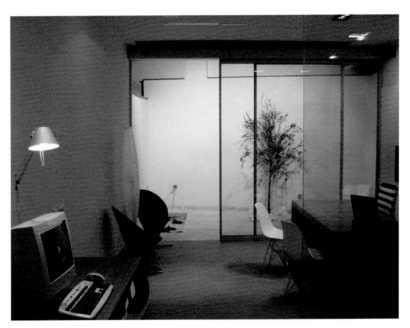

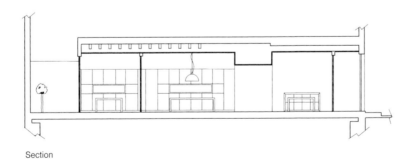

Section

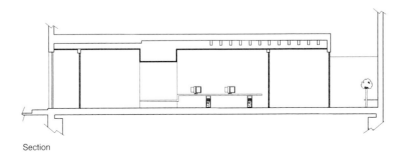

Section

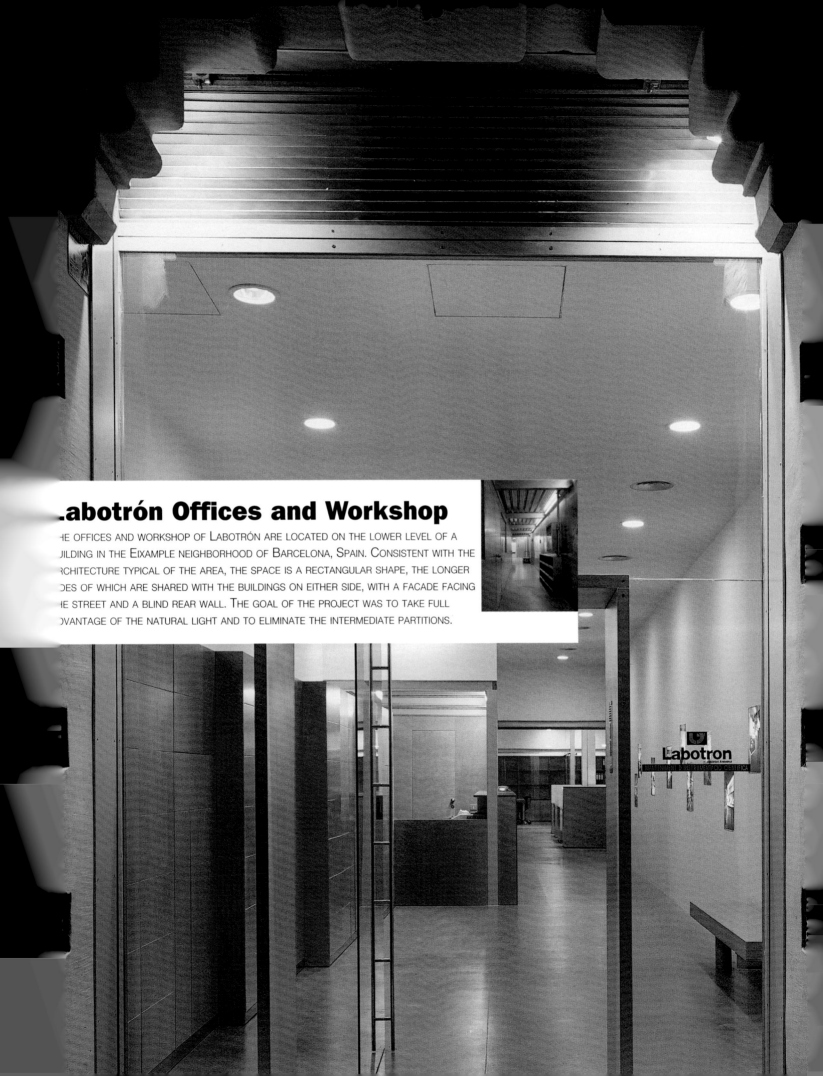

Labotrón Offices and Workshop

THE OFFICES AND WORKSHOP OF LABOTRÓN ARE LOCATED ON THE LOWER LEVEL OF A
BUILDING IN THE EIXAMPLE NEIGHBORHOOD OF BARCELONA, SPAIN. CONSISTENT WITH THE
ARCHITECTURE TYPICAL OF THE AREA, THE SPACE IS A RECTANGULAR SHAPE, THE LONGER
SIDES OF WHICH ARE SHARED WITH THE BUILDINGS ON EITHER SIDE, WITH A FACADE FACING
THE STREET AND A BLIND REAR WALL. THE GOAL OF THE PROJECT WAS TO TAKE FULL
ADVANTAGE OF THE NATURAL LIGHT AND TO ELIMINATE THE INTERMEDIATE PARTITIONS.

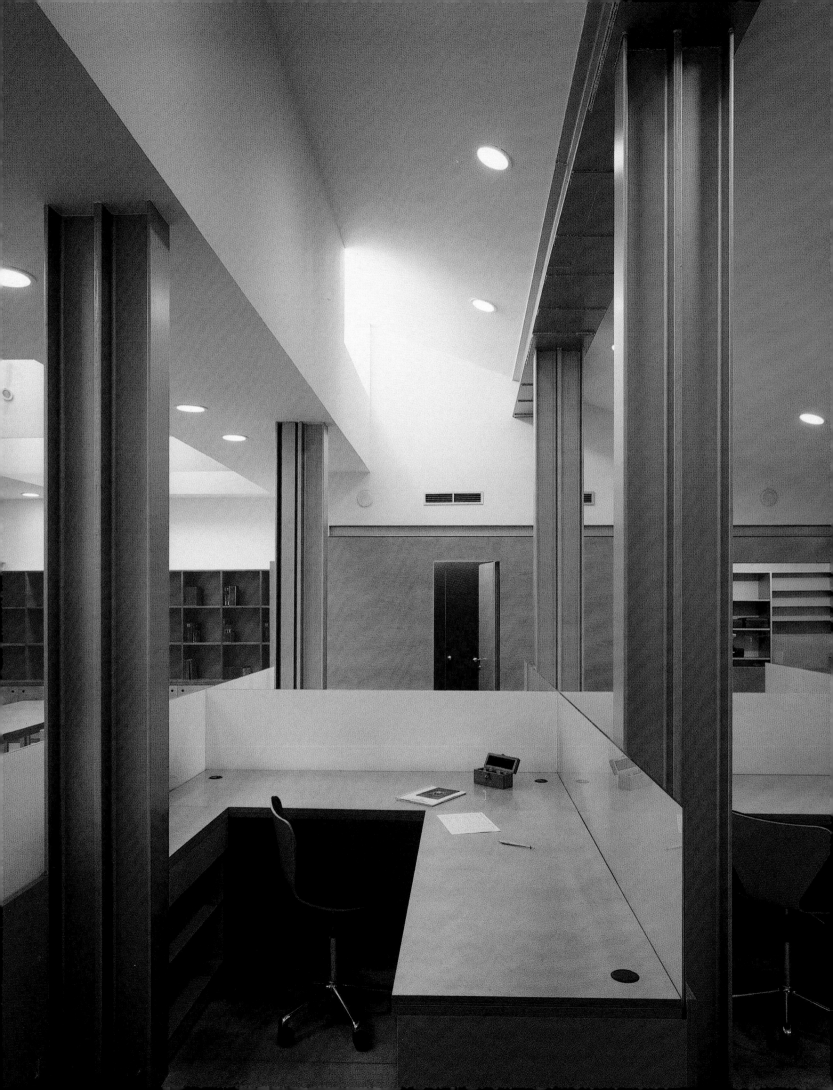

Labotrón Offices and Workshop

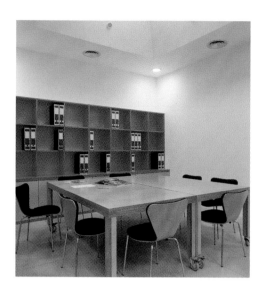

Architect: **Pep Zazurca**
Interior Designer: **Mar Ruiz**
Collaborator: **Isabel Figuera (Interior Designer)**
Client: **Labotrón**
Location: **Barcelona, Spain**
Construction Date: **1999**
Photography: **Eugeni Pons**

A small rectangle piercing the center of the wall facing the street extends halfway into the building and houses the doorman's office and vertical access to the building. This divides the floor plan of the space, which is about 3,928 square feet, into two lateral hallways and a large room at the back located under an inner courtyard. Entry to the facilities is gained through one of the hallways, where the reception counter is located. This area receives natural light through the street door entrance, which is made of glass.

The administrative area and the individual offices are located within the large room that communicates with the hallway. Located under the courtyard, the space is fully bathed in natural light due to the geometric skylights.

The workshop is situated in the other hallway. Its natural light comes from the opening to the street, which is visually protected with an acid-etched glass window. Both side hallways follow the common neighboring walls and enter the central area, forming a series of cubicles where the restrooms and storage are located.

Poured concrete was the treatment chosen for the floors. Screens made of light-colored laminated wood and glass doors were selected to prevent the loss of natural light and visual distractions.

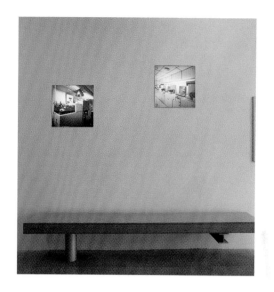

The interiors have been decorated with exquisite restraint and maximum efficiency. All furniture pieces throughout the different areas were especially designed for these offices. In this instance, the laminated wood becomes the protagonist.

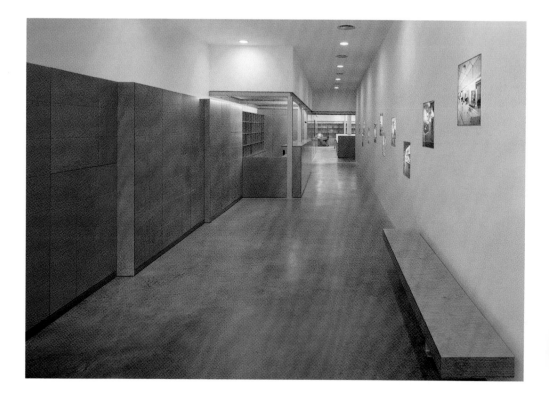

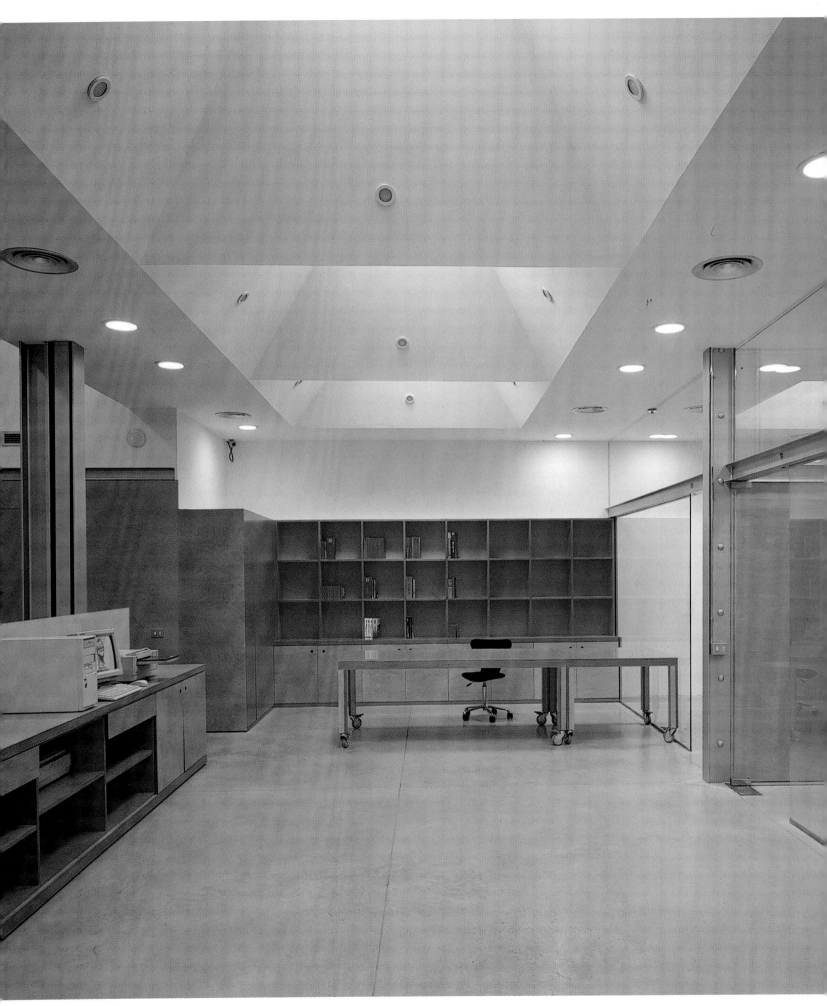

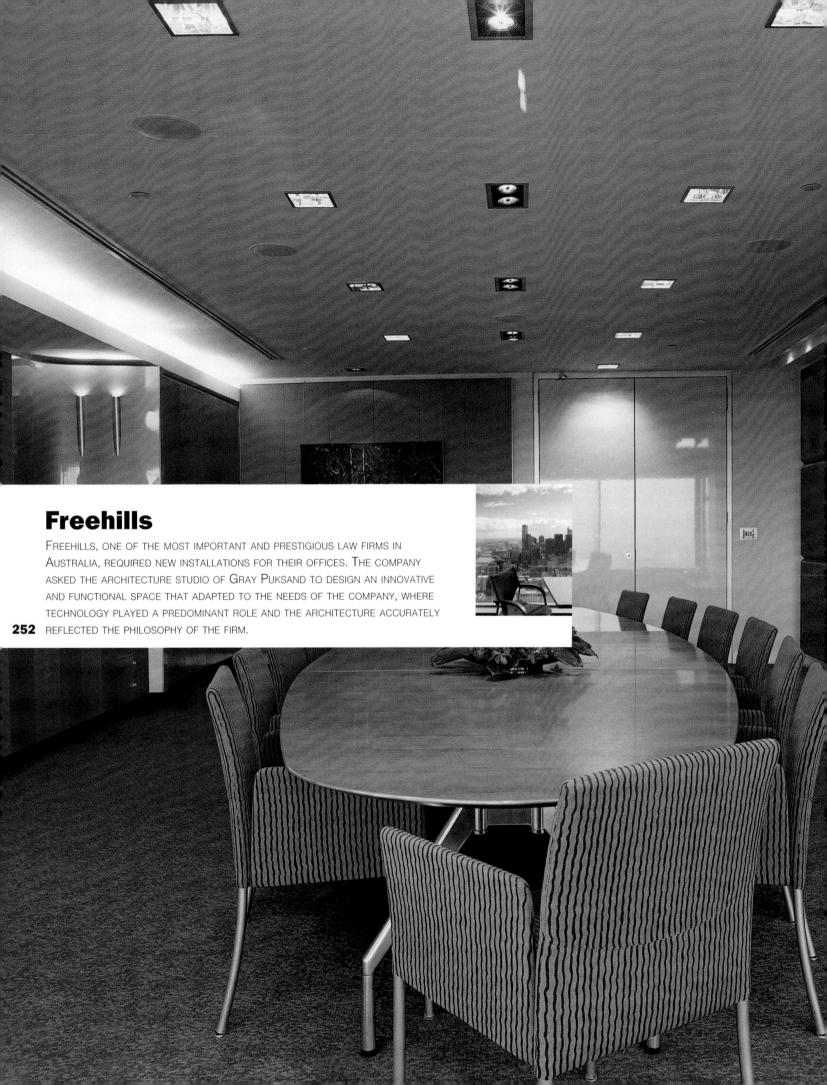

Freehills

FREEHILLS, ONE OF THE MOST IMPORTANT AND PRESTIGIOUS LAW FIRMS IN AUSTRALIA, REQUIRED NEW INSTALLATIONS FOR THEIR OFFICES. THE COMPANY ASKED THE ARCHITECTURE STUDIO OF GRAY PUKSAND TO DESIGN AN INNOVATIVE AND FUNCTIONAL SPACE THAT ADAPTED TO THE NEEDS OF THE COMPANY, WHERE TECHNOLOGY PLAYED A PREDOMINANT ROLE AND THE ARCHITECTURE ACCURATELY REFLECTED THE PHILOSOPHY OF THE FIRM.

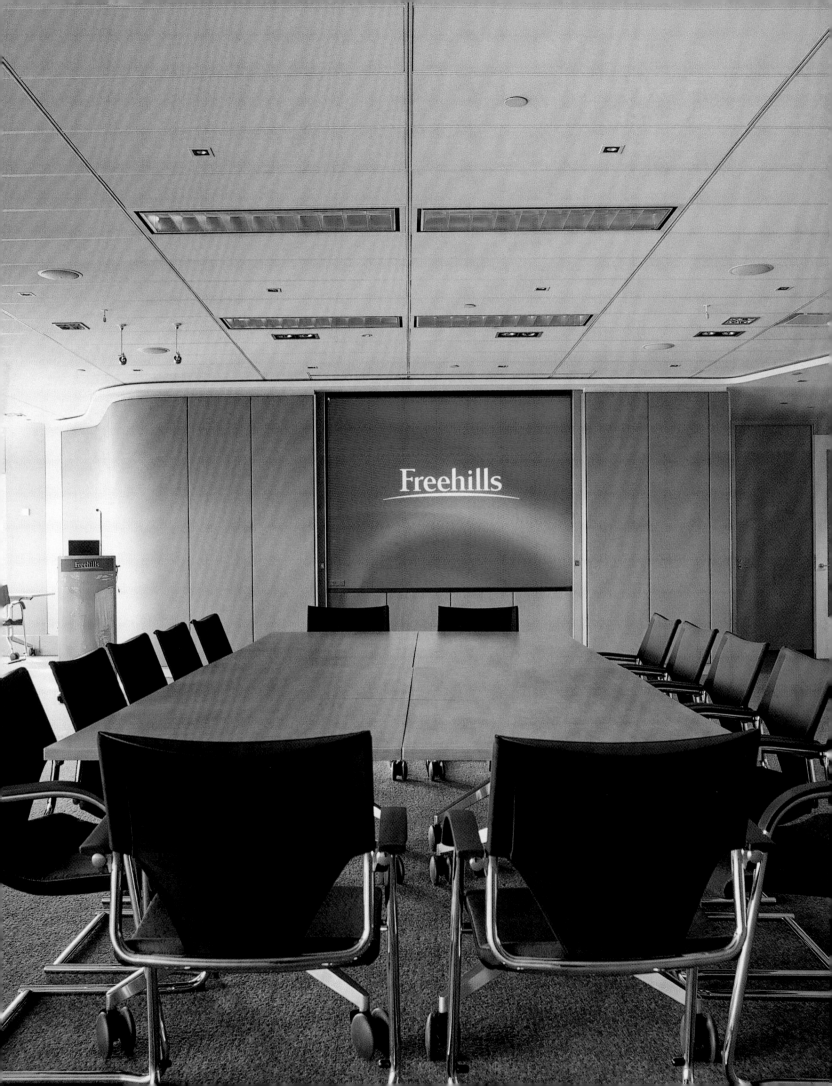

Freehills

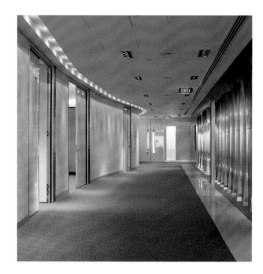

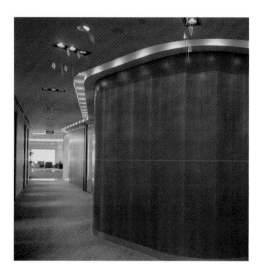

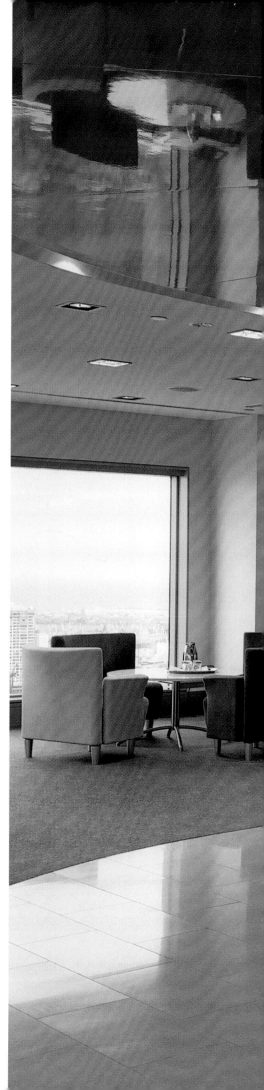

The offices are located on the 42nd floor of an already existing building in Melbourne, Australia. The goal of the project was to preserve part of the original characteristics of the building while at the same time responding to the guidelines of the client. Therefore, the functional requirements dictated the design of a free-flowing and flexible space where the different work areas—meeting rooms, offices, common areas, dining room, teleconferencing rooms, and reading rooms—are connected in a natural and organized manner, allowing the functions for which they were intended to take place with maximum comfort. The architectural solutions delineate functional and comfortable spaces that encourage the discovery of warm and informal spaces in line with the formal beauty yet respectful of the practical and ergonomic needs to guarantee the best performance.

Playing with the concept of "open and shut," public spaces and closed spaces (offices and more private areas where there is less traffic) are created by defining and designing the rooms according to their function and activities.

A contemporary and austere decorative style has been used for the different rooms and areas, free of excess and the superfluous elements that come from combining different styles. The result is a highly functional space that is visually very attractive and ordered.

Architect: **Gray Puksand**
Client: **Freehills**
Location: **Melbourne, Australia**
Construction Date: **2001**
Photography: **Shania Shegedyn**

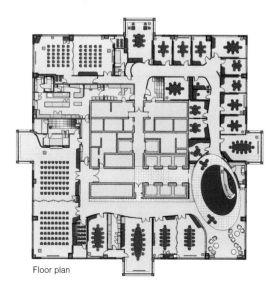

Floor plan

In some spaces, including the reception area and the lobby, the light, materials, and the color tones are skillfully handled to achieve attractive results. The play of reflections and combinations creates a comfortable and functional environment.

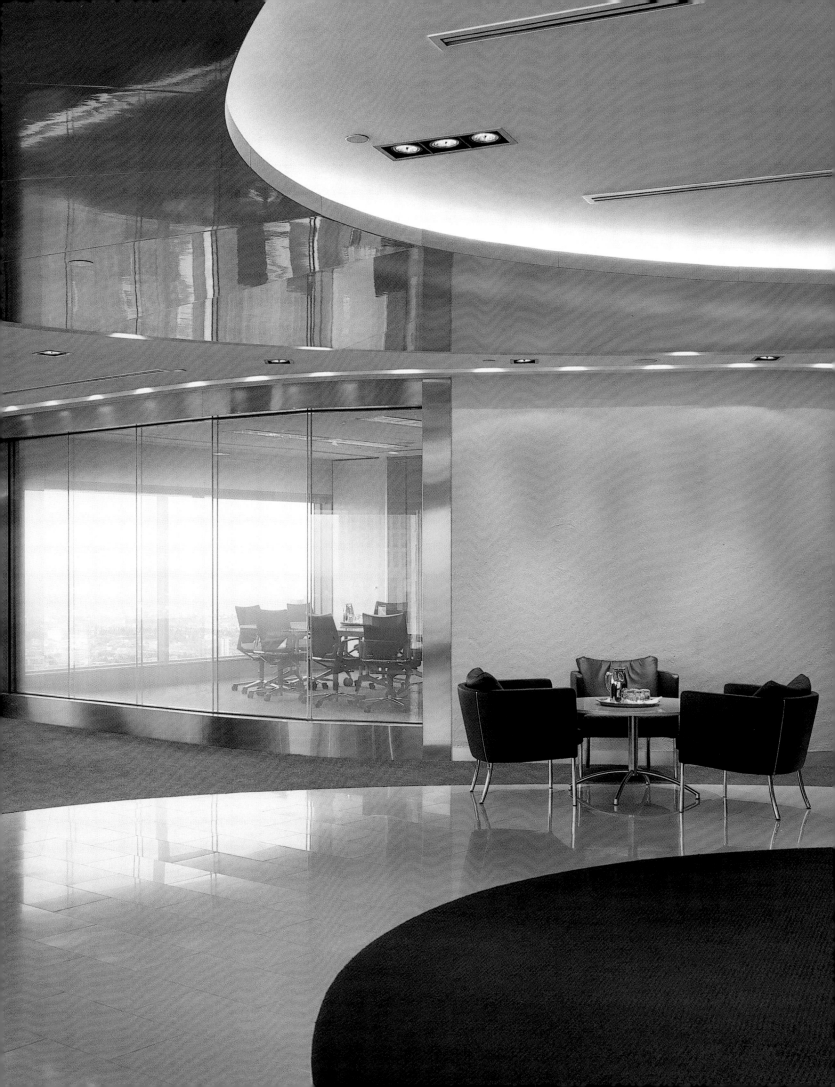

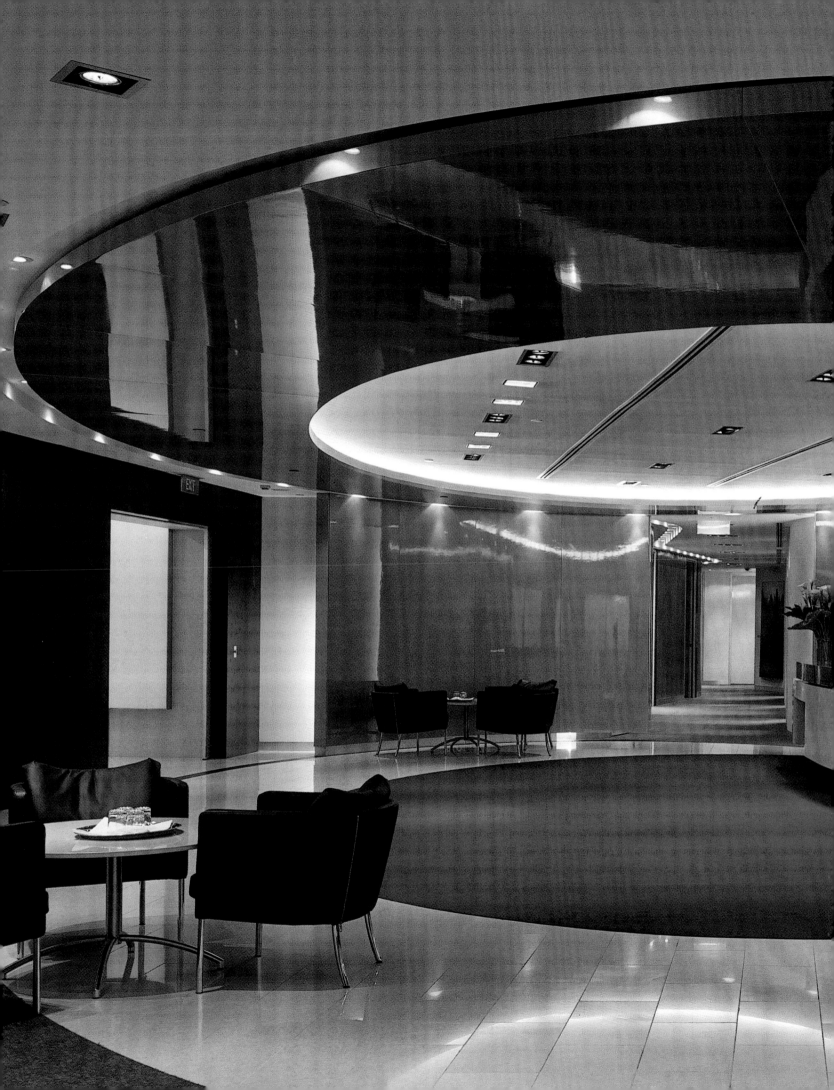

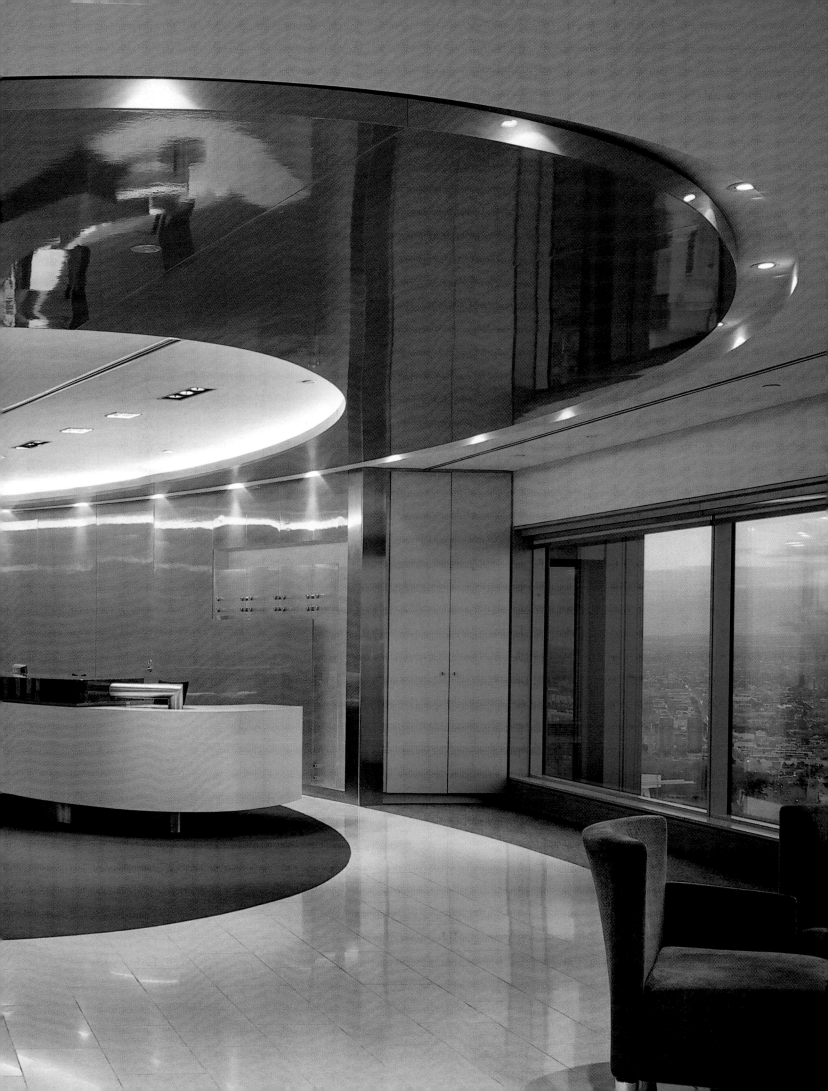

Remodeled Spaces

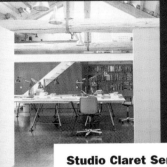

Studio Claret Serrahima

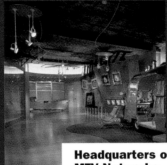

**Headquarters of
MTV Networks**

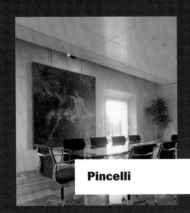

Pincelli

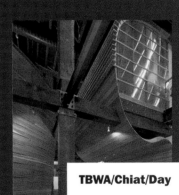

TBWA/Chiat/Day

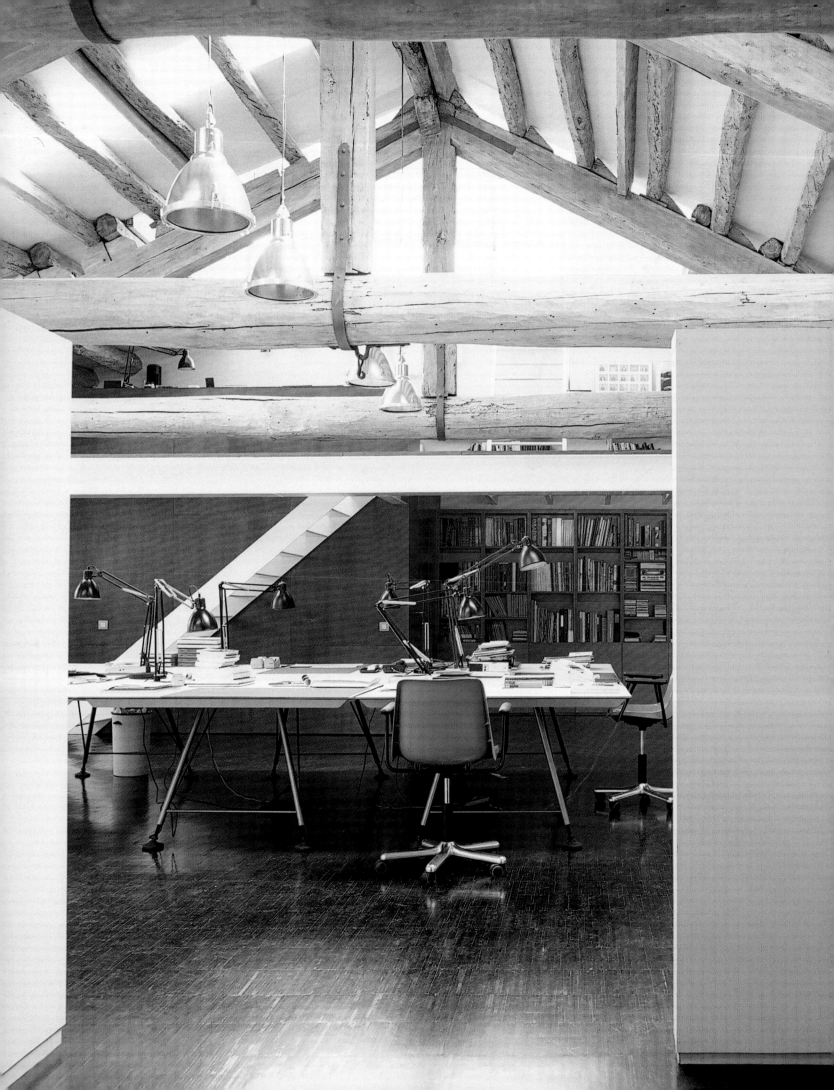

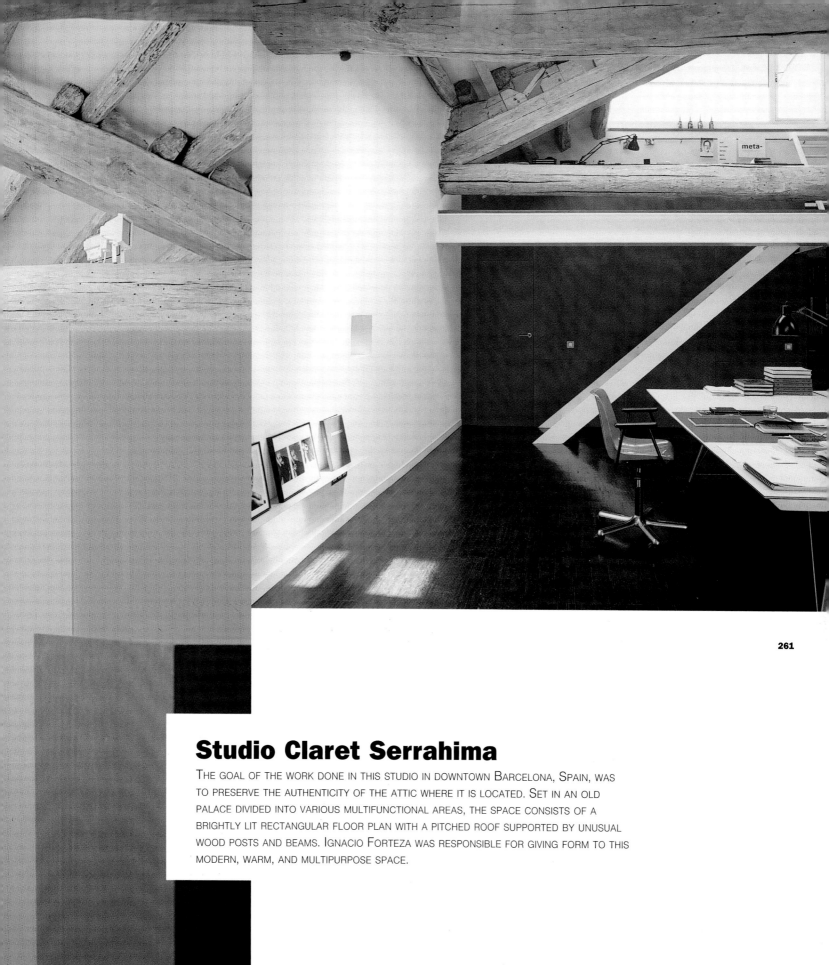

Studio Claret Serrahima

THE GOAL OF THE WORK DONE IN THIS STUDIO IN DOWNTOWN BARCELONA, SPAIN, WAS
TO PRESERVE THE AUTHENTICITY OF THE ATTIC WHERE IT IS LOCATED. SET IN AN OLD
PALACE DIVIDED INTO VARIOUS MULTIFUNCTIONAL AREAS, THE SPACE CONSISTS OF A
BRIGHTLY LIT RECTANGULAR FLOOR PLAN WITH A PITCHED ROOF SUPPORTED BY UNUSUAL
WOOD POSTS AND BEAMS. IGNACIO FORTEZA WAS RESPONSIBLE FOR GIVING FORM TO THIS
MODERN, WARM, AND MULTIPURPOSE SPACE.

Studio Claret Serrahima

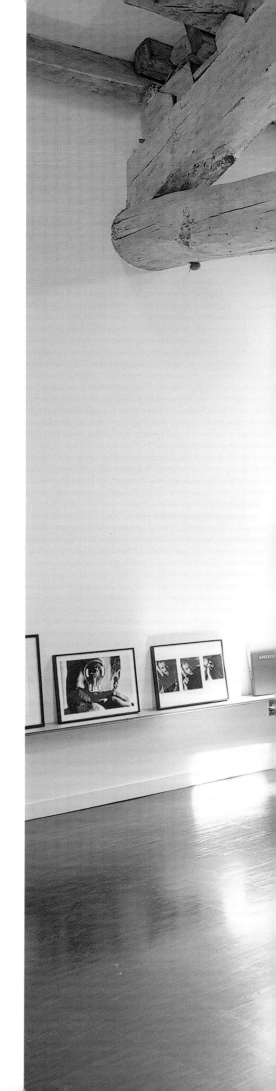

Interior Designer: **Ignacio Forteza**
(Forteza Carbonell Associats)
Client: **Studio Claret Serrahima**
Location: **Barcelona, Spain**
Construction Date: **1999**
Photography: **Eugeni Pons**

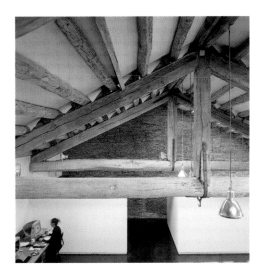

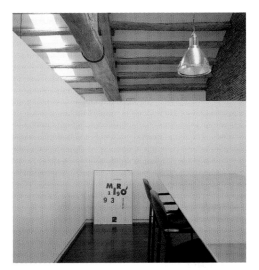

One of the main objectives for the construction was to direct natural light into the space, to give the environment a functionality that was non-existent, and to achieve a balanced and modern feeling.

The renovation required the remodeling of an empty space about·1,184 square feet and of a considerable height (11.5 feet at the lowest point) as well as to create an entry to a 484-square-foot terrace that was inaccessible until then. A mezzanine was created to get to the terrace. The library, bathroom, and kitchen are located below this area.

Due to the characteristics of the space and to the activity for which it was intended (a graphic design studio), separate workrooms are not needed. It was decided from the beginning to create zones without visually breaking up the space. This allows the rest of the area to be seen from the reception zone and the meeting room.

In front of the reception area, an L-shaped divider creates a space that is used as a meeting room. The work area is defined by a large central table (made by combining three tables), which does not need to be computerized, and a custom-designed side table that holds computer hardware.

The natural light enters the space through a glass wall that faces the terrace and through new large skylights. Artificial light comes from the large, industrial-type fixtures that hang from the ceiling and provides more general lighting. Flexor lamps are used for task lighting.

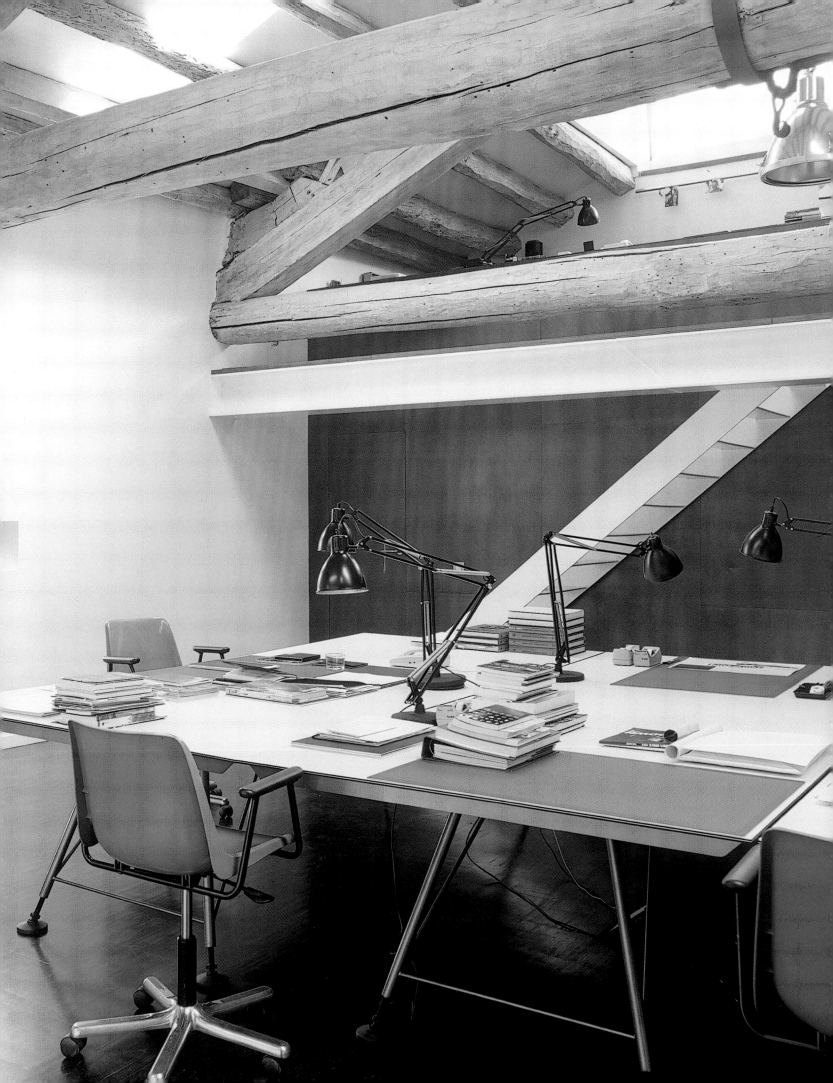

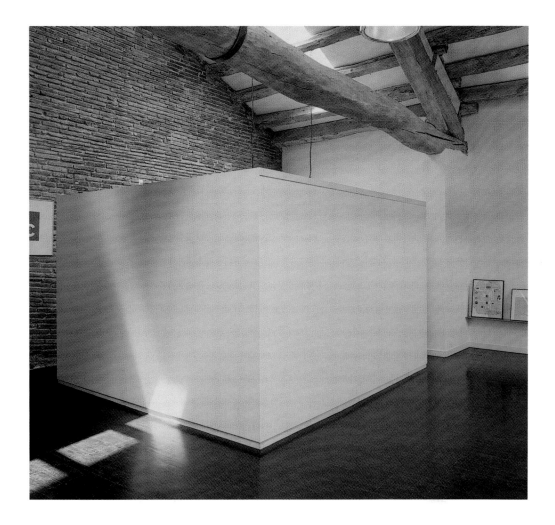

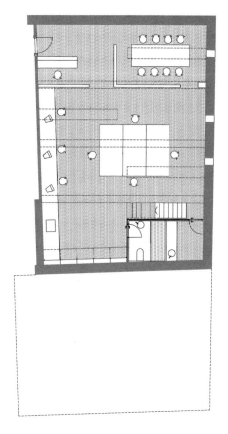

Ground floor

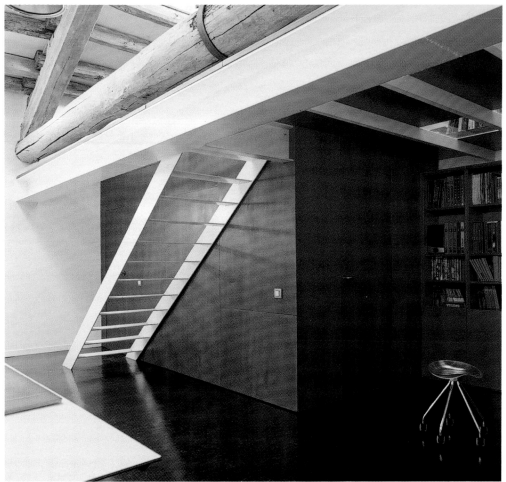

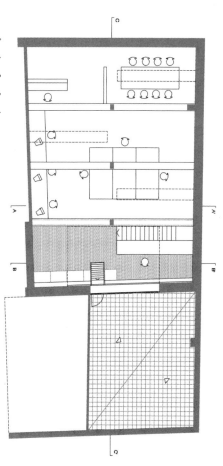

Mezzanine

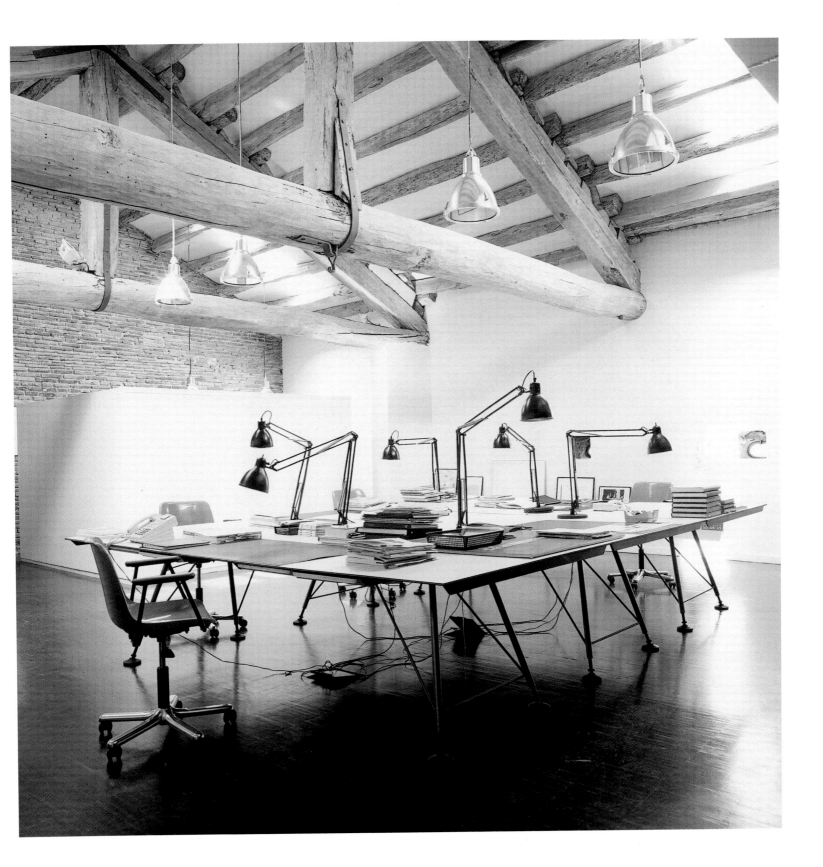

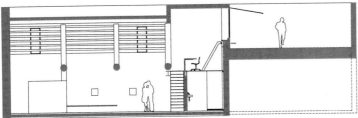

Section

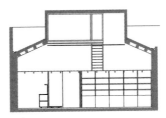

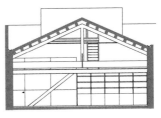

Section

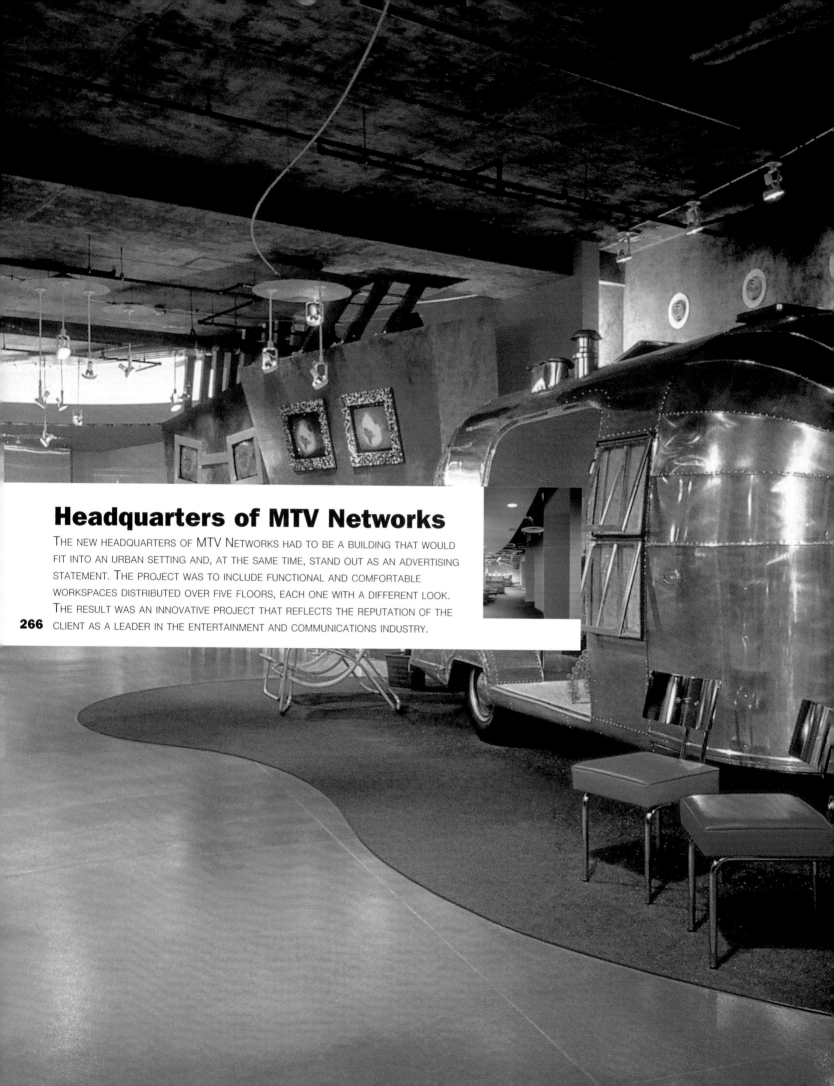

Headquarters of MTV Networks

THE NEW HEADQUARTERS OF MTV NETWORKS HAD TO BE A BUILDING THAT WOULD FIT INTO AN URBAN SETTING AND, AT THE SAME TIME, STAND OUT AS AN ADVERTISING STATEMENT. THE PROJECT WAS TO INCLUDE FUNCTIONAL AND COMFORTABLE WORKSPACES DISTRIBUTED OVER FIVE FLOORS, EACH ONE WITH A DIFFERENT LOOK. THE RESULT WAS AN INNOVATIVE PROJECT THAT REFLECTS THE REPUTATION OF THE CLIENT AS A LEADER IN THE ENTERTAINMENT AND COMMUNICATIONS INDUSTRY.

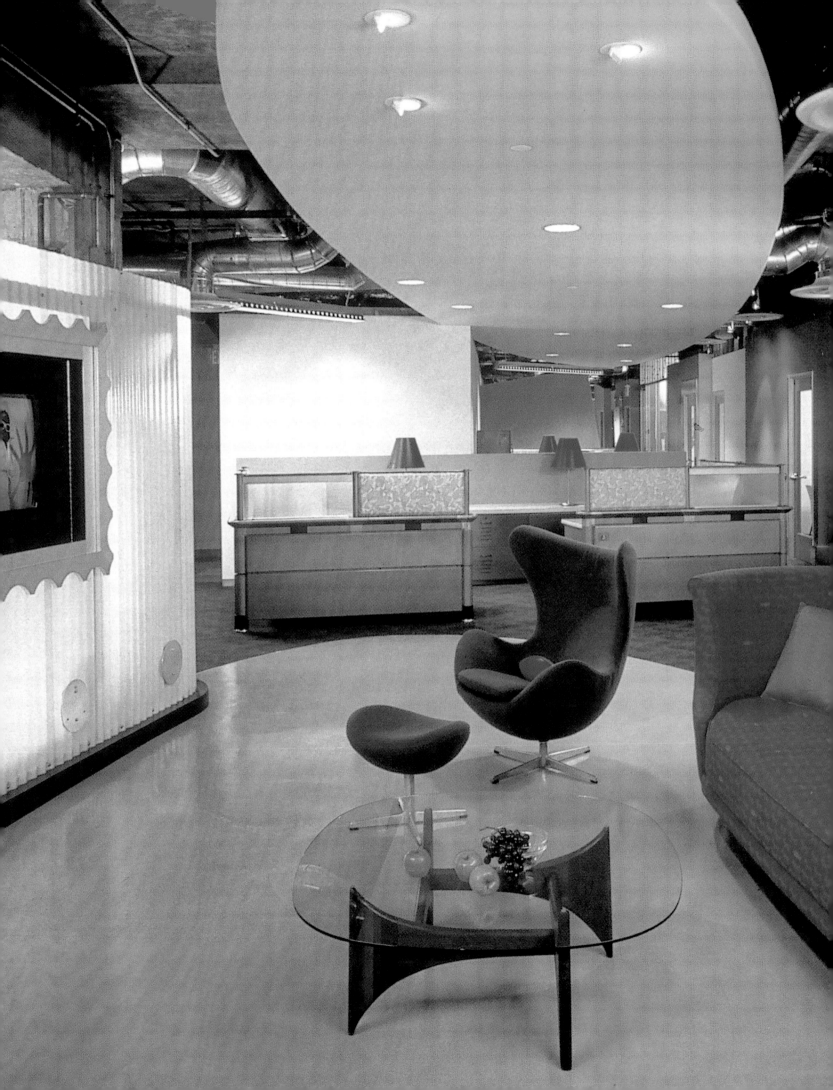

Headquarters of MTV Networks

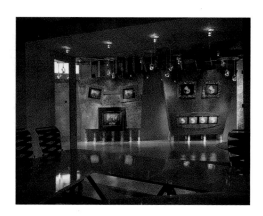

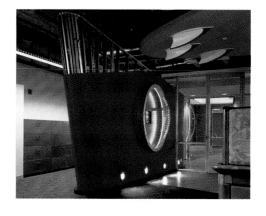

Architect: **Felderman & Keatinge Associates**
Client: **MTV Networks**
Location: **Santa Monica, California, United States**
Construction Date: **1999**
Photography: **Toshi Yoshimi**

One of the requirements was to come up with a lobby whose structure would relate to the ocean and the surrounding vegetation. The solution was to create a plaza with a sand-colored pavement that projects into the lobby and reflects the entryways of the traditional architecture of the area, where the division between outdoors and indoors is blurred.

The facade consists of metal panels that rise three and five stories high, creating a profile that is evocative of the ocean waves. A huge sign in the form of a ship displays the name of the company in wavy steel letters.

Inside, a 1957 aluminum trailer welcomes visitors and functions as a waiting room. A pink rug, black-and-white linoleum floors, and the Formica of the kitchen table are some of the decorative elements that recreate the '50s flavor. Six television screens built into the wall next to the trailer reproduce the shapes of faces. The reception counter, which is the hull of a boat clad in aluminum, and a copper-top table for meetings are also located in this area.

The office spaces are separated with low partition walls that resemble houses with painted windows and trim, and fences with hedges and bushes. The different areas, according to the clients' wishes, had to be informal and dynamic. This is why the conference room, for example, was designed as a living room, with television sets, rugs, and sofas.

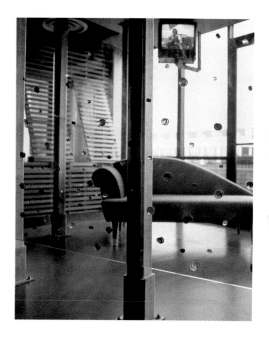

The fixtures and structure can be perceived among the decorative details and the actual office spaces. The interior combines a stark concrete framework with sophisticated coverings, finishes, and materials, such as painted wood, tweed wool fabrics, sheer drapery, and metal panels.

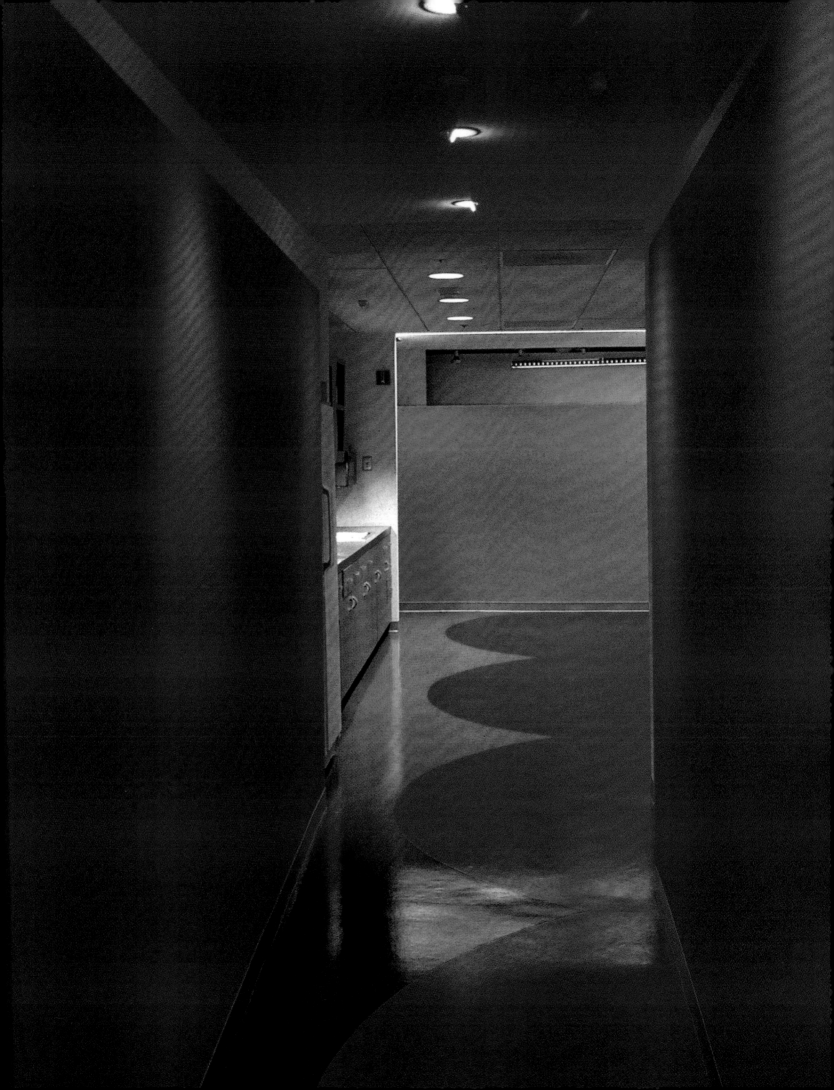

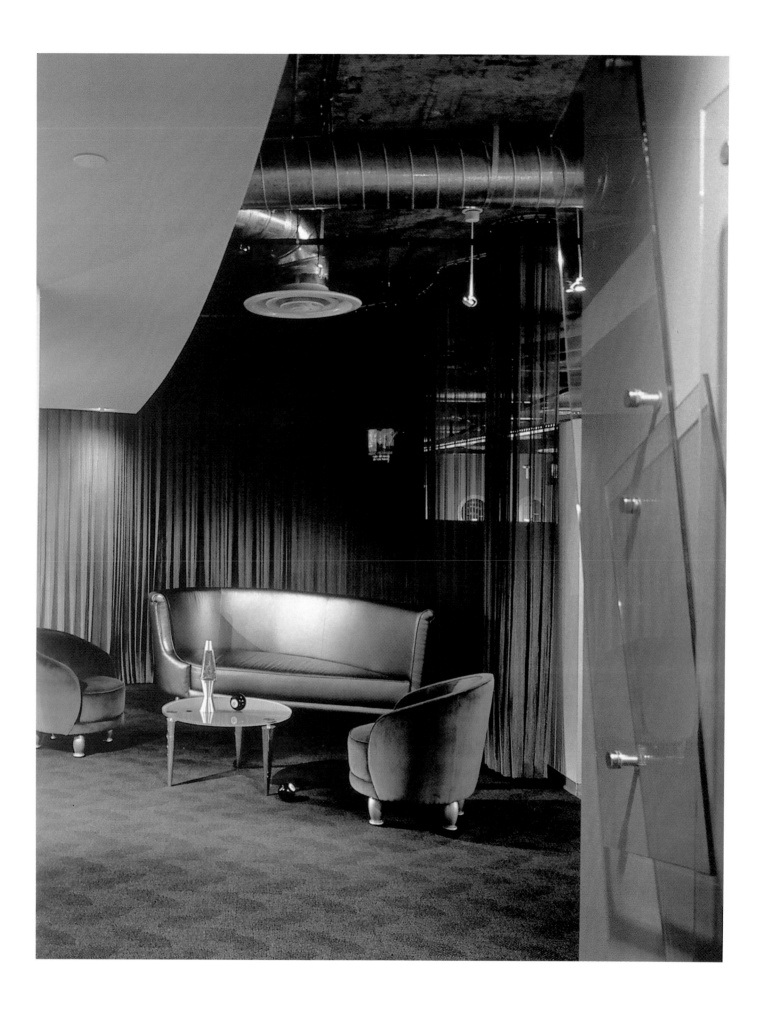

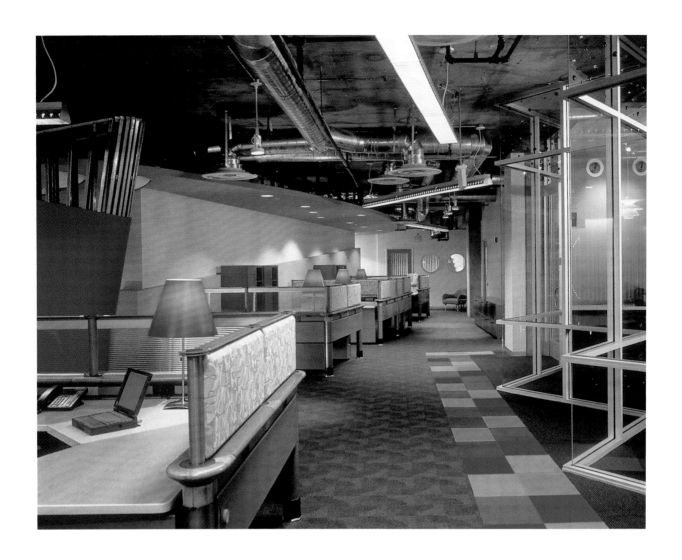

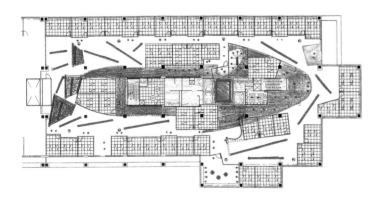

First floor

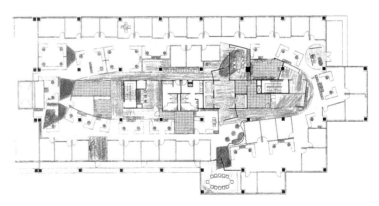

Third floor

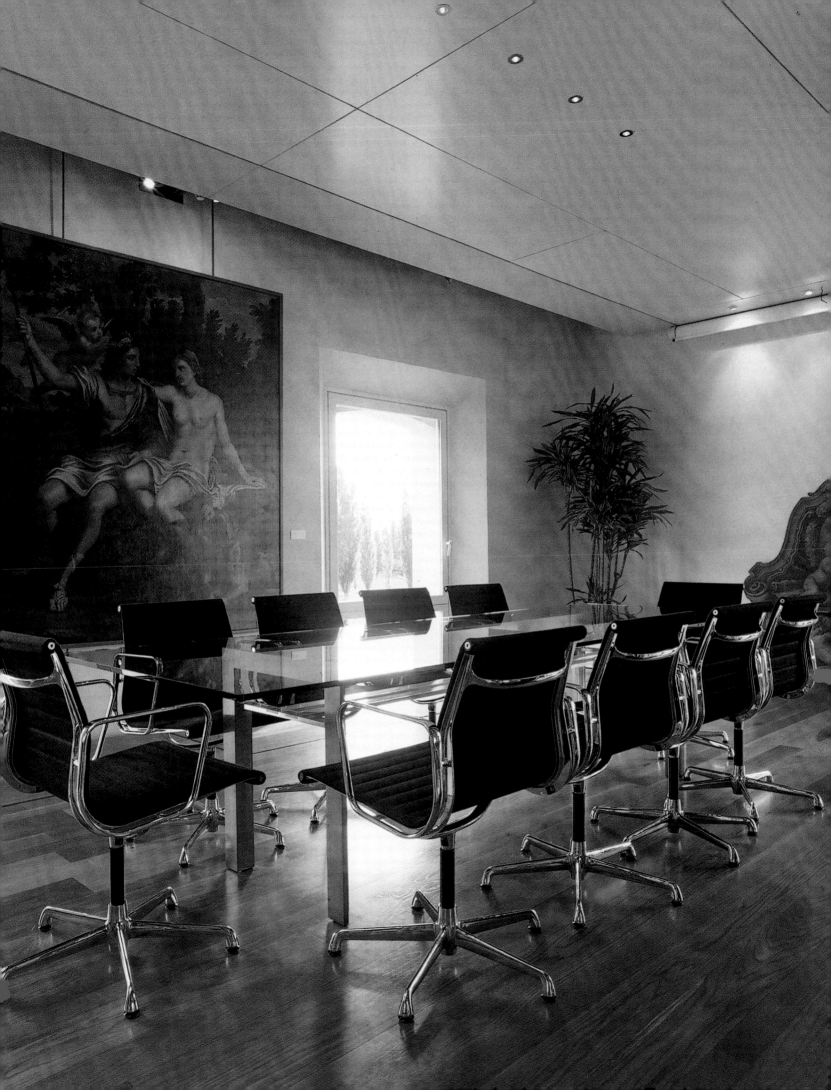

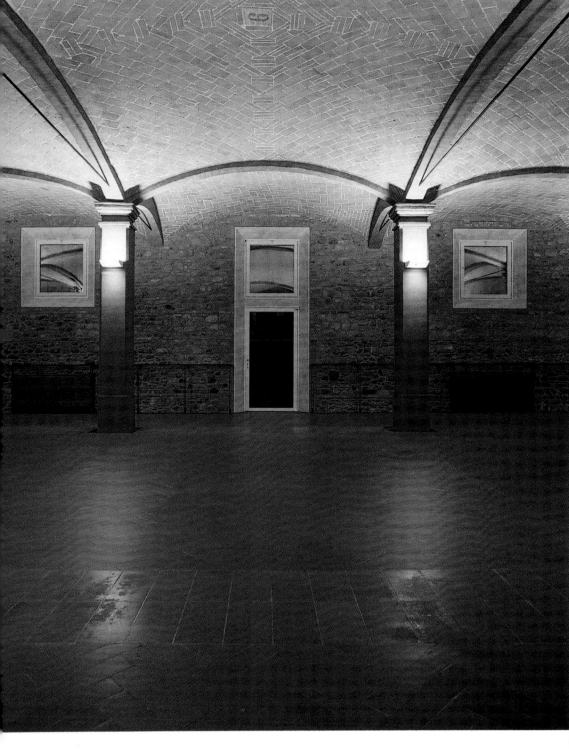

Pincelli

These offices are located in the old stables of a duke, an impressive property built in 1781 that belonged to the aristocratic family Estense de Sassuolo. Before the renovation, which made it possible to save the building while refurbishing it with everything needed for a new function, the structure was in very poor condition. The rehabilitation allowed for the recovery of an emblematic building and the construction of modern and efficient installations in which past and present go hand in hand.

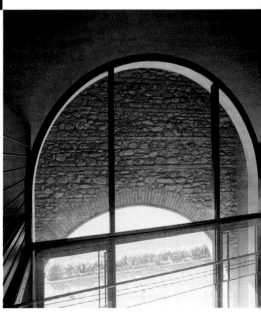

Pincelli

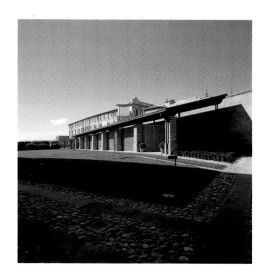

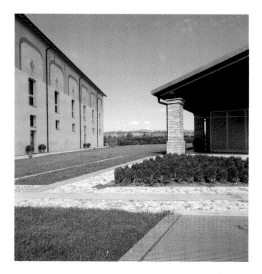

Architect: **Domenico Biondi, Progettisti Associati**
Client: **Pincelli**
Location: **Sassuolo, Italy**
Construction Date: **1999**
Photography: **Matteo Piazza**

The first phase of the remodeling consisted of saving the structure while preserving, whenever possible, the least-damaged original features. Therefore, the original cross beams and roof were put back into place, and the structural walls and the profiles of some of the vaulted arches were repaired. Another significant phase of the project was the restoration of the colors of the exterior walls, which were covered with graffiti.

The project designated the first floor of the building, which has different levels, as the headquarters of an important commercial consulting firm that needed its own modern and comfortable space. This requirement determined the treatment of the site as a modern and rational volume of iron and glass, whose rooms were organized based on their function. This solution allowed the original spaces to be preserved while adapting them using reversible methods. This complex undertaking achieved a balance between past and present. Stone, wood, iron, and glass bring to life this suggestive and successful combination of styles and periods. The stone and the wood are reminders of the building's past, while the iron evokes the present.

Enclosing several walls with glass allows the light to filter through, creating a subtle and attractive play of light and shadow while opening the interiors to the exceptional surroundings of the building. The final result is a project combining numerous successful and efficient solutions.

The remodeling operation has respected the original construction at all times, faithfully preserving the volume and lines of the old building as well as the exceptional site where it is located. The project has created a new space that encompasses the beauty and the stateliness of the past and the efficiency and functionality of the present.

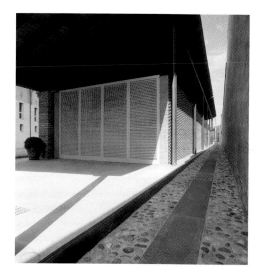

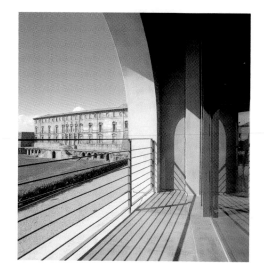

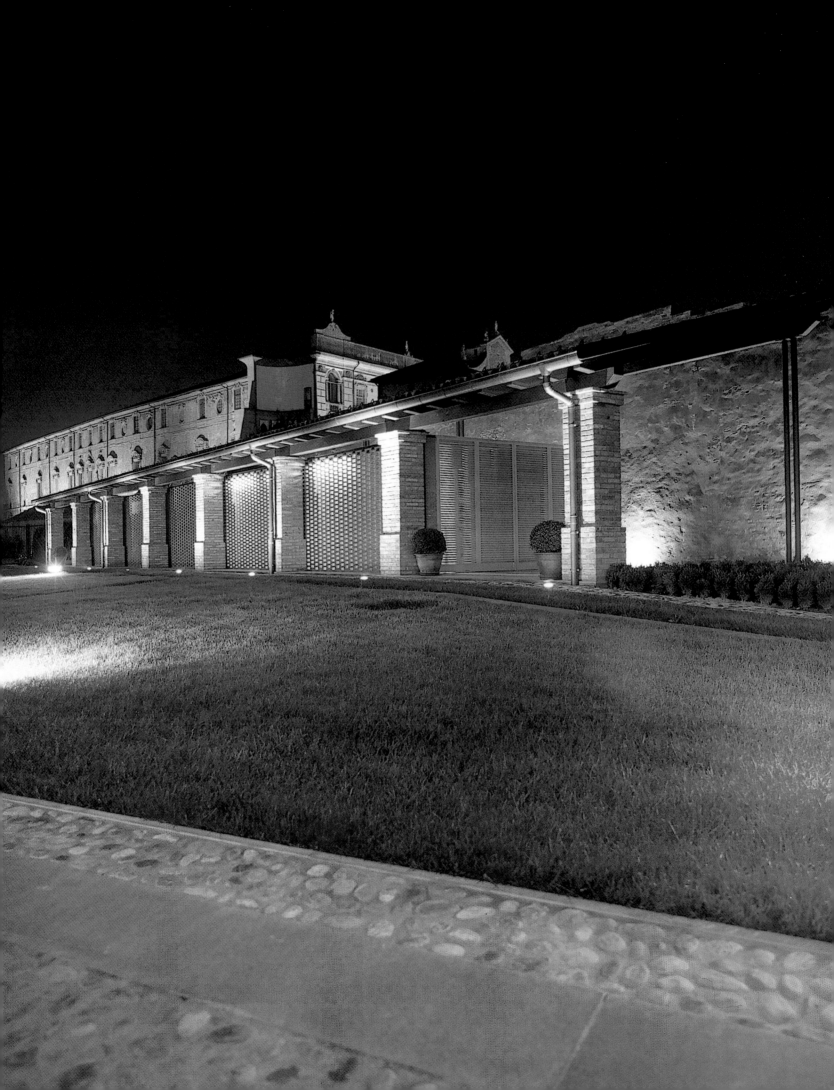

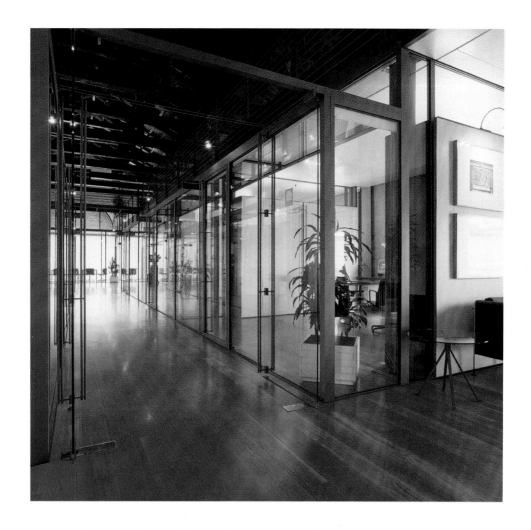

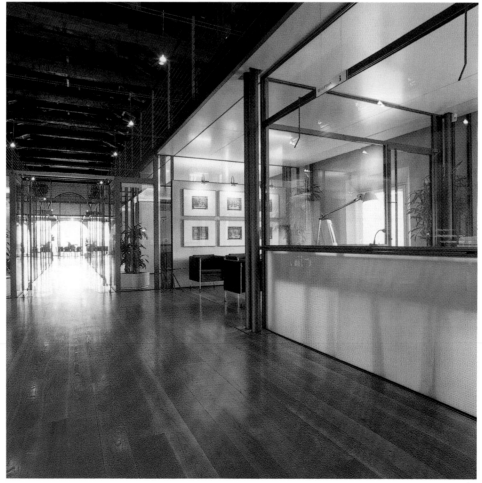

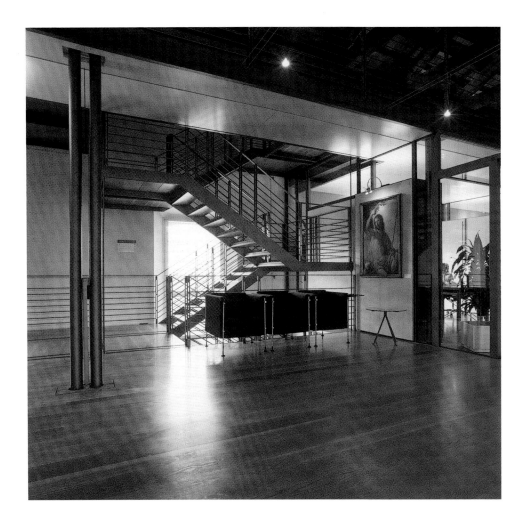

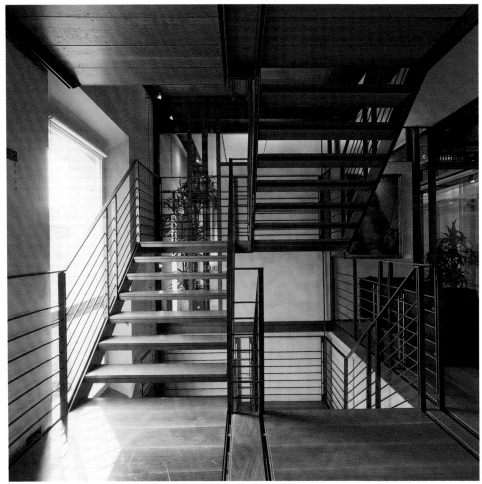

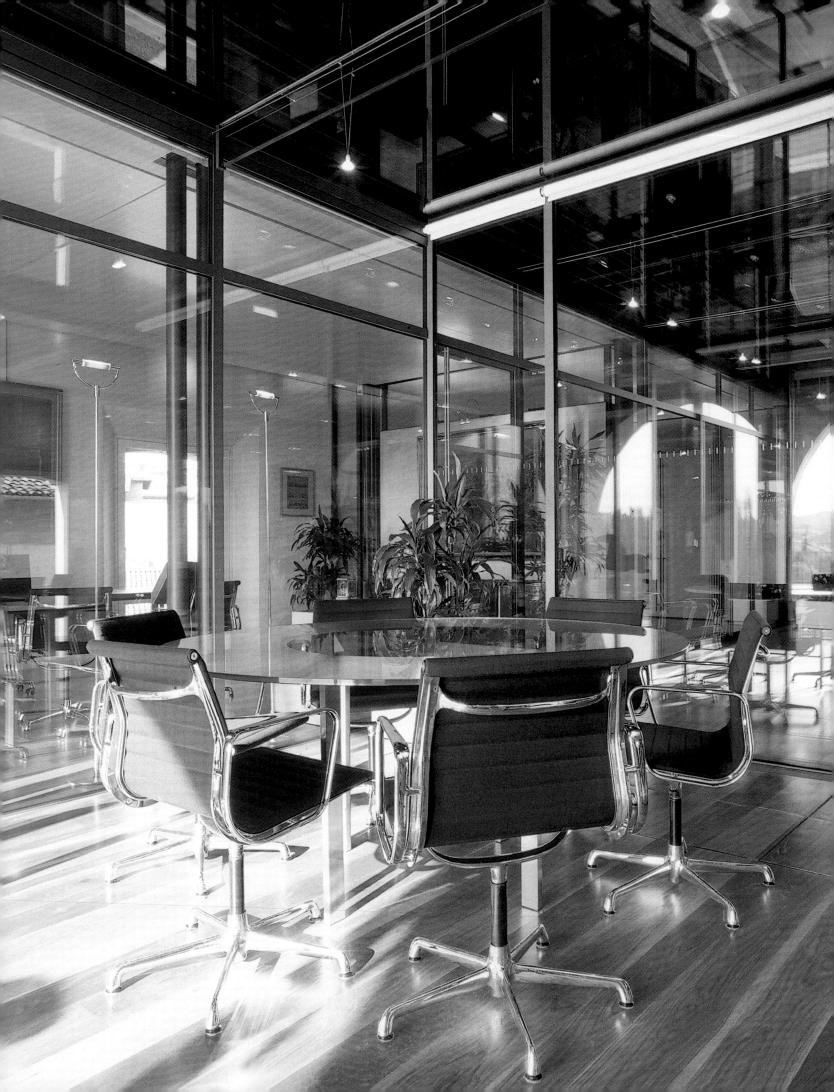

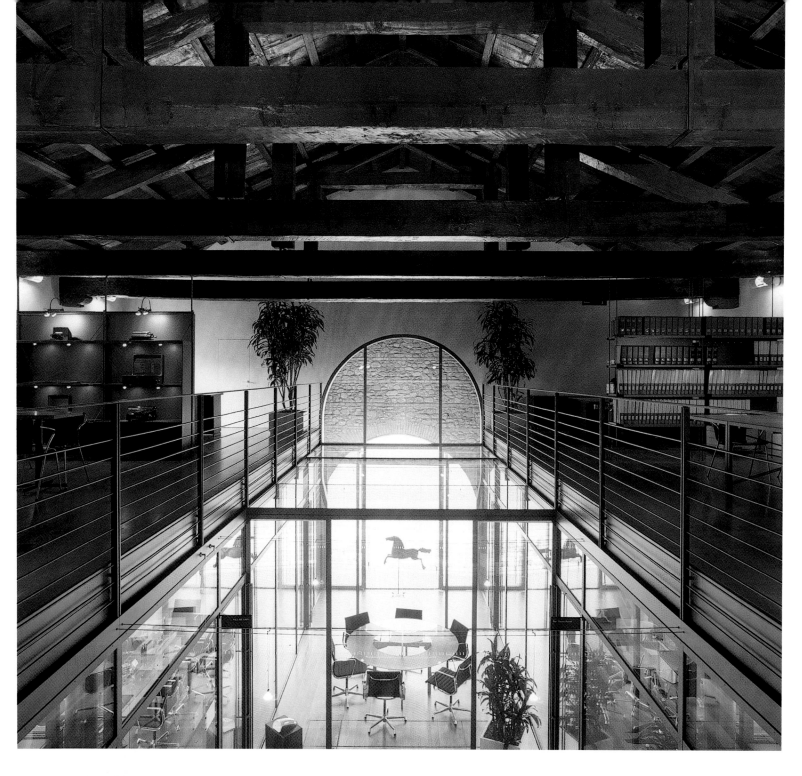

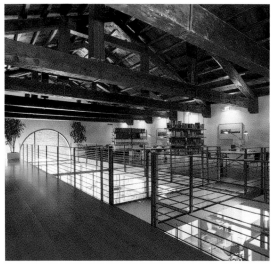

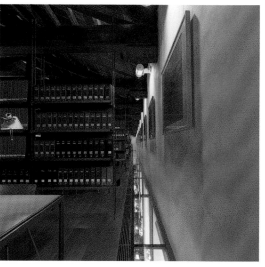

The interiors are decorated with great
care to allow the architecture to be the
true protagonist. The fluidity of the spaces,
the aesthetic beauty, and the functionality
are the key elements of its success.

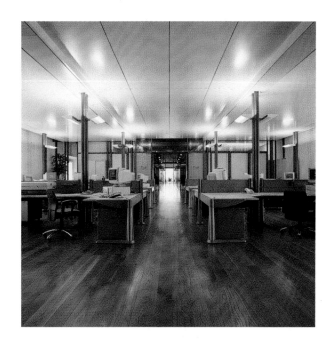

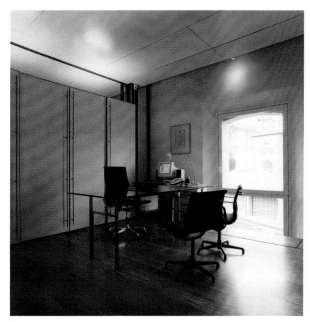

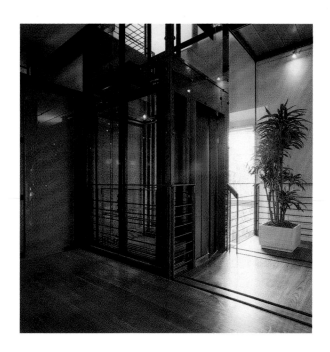

The furnishings were conceived following the same design criteria, attempting to minimize the use of materials to convey a unified and compact image with a reduced but successful palette of colors and elements.

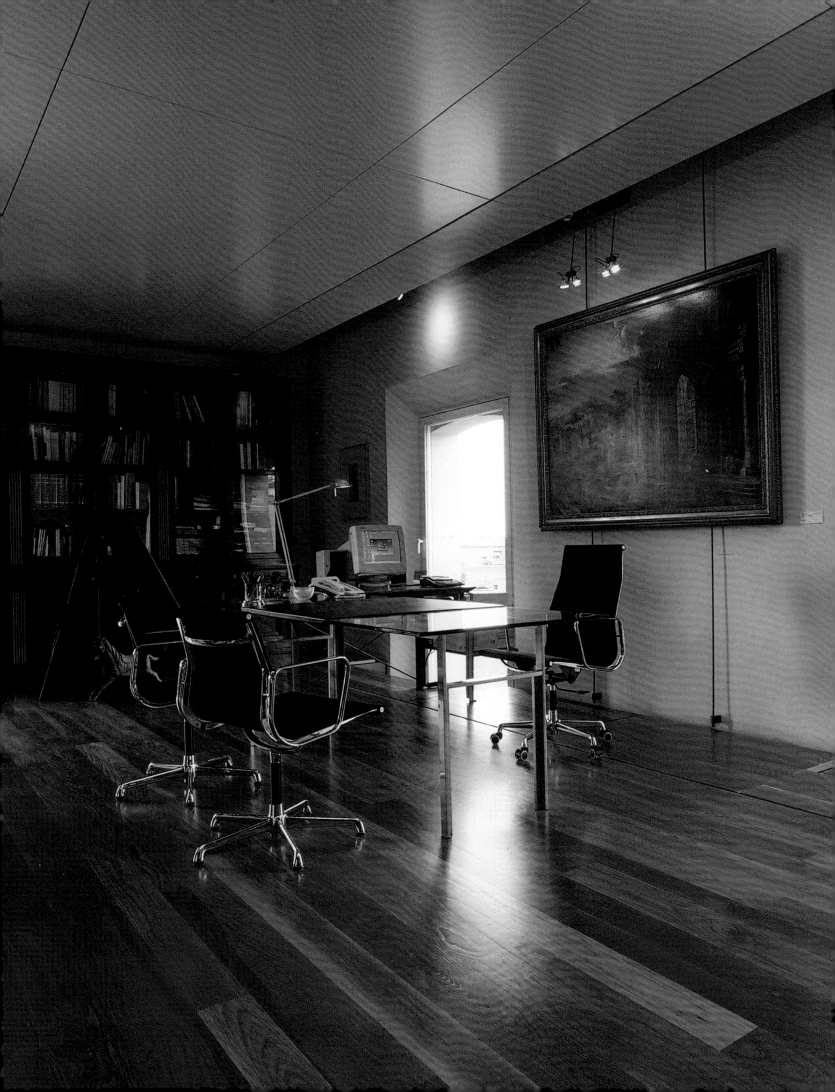

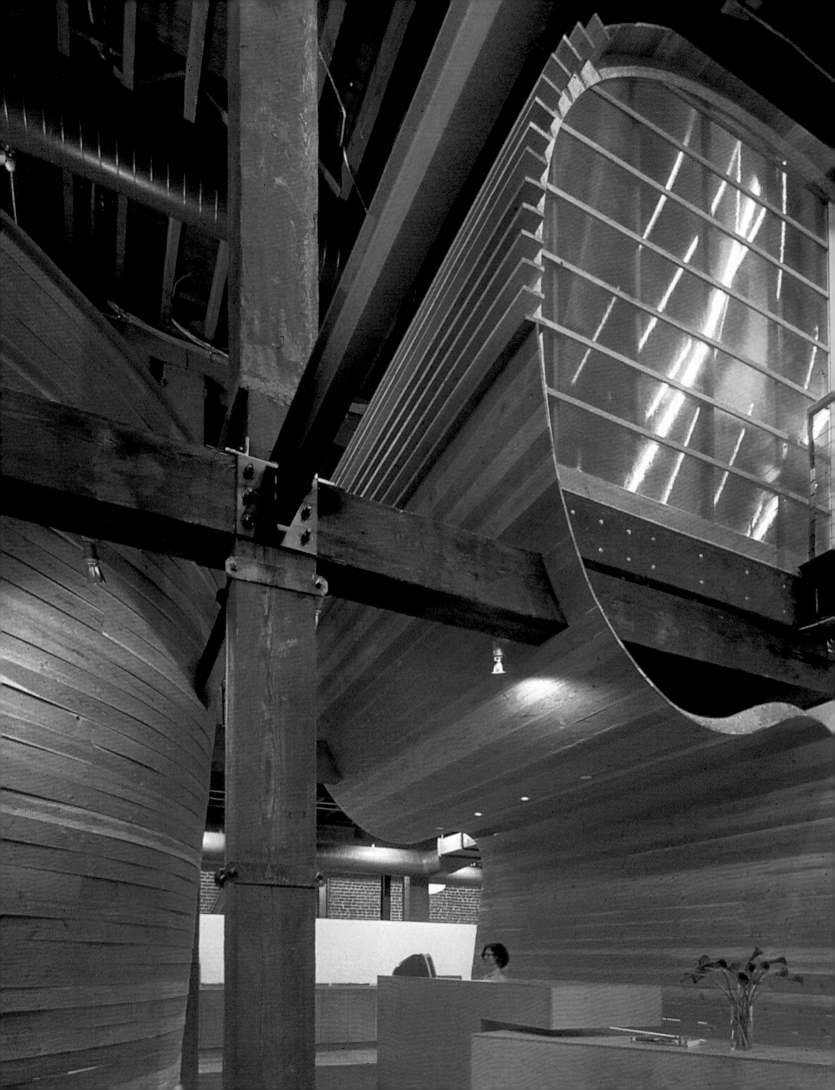

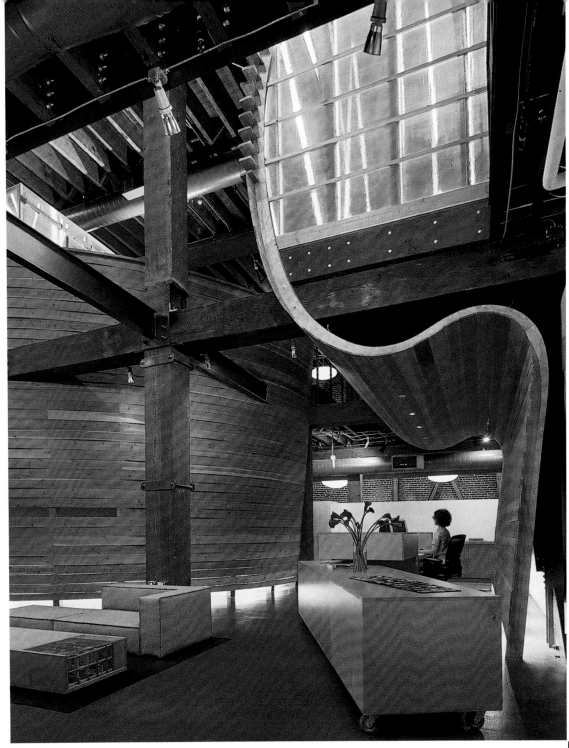

TBWA/Chiat/Day

THE RENOVATION OF THIS BUILDING ALLOWED THE CREATION OF A NEW AND PERSONAL ARCHI-
TECTURAL IDENTITY FOR THE OFFICE OF THE TBWA/CHIAT/DAY AGENCY IN SAN FRANCISCO,
CALIFORNIA. THE PROJECT GAVE FORM TO A CAPTIVATING AND IMAGINATIVE DESIGN THAT
DOES NOT IGNORE THE FUNCTIONALITY OF THE INSTALLATIONS DESPITE THE BEAUTY AND
UNIQUENESS OF THEIR FORMS. THIS IS A PROJECT THAT REINVENTS THE TRADITIONAL
CONCEPT OF THE OFFICE AND PROPOSES NEW WAYS OF UNDERSTANDING WORKSPACES.

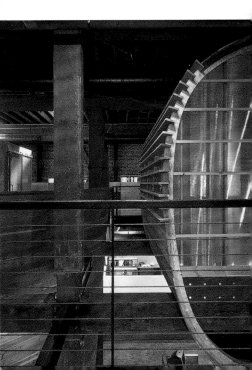

TBWA/Chiat/Day

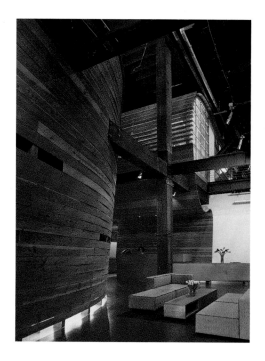

Architect: **Marmol Radziner + Associates**
Client: **TBWA/Chiat/Day**
Location: **San Francisco, California, United States**
Construction Date: **2001**
Photography: **Benny Chan**

The client approached the architecture studio of Marmol Radziner + Associates with one clear requirement: to design a creative, warm, modern, and visually striking space capable of accommodating 170 employees. The design plan, which involves different levels, incorporates vertical connections between spaces so that natural light abounds and bathes every corner, creating an evocative play of light and shadow.

Since the structure of the existing construction, including brick walls, wood ceilings and columns, and large glass windows, was preserved, the project began with a head start. An open space was created, taking advantage of all these elements, and connects the different areas and departments in a fluid and natural way. A large, curved wood structure becomes the element that defines and connects the first and second levels. It is a striking curvilinear volume of unquestionable visual power around which the space is distributed. The reception area is located below this. Here, the sinuous movement unfolds vertically to delineate the ceiling of the second floor, encompassing a unique meeting room and conference room.

The furniture has been carefully selected and is arranged to create several informal, relaxed, warm, and modern spaces where ideas flow freely and work becomes a pleasant task.

The choice of wood as one of the main materials, the clever combination of colors, and the successful handling of light helped create interiors that are well-balanced, warm, and flowing. Here, the architecture is the true protagonist, and work ceases to be routine.

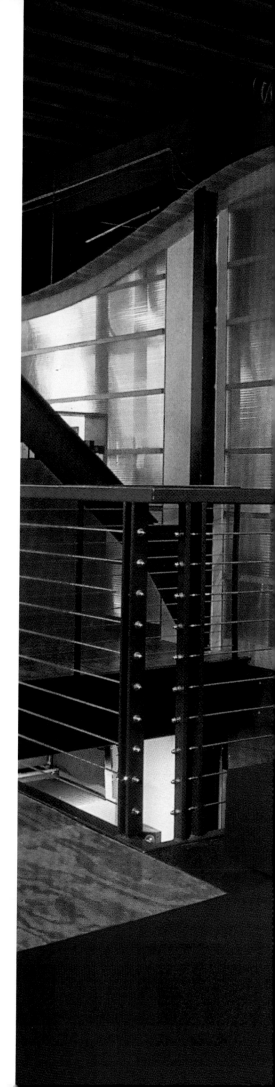

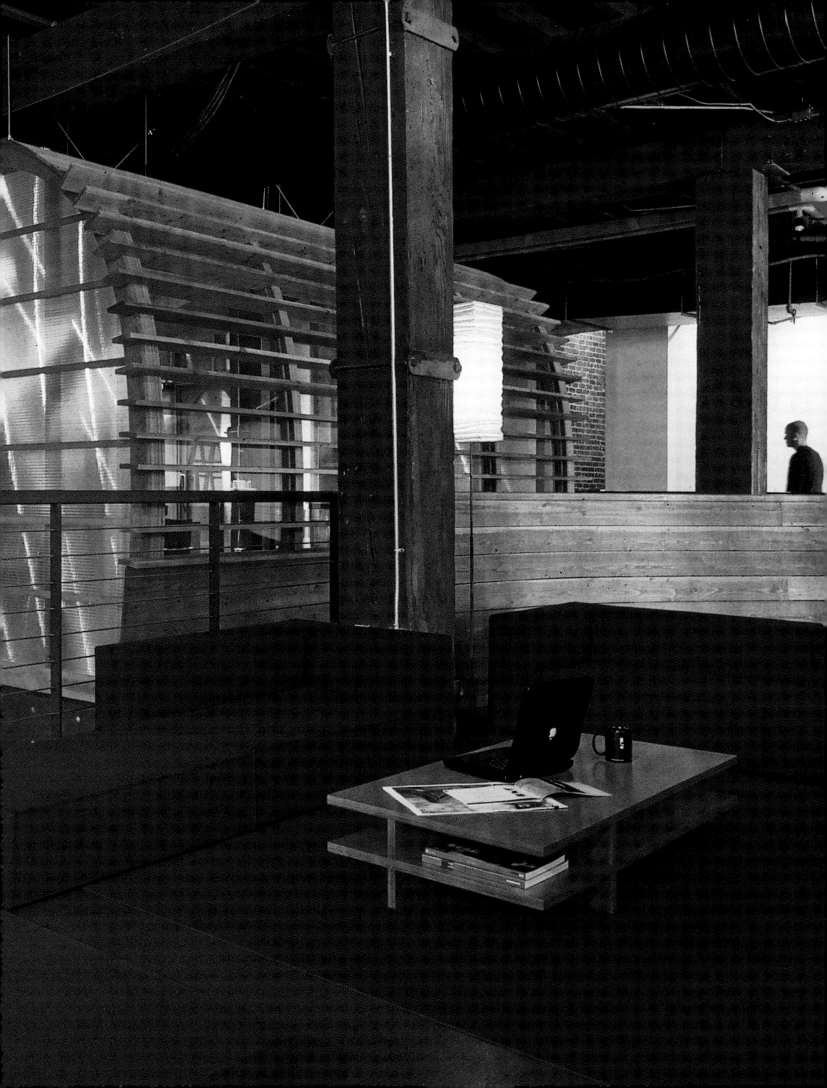

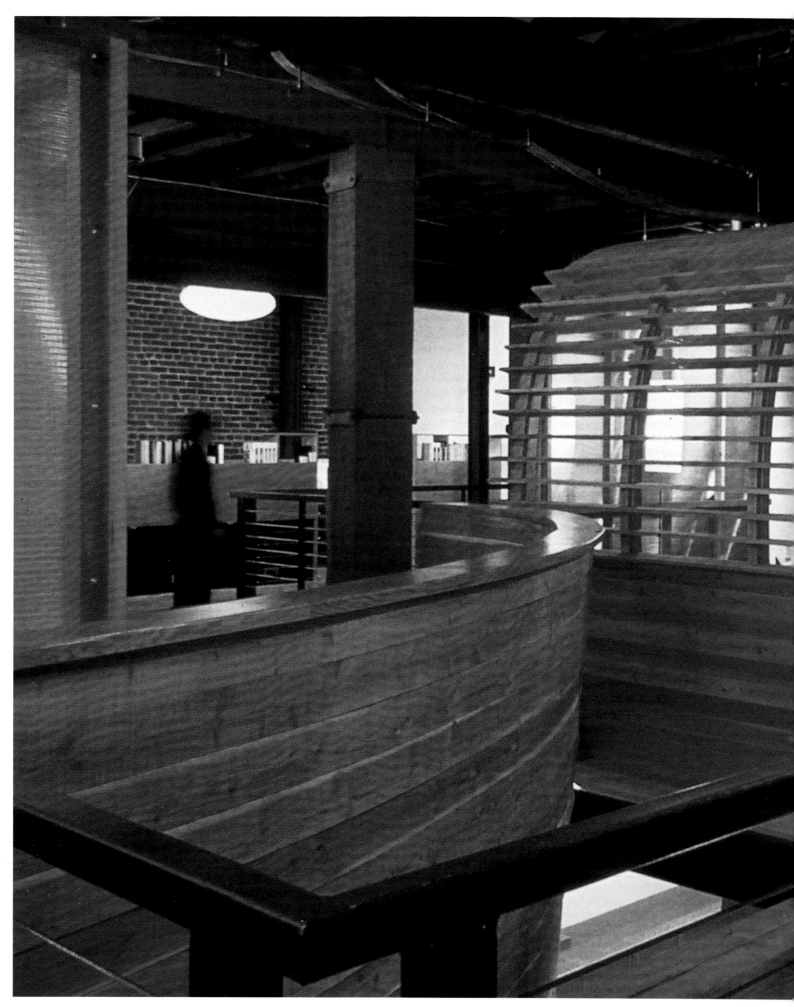

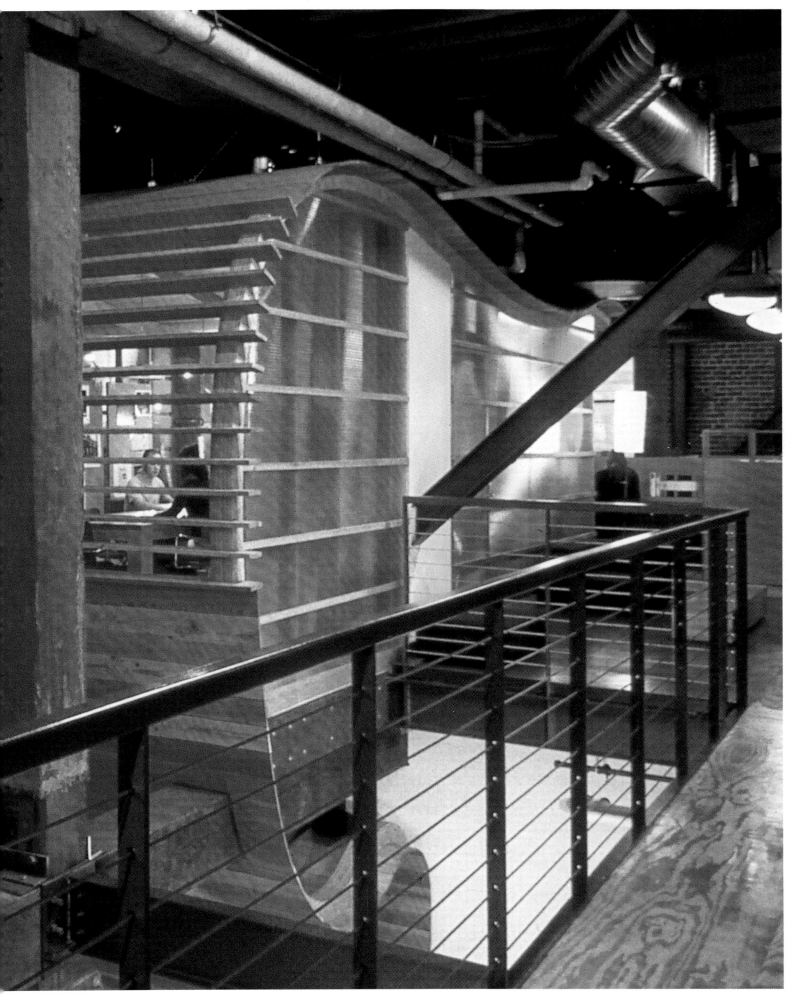

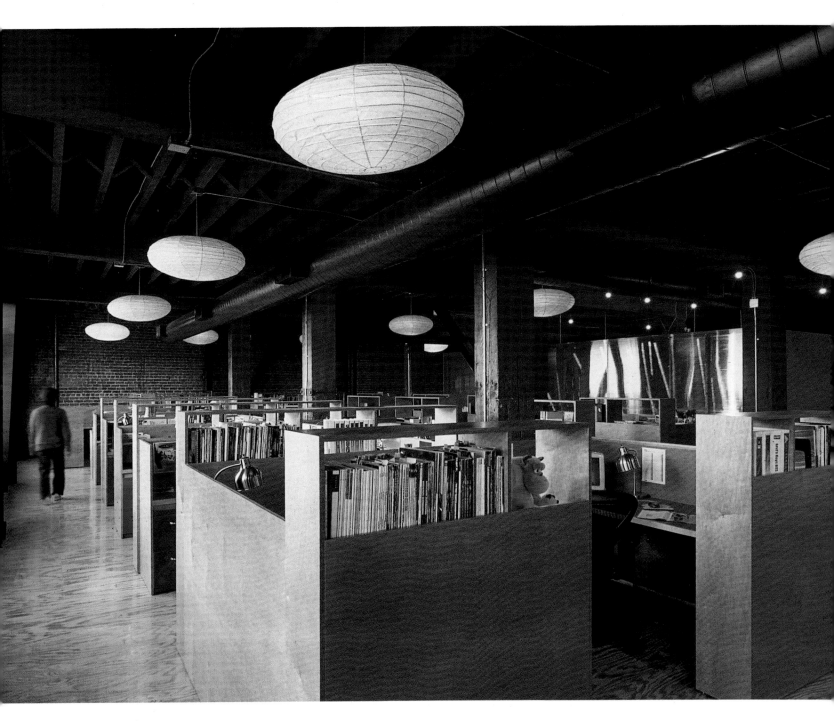

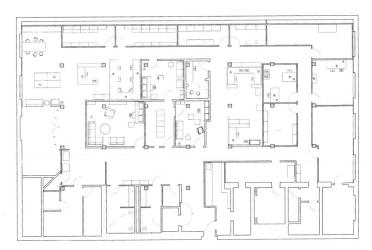

Ground floor

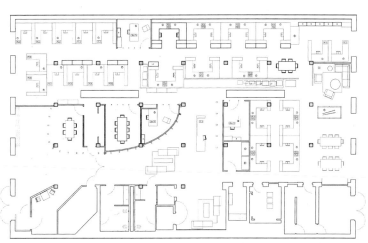

First floor

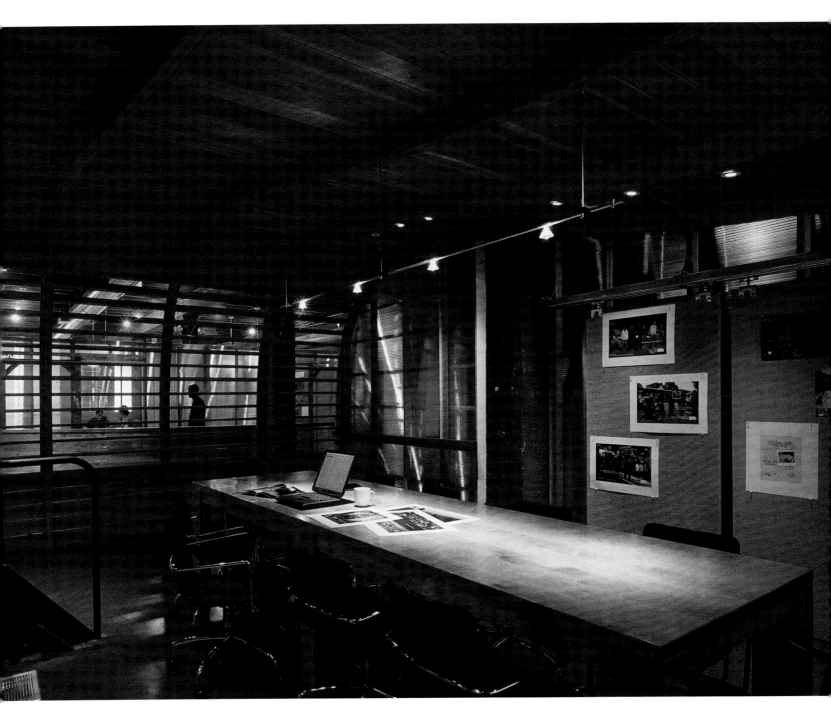

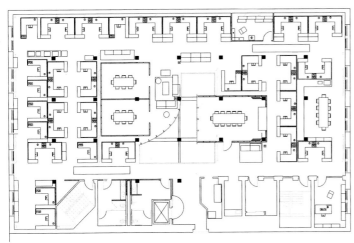

Second floor

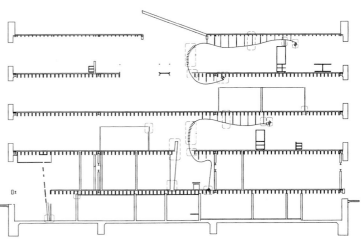

Longitudinal section

Industrial Design

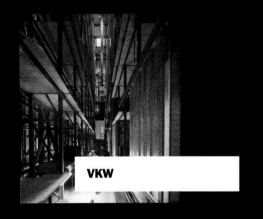

VKW

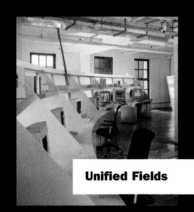

Unified Fields

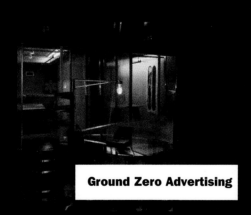

Ground Zero Advertising

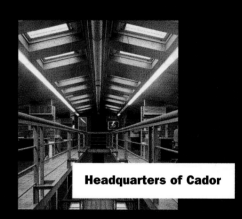

Headquarters of Cador

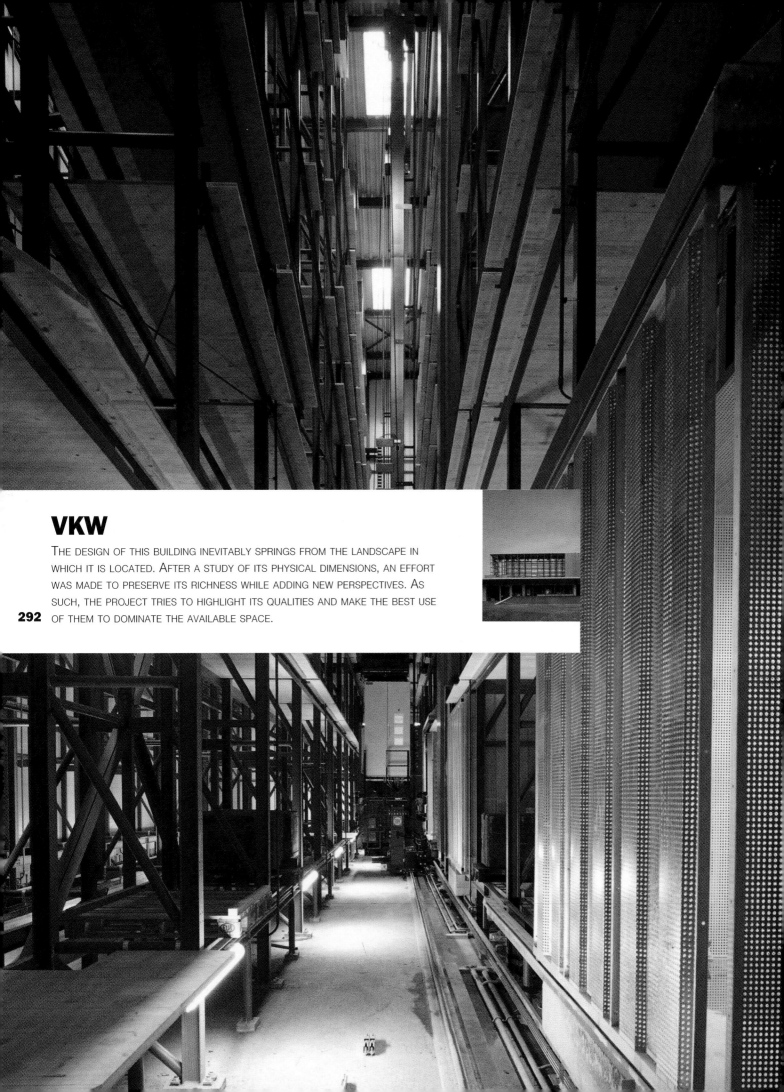

VKW

The design of this building inevitably springs from the landscape in which it is located. After a study of its physical dimensions, an effort was made to preserve its richness while adding new perspectives. As such, the project tries to highlight its qualities and make the best use of them to dominate the available space.

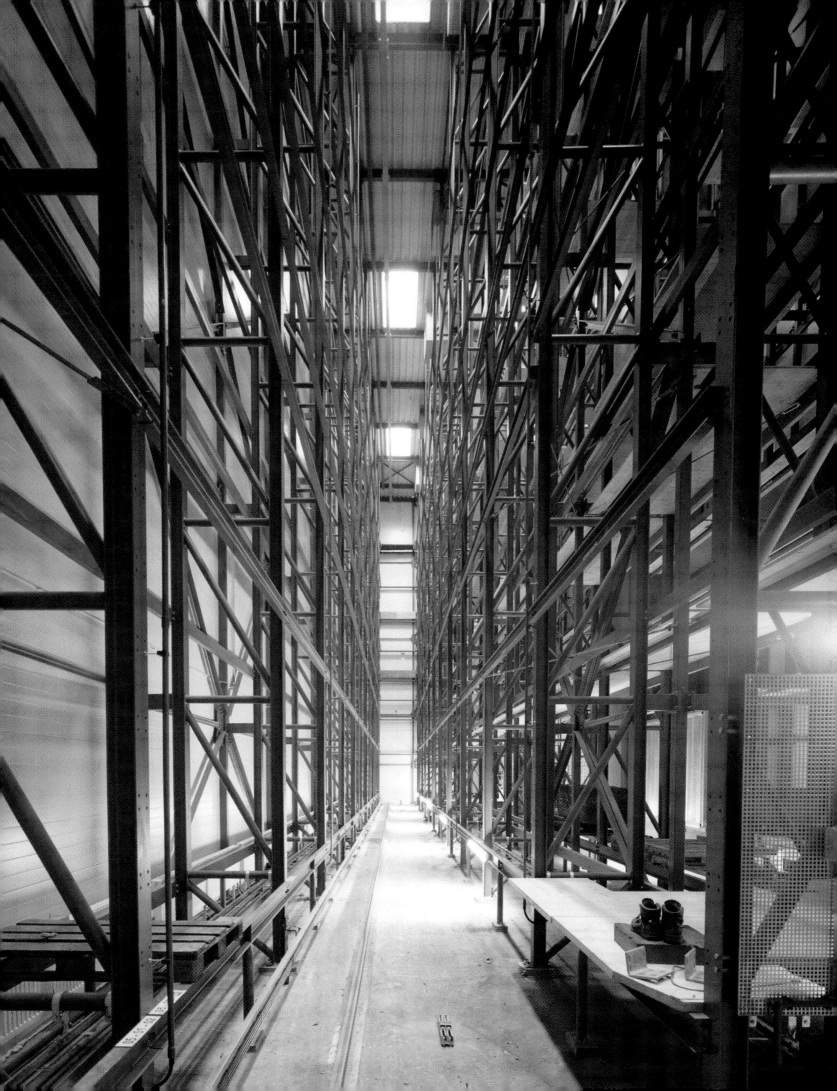

VKW

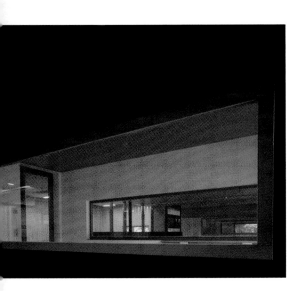

Architect: **Dietrich / Untertrifaller Architects**
Client: **VKW**
Location: **Bregenz, Austria**
Construction Date: **2002**
Photography: **Ignacio Martínez**

Visually, the exterior lines of the building may appear somewhat aggressive. Formally, the construction was erected following the guidelines of high-tech architecture. The plan includes a geometric volume with an L-shaped floor plan whose structure of radical rectitude gives the building a singular rationalism. All these characteristics create extraordinary functionality on all floors of the building, converting it into an ideal property capable of housing high-quality office spaces. The attractiveness lay in its austerity and restraint, which make it possible to create modern, efficient, and personalized interiors. All these features give form to original interiors.

Order and symmetry are without a doubt the protagonists of the interior spaces. Both remain constant throughout the building. Everything is perfectly calculated to achieve the desired effect. The architectural and decorative solutions make every part of the building flow. The spaces are defined with great flexibility, and there is an interesting play of relationships between the different volumes. Also, the transparency of glass and the delicacy of metal, which visually connect the different spaces with the exterior, are used to contrast the rigidity of the lines and to soften the forms.

Homogeneity, good intentions, and a wise combination of features are keys to success. The careful selection of materials, neutral colors, successful finishes, and sensible lighting are responsible for the particular feeling this building emanates.

The choice of glass and metal for certain parts of the facade contributes to an abundance of natural light and a permanent visual relation with the exterior. The various spaces created inside the building and their relationship with the exterior can be seen from the main lobby.

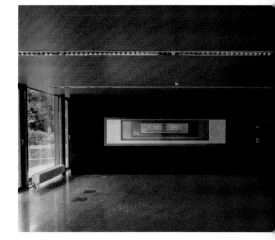

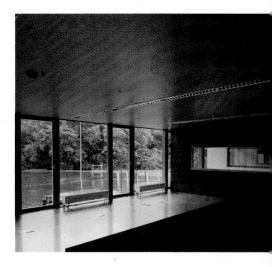

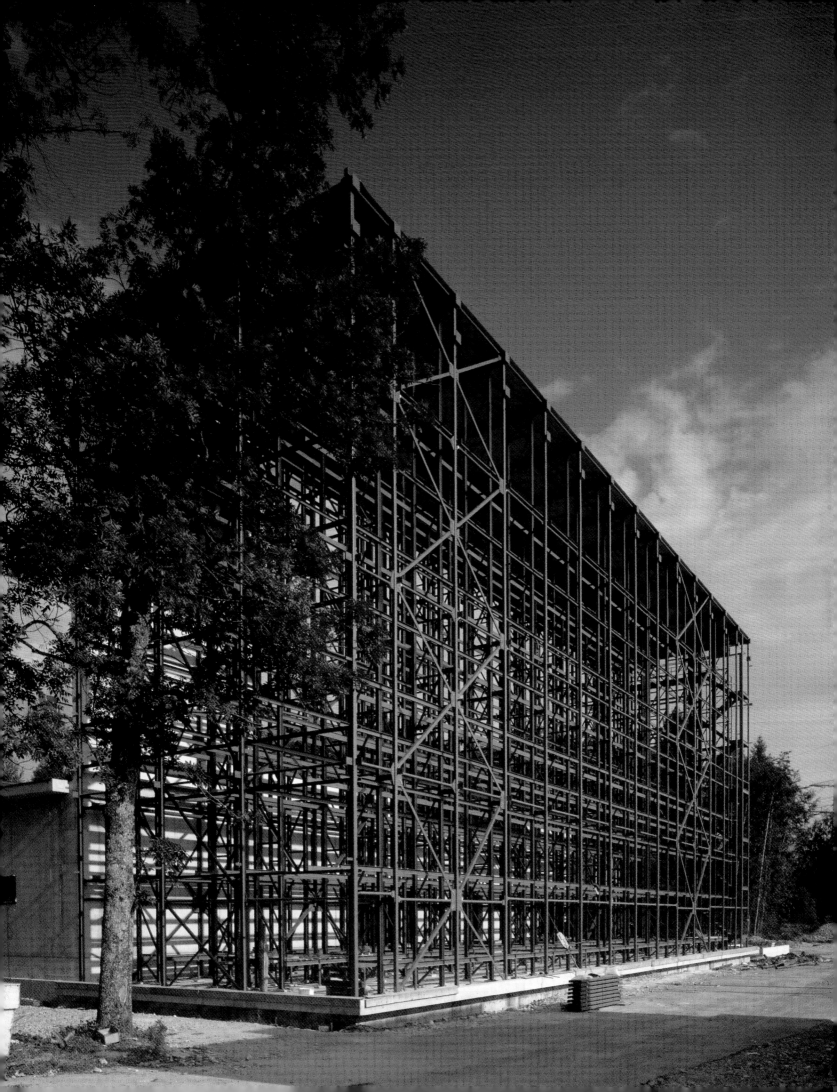

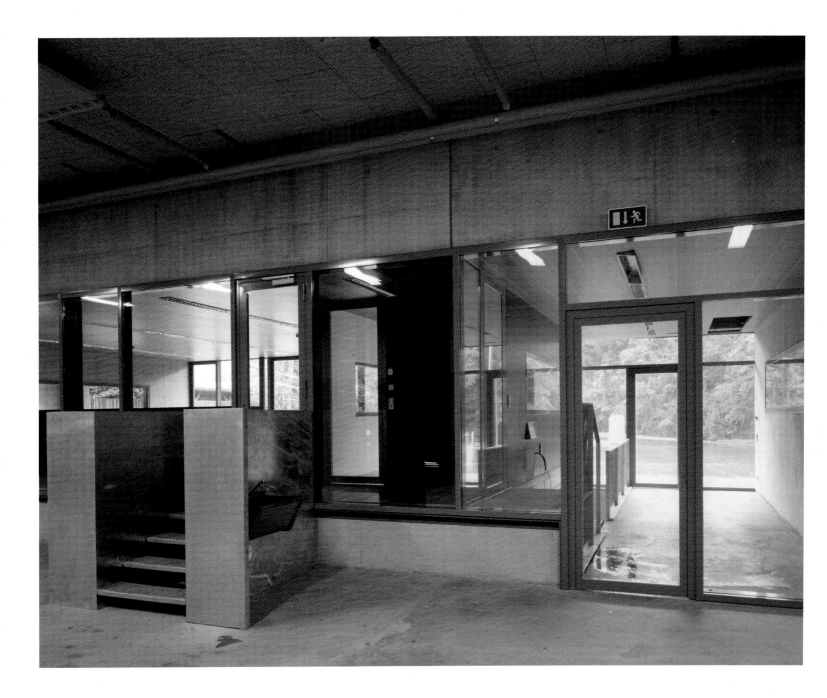

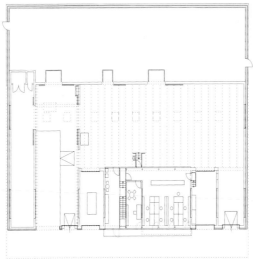

Ground floor

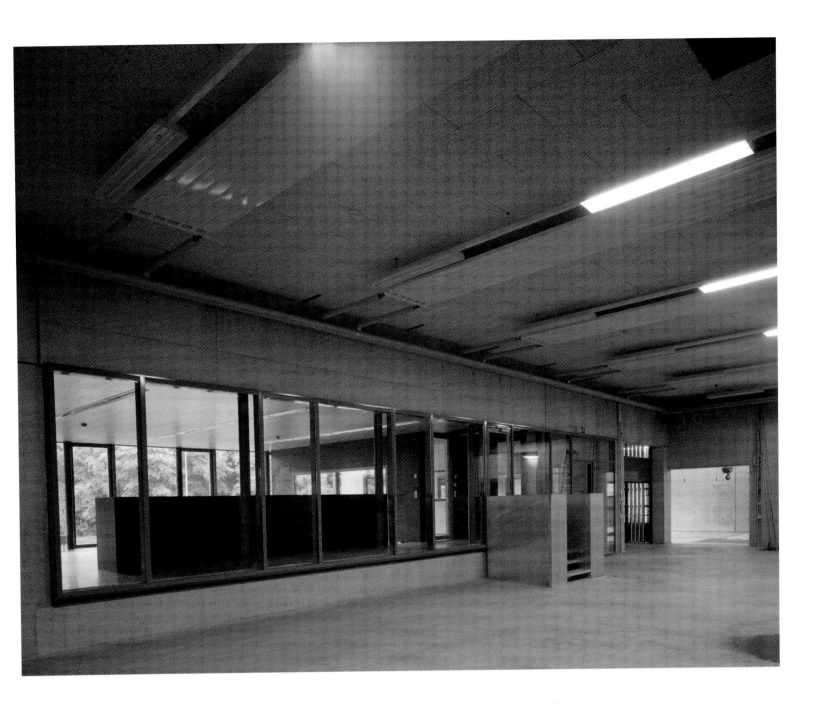

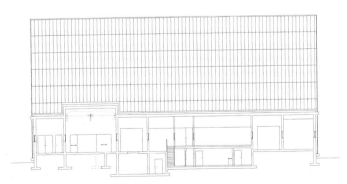

Section

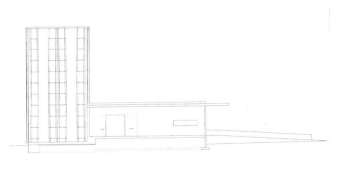

Section

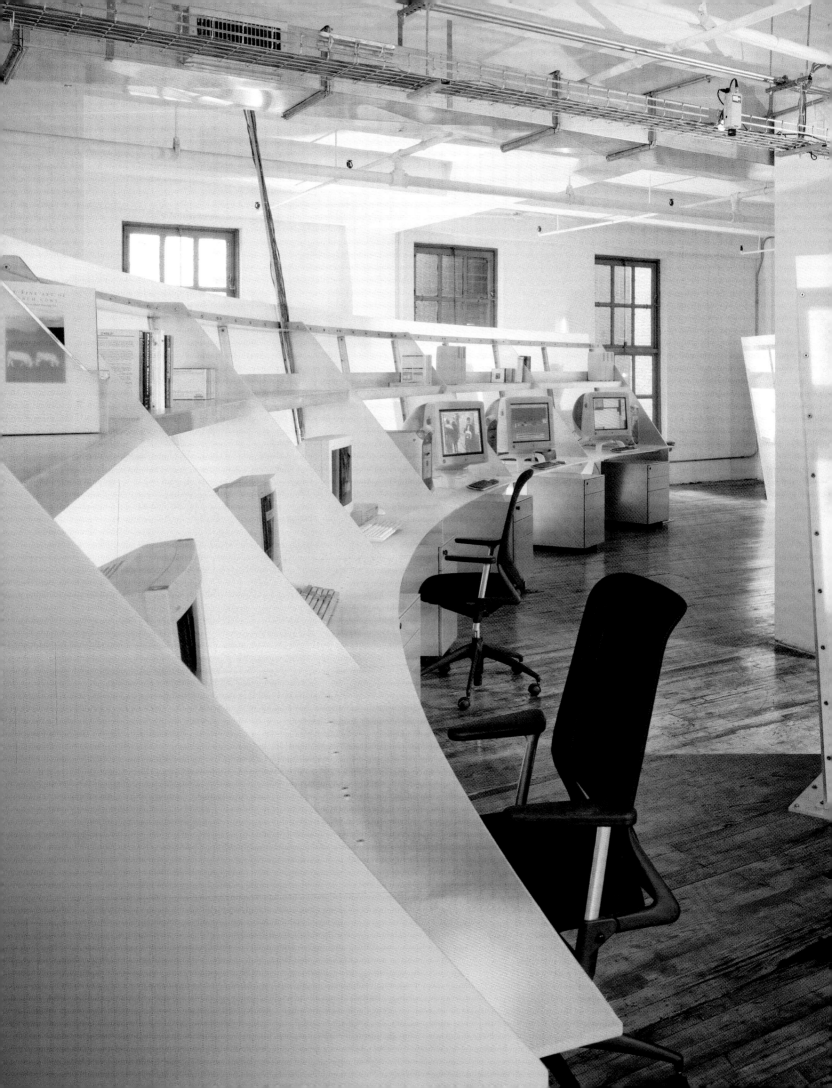

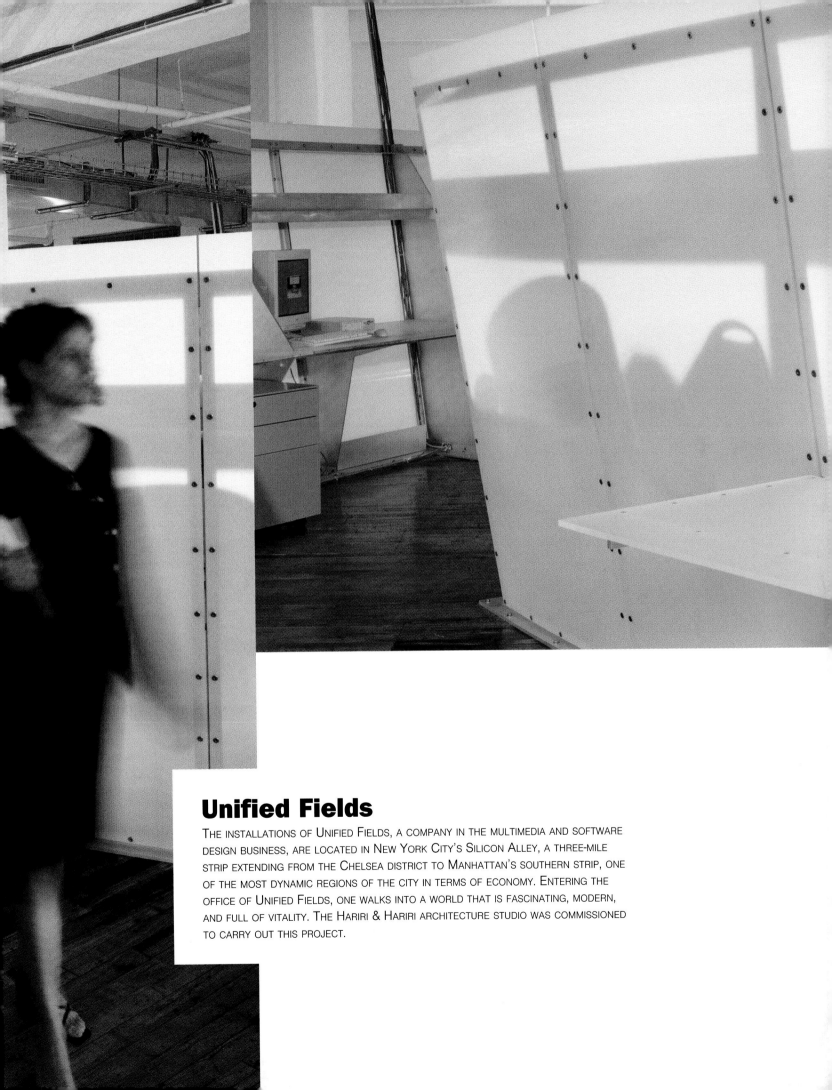

Unified Fields

THE INSTALLATIONS OF UNIFIED FIELDS, A COMPANY IN THE MULTIMEDIA AND SOFTWARE DESIGN BUSINESS, ARE LOCATED IN NEW YORK CITY'S SILICON ALLEY, A THREE-MILE STRIP EXTENDING FROM THE CHELSEA DISTRICT TO MANHATTAN'S SOUTHERN STRIP, ONE OF THE MOST DYNAMIC REGIONS OF THE CITY IN TERMS OF ECONOMY. ENTERING THE OFFICE OF UNIFIED FIELDS, ONE WALKS INTO A WORLD THAT IS FASCINATING, MODERN, AND FULL OF VITALITY. THE HARIRI & HARIRI ARCHITECTURE STUDIO WAS COMMISSIONED TO CARRY OUT THIS PROJECT.

Offices of Unified Fields

Architect: **Hariri & Hariri-Architecture**
Client: **Unified Fields**
Location: **New York City, United States**
Construction Date: **2001**
Photography: **Arch Photo, Inc. - Eduard Hueber**

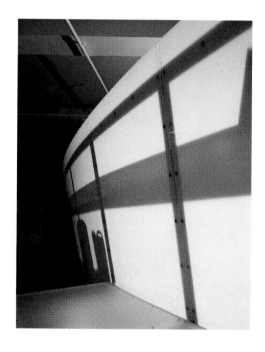

The client's guidelines for the architects were clear: to design a new space that faithfully reflects the activities of the company. It had to be a flexible and dynamic plan, and the resulting space had to allow the team of programmers, designers, and collaborators to carry out their tasks as comfortably as possible, in a relaxed and modern atmosphere, with innovative and engaging aesthetics.

According to the client's decision, the space was planned following the design principles for a loft; that is, large, bright, continuous, open areas that have been given an industrial treatment. It was decided to create a changing and dynamic atmosphere where there was ample space, in addition to the necessary work areas—meeting and conference rooms and various spaces among which are a small library and a kitchen. Visually, the most important architectural element is the curved shape in which the work areas are located. These are made of aluminum and Plexiglas, which allows light to filter through. This solution makes it possible to organize the work areas in a small space while giving the occupants a sense of privacy, even though they are in an open and common area that encourages communication. The reception area includes a table-counter with straight lines and the translucent sliding panels behind which are the meeting room and the multimedia rooms. In this area, as in the rest of the building, the materials highlight the industrial and modern feeling of the plan.

When designing the space, the goal was to create flexible, dynamic, practical, and functional spaces where work could be carried out as comfortably as possible. To achieve this, the appropriate resources and materials were used, such as the movable panels; wood, aluminum or Plexiglas; or the carefully planned spatial organization.

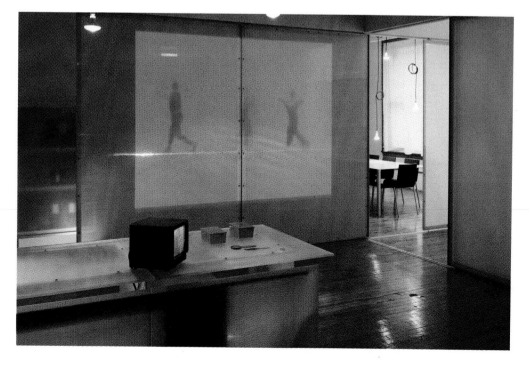

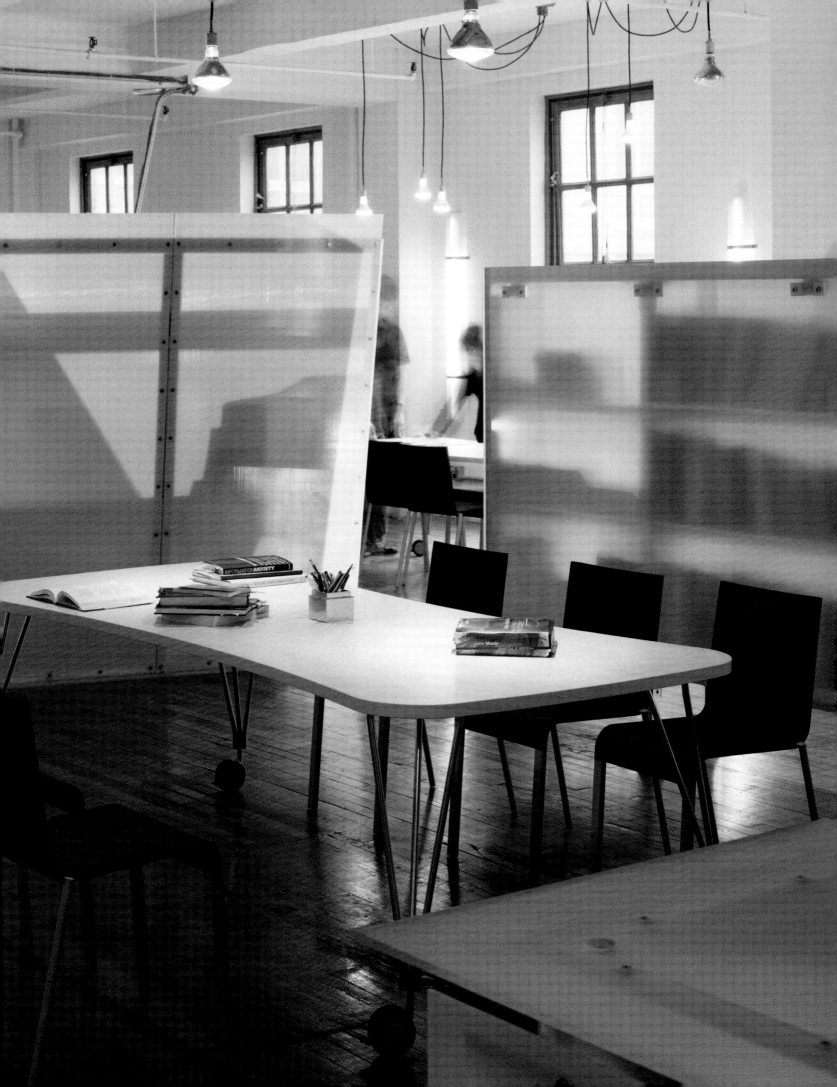

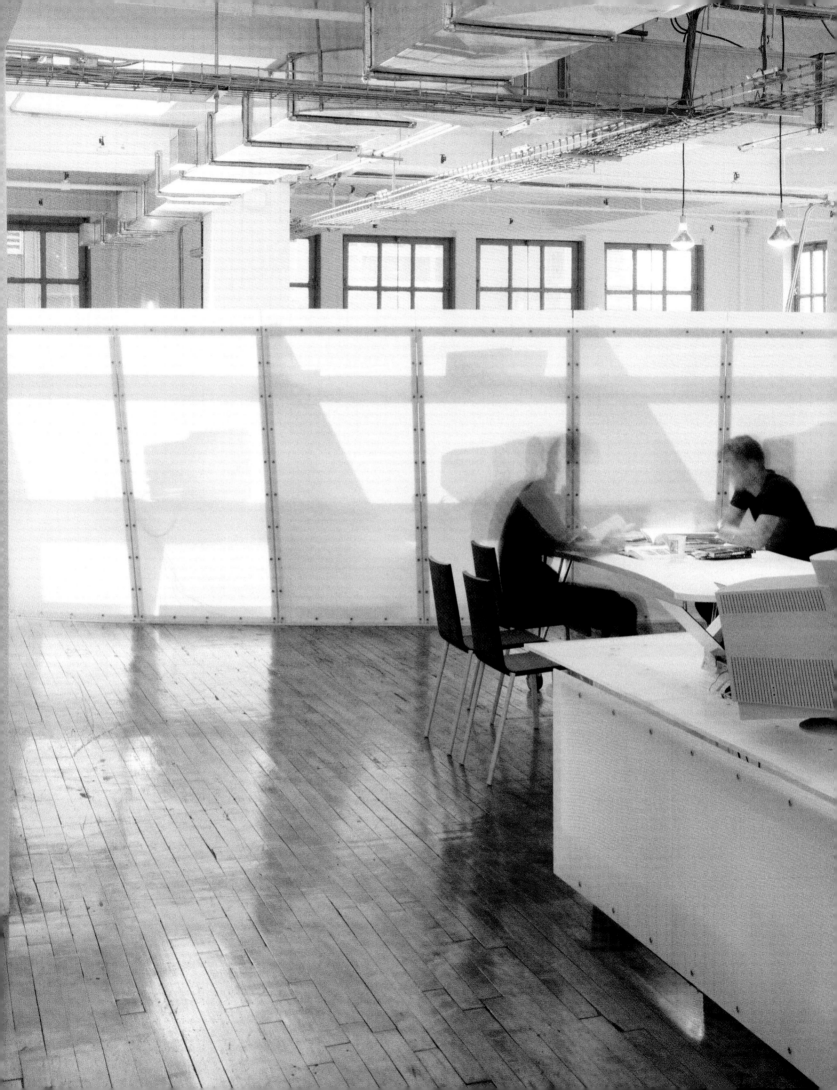

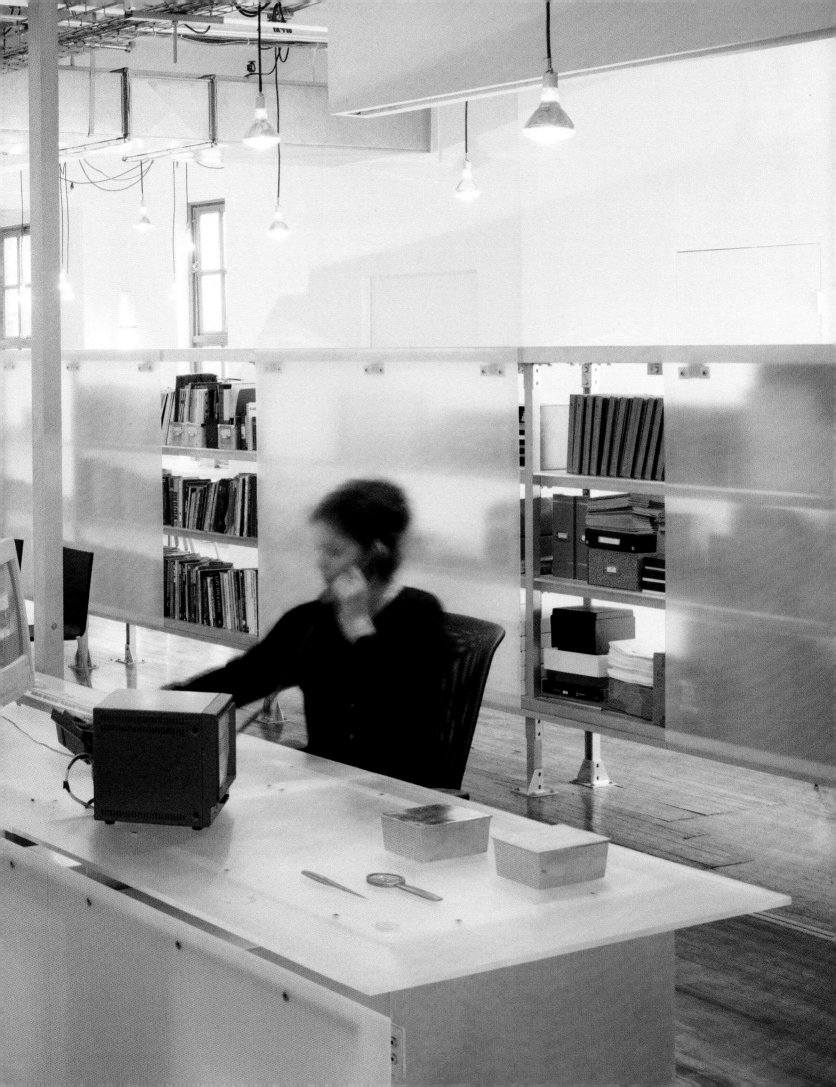

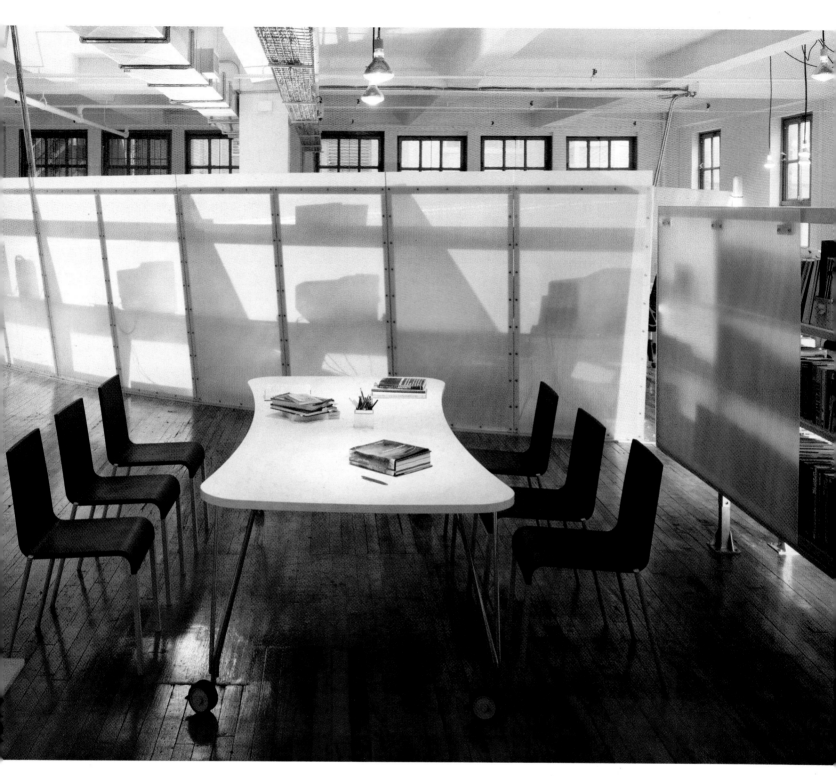

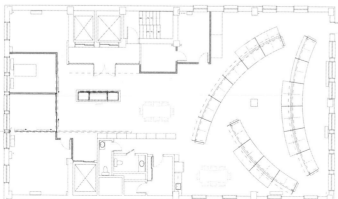

Floor plan

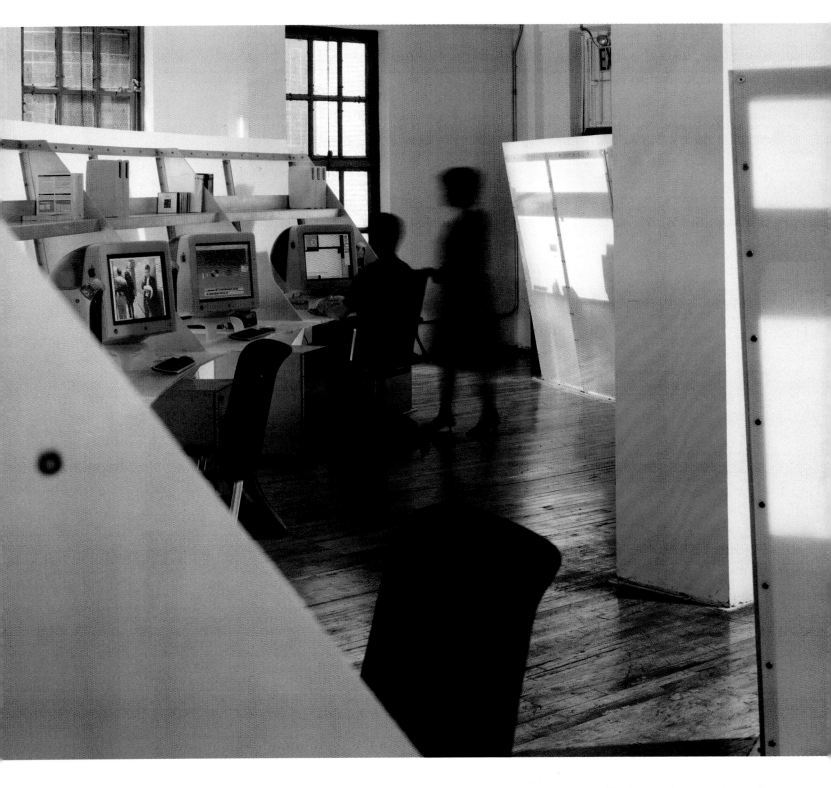

Grouping the work areas in a single curvilinear module presents numerous advantages while becoming an additional decorative element. The aluminum and Plexiglas, materials used in the construction, provide an evocative visual play when properly illuminated, where concepts like light–shadow, concave–convex, or indoors–outdoors take part.

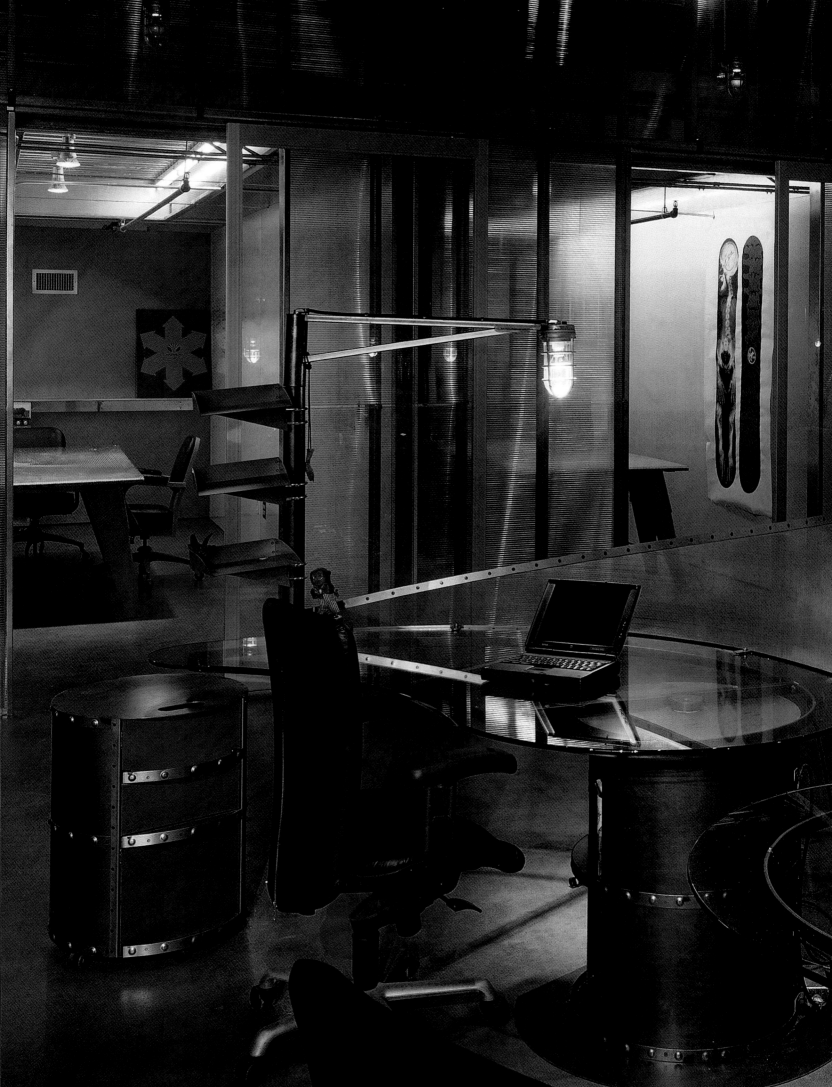

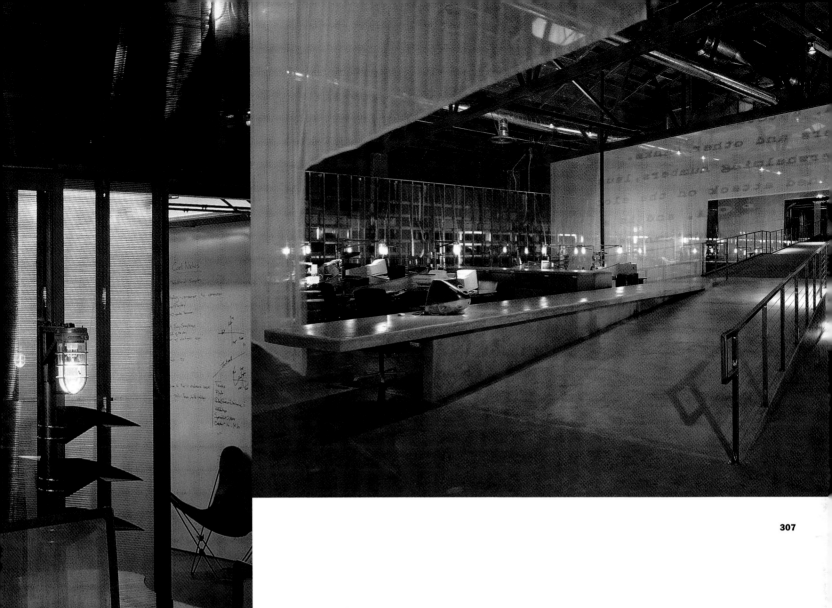

Ground Zero Advertising

THE GENERAL HEADQUARTERS OF THE AWARD-WINNING AND PRESTIGIOUS PUBLICITY AGENCY GROUND ZERO IS LOCATED IN AN OLD WAREHOUSE AND FILM PRODUCTION STUDIO. SHUBIN + DONALDSON RESPONDED TO THE WISHES OF THE CLIENT, WHO REQUESTED OPEN AND CREATIVE SPACES CAPABLE OF HOUSING 70 EMPLOYEES. AS SUCH, THE ARCHITECTS DESIGNED THESE FUTURISTIC AND UNIQUE SPACES LOCATED IN MARINA DEL REY, CALIFORNIA.

Ground Zero Advertising

Architect: **Shubin + Donaldson Architects**
Client: **Ground Zero**
Location: **Marina del Rey, California, United States**
Construction Date: **1999**
Photography: **Tom Bonner**

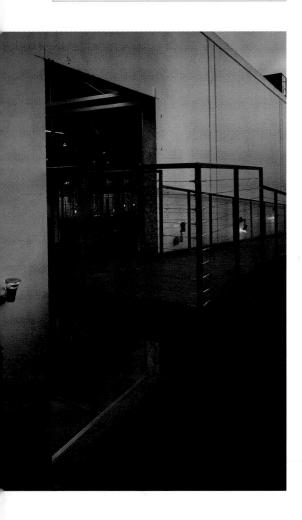

The original building was completely demolished to begin the modern construction, the concept of which originated with the idea of a black box theater. Based on this enclosed and concise geometric structure, an open plan had to be devised that included a reception area, services, administrative offices, three conference rooms, meeting rooms, audio and video screening and post-production rooms, and a library.

The project conceived the workspaces as open plans and areas continually connected and intersected by walls made of anodized aluminum, wood, steel, and acrylic panels. All of this was combined with a futuristic and industrial flair that was accentuated with a cold chromatic palette, used theatrical lighting in some areas, and the treatment of the spaces as if they were traditional lofts.

With innovative and ergonomic furniture designed by the architects themselves, the decoration of the interiors generates an attractive visual play in which eccentricity and futuristic themes are brought into being through the use of a daring and successful combination of textures and materials. This contemporary and dynamic space features some imaginative, vibrant, and fun installations that at no time lose their functionality.

The access to the reception area is via a ramp that extends into the space and divides it into two levels. The attractive structural forms that can be seen from the entrance are a pleasant precursor to the design solutions and decoration of the interiors, where the combination of materials and textures used results in a highly personal and futuristic aesthetic.

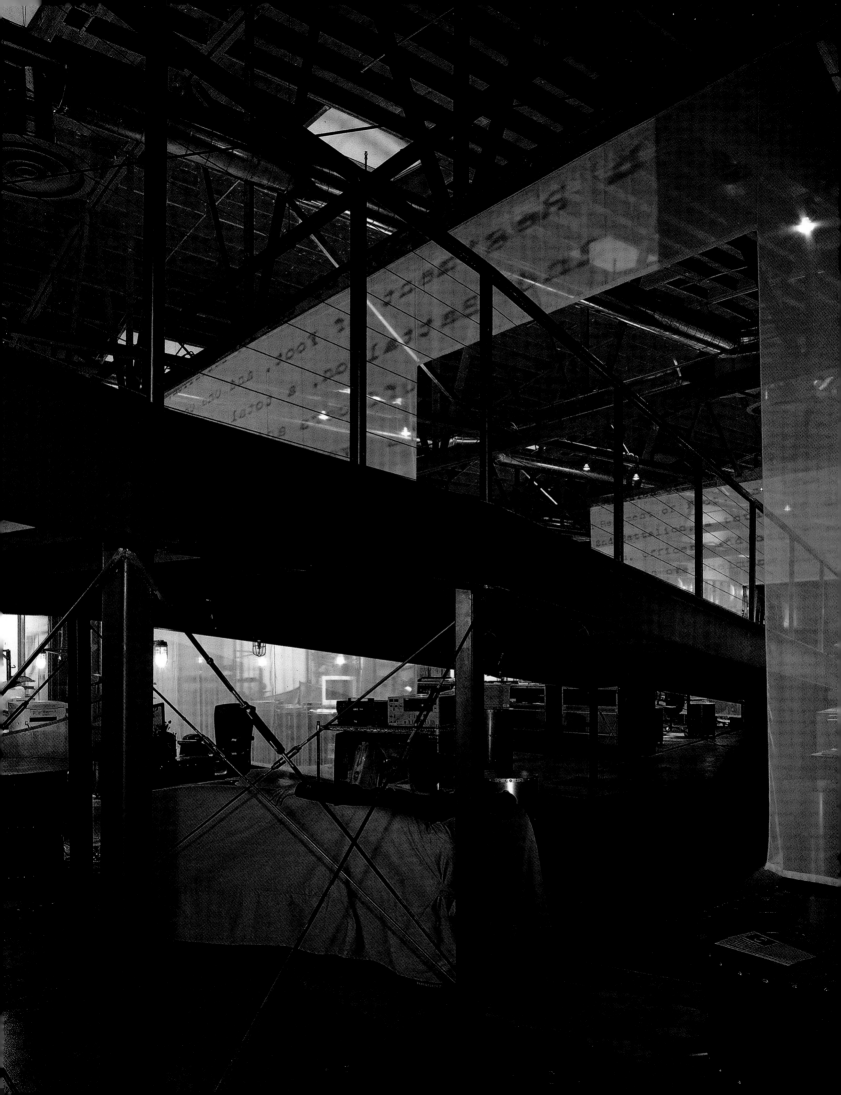

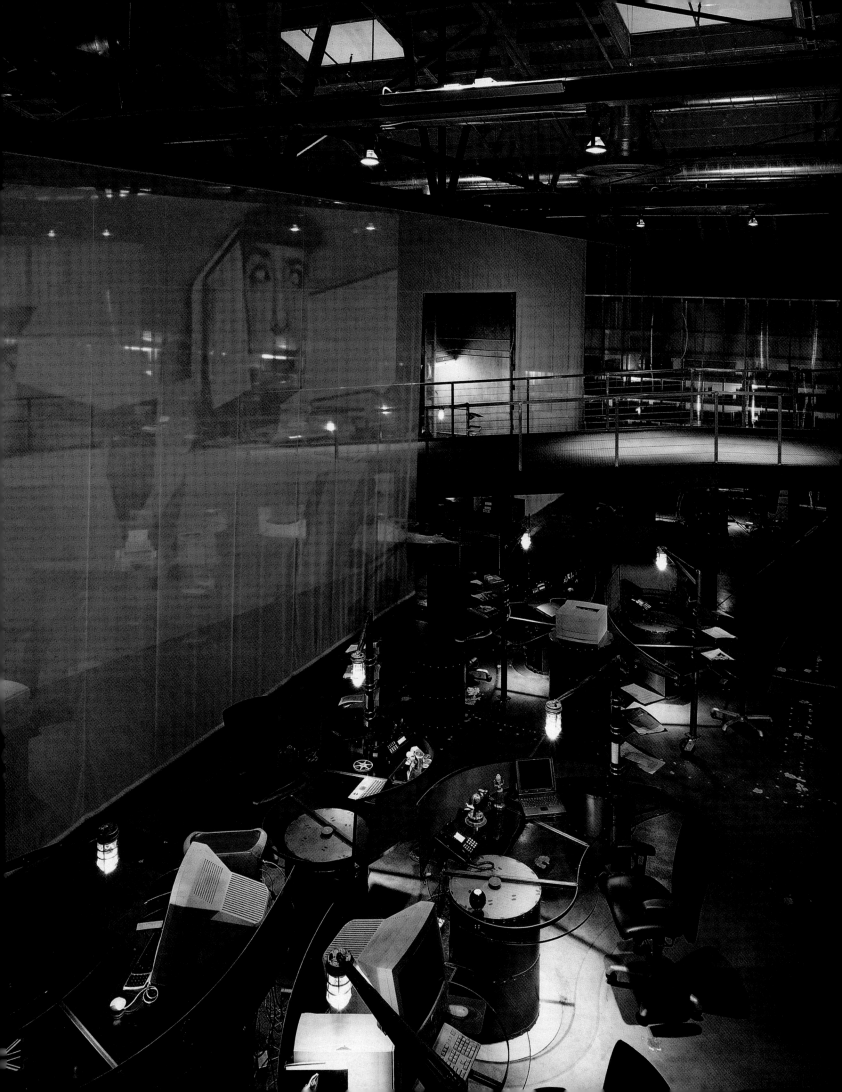

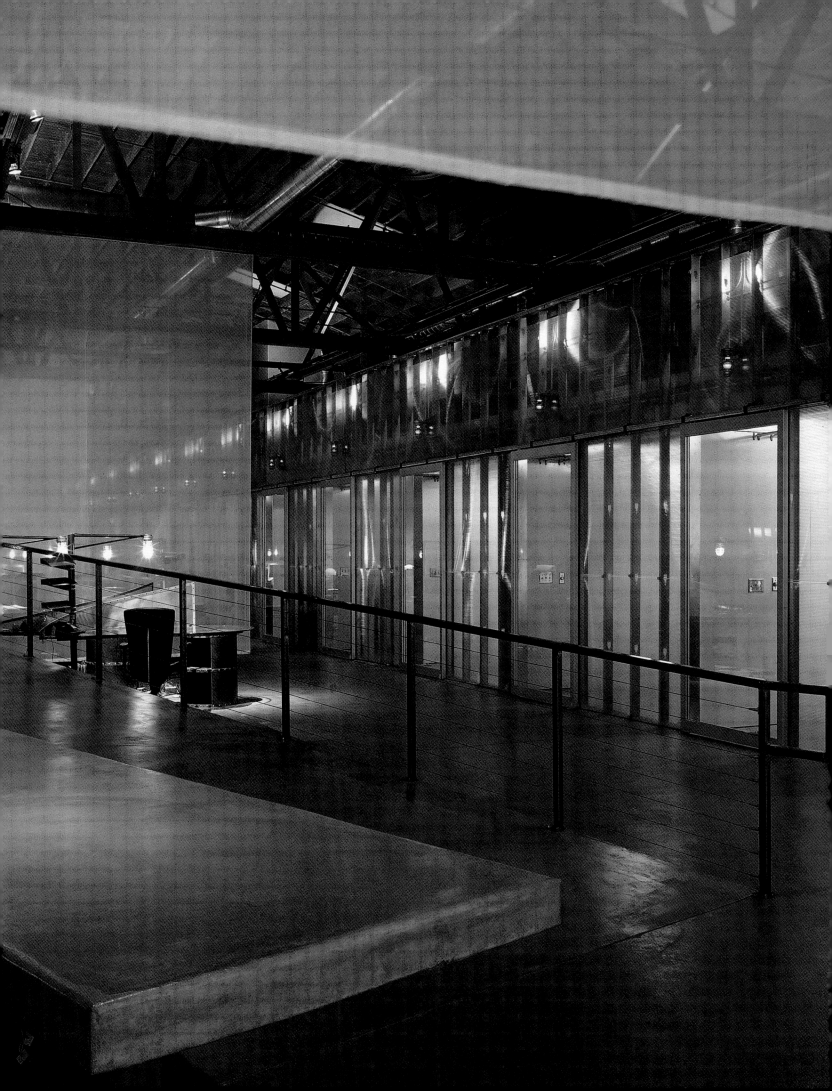

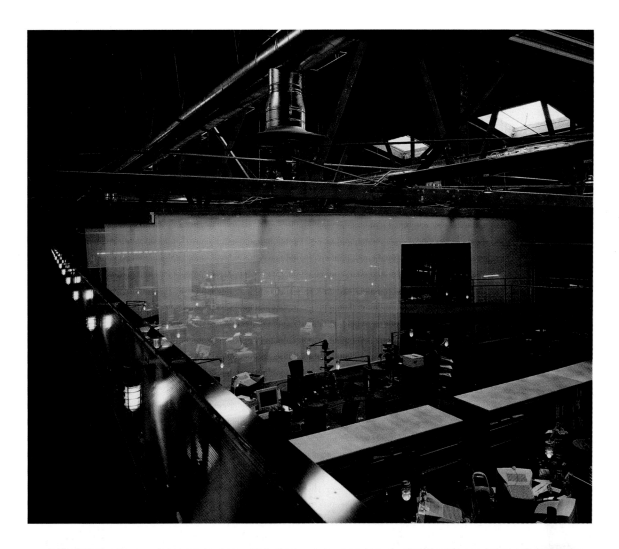

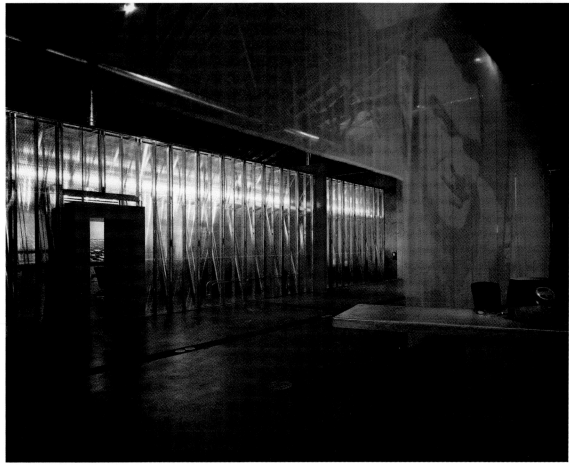

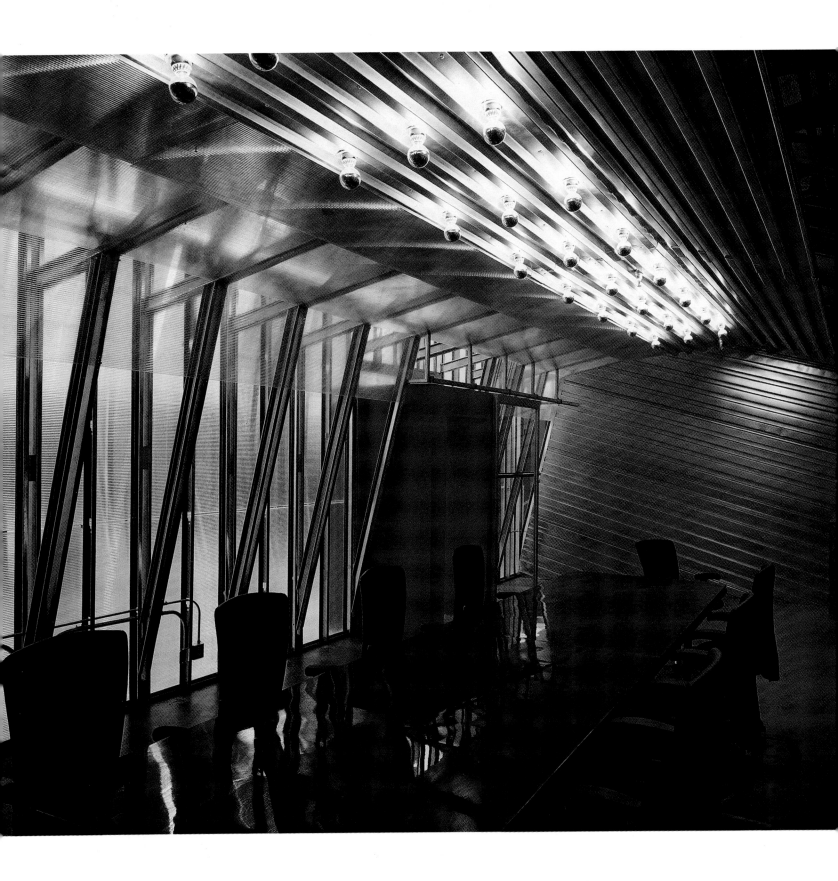

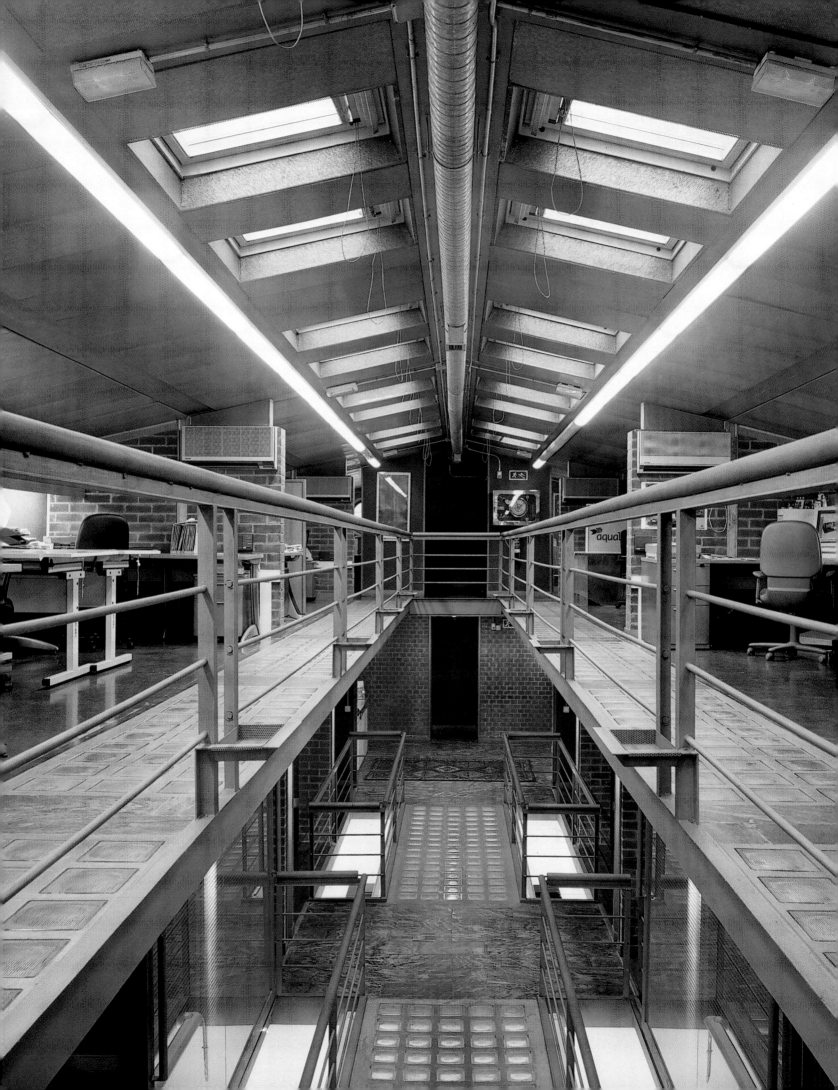

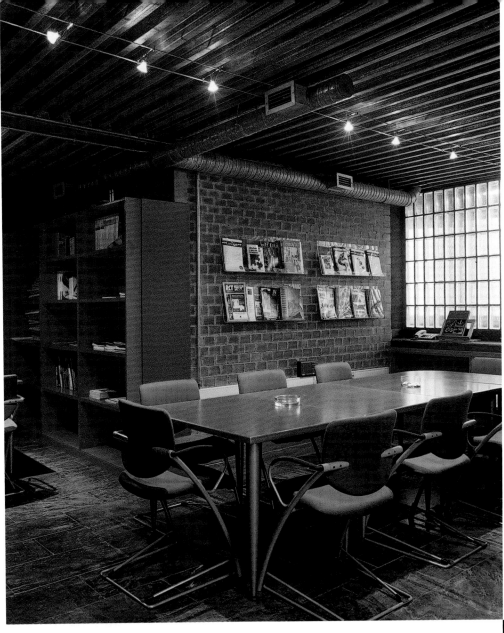

Headquarters of Cador

THE MADRID OFFICES OF CADOR, A COMPANY THAT SPECIALIZES IN SOLUTIONS FOR THE MANAGEMENT OF WORKSPACES, ARE AN EXAMPLE OF THE EVOLUTION THAT IS TAKING PLACE IN THE DESIGN OF OFFICES AND WORKSPACES. THEIR STRUCTURES ABANDON THE OLD BUREAUCRATIC DICTATES AND CREATE AN ENVIRONMENT WHERE EVERYTHING IS RECONFIGURED ACCORDING TO THE NEEDS OF THE MOMENT AND TO EACH ACTIVITY.

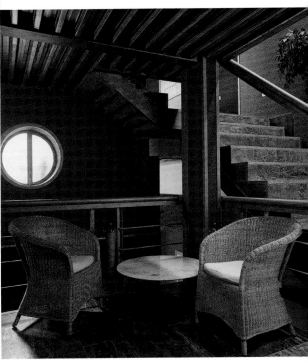

Headquarters of Cador

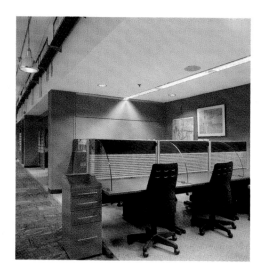

Interior Design: **Cador**
Client: **Cador**
Location: **Madrid, Spain**
Construction Date: **2000**
Photography: **Jordi Miralles**

For their installations in Madrid, Cador chose a building that had first been a soap factory and then an urban design, architecture, and engineering office. Architecturally speaking, the building is interesting because it was erected on a foundation of individual pads of reinforced concrete. The structure of the first floor is supported by pillars of reinforced concrete and steel beams, and the sub floor is made of prefabricated hollow blocks of concrete. The second floor is supported by bearing walls, with a base of exposed brick footings and a sub floor of parallel sheets of corrugated steel. The walls are solid brick with an air space and injected polyurethane insulation. The windows are vinyl with double glass panes. The roof is lacquered steel insulated on the underside; part of it was left flat and covered with gravel so it can be walked on.

The intention of the project was to create open spaces where all the offices were the same size, regardless of hierarchy, and where every two offices would be connected by a sliding door. There would be areas for informal meetings, non-designated spaces for commercial and technical personnel, and facilities for breaks and sports. The result is a contemporary, flexible, dynamic, and efficient space where work activities can be carried out with the greatest harmony.

A glass-brick passageway located in the center of the enclosure functions to organize the traffic on the first floor. The sides have been left open and the lower level is visible. On the second floor, the walkway recedes slightly to allow a full view of all three levels.

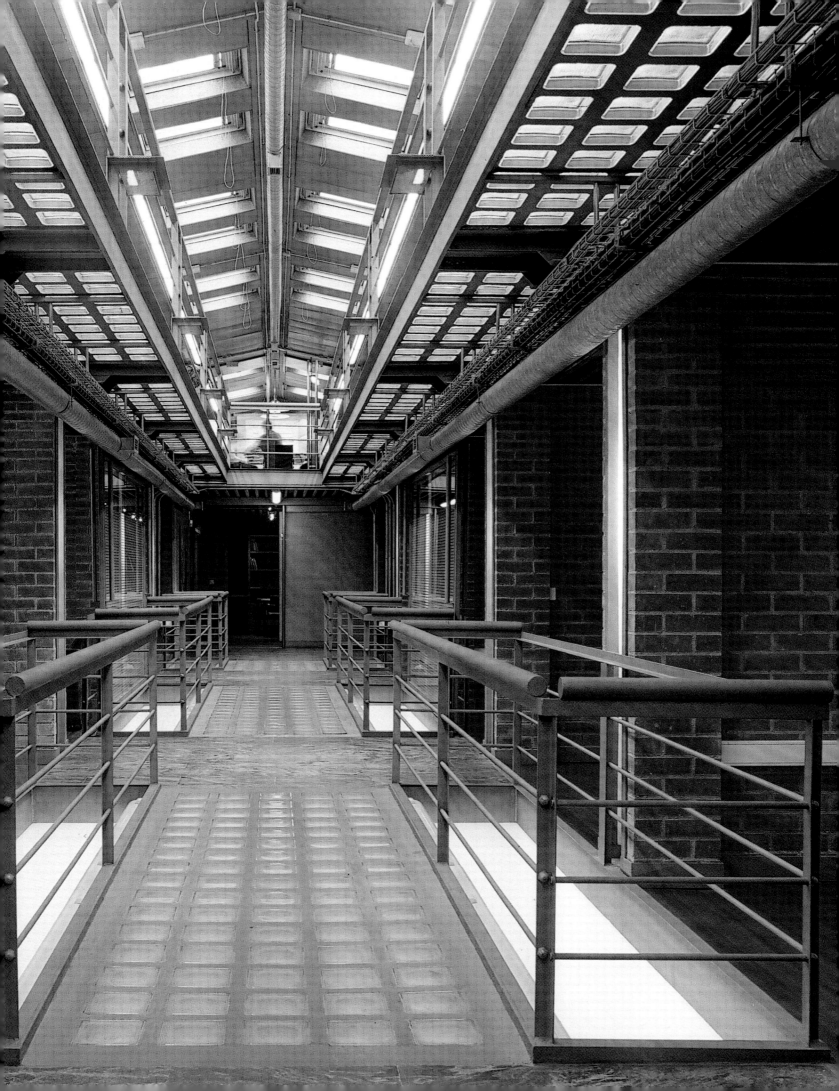

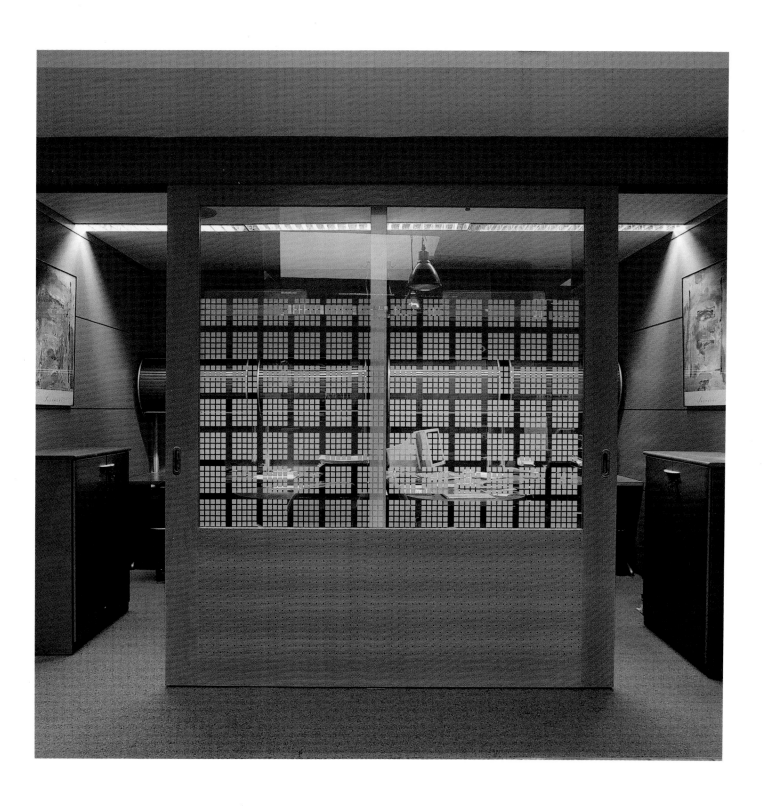

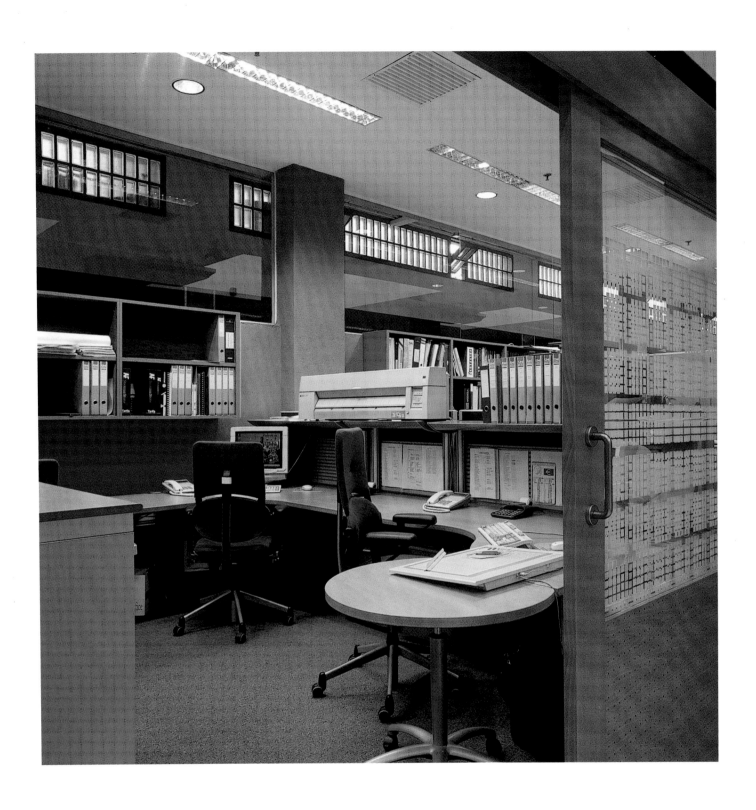

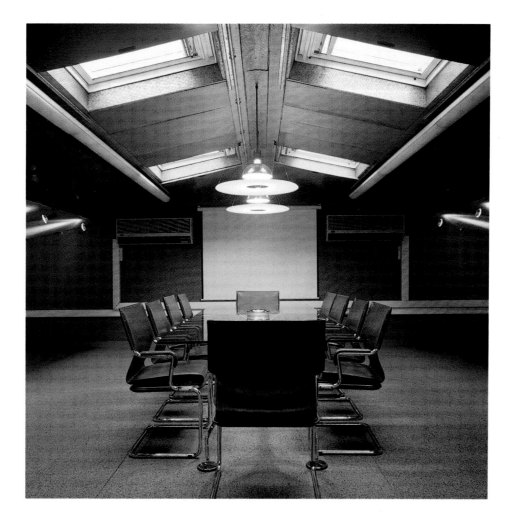

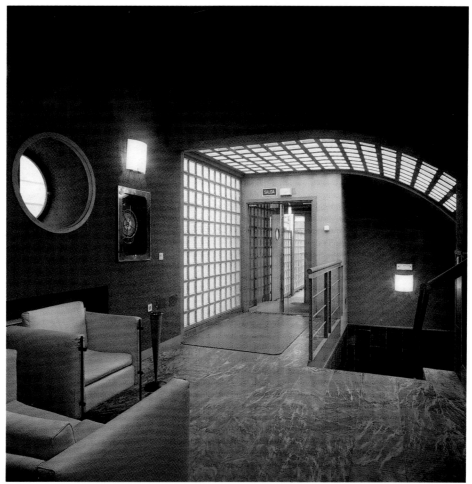

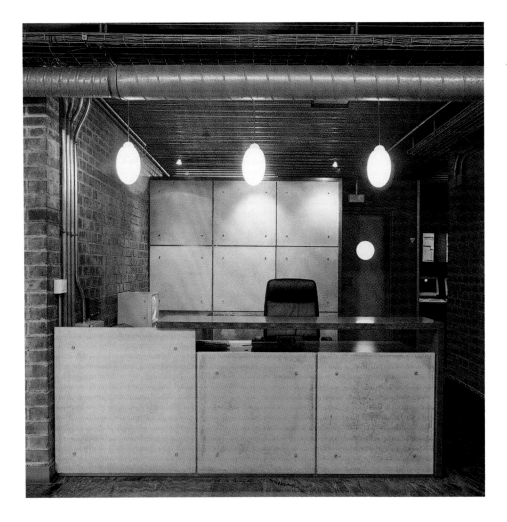

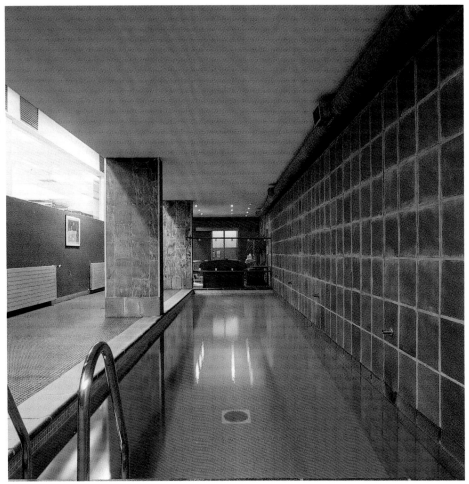

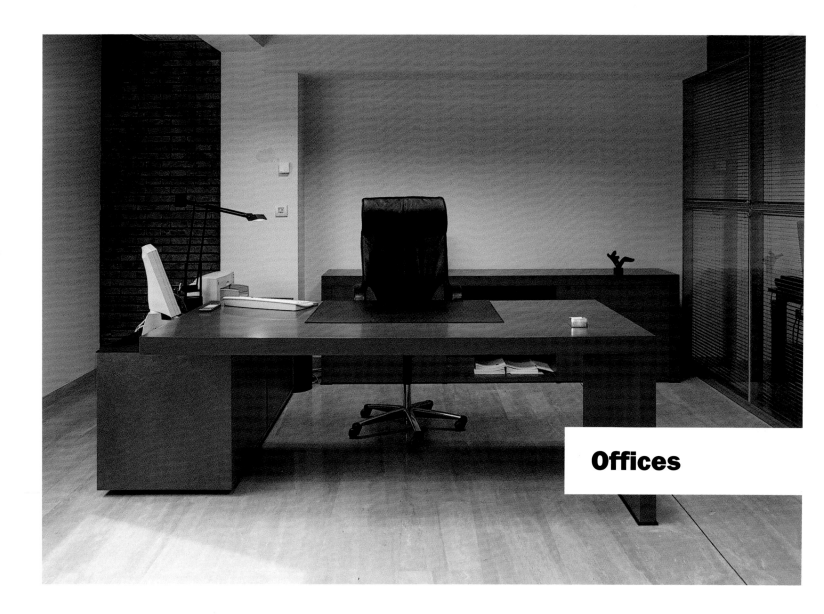

Offices

When conceptualizing and designing the interiors of an office it is necessary to fulfill a series of functional requirements to guarantee the comfort of the person who will work there. The formal aspects of the offices themselves dictate a certain way of understanding space. The physical distribution of the work area will vary depending on the activity being carried out (the type of installation needed will depend on this) and on the number of employees that belong to the company (it is not the same thing to house five people as it is 100). Planning, then, should not be taken lightly since it will have a profound effect on the productivity of the personnel. Simple changes, like the placement of objects or the telephone, good ventilation, the layout of a well-equipped office space, ergonomic furniture, proper lighting or the maintenance of the environment in which the employee has to carry out his or her tasks, can help to conserve energy and motivate the worker and will result in greater efficiency. The influence of the work environment on the productivity of workers has been repeatedly proven, therefore it is necessary to create a pleasant, functional, and practical atmosphere. Comfort is a major requirement and it is easy to achieve as long as the chosen setting does not impede the proper development of the activity.

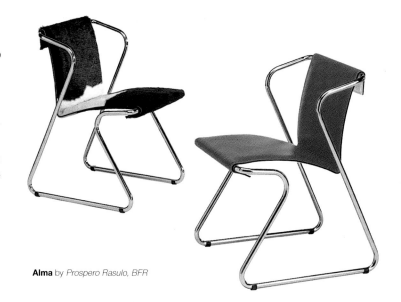

Alma by *Prospero Rasulo, BFR*

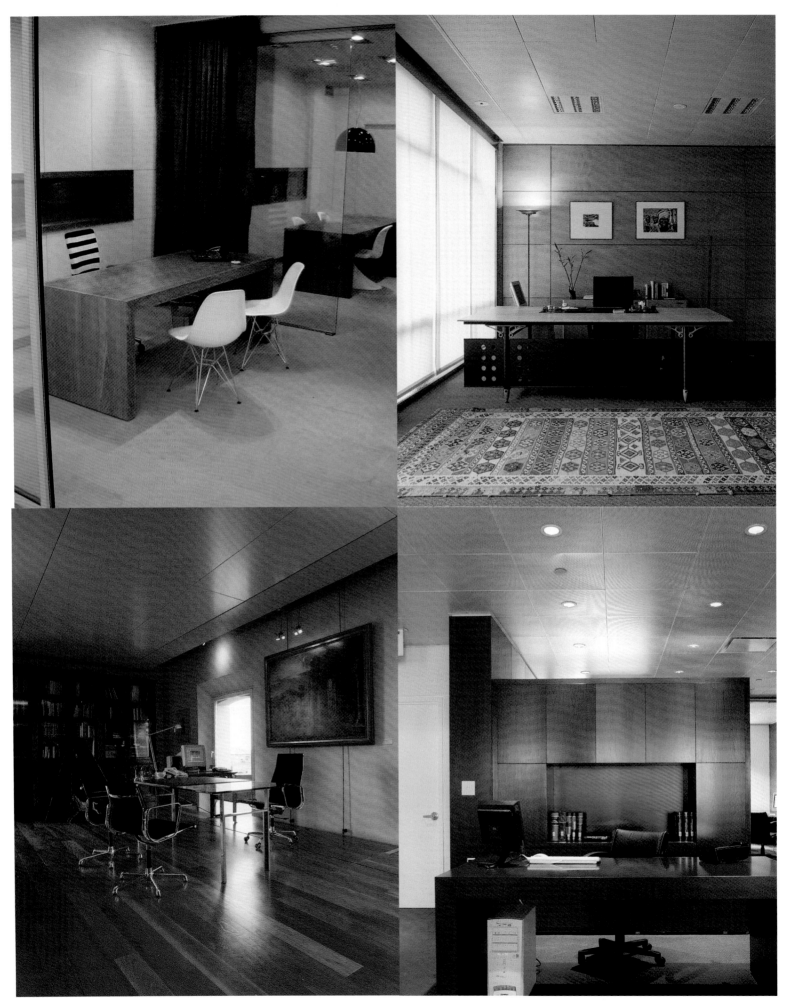

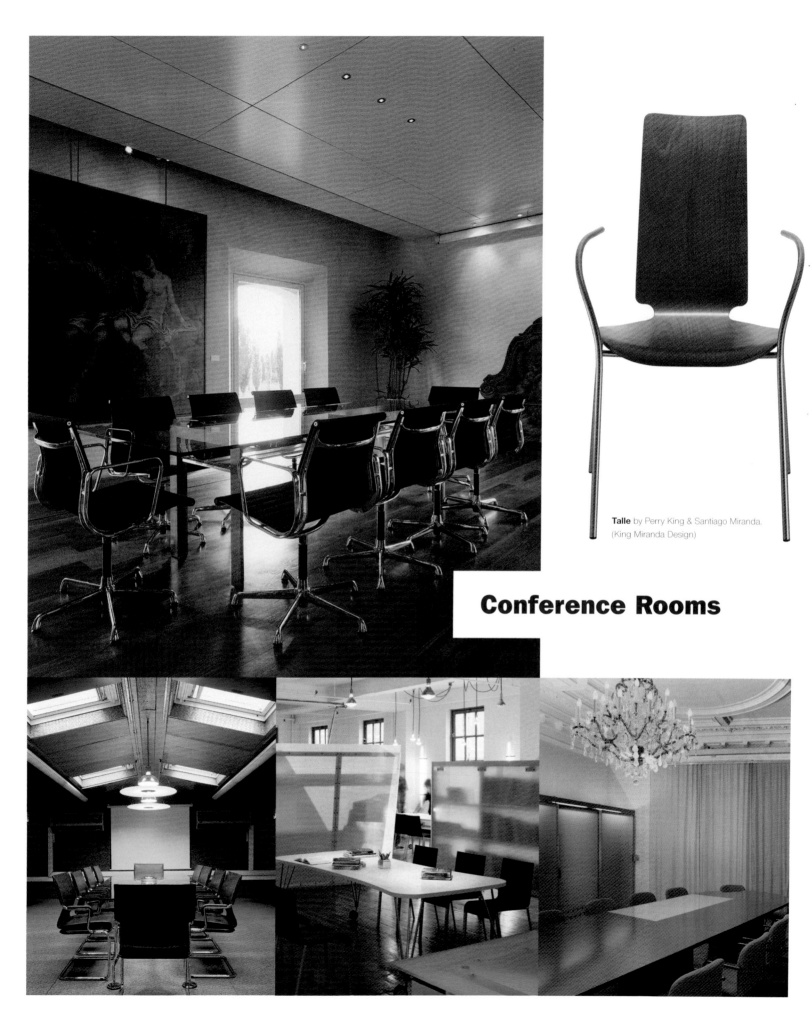

Talle by Perry King & Santiago Miranda.
(King Miranda Design)

Conference Rooms

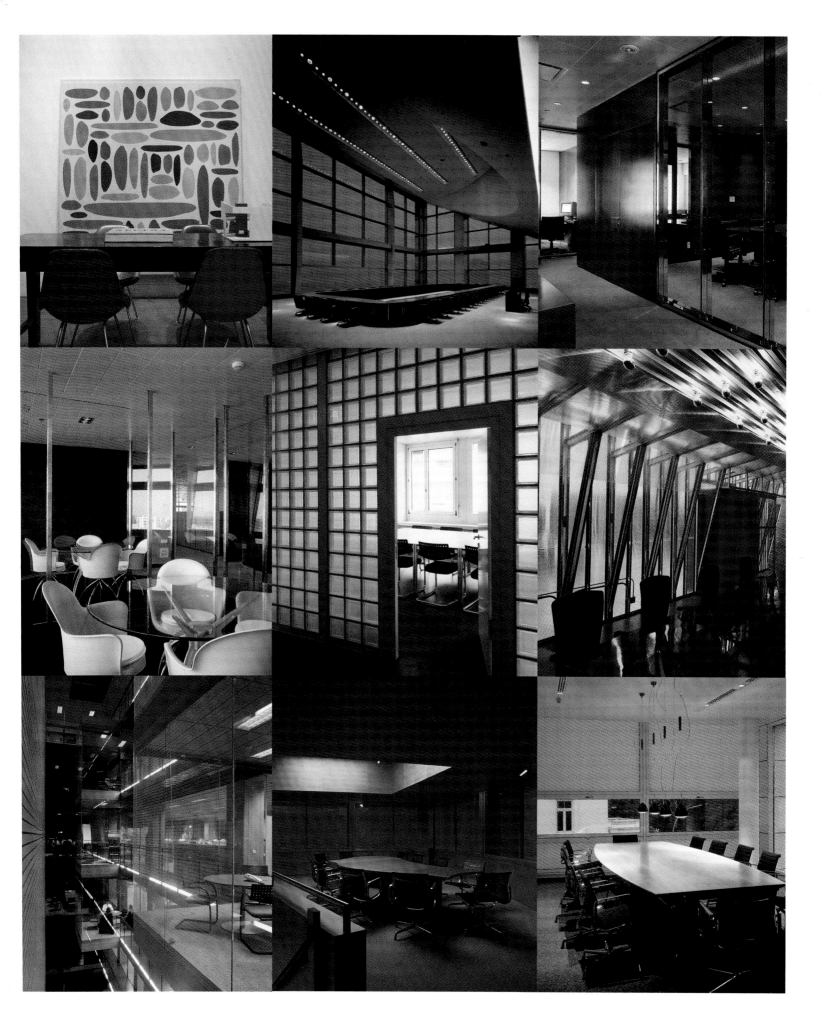

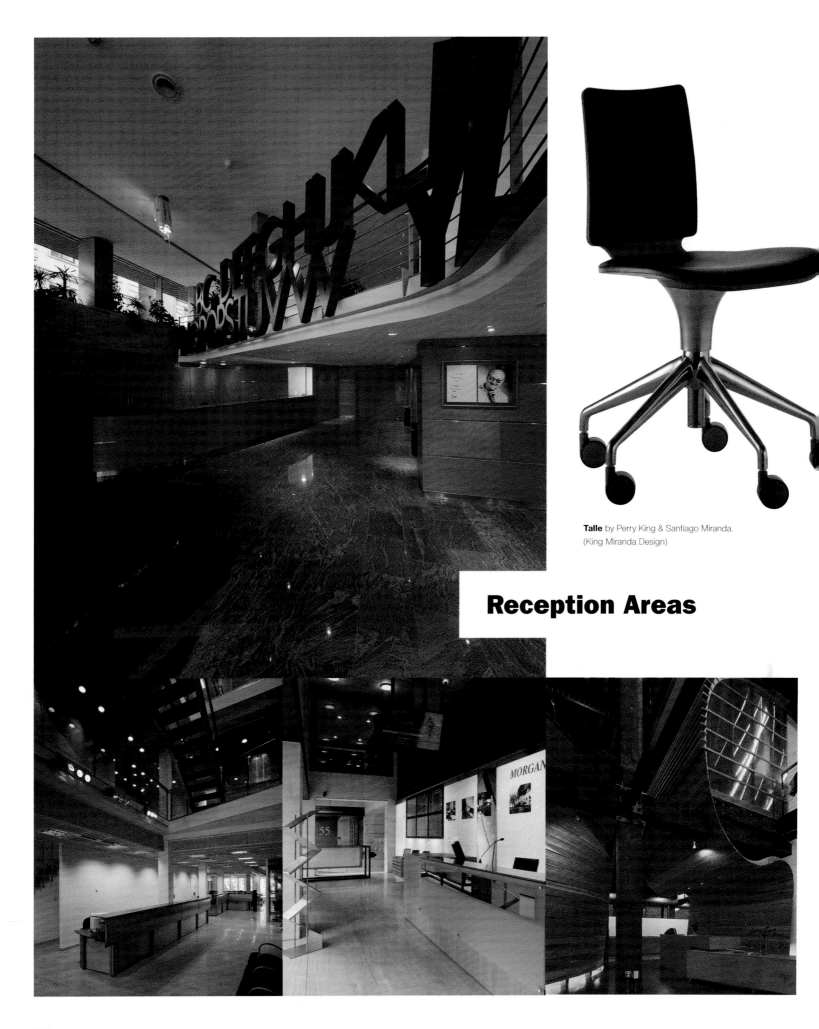

Talle by Perry King & Santiago Miranda.
(King Miranda Design)

Reception Areas

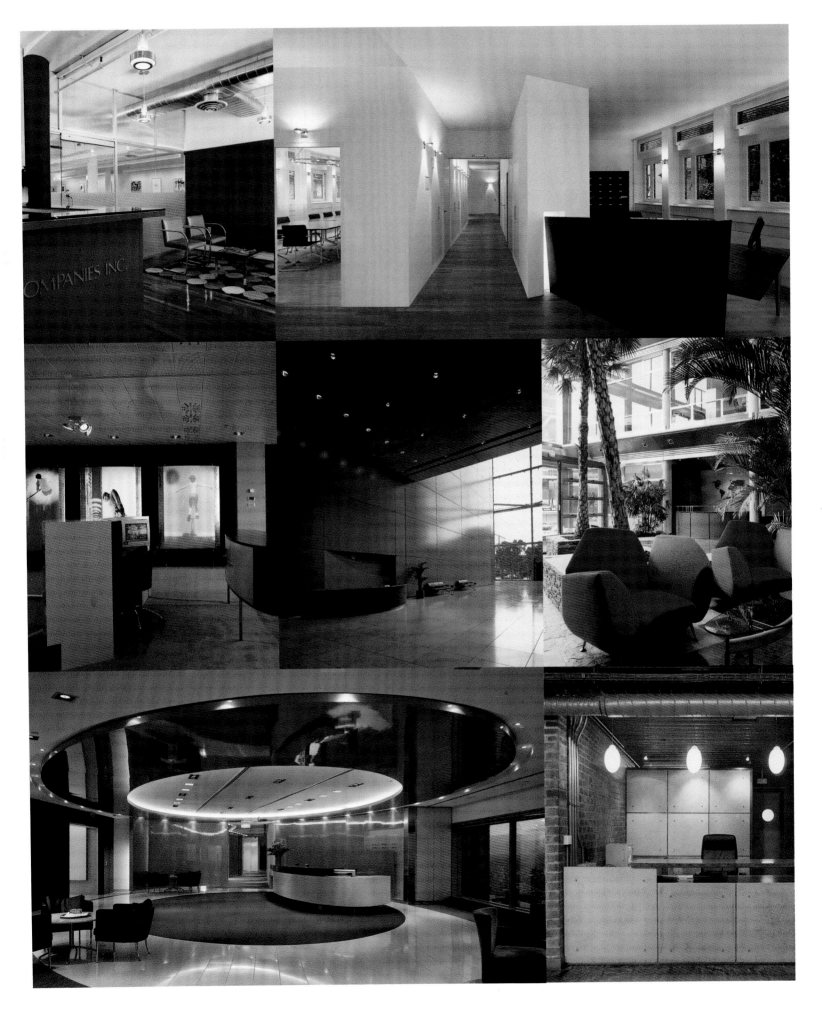

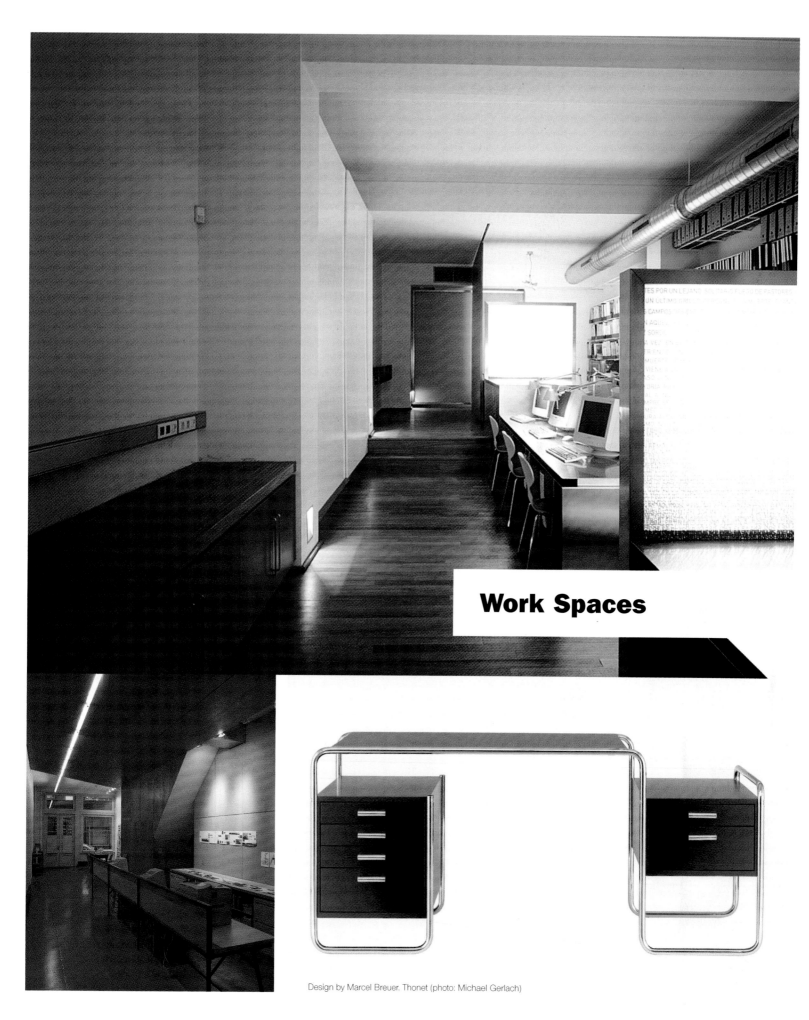

Work Spaces

Design by Marcel Breuer. Thonet (photo: Michael Gerlach)

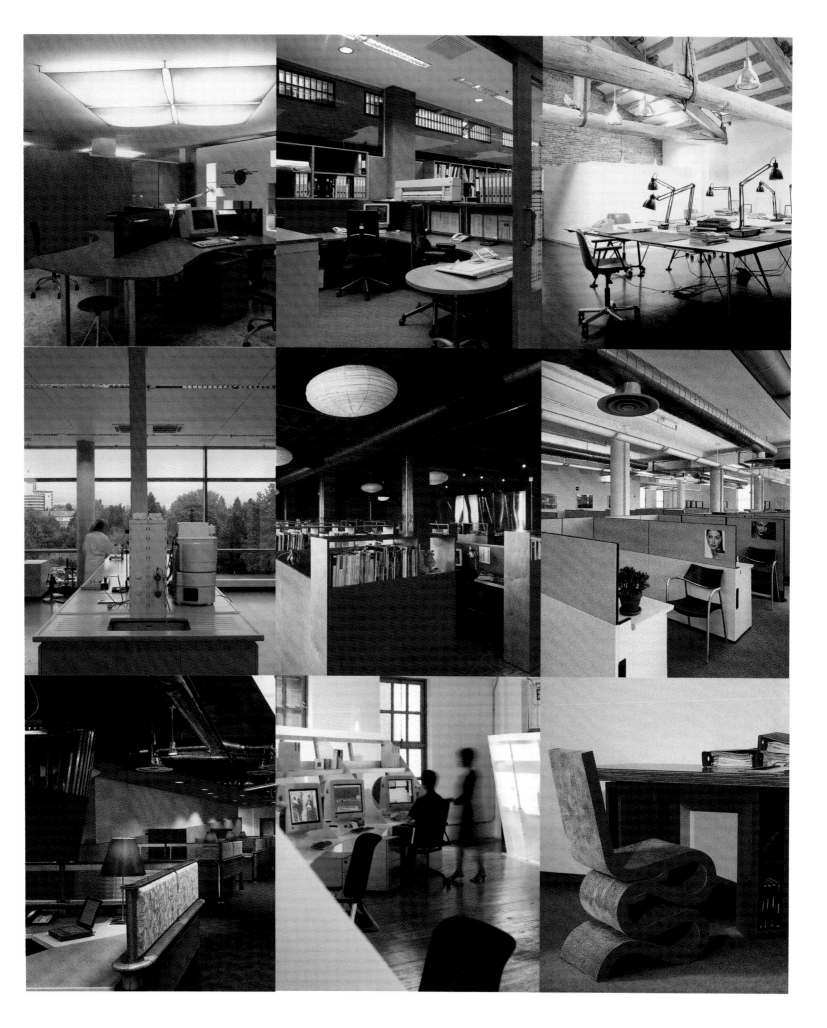